Fields of Greens

FIELDS *of* GREENS

New Vegetarian Recipes from the

Celebrated Greens Restaurant

ANNIE SOMERVILLE

 BANTAM BOOKS / New York · Toronto · London · Sydney · Auckland

FIELDS OF GREENS

A Bantam Book / May 1993

Book design by David Bullen.
Illustrations by Cynthia Schafer.
Composition by Wilsted & Taylor.

Library of Congress Cataloging-in-Publication Data
Somerville, Annie.
    Fields of greens : new vegetarian recipes from the celebrated
Greens Restaurant / Annie Somerville.
      p. cm.
    Includes index.
    ISBN 0-553-09139-5
    1. Vegetarian cookery.   2. Greens (Restaurant : Fort Mason,
Calif.)   I. Title.
TX837.S668   1993
641.5'636—dc20   92-42931
                                        CIP

This book is dedicated to Shunryu Suzuki Roshi, who planted a small seed of Buddhism in America

Table of Contents

Pizza 167

Curries and Stews 183

Gratins 203

Frittatas, Omelets, and Scrambled Eggs

Sandwiches

Breads   *309*

Sauces   *323*

Morning Breads and Pancakes

Desserts

Acknowledgments

This book is the work of many hearts, minds, and hands. Deepest thanks to Wendy Johnson, the head gardener at Green Gulch Farm, for writing the chapter on organic gardening and for her pearls of gardening lore. I'm equally indebted to Rick Jones, our general manager and wine buyer, for writing the chapter on pairing wine with vegetarian food, and to Greg Tompkins, who wrote the chapter on Tassajara breads. Their inspiring work has greatly enriched this book.

Laurie Senauke worked with me at every step of writing and editing. Dana Tommasino and Alison Wilmarth contributed their writing talent and love of cooking. Cathy Ehrhard tested the recipes in my home kitchen; her warmth and humor were always present. Carole Forrest, our former pastry chef, tested the pastry recipes. Karin Gjording dug up gardening sources and worked closely with Wendy on the gardening chapter. Danielle Tompkins, Marcella Smith, and Kyra Lowther assisted Greg with the bread recipes. Lisa Anderson and Rosalie Curtis contributed their editing skills. Special thanks to the Water Street tasters and to the Great Blue Heron for weaving richness into everyday life.

My deepest gratitude to our chef, J Kenyon, whose sustaining spirit and creative style are at the center of our cooking, and again to Rick Jones; their tremendous support made all of this work possible. To our chefs, past and present, whose inspiration and recipes grace these pages: Diana Adkins-Glassman, Susan H. Brinkley, Michael McNamara, Laura Levin, Greg West, Ulysses Lowry, Richard Porto, Mark Hall, Donna Nicoletti, Jito Yumibe, Lea Bergen, Allison Henderson, and Mary Downs. Bruce McCallister and Tom Girardot have enhanced our wine list over the years. Thanks to Philip Horn, Joyce Franklin, Jane Haseldine, Bo Thompson, and all the staff at Greens.

The groundbreaking *Greens Cookbook* laid the foundation for this book; Deborah Madison and Edward Espe Brown changed forever the way we think about vegetarian food. The recipes of Marion Cunningham, Lindsey Shere, Julie Sahni, Barbara Tropp, and Joyce Goldstein are particularly rich sources of inspiration. Sibella Kraus offered her invaluable ideas and her recipe for Firecracker Potatoes. Peter Rudnick shared his extensive knowledge of organic farming gleaned from more than fifteen years of working the Green Gulch fields. Rosalind Creasy recommended her favorite gardening reading. Alice Waters's words "Eat fresh from the garden" have encouraged us for years.

David Bullen designed the book with a fine hand and the patience of a saint. The striking illustrations are the work of Cynthia Schafer. Catherine Anderson's watercolor of the Green Gulch hills embraces the cover.

Deepest thanks to my agent, Michael Katz, who encouraged me in every way; his thoughtful questions helped shape the book from the very beginning. Jane Hirshfield's well-chosen words are greatly appreciated. My editor, Fran McCullough, was my guiding light; her sharp insights and wise comments really put me to work, and her gifts of levity and laughter always kindled my spirits. Richard Baker's far-reaching vision established Greens; without it, Greens wouldn't be what it is today. My gratitude to Michael Wenger for inviting me to write this book, and, finally, to Zen Center for this rare opportunity.

Introduction

The spirit of the Greens kitchen is found in the bustling activity of open-air markets, in backyard gardens, and in the richly laid fields of Green Gulch Farm—wherever fresh vegetables, fruits, and herbs are cultivated or change hands with a lively exchange of words. This engaging way of life and work is our constant source of inspiration.

We've worked closely with the gardeners at Green Gulch Farm since the day Greens opened, planning the crops of tender lettuces and salad greens, Bloomsdale spinach, sugar pumpkins, fingerling potatoes, and herbs we'll serve in the upcoming seasons. A walk to the ocean through the Green Gulch fields is a feast for the senses: rows of shiny lettuces and radicchio heading up, fragrant English thyme in full bloom, the lingering scent of black peppermint, and the lemony French sorrel that's sure to take over the greenhouse if we don't use it soon. We've drawn on the resources of that cool, coastal valley year after year and always with the spirit of giving back what we've taken.

Planting your own garden spot or making early morning trips to the farmers' market will give you the same sense of the abundant resources close at hand; there's a world of garden-fresh produce out there rarely found in most supermarkets. If there isn't a farmers' market in your area, find a local market that features fresh produce and seek out the ethnic markets. The boxes scattered through the book give you some ideas of particularly interesting varieties to search for. We've included a chapter on organic gardening at Green Gulch Farm to encourage you; even if you don't have the time or space for a full kitchen garden, plant a window box with your favorite herbs or a small bed of salad greens; they're sure to bring fresh tastes to your kitchen. There's also a source list of gardening books, seed suppliers, and farmers' markets to help you get started.

Our distinctive culinary style was developed by Deborah Madison, the founding chef of Greens; though our dishes have evolved over the years, her creative inspiration remains at the heart of our kitchen. We combine the freshest seasonal produce with pasta, dried beans, and grains; even the humblest ingredients are prepared with attention and care. Our recipes are a little leaner now, with less emphasis on cream and butter. Though dairy products and eggs are still essential ingredients, we use them with a lighter hand. We use olive oil for most of our sautéing, but when it really makes a difference of course we use butter. We look for "big flavors" in most of the dishes, but leave the final seasoning of salt, pepper, and vinegar to your taste.

We don't think of our ingredients as fancy, but they're always fresh and of the highest quality. Stocking your pantry with a few good oils and vinegars, dried mushrooms and chilies, sun-dried tomatoes, olives, and capers may seem expensive, but just a little of these fine ingredients will go a very long way to enhance your cooking. Cheese is no exception: there's a world of difference between a good aged Parmesan or provolone and domestically processed cheese. Pine nuts cost a small fortune, but a tablespoon or so is all that's needed in most of the dishes. Make sure they're fresh when you buy them and keep them in the freezer.

The seasonal celebration menus will assist you in planning menus for special occasions from recipes in this book, and we hope they'll inspire your palate. The complex dishes like lasagne, filo, and some of the stews have lengthy preparation times, and we've made note of this in the recipe introductions. Plan to make a complex dish the focus of the meal, then pair it with simpler dishes to save yourself a lot of time. We've also included a chapter on pairing wine with vegetarian food to help you select wines to go with our dishes.

A salad of vegetables, beans, or grains is a good way to begin almost any meal, and most of these dishes can be made ahead of time. Pasta and risotto are always delicious served with a leafy green salad, an antipasto, or vegetables grilled ahead of time or, if you can manage it, hot off the grill. A hearty stew is a meal in itself served over basmati rice, couscous, or polenta. Most stews, soups, and dishes of beans and grains are even better the following day; be sure to save your leftovers.

Fresh fruit at its peak is a wonderful way to end a meal, particularly if you're short on time. Dress up a bowl of sliced peaches and berries with a pitcher of crème anglaise or a drizzle of fresh raspberry puree. Our desserts are simple yet elegant in their own way, and most can be made in advance or partially prepared ahead of time.

Most restaurant cookbooks present challenges to the home cook, who doesn't have a *batterie de cuisine* or a large prep staff on hand. Not this one; the recipe testing took place in my home, a funny little house on a back street in San Francisco's North Beach. Mine is a modest, old-style kitchen: an airy room with a sturdy old four-burner gas stove with a single oven, and two butcher block tables. Our tools were a set of stainless steel pans, a KitchenAid mixer, a tiny food processor, a reliable old blender, a citrus zester, a few sharp knives, and a pizza stone. Of course there were plenty of bowls, measuring utensils, and all the rest, but you won't need a state-of-the-art kitchen to make these dishes.

The equipment in the open, light-filled Greens kitchen is well-worn from many years of good use, but there's a tradition in the way we work together that makes it shine. The loading-dock view is spectacular, with Angel Island in sight just outside our door and pelicans out over the Bay. In the morning the dock is loaded with all kinds of fruits and vegetables and fresh herbs waiting to go to the walk-in. On warm spring and summer afternoons it's the spot to shell fava beans and peas or shuck sweet white corn.

It's been nearly fourteen years since we opened Greens, and many people have passed through our double wooden doors—customers, staff, and all kinds of friends. There's a tangible sense of place that you can almost feel in the woodwork and walls; I've often described Greens as having a life of its own. It's a lively scene in the spacious, open dining room with floor-to-ceiling windows: people of all ages and walks of life gathering for a special occasion or enjoying a simple meal. We hope our cooking offers a taste of something fresh and slightly different to this busy and uncertain world: a salad green or vegetable you've never tried before, a new dish you'll come back to try again, or, better yet, a dish that's so delicious you're inspired to make it at home.

Organic Gardening at Green Gulch Farm

by Wendy Johnson

In early spring the fields of Zen Center's Green Gulch Farm—in a valley in the Marin head-lands just north of San Francisco—are a brocade of every shade of green. The soft blue-green of new fava leaves, the dark forest green of wild stinging nettles, the pale, trans-lucent yellow-green of miner's lettuce—interlace in a tapestry that unfolds out toward the Pacific Ocean. Out of these bountiful fields we harvest organic vegetables for Greens restaurant, for our meditation centers, kitchens, and for local markets.

As summer begins on the northern California coast, we're harvesting 14 varieties of lettuce, dark Bloomsdale spinach, rich burgundy radicchio, and the first new potatoes. The subtle whites, mauves, and lavenders of the perennial flowers yield to a riot of brightly colored annual blooms. Snapdragons, campanulas, clove-scented stock, and lo-tus dahlias rule the summer garden with their vivid bright pink, deep orange, and dark red. In the fall harvest our farm fields are covered with pumpkins, winter squash, Rosefir potatoes, and huge globe beets, their red shoulders lifting out of the ground. Lettuce con-tinues into the new year, yet long before then we see the tracings of the winter garden: neat rows of young leeks, garlic, broccoli, kale, cauliflower, and cabbage.

Zen Center farmers first began to work the rich bottomland soil of Green Gulch Farm in the spring of 1972. From the beginning, there has always been a vital connection between kitchen and garden. We were lucky to have some wonderful gardening teach-ers, English horticulturalist Alan Chadwick and Yurok Indian teacher and botanist Harry Roberts. These inspiring mentors taught us the value of farming organically— both for taste and as a fundamental way to care for the soil.

In these few pages we offer you a taste of gardening for your own kitchen. Through-out the book we've "intersown" growing information for a wide variety of herbs and vegetables—many familiar plants as well as some of the unusual varieties we've come to love. The particular focus is on plants that are incomparably better garden fresh or that may be difficult to find in your local produce markets. For more information about gar-dening, see Sources (page 419).

What to Grow

Starting small is of vital importance for beginners. This way you can expand your garden as your knowledge develops. You might begin with a window box of Mediterranean herbs—rosemary, thyme, and marjoram. Just a few of these perennial plants will give a fresh accent to your cooking year after year. A healthy chard plant or two near your back door can provide you with tender greens for many months. You could even grow a small Meyer lemon tree or semidwarf apple in a large redwood planter; surround the tree with Marvel of Four Seasons lettuce, which looks like huge roses. Lacking a garden or a ter-race, the potted Meyer lemon could live indoors in front of a large sunny window.

A small plot in your backyard might contain sweet basil, opal basil, and a variety of tomatoes to create mouth-watering summer salads for picnics and potlucks. A 12- by 3-foot bed planted in the spring with a trellis of sugar snap peas flanked by lettuce and spinach could give way to a late summer planting of winter carrots, kale, broccoli, and frisée. Sow the corners of the garden with a mix of edible flowers; borage, calendula, and Johnny-jump-ups, enhancing both garden and table.

Annual herbs (which need to be replanted every year) are easy to grow and particularly rewarding; many varieties are unavailable in markets, and even those that are often arrive wilted. Cilantro, chervil, and arugula grow nicely together. Start a container with your favorite annual herbs, then sow again every month to extend the harvest season.

Perennial Mediterranean herbs will thrive in mild climates under the conditions of their homeland—sun, warmth, and light, well-drained soil. Wrap a few aromatic bundles and give them to friends as a thanksgiving to the earth.

Gardening Essentials

CULTIVATING THE SOIL

Most plants flourish in a loose, open soil that "breathes," allowing for air circulation, deep root growth, and perfect drainage. Good garden cultivation begins with loosening the topsoil, removing large rocks and roots, and being careful to keep the topsoil on top. A spading fork is a great cultivating tool, one that prevents you from inverting the soil layers. The soil is ready for digging in the spring when a ball of earth crumbles lightly in your hand, not too wet or too dry. If you're gardening in a container, make sure the soil mix is loose and friable and alive with plenty of organic matter. Open, friable soil is kept in good heart by protecting the skin of the soil with a light layer of organic mulch material such as old rotted hay or aged compost. Once you begin to work the soil, the garden will teach you what to do.

FEEDING THE EARTH

The Green Gulch kitchens and farmlands generate a steady supply of organic matter. I love to see these kitchen scraps recycled into garden compost. Humus, the end product of composting, has nine times the water-holding capacity of sand, warms the ground in spring, hosts a multitude of soil organisms, leads to better oxygen utilization, and stimulates sugar production in plants.

Garden fertility is also maintained by planting "cover crops" that are turned back into the earth at the start of each new growing season. This method of building soil fertility is advisable no matter what your scale of operation. It's lovely to see an early spring planting of flowering buckwheat sown on a dormant vegetable bed. The seed of buckwheat, a plant rich in phosphorus, is readily available from a health food store. Scatter the seed generously over the bed and rake it in. After about eight weeks the buckwheat can be dug back into the soil to provide a rich bed for summer crops. Other beneficial cover crops include fava beans, purple vetch, and alfalfa, as well as many ornamental clovers.

To enrich the soil even more, good organic products such as fish emulsion, seaweed sprays, and rock powders can be applied throughout the growing season.

WATERING

One of the most effective ways to water is to go from plant to plant with a hand-held hose. In California water conservation is of primary importance. Hand watering a small garden is conservative and allows you a chance to notice what's going on in your garden. It's best to water in the early morning; drops of water on the foliage in the heat of the day will magnify the sun's intensity and burn the plant. Unless the nights are warm and dry, watering in the evening will make crops susceptible to mold and fungus.

If you don't have a hose or if your garden is indoors, a watering can that lets the water out slowly and evenly works fine. If you're gardening on a larger scale, drip irrigation is the most efficient method of offering a slow application of water to the root zone. Be sure to note and remember the different water requirements of the plants you grow.

PESTS AND WEEDS

A well-cultivated and fertilized garden irrigated with care and awareness creates healthy plants. Vigorous plants are far less susceptible to insects and disease. Many popular plant varieties are naturally resistant—some insect pests cause only minor blemishes. There are organic solutions to more serious problems.

I have a somewhat unconventional approach to weeding. I am uneasy of a garden that's completely weed-free; weeds indicate a vital, fertile environment, and many can enhance fertility if they're turned back into the soil before they go to seed. But if you let weeds take over, they'll absorb the moisture and nourishment crops need to flourish. So weed regularly, taking particular care to protect annual crops—young lettuce, the first radishes, and tender carrots grow best in a well-weeded soil.

STARTING YOUR PLANTS

At Green Gulch seed propagation is our passion and joy. At one point we were growing 70 varieties of flowers from seed gathered all over the world. As a beginner you may want to purchase seedlings from a local plant nursery. Of course I think every beginning gardener should do a little growing from seed just to experience the mystery of life starting from a tiny seed capsule. Tender French green beans are ideal to start directly from seed, since beans cannot be transplanted. They like full sun and loose soil with plenty of organic matter. We sow them here in early May and have beans on the table by mid-July. If the crop is particularly tasty, you can let some of the beans ripen on the bush and save the dried bean seeds for the next growing season.

For both seeds and transplants we follow the lunar calendar, which has assisted gardeners since the beginning of agriculture. We sow seeds in the "bright of the moon," beginning two days before the new moon, up until two days before the full moon, the period of time for maximum top growth. In the "dark of the moon"—that time following the full moon until the new moon—we transplant, knowing that this is an excellent time for root growth and underground activity. During the dark of the moon in early autumn we divide and take cuttings from our perennial plants.

KEEP RECORDS

As you plant seeds and raise garden crops, keep careful records of what you are learning from the garden. Remember the crops you love and how to grow them well. Season after season, let your own "recipes" for garden success continue to grow.

ASK QUESTIONS

Draw from local resources to learn about your particular place. Older gardening neighbors or the farm extension service can be invaluable in helping you learn about soil and climate, dates of the first and last frosts, length of growing season, when to start your early crops, availability of water and fertilizer, what pests have caused problems in your neighborhood and how to work with them, and much more. Don't hesitate to venture into a particularly enticing garden for a chat. Our experience at Green Gulch has taught us to ask questions and to closely observe the consequences of our activity. Zen Center's founder, Shunryu Suzuki Roshi, taught us that "beginner's mind" is our greatest asset: "In the beginner's mind there are many possibilities, but in the expert's there are few." So I encourage you to keep your beginner's mind as you garden and as you cook; be ready and willing to learn from everything you do. Listen as your spot of good earth speaks to you.

At the Zen Center and Green Gulch Farm, we continue to cook and garden together because we love this way of life. Committed to good taste and to caring for our world, cook and farmer draw their inspiration from each other, from the seasons, and from the fruit of the earth. If you are in the San Francisco Bay Area, please visit us at Green Gulch Farm and enjoy a long, slow walk out to the Pacific Ocean through our endless fields of greens.

Salads: Leafy Greens, Beans and Grains, Marinated Vegetables

Leafy Greens

The freshest, most extraordinary lettuces, all organically grown, come to us year-round from Green Gulch Farm and Star Route Farms in Bolinas. For both shoppers and gardeners, the marketplace has recently expanded to include all kinds of delicious field greens—mizuna and mustard greens, rocket (arugula), field cress, tat soi, and mâche—all easy and quick to grow. Even radicchio and Belgian endive, once exotic imports, are grown locally.

We love the bitter greens and feature them in the fall and winter—they're wonderful with citrus, apples, or pears, tossed with a tangy citrus or sharp sherry vinaigrette. When you see a large head of chicory or escarole in the market, remember that the pale green hearts are incredibly delicious in salads; the tough outer leaves can be sautéed with chard, beet greens, and kale. Sprigs of watercress add a peppery lift to any salad, while lacy frisée, or curly endive, adds loft and a bit of crunchy texture.

Good old romaine is still a favorite, ribs and all—its crispy hearts and dark outer leaves make a wonderful salad; just remember to make a sharp vinaigrette and toss the leaves generously with the dressing.

We often add light-tasting annual herbs to our green salads—sprigs of chervil or Italian parsley, thin ribbons of lemony French sorrel, and whole leaves of black peppermint or opal basil. Herbs can also be chopped and added to the vinaigrette. In spring and summer we toss in borage flowers, chive blossoms, and petals of calendulas and nasturtiums. The peppery nasturtium leaves can be torn or thinly sliced and included as well.

Very clean hands are the best tools for tossing a salad. Toss the greens gently, being careful not to overdress them; you want to be able to taste them and enjoy their fresh flavor. The heartier greens like a sharper vinaigrette and need to be dressed a little more generously than the tender lettuces and field greens.

A word on preparing greens: We like to keep small, inner leaves whole, cutting—with a non-corrosive knife—the larger leaves in pieces that maintain the integrity of each leaf. You can also tear lettuces; just handle the greens gently, especially when washing and drying them—they bruise and tear easily. Spinach often needs an extra rinse or two to remove the last grains of sand, an extra step that's well worth the time. A salad spinner is invaluable for both washing and drying and can be used for rinsing vegetables as well. Dry your salad greens well, or the wet leaves will dilute the flavor of even the tastiest vinaigrette and give you a soggy salad.

OILS AND VINEGARS

We use a fairly high ratio of vinegar (or acid) to oil when making vinaigrettes, often combining two different vinegars to sharpen or accent the flavors. The quality of the oil and vinegar makes all the difference here, so stock your kitchen with a few flavorful oils and favorite vinegars, keeping the oils in a cool cupboard or refrigerating them. Dark sesame oil and nut oils are particularly prone to rancidity, so buy them in small bottles from a reliable source and be sure to refrigerate after opening.

We use two grades of olive oil for our vinaigrettes—a California extra virgin olive oil made by the Sciabica family in Modesto and an imported pure (or light) olive oil. We like the fruity flavor of the extra virgin for assertive balsamic, sherry, and red wine vinaigrettes. For more delicate citrus vinaigrettes we prefer the lighter taste of pure olive oil and often combine it with hazelnut or walnut oil.

Our favorite vinegars range from smooth, almost sweet-tasting balsamic to sharp sherry and red wine vinegars. The clear, clean flavor of Champagne and rice wine vinegars is an excellent accent for citrus juice as well as other vinegars. A tasty apple cider vinegar will add sparkle to fall and winter salads. Vinegars last virtually forever, so it's well worth keeping an interesting variety of them on hand.

Vinaigrettes can be made up ahead and refrigerated; the one exception is citrus vinaigrettes—one of our favorites—which should be made just before the salad is tossed.

Beans and Grains

We feature salads of beans and grains daily on our menu, often with two or three vegetable salads as an antipasto. We season these hearty salads generously—a splash or two of vinegar or an additional sprinkle of salt and pepper is often all that's needed to make the flavors sparkle.

We use a wide variety of beans here, each distinctive in its own way. Little French lentils are wonderful for salads, and unlike the larger lentils, they hold their shape while cooking. Chick-peas have an unusual sweetness—they're slow-cooking beans, so be generous with their cooking time. Small black turtle beans are a mainstay of our menu, as are small white beans and slightly larger Great Northerns. Cannellini, Pueblo, and Black and White Runner Beans are among our favorites, with exceptionally smooth, buttery flavor.

Lentils cook quickly, but we soak all of our other beans overnight to speed the cooking time, covering them generously with water. If you're short on time, cover the beans with boiling water and allow them to sit for at least an hour before cooking. (For the larger, starchier beans, such as cannellinis and Black and White Runners, it's best to soak them overnight.) We always drain the beans and cook them in fresh, unsalted water. We never salt the cooking water—in our experience, it constricts the skins and increases the cooking time. A bay leaf or two and a few fresh herb sprigs add welcome flavor and earthy fragrance to a simmering pot of beans.

The texture of the beans is essential, affecting both the flavor and appearance of a salad, so cook them uncovered at a gentle boil and watch them closely during the final minutes of cooking. At this point, taste the beans to make sure that they're perfectly tender. If not, cook them for another minute or two, then drain them and season immediately—the warm beans will soak up all the delicious flavors.

There's a lightness to our grain salads, and we find that very little oil is needed. We use citrus and Champagne vinegar to brighten the flavors, chilies and herbs for freshness, and dried fruits to add a touch of sweetness. Couscous and bulgur are already precooked—they require a little less attention than basmati and wild rice, which we often serve together, though we find it's best to cook them separately. We're careful not to over-dress our couscous, rice, or bulgur salads so they don't lose their light texture.

Virtually all of these salads can be made ahead, and most of them are even tastier the next day.

Marinated Vegetables

Our favorite salads are often the simplest, and it's always the freshness of the vegetables that makes them so remarkable. Roasted red and yellow peppers are delicious marinated in their own juices with balsamic vinegar, olive oil, and fragrant leaves of basil, while tender, fresh beans are perfectly seasoned with fresh tarragon and a zesty lemon vinaigrette. Black and green olives, sun-dried tomatoes, capers, and toasted pine nuts offer a range of tastes from salty and piquant to nutty sweetness—delightful accent flavors that really brighten and enliven our vegetable salads.

Cut the vegetables with care, making the shapes distinctive and of consistent size so they appeal to the eye and cook evenly. We include stems whenever possible—broccoli, for instance—and slice them diagonally to add length and an elegant touch.

For fresh, clean tastes and textures we cook the vegetables in boiling water until just tender, then quickly rinse them under cool water to retain their vibrant color—this works particularly well with green vegetables, such as asparagus, broccoli, fresh peas, and beans. To keep their color bright, toss the vegetables with the vinaigrette just before serving or marinate them in the olive oil, and then add the vinegar or citrus at the last moment. Jícama, fennel, and cabbage are at their best when simply sliced and marinated; make sure that the flavors are lively to accentuate their crisp freshness.

For softer flavors we turn to the oven for roasting—eggplant, garlic, beets, peppers, and potatoes are delicious prepared this way and free the stove top for dishes that may need more immediate attention.

NASTURTIUMS

With a range of deep orange and yellow hues, spicy nasturtium petals are a stunning addition to leafy summer greens. The leaves, thinly sliced into ribbons, will add peppery flavor to the salad.

This annual flower propagates from seed quite easily; in California the seeds ripen, roll down hillsides, and grow in profusion. In mild climates nasturtiums flower in spring and fall and will reseed year after year. These sun lovers will grow long stems to get their sunlight. Grown in the shade, the leaves will be more tender.

Romaine Hearts with Sourdough Croutons and Parmesan Cheese

The tangy Lemon Vinaigrette coats the romaine leaves and settles on the crisp ribs with the grated Parmesan and chopped Gaeta olives. The sourdough croutons add crunch and good strong garlic flavor. If you're a true garlic lover, add an extra clove to the vinaigrette.

2 heads of romaine lettuce
1 garlic clove, finely chopped
Extra virgin olive oil
4 thick slices of sourdough bread, cut into ½-inch cubes, about 1 cup
Lemon-Garlic Vinaigrette (recipe follows)
8 Gaeta or Niçoise olives, pitted and coarsely chopped
1 ounce Parmesan cheese, grated, about ⅓ cup
Pepper

Discard the tough outer leaves of the romaine and use the whole leaves and the hearts, which should be pale green or yellow and firm. Wash the leaves and dry them in a spinner; wrap loosely in a damp towel and refrigerate.

Preheat the oven to 375°F. Add the garlic to 1 tablespoon olive oil and toss with the cubed bread. Spread the cubes on a baking sheet and bake for 7 to 8 minutes, until golden brown. Set aside to cool. Make the vinaigrette.

When you're ready to serve the salad, place the lettuce in a large bowl. Add the olives and toss with the vinaigrette, coating all of the leaves. Add the croutons and Parmesan; toss again. Sprinkle with freshly ground black pepper and serve.

MAKES TWO LARGE OR FOUR SMALL SALADS

Lemon-Garlic Vinaigrette

½ teaspoon minced lemon zest
3 tablespoons fresh lemon juice
¼ teaspoon salt
1 garlic clove, finely chopped
5 tablespoons extra virgin olive oil

Combine everything but the oil, then whisk it in. The vinaigrette should be very lemony and bright.

MAKES ABOUT ½ CUP

Garden Lettuces and Rocket with Summer Beans, Goat Cheese, and Hazelnuts

Toasted hazelnuts, creamy goat cheese, and tender beans fresh from the garden make this a delectable summer salad. We use a wide variety of lettuces grown at Green Gulch and Star Route farms and like to mix them in our salads. The lettuces themselves are extraordinary, and their names are even more so—Marvel of Four Seasons, Red and Green Oak Leaf, Red Butter, and Lollo Rossa, a crinkly red-hued lettuce whose ruffled leaves catch the richly flavored Hazelnut-Shallot Vinaigrette.

Salt
¼ pound Blue Lake or yellow wax beans, trimmed and cut into 2-inch lengths
Light olive oil
Pepper
Sherry vinegar
Hazelnut-Shallot Vinaigrette (recipe follows)
9 to 10 cups garden lettuces
1 small head of radicchio
1 handful of rocket (arugula) leaves
¼ cup hazelnuts, toasted (page 263)
1 or 2 ounces mild, creamy goat cheese such as chèvre or Montrachet, crumbled

Bring a small pot of water to a boil and add ½ teaspoon salt. Drop the beans into the water and cook them for 3 to 4 minutes, until just tender. Drain and rinse the beans under cold water, then toss with a little olive oil and a sprinkle of salt and pepper. Just before you're ready to toss the salad, add a splash of sherry vinegar to brighten their flavor.

Make the vinaigrette. Discard any bruised or wilted leaves of lettuce. Cut or tear the larger leaves and keep the small leaves whole. Trim the base of the radicchio and carefully separate the leaves; cut or tear them into large pieces. Sort through the rocket and trim off the stems. Wash the greens and dry them in a spinner.

Combine the salad ingredients in a large bowl and toss with the vinaigrette. Sprinkle with freshly ground black pepper.

SERVES FOUR

Hazelnut-Shallot Vinaigrette

2 tablespoons sherry vinegar
1 small shallot, diced
¼ teaspoon salt
2 tablespoons hazelnut oil
2 tablespoons light olive oil

Combine everything but the oils in a bowl, then slowly whisk in the oils.

MAKES ABOUT ⅓ CUP

MÂCHE

This old-time salad green is also known as lamb's lettuce or corn salad. The dark green leaves form in charming rosettes and add a soft, buttery flavor to salads—delicious with a mix of lettuces and rocket.

Plant a few seeds in the spring, as soon as the ground can be worked, and then every 2 weeks until the end of July. Mâche will need some shade; try interplanting with tomatoes, broccoli, or other tall plants. You can also plant in the fall, before the hard frost; mulch well and you'll be rewarded with extra early fresh greens the following spring. Or allow a few plants to go to seed, and they'll come up next year on their own.

Red and Green Romaine Hearts with Avocado, Mango, and Ginger

Green Gulch Farm grows red romaine for us, and though it's uncommon, it can sometimes be found at farmers' markets. If red romaine is unavailable, use the green romaine on its own or replace it altogether with butter lettuce. The Zesty Ginger Vinaigrette is blended and emulsified to a creamy texture.

1 head of green romaine lettuce
2 to 3 heads of red romaine lettuce or 1 more head of green romaine
1 ripe mango
Zesty Ginger Vinaigrette (recipe follows)
1 tablespoon pine nuts, toasted (page 263)
1 avocado, peeled and sliced ¼ inch thick on a slight diagonal
Pepper

Discard the bruised outer leaves of the green romaine. Use the pale green inner leaves, keeping the small leaves whole and cutting or tearing the larger leaves into halves or quarters. The heads of red romaine will be smaller and somewhat delicate. Discard the bruised leaves; cut or tear the large leaves, keeping the small leaves whole. Wash the lettuce and dry it in a spinner. Wrap loosely in a damp towel and refrigerate.

Peel the mango with a paring knife; carefully slice the fruit off the pit in long sections, using the knife to feel the contours of the flat oval-shaped pit. Cut the sections lengthwise into ¼-inch slices. Prepare the vinaigrette.

Place the romaine leaves in a large bowl and sprinkle with the pine nuts. Pour the vinaigrette over and toss thoroughly, coating all of the leaves. Add the avocado and the mango; gently toss to distribute the fruit and coat with the vinaigrette. Sprinkle with freshly ground black pepper and serve.

MAKES TWO LARGE OR FOUR SMALL SALADS

Zesty Ginger Vinaigrette

¼ teaspoon minced lime zest
¼ teaspoon minced orange zest
2 tablespoons fresh lime juice
1 tablespoon fresh orange juice
¼ teaspoon salt
1 teaspoon grated fresh ginger
3 tablespoons light olive oil

Combine everything but the zests in a blender jar; blend, then whisk in the zests.

MAKES ABOUT ⅓ CUP

Wilted Spinach Salad with Roasted Peppers

In this delicious variation on our classic spinach salad, the slightly bitter flavor of the frisée balances the sweetness of the roasted peppers and the balsamic vinegar. The greens are tossed with very hot olive oil, which wilts the leaves and brings the flavors of the salad together. This is a wonderful way to feature Bloomsdale spinach, known for its crinkly dark green leaves and exceptional flavor.

1 medium-size red or yellow bell pepper, roasted, peeled, and sliced into ¼-inch strips (page 55)
6 tablespoons extra virgin olive oil
Salt and pepper
¼ medium-size red onion, thinly sliced
8 to 12 thin baguette slices for croutons
1 large bunch of spinach or 3 heads of Bloomsdale spinach, about 12 cups leaves
2 handfuls of frisée or chicory
3 tablespoons balsamic vinegar
1 garlic clove, finely chopped
10 Niçoise or Gaeta olives, pitted
1 ounce Parmesan cheese, grated, about ⅓ cup

Preheat the oven to 375°F. Toss the peppers with ½ tablespoon olive oil and a few pinches of salt and pepper; set aside to marinate. Cover the onion slices with cold water to leach out their strong onion flavor and set aside.

Place the baguette slices on a baking sheet and brush them lightly with olive oil, using about 1½ tablespoons. Toast them until crisp and lightly browned, about 8 minutes.

Discard the bruised outer leaves of the spinach and trim off the stems, keeping the leaves whole. Cut off the stem end of the frisée and discard the tough outer leaves; use only the tender inner leaves. Wash the greens well and dry them in a spinner.

Drain the onions just before you make the salad. In a large bowl, combine the vinegar, the garlic, ½ teaspoon salt, and a few pinches of pepper. Add the greens, onions, peppers, and olives. Be sure to include the sweet juice of the peppers, because it adds flavor to the salad. Heat the remaining ¼ cup olive oil in a small skillet until it is very hot, just below the point of smoking. Immediately pour it over the salad and toss with a pair of metal tongs to coat and wilt the leaves, sprinkling in the Parmesan as you toss. Add the croutons and serve immediately.

MAKES TWO LARGE OR FOUR SMALL SALADS

Variation: In summer, we toss small leaves of opal basil into the salad. The purple leaves are very beautiful and add a mintlike flavor. In fall, we add escarole and radicchio to the spinach and frisée, using equal amounts of the greens.

Butter Lettuce and Radicchio with Avocado, Ruby Grapefruit, and Pecans

Pale green leaves of butter lettuce and deep red radicchio blend beautifully with the rich avocado, toasted pecans, and citrus flavors. This lovely salad often includes Red Butter, an exceptional variety of lettuce grown for us at Green Gulch. Its light green leaves are tinged with rust-colored tips, adding subtle beauty to the salad. Handle the lettuce delicately to keep the tender leaves from bruising. A sprinkling of fresh pomegranate seeds adds tangy flavor and highlights the colorful greens.

1 to 2 heads of butter lettuces or mixed garden lettuces
1 small head of radicchio
1 large ruby grapefruit
Grapefruit Vinaigrette (recipe follows)
1 pomegranate (optional)
1 avocado, peeled and sliced ¼ inch thick on a slight diagonal
¼ cup pecan pieces, toasted (page 263)

Discard the bruised outer leaves of the butter lettuces. Use the tender inner leaves, keeping the small leaves whole and cutting or tearing the larger outer leaves. Trim the base of the radicchio and carefully separate the leaves, tearing or cutting the larger leaves. Wash and dry the greens in a spinner.

Using a sharp knife, remove the peel and white pith from the grapefruit, slicing off the top and the bottom, then working down the sides. Hold the grapefruit over a bowl to catch the juice (save for the vinaigrette) and cut each section loose by slicing next to the membrane. Make the vinaigrette.

Cut the pomegranate in half crosswise, gently pull it apart, and remove the seeds from the membrane. Assemble all the ingredients except the pomegranate seeds in a large bowl. Gently toss with the vinaigrette to keep the avocado slices from breaking. Sprinkle with 1 tablespoon pomegranate seeds.

MAKES TWO LARGE OR FOUR SMALL SALADS

Grapefruit Vinaigrette

2 tablespoons fresh grapefruit juice
½ tablespoon Champagne vinegar
¼ teaspoon salt
1 shallot, finely diced
2½ tablespoons light olive oil

Combine everything but the oil in a small bowl, then gradually whisk in the oil.

MAKES ABOUT ⅓ CUP

Variation: For an exquisite fall variation, use thin slices of pale orange Fuyu persimmons in place of the grapefruit and make a Citrus Vinaigrette (page 15). The crisp persimmons are exceptionally delicious with the pomegranates, toasted pecans, and contrasting greens.

LETTUCES

A salad of tender lettuces, fresh herbs, and peppery greens is unbeatably delicious, particularly if it's grown from your own window box or garden patch. There's a wondrous satisfaction in taking shiny, vibrant lettuces from tiny seedlings to the table—you can even harvest the outer leaves as you need them, keeping the heads of lettuce producing. If you have time to weed and water, lettuce is a good bet for a small home garden plot. It likes the cooler temperatures of spring and fall; most varieties will become bitter or go to seed in very hot weather. In rich, moist soil, lettuce grows easily and quickly; you'll have fresh garden greens on your table in about two months. Lettuce also grows well in a container. Our favorite Green Gulch lettuces—with a wonderful range of colors, tastes, and textures that we mix daily for the most delicious garden salads—follow.

Oak Leaf: The graceful leaves of this sturdy lettuce are notched like an oak leaf with long, slender fingers. Red Oak Leaf ranges from earthy brown to tips of deep red. The warm shade of Green Oak Leaf is a lively contrast. In mild climates, this lettuce is a year-round staple.

Red romaine: The tender, flat leaves have beautiful rose-colored edges and a satisfying texture. This lettuce is delicate compared to crisp green romaine—tossed together, they contrast beautifully and like a robustly flavored lemon vinaigrette. You can harvest the reddish-brown leaves one at a time and keep the head producing.

Lollo Rossa: A lovely Italian loose-leaf lettuce with crinkly ruffled leaves that hold on to a vinaigrette. The green centers turn to warm red hues at the tips. This quick-growing lettuce adds a light, buoyant touch to salads. Show off its beauty in a mixture of greens, including mizuna and Red and Green Oak Leaf.

Marvel of Four Seasons: This marvelous lettuce speaks for itself—the mottled heads of red and pale green are a kind of Red Butter lettuce. The tender, slightly cupped leaves make a beautiful bed for marinated vegetables—tossed into a mixture of leaves, they're stunning. If you're starting from seed, oversow a bit, because the seed is fragile. It's resistant to bugs and will grow year-round in a mild climate.

Red Butter: This silky butter lettuce with rust-colored tips has a crisp and clean flavor. Combined with Green Butter lettuce, toasted pine nuts, and a sweet citrus vinaigrette, it makes the most delicate of summer salads. In fall it's lovely with kumquats, pecans, and tangerines.

Fall Greens with Marinated Mushrooms, Fennel, and Gruyère Cheese

A late September walk through the Green Gulch fields inspired this salad of fall and winter greens. Red and Green Oak Leaf lettuces are shiny and vibrant, ranging from pale green to brilliant cranberry and deep, earthy red. Radicchio and Belgian endive add a slightly bitter taste, while the rocket comes through nutty and light. Select firm, fresh mushrooms and marinate them with the fennel in a little vinaigrette. Slivers of nutty Gruyère add the finishing touch. Serve with a crusty hearth bread and Butternut Squash Soup with Apple Confit (page 98).

¼ pound white mushrooms with closed caps
Balsamic Vinaigrette (recipe follows)
1 small fennel bulb, quartered lengthwise, cored, and thinly sliced
Salt and pepper
Balsamic vinegar if needed
9 to 10 cups garden lettuces
1 small head of radicchio
1 head of Belgian endive
1 or 2 ounces Gruyère cheese, cut into thin strips
1 tablespoon pine nuts, toasted (page 263)

Rinse the mushrooms quickly under cool water and pat them dry. Trim the bottom of the mushroom stems to even them, then cut the mushrooms in half. Make the vinaigrette and marinate the fennel and mushrooms in half of it for 30 minutes. Save the rest to toss with the salad. Season the mushrooms and fennel with salt, pepper, and a splash of balsamic vinegar if needed.

Sort through the lettuces, discarding any leaves that are wilted or bruised. Cut or tear the large leaves, keeping the small leaves whole. Trim the base of the radicchio and gently separate the leaves, tearing or cutting the larger leaves. Wash the greens and dry them in a spinner; wrap in a damp towel and refrigerate.

Separate the endive leaves, cutting the larger leaves in half lengthwise. Combine the salad ingredients in a large bowl, drizzle with the remaining vinaigrette, and toss. Sprinkle with freshly ground black pepper.

SERVES FOUR

Balsamic Vinaigrette

2 tablespoons balsamic vinegar
Salt
1 garlic clove, finely chopped
¼ cup extra virgin olive oil
Pepper
Sherry vinegar

Combine the balsamic vinegar, ¼ teaspoon salt, and the garlic in a small bowl; whisk in the oil. Add salt, pepper, and a splash of sherry vinegar to season.

MAKES ABOUT ⅓ CUP

FRENCH SORREL

The tangy flavor of this tender-leafed perennial is distinctly lemony. The leaves add spunk to salads and make a classic potato soup. They're torn, or bundled and sliced into thin ribbons, then simmered with the potatoes in their broth—don't worry when the leaves discolor; sorrel leaves always do. Finish the soup with a touch of cream or crème fraîche and it will come together instantly.

This wonderful herb propagates like mad, growing easily from a plant division or from seed. It likes rich, moist, well-drained soil and plenty of sun and water. (The foggy Green Gulch climate is damp, so we grow ours in the greenhouse.) Harvest the sorrel when very young and tender and keep it well cut, right down to the nub. Untended, the leaves will get large and stringy and provide a great hideout for snails. Sorrel is an ideal candidate for a patio or indoor container. Let a few plants go to seed; the long-stemmed coral-pink flower is gorgeous.

Citrus Salad with Bitter Greens

Juicy rounds of tangerines, ruby grapefruit, and oranges are arranged atop a bed of watercress and frisée, then drizzled with a vinaigrette made of their juices. The slightly bitter greens balance the sweetness of the vinaigrette. Select a variety of tangerines or tangelos with as few seeds as possible, such as Satsumas, Mineolas, or Fairchilds. If blood oranges and kumquats are available, be sure to use them—the crimson blood oranges contrast beautifully with the greens, and the thinly sliced kumquats add a delicate tartness to the salad.

> *1 handful of escarole hearts*
> *1 small head of radicchio*
> *1 handful of watercress or frisée hearts or a mixture*
> *Citrus Vinaigrette (recipe follows)*
> *2 or 3 kumquats, thinly sliced and seeded*
> *2 navel or blood oranges*
> *2 tangerines*
> *1 large ruby grapefruit*

Remove and discard the outer leaves of the escarole; cut or tear the tender light green inner leaves into large pieces. Trim the base of the radicchio, carefully separate the leaves, and cut or tear them. Sort through the watercress and pluck the small sprigs, discarding the long stems and bruised leaves. Wash and dry the greens in a spinner; wrap loosely in a damp towel and refrigerate until needed.

Make the vinaigrette, then toss the kumquats in a little of it to soften their acidity.

Using a sharp knife, remove the peel and white pith from the fruit, slicing a piece off the top and bottom, then working down the sides. Be sure to remove all of the outer white membrane. Slice the oranges and tangerines into rounds; slice the grapefruit in half lengthwise, then into half-moons. Remove all seeds.

Place the greens in a bowl and toss with half of the vinaigrette. Arrange them on a platter or individual plates and place the fruit on top, alternating the slices. Sprinkle on the kumquats and drizzle with the remaining vinaigrette.

SERVES FOUR

Citrus Vinaigrette

½ teaspoon minced orange zest
2 tablespoons fresh orange juice or 1 tablespoon each orange and tangerine juices
1 tablespoon Champagne vinegar
¼ teaspoon salt
3 tablespoons light olive oil

Combine everything but the oil in a small bowl, then whisk in the oil.

MAKES ABOUT ⅓ CUP

RADICCHIO

The cupped leaves of this endive are a deep crimson color with white ribs running through. The heads open like flowers, so shiny and vibrant you'll be tempted to leave them in the ground. Crisp and slightly bitter in taste, radicchio is a beautiful contrast to young lettuces and both hearty and peppery greens. The leaves can be sliced into ribbons and tossed with pasta or filled and grilled over coals—the heat draws out a wonderful bittersweet flavor.

Start this gorgeous plant from seed in mid-February. We recommend Johnny's in Maine for seeds. Do four successive plantings, then repeat at the beginning of fall. Radicchio likes an early morning watering. Don't give too much water when the head is forming—avoid watering the head itself, or rot is sure to form. It will be about 3 months from seed to table. Harvest the whole plant, because the inside leaves are the tastiest.

Winter Greens with Apples, Pecans, and Stilton Cheese

Watercress, both tender and peppery at its peak, finds its way into many of our salads. Our watercress is grown on a terraced hillside in Sausalito and is often delivered in a French fishing basket worn on the grower's back.

In this classic Greens salad, watercress mingles with hearty escarole and silky leaves of Belgian endive. Flavorful crisp apples, crumbled Stilton, and well-toasted pecans nestle into this lively mix of winter greens.

1 large head of escarole, about 6 cups
1 small bunch of watercress
Sherry-Shallot Vinaigrette (recipe follows)
1 head of Belgian endive
1 crisp apple, such as Sierra Beauty, McIntosh, or Granny Smith
¼ cup pecan pieces, toasted (page 263)
1 or 2 ounces Stilton cheese, crumbled
Pepper

Remove the outer leaves of the escarole and use only the tender, light green inner leaves. Pluck the small sprigs of watercress, discarding the long stems and bruised leaves. Wash the greens and dry them in a spinner; wrap loosely in a damp kitchen towel and refrigerate. Make the vinaigrette.

Separate the endive leaves, cutting the larger leaves in half lengthwise. Cut the apple into quarters, remove the core, and thinly slice. Place the greens in a large bowl with the apples, pecans, and cheese. Toss with the vinaigrette and sprinkle with freshly ground pepper.

MAKES TWO LARGE OR FOUR SMALL SALADS

Sherry-Shallot Vinaigrette

1½ tablespoons sherry vinegar
1 small shallot, thinly sliced
¼ teaspoon salt
¼ cup light olive oil

Combine everything but the oil, then whisk it in.

MAKES ABOUT ⅓ CUP

Garden Lettuces, Watercress, and Escarole with Goat Cheese and Sun-Dried Tomatoes

Begin with tender inner leaves of winter escarole, peppery watercress, and the rich flavors of sun-dried tomatoes and toasted pine nuts. Add delicate garden lettuces, perhaps Marvel of Four Seasons—a superior red lettuce with subtle ruby-tipped leaves. Toss with Balsamic Vinaigrette and sprinkle with crumbled goat cheese. Serve with a savory winter stew or pastry turnover.

8 to 9 cups tender garden lettuce leaves
1 handful of tender inner escarole leaves
1 small bunch of watercress, 2 handfuls of small sprigs
Balsamic Vinaigrette (page 13)
1 tablespoon pine nuts, toasted (page 263)
2 sun-dried tomatoes packed in oil, drained and thinly sliced
1 or 2 ounces creamy, mild goat cheese such as chèvre or Montrachet
Pepper

Keep the inner lettuce leaves whole and cut or tear the larger ones. Cut or tear the escarole leaves into large pieces. Wash the greens and dry them in a spinner; wrap in a damp towel and refrigerate until needed. Make the vinaigrette.

Toss the lettuce, escarole, watercress, pine nuts, and sun-dried tomatoes with the vinaigrette. Crumble the goat cheese onto the salad and toss again. Sprinkle with freshly ground black pepper.

MAKES TWO LARGE OR FOUR SMALL SALADS

Winter Greens with Pears, Walnuts, and Warm Roquefort Croutons

Tossed escarole hearts, radicchio, watercress, and frisée blend beautifully with toasted walnuts and the smooth sweetness of pears. We often use Red Bartletts for their gorgeous color, though the delicate flavor of Comice or French Butter pears is hard to surpass. For all its elegance, this is a relatively easy salad to make. Have the Roquefort Croutons ready and toast them at the last minute as you toss the salad. Serve the salad with the croutons crisp and bubbly from the oven.

About 6 cups inner leaves of escarole, 1 to 2 heads
1 small head of radicchio
A handful of small watercress sprigs
A handful of frisée hearts
Roquefort Croutons (recipe follows)
Walnut-Shallot Vinaigrette (recipe follows)
1 ripe, flavorful pear
¼ cup walnut pieces, toasted (page 263)
Pepper

Cut or tear the escarole leaves into large pieces. Carefully separate the radicchio leaves and cut or tear into large pieces. Discard any bruised watercress leaves. Trim the base of the frisée hearts. Wash and dry the greens in a spinner; wrap loosely in a damp towel and refrigerate.

Prepare the croutons and the vinaigrette.

When you're ready to serve the salad, set the oven to broil. Halve the pear, trim away the core, and slice lengthwise. Combine the greens, pear slices, and walnuts in a large bowl; gently toss with the vinaigrette. Sprinkle with freshly ground black pepper. Toast the croutons in the broiler until the cheese is bubbly, 1 to 2 minutes. Tuck them into individual salads or serve them separately with the salad.

SERVES FOUR

Roquefort Croutons

12 baguette slices, cut about ¼ inch thick on a diagonal
Olive oil
2 ounces Roquefort cheese
1 tablespoon unsalted butter
Pepper

Preheat the oven to 375°F. Brush the sliced bread with olive oil and bake until crisp and golden, about 8 minutes. Cream the cheese with the butter and a few pinches of pepper. Spread the croutons generously with the Roquefort butter.

MAKES 12 CROUTONS

Walnut-Shallot Vinaigrette

2 tablespoons sherry vinegar
1 small shallot, finely diced
¼ teaspoon salt
A few pinches of pepper
2 tablespoons light olive oil
2 tablespoons walnut oil

Combine everything but the oils in a small bowl, then whisk in the oils.

MAKES ABOUT ⅓ CUP

FRISÉE

The frilly leaves of this green, with their sturdy crisp ribs, add lift and texture to salads. Also known as curly endive, *frisée is particularly good tossed into a warm spinach salad or quickly braised with escarole and radicchio in the fall.*

Frisée likes cooler weather and moist, rich soil with excellent drainage. For an early spring harvest, sow a row of seeds indoors in flats in early January and plant the young seedlings outdoors as soon as the ground can be worked.

Romaine Hearts with Avocado, Jícama, and Orange

Crispy green romaine hearts and thinly sliced jícama work together to make this spirited salad. There's just enough cumin in the vinaigrette to heighten its flavor without overpowering the avocado and orange. The jícama is marinated with orange juice and Champagne vinegar—a touch of cayenne adds heat and accents its clean flavor.

2 heads of romaine lettuce, 8 to 10 cups hearts
1 large navel orange
½ medium-size jícama, about ¼ pound
3 tablespoons fresh orange juice
1 teaspoon Champagne vinegar
⅛ teaspoon salt
Cayenne pepper
1 avocado
Citrus-Cumin Vinaigrette (recipe follows)
Pepper

Trim the base of the romaine, discarding the tough outer leaves; save the light green inner leaves or hearts. Cut the larger leaves in half down the length of the rib; cut into quarters if long and keep the smaller leaves whole. Wash the lettuce and dry it in a spinner; wrap it in a damp towel and refrigerate.

Using a sharp knife, remove the peel and white pith from the orange, slicing a piece off the top and bottom, then working down the sides. Slice the orange in half through the stem end; remove any seeds or pith in the center. Slice across the orange, making ¼-inch-thick half-moons.

Peel the jícama and slice into thin matchsticks, about 2 inches long. Combine the orange juice, vinegar, salt, and a few pinches of cayenne; marinate the jícama for 10 to 15 minutes. (It will pick up the citrus flavor and the heat of the cayenne.)

When you're ready to serve the salad, cut the avocado in half; peel and thinly slice it on a slight diagonal.

Place the lettuce, orange slices, and jícama in a large bowl and toss with the vinaigrette until the leaves are coated. Add the avocado and toss again, carefully, to keep the slices from breaking. Sprinkle with freshly ground black pepper.

MAKES TWO LARGE OR FOUR SMALL SALADS

Citrus-Cumin Vinaigrette

½ teaspoon minced orange zest
2 tablespoons fresh orange juice
1 tablespoon Champagne vinegar
⅛ teaspoon cumin seed, toasted and ground (page 89)
¼ teaspoon salt
3 tablespoons light olive oil

Combine everything but the orange zest in a blender; blend, then whisk in the zest.

MAKES ABOUT ⅓ CUP

Serving Note: If you're serving the salad on individual plates, toss the romaine hearts and jícama with the vinaigrette, reserving a little vinaigrette for the avocado. Gently toss the avocado in a small bowl with the remaining vinaigrette. Place the salad on chilled plates and tuck the avocado and orange slices into the leaves. Sprinkle with freshly ground black pepper.

Variation: Watercress and hearts of escarole are a delicious addition to the romaine. Substitute the greens for one head of romaine or make the salad entirely with escarole and watercress. The peppery watercress and slightly bitter escarole work well with the strong flavors of this salad. You can also use ruby grapefruit in place of the orange.

CALENDULAS

Known as "poor man's saffron," this edible flower has wispy golden to orange petals offering bright color and subtle flavor to salads, rice pilafs, and egg dishes. Planted as a cover crop, calendulas will keep the garden clean, giving refuge to beneficial insects. Start with seed or bedding plants; calendulas are annuals but naturalize like wildfire. These cheerful flowers like cold weather—at Green Gulch we sow in early October and they begin to flower in November. Pacific Beauty is a large-petaled variety that lends itself particularly well to the kitchen.

Mango-Papaya Salad with Citrus-Ginger Vinaigrette

This simple salad is heavenly in the summer, when mangoes and papayas are at their peak—the sweet, succulent fruit is perfectly balanced with the fresh flavors of ginger and lime. Delicate leaves of pale green mizuna and crisp, lacy frisée contrast beautifully with the vivid orange tropical fruit.

2 handfuls of mizuna or red mustard greens
1 ripe mango
1 ripe papaya
Citrus-Ginger Vinaigrette (recipe follows)

Remove and discard the long stems of the greens, then wash leaves and dry them in a spinner; wrap loosely in a damp towel and refrigerate.

Peel the mango with a paring knife; carefully slice the fruit off the pit in long sections, using the knife to feel the contours of the flat oval-shaped pit. Cut the sections lengthwise into ¼-inch slices. Peel and halve the papaya and scoop out the seeds. Cut across the papaya diagonally to make ¼-inch slices.

Prepare the vinaigrette, toss the greens with 2 tablespoons of it, and arrange the greens on a plate. Place the fruit on the greens, alternating the slices of mango and papaya. Drizzle the remaining vinaigrette over the fruit and serve.

SERVES FOUR TO SIX

Citrus-Ginger Vinaigrette

¼ teaspoon minced lime zest
1 tablespoon fresh lime juice
1 tablespoon fresh orange juice
½ tablespoon Champagne vinegar
½ teaspoon grated fresh ginger
⅛ teaspoon salt
3 tablespoons light olive oil

Combine everything but the lime zest in a blender; blend, then whisk in the zest.

MAKES ABOUT ⅓ CUP

Spinach Salad with Tangerines, Red Onions, and Sesame-Ginger Vinaigrette

The rich flavor of sesame blends with sweet tangerine juice and freshly grated ginger to create a sparkling vinaigrette. It's tossed with tender spinach leaves, delicate tangerines, and toasted sesame seeds. A refreshing salad to enjoy year-round—oranges will substitute splendidly when tangerines aren't available.

2 handfuls of frisée or chicory
1 1-pound bunch of spinach, stems removed, about 8 cups leaves
¼ medium-size red onion, thinly sliced
Rice wine vinegar
2 or 3 tangerines: Satsuma, Mineola, or Fairchild
Sesame-Ginger Vinaigrette (recipe follows)
1 teaspoon sesame seeds, toasted (page 263)

Cut off the stem end of the frisée and discard the tough outer leaves, using the pale green inner leaves. Wash the greens and dry them in a spinner; wrap loosely in a damp towel and refrigerate.

Toss the onion with a splash of rice wine vinegar to draw out its pink color. Peel and section the tangerines, removing any seeds, pith, or threads. Make the vinaigrette. Combine the greens, tangerines, and onion in a large bowl. Toss with the vinaigrette and sprinkle with the sesame seeds.

SERVES FOUR

Sesame-Ginger Vinaigrette

1 teaspoon minced tangerine zest
2 tablespoons fresh tangerine juice
2 teaspoons grated fresh ginger
2½ tablespoons rice wine vinegar
2 tablespoons light olive oil
1 tablespoon dark sesame oil
1 teaspoon soy sauce
¼ teaspoon salt

Combine everything but the zest in a blender; blend, then whisk in the zest.

MAKES ABOUT ½ CUP

Late Summer Salad—Figs and Melon with Orange Vinaigrette

This lovely salad is on our menu at the end of the summer, with autumn well on the way. Choose a flavorful melon—cantaloupe, Sharlyn, or Ambrosia—and the ripest figs. The most delicious figs are often a little bruised—be sure to include them and show off their voluptuous shape by leaving the stem end on. We've chosen rocket (arugula) for this salad, but delicate leaves of peppery mizuna and red mustard greens are also delicious.

> *2 handfuls of rocket, mizuna, or red mustard greens*
> *Orange Vinaigrette (recipe follows)*
> *1 small melon*
> *8 to 10 ripe fresh figs: any combination of Kadota, Black Mission, or Calmyrna*
> *1 tablespoon pine nuts, toasted (page 263)*

Sort through the rocket; trim the stems and discard any bruised leaves. Wash the greens and dry them in a spinner; wrap in a damp towel and refrigerate. Make the vinaigrette.

Cut the melon in half and scoop out the seeds; thinly slice and peel, following the contour of the rind. Rinse the figs under cool water and pat dry. Cut them into halves or quarters, leaving the stem end on.

Arrange the rocket on a serving platter and loosely arrange the melon and figs on it. Drizzle the vinaigrette over the fruit and sprinkle with pine nuts. (You can also toss the pine nuts with a little vinaigrette to make them shiny.)

SERVES FOUR

Orange Vinaigrette

> *¼ teaspoon minced orange zest*
> *2 tablespoons fresh orange juice*
> *½ tablespoon Champagne vinegar*
> *¼ teaspoon salt*
> *3 tablespoons light olive oil*

Combine everything but the oil in a small bowl, then whisk in the oil.

MAKES ⅓ CUP

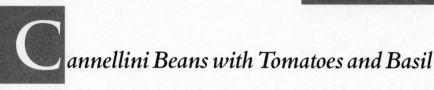Cannellini Beans with Tomatoes and Basil

Italian white kidney beans, known as *cannellini,* are one of our antipasto favorites. Starchy and full of flavor, they create their own delicious sauce when tossed with vine-ripened tomatoes, olive oil, and vinegar. For a wonderful light summer meal, serve with grilled sourdough bread, fresh mozzarella cheese, and an assortment of black olives.

1½ cups dried cannellini beans, about 9 ounces, sorted and soaked overnight
1 bay leaf
A few sprigs of fresh herbs: marjoram, thyme, and sage
¼ medium-size red onion, diced, about ½ cup
Champagne vinegar
2 tablespoons red wine vinegar
Zest of 2 lemons, minced, about 2 teaspoons
2 garlic cloves, finely chopped
Salt and pepper
⅓ cup extra virgin olive oil
½ pound tomatoes
¼ cup chopped fresh basil

Drain and rinse the beans and place them in a large saucepan. Cover generously with the cold water, then add the bay leaf and herb sprigs. Bring to a boil, then reduce the heat and cook at a gentle boil until tender, about 20 to 25 minutes. Taste the beans to be sure that they're cooked through. If the skins are still tough, cook them a little longer until the skins loosen and the beans begin to open up.

While the beans are cooking, bring a small pot of water to a boil. Drop the onion in and cook for 15 seconds; scoop out and toss with ½ tablespoon Champagne vinegar. Combine the red wine vinegar, lemon zest, garlic, ¾ teaspoon salt, and ¼ teaspoon pepper in a bowl and whisk in the oil. Core and seed the tomatoes; cut into large pieces.

Drain the cooked beans and toss them immediately with the vinaigrette. The hot beans will soak up all the good flavors. Cool, then add the tomatoes, onion, and basil. It's best to marinate the beans for an hour or two. Season to taste with salt and pepper and a splash of Champagne vinegar if needed; serve at room temperature.

SERVES FOUR TO SIX

Tip: Make this dish a day in advance, since the beans are even more delicious the second day. They'll need to be reseasoned, and they may need more lemon zest. Be sure to bring them to room temperature before serving.

White Beans and Flageolets with Summer Beans, Lemon, and Tarragon

We like to make this salad when green beans and yellow wax beans are tender on the vine. The crunchy texture of the fresh beans contrasts nicely with the dried beans, especially the smooth, subtle character of the pale green flageolets. Tarragon is distinctive here, and the bright, clean flavor of the lemon comes through. Serve with thick slices of vine-ripened tomatoes, sprinkled with salt and pepper and drizzled with olive oil.

½ cup dried flageolet beans, about 3 ounces, sorted and soaked overnight
2 bay leaves
2 fresh tarragon sprigs
1 cup dried small white beans, about 6 ounces, sorted and soaked overnight
Salt
¼ pound Blue Lake green beans or yellow wax beans, stem ends trimmed, cut into 2-inch lengths on a diagonal
1 small carrot, diced, about ½ cup
½ celery rib, diced, about ½ cup
Vinaigrette (recipe follows)
2 shallots, thinly sliced
1 heaped tablespoon coarsely chopped fresh tarragon

The flageolets will take nearly twice as long to cook as the white beans, so cook the beans separately. Drain and rinse the soaking flageolets and place in a medium-size saucepan; cover generously with cold water and add 1 bay leaf and a tarragon sprig. Bring to a boil, then reduce the heat and cook at a gentle boil until tender, 50 to 60 minutes. Watch the flageolets closely during the last 10 minutes; taste them to be sure they're tender before draining them. Put the white beans in another medium-size saucepan, cover them generously with cold water, and cook them with the remaining tarragon sprig and bay leaf; they will take 25 to 30 minutes.

While the beans are cooking, blanch the vegetables. Fill a medium-size saucepan with water, bring to a boil, and add ½ teaspoon salt. Cook the fresh beans until just tender, 4 to 5 minutes. Scoop them from the water with a slotted spoon and rinse under cold water. Set them aside to be added to the salad later. Blanch the carrots for about 1 minute, adding the celery for the last 30 seconds. Drain in a colander and rinse under cold water. Make the vinaigrette.

When the flageolets and white beans are tender, drain them and, while still warm, toss with the carrots, celery, shallots, and vinaigrette. Marinate for 30 minutes to 1 hour. Toss with the chopped tarragon and fresh beans; serve at room temperature.

SERVES FOUR TO SIX

Vinaigrette

2 teaspoons minced lemon zest
¼ cup fresh lemon juice
1 tablespoon sherry vinegar
2 garlic cloves, finely chopped
1 teaspoon salt
¼ teaspoon pepper
⅓ cup extra virgin olive oil

Combine everything but the oil in a small bowl, then gradually whisk in the oil to emulsify the vinaigrette.

MAKES ABOUT ¾ CUP

FRENCH TARRAGON

This essential herb has a tangy aniselike flavor that adds a bright touch to leafy green salads, grilled or roasted potatoes, and beans, fresh or dried. The classic French combination—lemon juice or red wine vinegar, Dijon mustard, and tarragon—appears on our menu throughout the year. In spring it's in a salad of asparagus, Chioggia beets, and sugar snap peas; in summer it's in a grilled Rosefir potato salad that mixes tender green beans, cherry tomatoes, and tarragon.

Be sure to grow true French tarragon; its Russian cousin is virtually tasteless. Tarragon grows from plant division, not seeds. If you see a sprig growing close to the ground, weigh it down with a twig and it will root a new tarragon plant. It likes full sun and rich, well-drained soil. In cold-weather climates, bring the entire plant indoors in a large pot. Tarragon flourishes in a window box with other sun-loving herbs.

Three-Bean Salad with Jícama and Orange

Perfect for a summer picnic, this salad is surprisingly light and full of pleasing textures. The beans take on the sweetness of the orange and the heat of the chilies, while the crunchy jícama adds fresh flavor. For a simpler salad, use one or two of the beans instead of all three. Serve with tortilla chips and Pickled Red Onions (page 399).

½ cup dried pinto beans, about 3 ounces, sorted and soaked overnight
½ cup dried black beans, about 3 ounces, sorted and soaked overnight
½ cup dried red beans, about 3 ounces, sorted and soaked overnight
Vinaigrette (recipe follows)
¼ medium-size red onion, diced, about ½ cup
Champagne vinegar
½ cup diced jícama, about 2 ounces
1 or 2 jalapeño chilies, seeded and finely diced
Salt
2 tablespoons coarsely chopped cilantro

The beans will vary in cooking time, so cook them separately. Although it may seem laborious, you'll avoid undercooking or overcooking the beans this way. Drain and rinse the pinto beans and place in a small saucepan; cover generously with cold water. Bring to a boil, then reduce the heat and cook at a gentle boil until tender, 40 to 45 minutes. Cook the black and red beans separately; cover generously with cold water, bring to a boil, then reduce the heat. Cook at a gentle boil until tender, about 25 to 30 minutes.

While the beans are cooking, prepare the vinaigrette and the rest of the salad ingredients. Bring a small pan of water to a boil and drop the onion in for 15 seconds. Drain well and toss with a splash of Champagne vinegar.

When the beans are tender, drain and transfer to a bowl. Toss the warm beans immediately with the vinaigrette, then add the onion, jícama, and chilies. Add salt to season. Sprinkle in the cilantro and serve at room temperature.

SERVES FOUR TO SIX

Vinaigrette

1 teaspoon minced orange zest
½ cup fresh orange juice
½ tablespoon Champagne vinegar
1 garlic clove, finely chopped
1 teaspoon cumin seed, toasted and ground (page 89)
1 teaspoon salt
2 tablespoons light olive oil
3 pinches of cayenne pepper

Combine all the ingredients in a small bowl and whisk together.

MAKES ABOUT ⅔ CUP

COMBINING CITRUS JUICE AND VINEGAR

*We like the way a splash or two of vinegar brightens a
citrus flavor and frequently combine the two in our
citrus vinaigrettes—this winning combination is exceptional in a couscous salad or with Artichokes with
Lemon and Mint.*

*Champagne vinegar or rice wine vinegar perfectly
accents the fresh juice of tangerines, oranges, lemons,
and limes. Sherry vinegar is delightful with orange
juice, though it sharpens lemon juice just as well—
enjoy it either way in a citrus vinaigrette tossed with
warm new potatoes, asparagus, and English peas.
A sprinkling of zest (citrus peel) brings the flavors to
life—we almost always include it in our citrus
vinaigrettes.*

Chick-Pea and Sun-Dried Tomato Salad

We serve this simple, satisfying salad year-round. Cook the chick-peas until they're quite tender, or they won't soak up the wonderful flavors. Let the salad sit for an hour or so before serving; the flavors will round and soften. Serve with crisp croutons and grilled eggplant (page 67).

1½ cups dried chick-peas, about 9 ounces, sorted and soaked overnight
1 bay leaf
1 fresh sage leaf
2 fresh marjoram or oregano sprigs
½ small red onion, diced, about ½ cup
Champagne vinegar
¼ cup red wine vinegar
1 garlic clove, finely chopped
Salt and pepper
2 tablespoons extra virgin olive oil
2 sun-dried tomatoes packed in oil, drained and diced, about ¼ cup
2 tablespoons chopped Italian parsley

Drain and rinse the beans and place them in a large saucepan. Cover generously with water; add the bay leaf and the fresh herbs. Boil gently for 50 to 60 minutes, tasting the beans to be sure they're tender; if they're undercooked, they won't absorb the flavors.

Meanwhile, bring a small pot of water to a boil, add the onion, and cook for 15 seconds. Drain and toss with a splash of Champagne vinegar. Combine the red wine vinegar, garlic, ¾ teaspoon salt, and a few pinches of pepper in a bowl. Gradually whisk in the oil.

Drain the beans when tender, then toss immediately with the vinaigrette, onion, and sun-dried tomatoes. Marinate for an hour; toss in the Italian parsley and serve at room temperature.

SERVES FOUR TO SIX

Spicy Black Beans with Chilies and Lime

Mint leaves, cilantro, and fresh lime give black beans a refreshing lift. We often crumble *queso fresco* (a Mexican cheese) over the beans and serve them with Jícama-Orange Salad (page 63), Pickled Red Onions (page 399), and sliced avocado.

1 ½ cups dried black beans, about 9 ounces, sorted and soaked overnight
Salt and pepper
½ medium-size carrot, diced, about ¼ cup
½ celery rib, diced, about ¼ cup
Zest of 2 limes, minced, about 1 ½ teaspoons
3 tablespoons fresh lime juice
2 tablespoons Champagne vinegar
1 garlic clove, finely chopped
3 pinches of cayenne pepper
¼ cup light olive oil
1 or 2 jalapeño chilies, seeded and diced
2 heaped tablespoons chopped cilantro
1 tablespoon chopped fresh mint

Drain and rinse the beans and place them in a large saucepan. Cover generously with cold water and bring to a boil. Reduce the heat and cook at a gentle boil for 20 to 25 minutes, until the beans are tender yet still hold their shape. Taste the beans to be sure they're cooked before draining them.

While the beans are cooking, bring a small pot of water to boil with ½ teaspoon salt. Drop the carrot into the water and cook for 1 minute, adding the celery for the last 30 seconds. Drain immediately and rinse under cold water. Make the dressing by combining the lime zest and juice, vinegar, garlic, cayenne, 1 teaspoon salt, and ¼ teaspoon black pepper. Gradually whisk in the oil.

When the beans are tender, drain and toss immediately with the dressing and the jalapeños. If the chilies are very hot, add half the amount to the salad, then add more to taste; the salad should be spicy. Marinate for 30 minutes. Season to taste with salt and pepper, then add the cilantro and mint before serving.

SERVES FOUR TO SIX

Lentil Salad with Curry Spices and Yogurt

This delicate salad is full of punch. Little French lentils are tossed with tangy yogurt, fragrant spices, and just enough cayenne pepper to add heat. Lemon juice and cilantro freshen and lighten the flavors. Serve with croutons or grilled pita bread.

1½ cups French lentils, about 9 ounces
1 bay leaf
¼ medium-size red onion, diced, about ½ cup
Champagne vinegar
1 small carrot, diced, about ½ cup
½ cup plain yogurt
3 tablespoons fresh lemon juice
1½ teaspoons cumin seed, toasted and ground (page 89)
½ teaspoon ground turmeric
¼ teaspoon ground coriander
1 teaspoon salt
⅛ teaspoon cayenne pepper
⅛ teaspoon black pepper
½ red bell pepper, diced, about ½ cup
2 tablespoons coarsely chopped cilantro

Rinse the lentils and place them in a medium-size saucepan; cover generously with cold water and add the bay leaf. Bring to a boil, then reduce the heat and simmer until tender, 15 to 20 minutes. Keep an eye on the lentils, being careful not to undercook or overcook them.

Meanwhile, bring a small pot of water to a boil and drop the onion in for 15 seconds. Scoop out with a strainer and toss with a splash of Champagne vinegar. Drop the carrot in for 1 minute, then drain and set aside.

In a small bowl, combine the yogurt, lemon juice, 1 tablespoon Champagne vinegar, spices, salt, cayenne, and black pepper.

Drain the lentils when tender; remove the bay leaf and immediately toss with the vegetables and the yogurt mixture. The lemon flavor will be strong at first, but the lentils will gradually absorb it. Toss in the cilantro just before serving.

SERVES FOUR TO SIX

Tip: French lentils are particularly good for marinating, so be sure to use them. They cook quickly and hold their shape and texture well. Watch them closely during the last few minutes of cooking—there's a fine line between undercooking and overcooking them.

Basmati and Wild Rice Salad with Tangerines and Pine Nuts

The nutty flavor of the wild rice and toasted pine nuts combined with the sweetness of currants and juicy tangerines makes this elegant salad a delightful addition to a holiday feast.

1 cup wild rice
7 cups water
Salt
½ cup basmati rice, rinsed and drained
¾ cup fresh tangerine juice, about 4 tangerines
½ cup dried currants
3 tangerines
Champagne vinegar
2 tablespoons light olive oil
2 tablespoons pine nuts, toasted (page 263)

Place the wild rice in a large saucepan; cover with 1 quart of water, add ½ teaspoon salt, and bring to a boil. Reduce the heat to a gentle boil; cover and cook until the grains are tender but still chewy, about 30 to 35 minutes.

Bring the remaining 3 cups water to a boil in a medium-size saucepan; add the basmati rice and ½ teaspoon salt. Cook for 8 to 10 minutes, until just tender. Drain and cool, then add to the wild rice.

In a small saucepan over medium heat, heat the tangerine juice just to boiling; pour it over the currants to plump them. Peel and section the tangerines, removing the seeds and threads.

Toss the rice with the currants, tangerine juice, ½ tablespoon Champagne vinegar, and the olive oil. If necessary, adjust the seasoning with salt and a splash of vinegar. Add the tangerines and the toasted pine nuts just before serving at room temperature.

SERVES SIX

Variation: Use oranges and their juice in place of the tangerines. Using a sharp knife, remove the peel and white pith from the orange by slicing off the top and the bottom, then working down the sides. Hold the orange over a bowl to catch the juice and cut each section loose by slicing down next to the membrane.

Corn and Bulgur Salad
with Cilantro and Lime

A zesty summer salad with a fresh, hearty taste that's quick and easy to put together. The bulgur has a nutty flavor and texture that mixes deliciously with the sweet kernels of corn.

½ cup bulgur
½ cup boiling water
1 tablespoon light olive oil
3 ears of corn, shaved, about 3 cups kernels
Salt
¼ medium-size red onion, diced, about ½ cup
1 jalapeño chili, seeded and thinly sliced
1 tablespoon fresh lemon juice
1 tablespoon fresh lime juice
Cayenne pepper
1 tablespoon coarsely chopped cilantro
1 tablespoon chopped fresh sage, about 5 large leaves

Place the bulgur in a medium-size bowl and pour the boiling water over it. Cover and let sit for 20 minutes.

Meanwhile, heat the oil in a sauté pan. Add the corn and ¼ teaspoon salt and sauté over medium heat for 5 minutes. Add the onion and sauté for about 3 minutes, until the corn is tender. Allow to cool, then toss with the bulgur, chilies, lemon and lime juices, ½ teaspoon salt, and a few pinches of cayenne. Add salt if necessary. Toss in the cilantro and sage just before serving.

SERVES FOUR TO SIX

Dolmas—Grape Leaves Stuffed with Fragrant Rice

Our dinner chef, Diana, learned to make these dolmas on the Greek island of Mykonos and brought the recipe to Greens. The rice is cooked with lemon threads and freshly ground cinnamon, then tossed with plump currants and toasted pine nuts. Its spicy, sweet flavor is a perfect contrast to the pungent grape leaves. These dolmas are absolutely delicious and surprisingly easy to make. Serve simply with wedges of lemon and Kalamata olives or alongside marinated Chioggia beets and Cucumbers with Yogurt and Mint (page 395).

2 cups water
Salt
1 cup long-grain white rice
¾ teaspoon cinnamon, preferably freshly ground
1 tablespoon sugar
1 tablespoon unsalted butter
Zest and juice of 1 lemon, about 2 tablespoons juice
¼ cup dried currants
¼ cup pine nuts, toasted (page 263)
Five-pepper mixture or black pepper
20 to 24 grape leaves packed in brine
Extra virgin olive oil

Bring the water to a boil in a medium-size saucepan; add 1 teaspoon salt, then stir in the rice, cinnamon, sugar, butter, and lemon zest. Allow the pot to return to a boil, then cover and cook over low heat until the rice is just tender, 15 to 20 minutes. The rice should be slightly undercooked at this point, since it will cook a little more when the dolmas steam.

Transfer the rice to a bowl and, while it's still hot, toss with the currants, pine nuts, and the lemon juice. Season to taste with salt and pepper.

Rinse and drain the grape leaves, pat them dry, and snip off the stems; spread them out on a work surface. Pack 1 tablespoon rice in your hands to compress it and place in the center of each grape leaf. Fold in the bottom and the two sides, then roll toward the top until the entire grape leaf has been rolled.

Brush the dolmas lightly with a little olive oil and set in a steamer basket. Place the steamer over boiling water, cover, and steam for 3 to 5 minutes, until heated through. Serve warm or at room temperature.

MAKES 20 TO 24 DOLMAS

Couscous Salad with Apricots, Pine Nuts, and Ginger

The tastes and textures of this delicious, light salad are wonderfully balanced—the couscous absorbs the sweetness of the plump dried fruit and the flavors of ginger and orange. Serve in the spring with watercress and asparagus spears tossed in sesame vinaigrette; in the winter with sliced blood oranges, black olives, and grilled pita bread. You can make the salad a few hours or even a day in advance. Just be sure to add the pine nuts right before serving to keep them crisp and nutty.

1 cup instant couscous
½ cup water
1 cup fresh orange juice
¼ cup light olive oil
Champagne vinegar
8 dried apricots, thinly sliced, about ⅓ cup
1 tablespoon dried currants
1 tablespoon golden raisins
2 teaspoons grated fresh ginger
Salt
¼ medium-size red onion, finely diced, about ½ cup
2 tablespoons pine nuts, toasted (page 263)

Pour the couscous grains into a small mixing bowl. Combine the water, orange juice, olive oil, and 2 tablespoons vinegar in a medium-size saucepan. Bring the liquid just to a boil and stir in the dried fruit, ginger, and ½ teaspoon salt; pour immediately over the couscous. Cover the bowl and let it sit for 20 minutes.

Bring a small pot of water to a boil and drop in the red onion for 15 seconds. Drain well; toss the onion with a few splashes of vinegar to draw out its pink color.

When the couscous is ready, gently fluff it with a fork and toss with the pine nuts and onion. Add salt to season and an additional splash of vinegar to brighten the flavor.

SERVES FOUR

Spicy Corn with Chilies and Cilantro

Plump sweet corn, juicy cherry tomatoes, scallions, and spicy chilies—a flavorful combination that makes this dish a summer favorite. Served on its own as a salad or a relish or alongside quesadillas brushed with Chipotle Puree (page 332) and filled with smoked cheese, it's a delicious way to enjoy corn and tomatoes when they're in season.

1 tablespoon light olive oil
4 ears of corn, shaved, about 4 cups kernels
1 or 2 jalapeño chilies, seeded and diced
Salt
2 teaspoons Champagne vinegar
4 teaspoons fresh lime juice
Cayenne pepper
1 scallion, white and green parts, thinly sliced on a diagonal
2 tablespoons coarsely chopped cilantro
1 cup cherry tomato halves, about ½ pint

Heat the olive oil in a wide skillet; add the corn, jalapeños, and ¼ teaspoon salt. Sauté over medium heat for 7 to 8 minutes, until the corn is tender. Transfer to a bowl and toss the warm corn with the vinegar, lime juice, ¼ teaspoon salt, and a few pinches of cayenne.

When the corn is cool, add the sliced scallion and cilantro. Season to taste with salt. Toss in the cherry tomatoes just before serving. For a spicier salad, add more cayenne or another jalapeño chili.

SERVES FOUR TO SIX

Fall Salad with Warm Gorgonzola Croutons

This beautiful salad is a Greens classic. Tart, crisp apples, freshly cracked walnuts, and feathery slices of pale green fennel offer flavorful texture. Sherry vinegar cuts through the richness of the Walnut Vinaigrette and defines the flavors with its sharp acidity. Gorgonzola cheese is creamed with just enough butter to soften the flavor, then spread over crisp croutons and toasted until golden and bubbly. Arrange the salad on a platter and pass the warm croutons at the table.

1 pound beets
⅓ cup walnut pieces
1 medium-size fennel bulb
2 handfuls of frisée
Gorgonzola Croutons (recipe follows)
Walnut Vinaigrette (recipe follows)
1 shallot, thinly sliced
Salt and pepper
Sherry vinegar
1 tart, crisp apple

Preheat the oven to 375°F. Trim away the beet greens and save them for pasta or a sauté. Wash the beets and place them in a small baking dish with ½ inch water. Cover and bake until tender, 40 to 45 minutes, depending on their size. Test the beets for doneness with a paring knife or a skewer. Remove from the oven and set aside. Toast the walnuts on a baking sheet until fragrant, about 8 minutes. Set aside to cool.

Trim the base of the fennel and remove the tough outer leaves. Cut the bulb lengthwise into quarters; trim away the core and thinly slice. When the beets are cool, peel and slice into wedges.

Trim off the root end and tough outer leaves of the frisée, saving the pale green inner leaves for the salad. Wash the leaves and dry them in a spinner; wrap them in a damp towel and refrigerate. Prepare the croutons and the vinaigrette.

Set the oven to broil. Toss the frisée with a little vinaigrette and arrange on a platter. Combine the beets and shallots and toss with half the vinaigrette. Season to taste with salt, pepper, and a splash of vinegar; arrange the beets on the frisée. (Dressing the beets separately will keep the beet juice from coloring the fennel and apples.)

Cut the apple into quarters, remove the core, and thinly slice. Combine the fennel, apple, and walnuts, toss with the remaining vinaigrette, and spread over the beets. Sprinkle with freshly ground pepper. When the salad is ready, toast the croutons in the broiler until the cheese is bubbly, 1 to 2 minutes; serve them with the salad.

SERVES FOUR TO SIX

Gorgonzola Croutons

12 baguette slices, cut about ¼ inch thick on a diagonal
Light olive oil
2 ounces Gorgonzola cheese
1 tablespoon unsalted butter, softened
Pepper and salt

Preheat the oven to 375°F. Brush the sliced bread with olive oil and bake until crisp and golden, about 8 minutes. Cream the Gorgonzola with the butter and a few pinches of pepper. Add salt if needed. Spread the croutons generously with the Gorgonzola butter.

MAKES 12 CROUTONS

Walnut Vinaigrette

2 tablespoons sherry vinegar
¼ teaspoon salt
A few pinches of pepper
3 tablespoons light olive oil
3 tablespoons walnut oil

Combine everything but the oils in a small bowl, then whisk in the oils.

MAKES ABOUT ⅓ CUP

GOLDEN AND CHIOGGIA BEETS

Chioggias are rosy, sweet beets with varying blush rings—when sliced, they show off their beautiful concentric circles. Golden beets are a deep rusty yellow throughout, with a slightly nuttier taste. At their best they need very little seasoning—a little walnut oil, a splash of vinegar, and a sprinkle of salt and pepper. Unlike red beets, they hold on to their color and can be marinated together or tossed into a salad. Be sure to save the tender greens—they make a delightful pasta dish or simple sauté.

Beets love sunlight and rich, well-drained, slightly alkaline soil—mix in a little wood ash or lime before planting. Sow the seeds an inch apart in the early spring or fall (they'll winter over) and keep the ground evenly moist throughout the growing season. Harvest the tender thinnings for a delicious sauté and leave the rest to grow to maturity.

Grilled Potato Salad with Chipotle Vinaigrette

This lively potato salad is a favorite year-round. Strips of sweet peppers, rings of red onions, and freshly harvested potatoes are grilled over coals, then tossed with spicy Chipotle Vinaigrette. The flavors really work together—the sweetness of the peppers and onions comes through, while the potatoes absorb the smoky heat of the chilies and the fresh flavor of cilantro. Yellow Finn, Bintje, or Rosefir potatoes are particularly delicious in this salad. Of course you can serve the potato salad on its own and skip the bed of greens.

> 2 pounds new potatoes
> Light olive oil
> Salt and pepper
> 1 medium-size red onion
> 1 red or yellow bell pepper
> 1 garlic clove, finely chopped
> A handful of salad greens: mizuna and frisée or sprigs of watercress
> Chipotle Vinaigrette (recipe follows)
> 1 tablespoon coarsely chopped cilantro

Prepare the grill.

Preheat the oven to 400°F. Toss the potatoes in a small baking dish with just enough olive oil to coat them lightly and sprinkle with a few pinches of salt and pepper. Cover and roast until tender, about 35 to 40 minutes. Set aside to cool. Cut the potatoes into halves, or quarters if they're large, then slide them onto skewers for grilling. (Skewers aren't necessary if the grill grates are close together.)

Slice the onion into ½-inch-thick rings, keeping each section of cut rings intact, then peel off the outer skin. Cut the pepper in half lengthwise, remove the membrane and seeds, and pull away the stem; cut lengthwise into 1-inch-thick strips. Add the garlic to a little olive oil and brush over the vegetables, then sprinkle with salt and pepper. Wash the greens and dry them in a spinner. Make the vinaigrette.

Place the vegetables on the grill, making sure that the cut side of the potatoes and the skin side of the peppers are facing the grill. Turn the onions after about 5 minutes and, if necessary, move the peppers and the potatoes to a cooler part of the grill while the onions continue to cook. The onions become very sweet as they cook slowly over the hot coals, so don't try to hurry them.

When the onions are tender and grilled on both sides, transfer to a bowl and toss with the potatoes, peppers, vinaigrette, and cilantro. Loosely arrange the greens on a platter, then spoon the vegetables over. Serve immediately.

SERVES FOUR TO SIX

Chipotle Vinaigrette

1 tablespoon Champagne vinegar
2 tablespoons fresh lime juice
½ teaspoon Dijon mustard
1 teaspoon Chipotle Puree (page 332)
1 garlic clove, finely chopped
½ teaspoon salt
5 tablespoons light olive oil

Combine the vinegar and lime juice in a small bowl. Whisk in the Dijon mustard, Chipotle Puree, garlic, and salt. Slowly whisk in the oil to emulsify.

MAKES ABOUT ½ CUP

MIZUNA

The finely cut leaves of this versatile Japanese mustard green have a flavor that's delicate and peppery. It's delightful tossed with Lollo Rossa and Oak Leaf lettuces, red mustard greens, and a sharp sherry vinaigrette. With frisée, it's a lofty green bed for warm potatoes, asparagus, and peas.

Mizuna germinates quickly and likes the same growing conditions as red mustard. For an instant salad, sow mizuna, rocket, and red mustard seeds together, or plant them together in a container. Harvest the leaves as needed and let the plant continue to grow.

Yellow Finn Potato Salad with Artichokes and Lemon-Tarragon Vinaigrette

This is a delightfully unusual potato salad. The potatoes are still warm when tossed with the vinaigrette, so they take in its full rich flavors—lemon, tarragon, extra virgin olive oil, and a little Dijon mustard for added sharpness. To allow the flavors to develop and soften, let the salad sit for an hour or two before serving. It's beautiful served on a bed of peppery watercress. For a delicious variation, include strips of roasted red pepper.

2 pounds Yellow Finn or new potatoes
Extra virgin olive oil
Salt and pepper
Artichokes with Lemon and Mint (page 53), the mint omitted
2 shallots or ¼ medium-size red onion, thinly sliced
Champagne vinegar
Lemon-Tarragon Vinaigrette (recipe follows)
1 teaspoon drained capers, rinsed
12 Gaeta or Niçoise olives

Preheat the oven to 400°F. Toss the potatoes with a little olive oil and sprinkle with salt and pepper. Place in a baking dish, cover, and roast until tender, about 35 to 40 minutes.

While the potatoes are roasting, prepare the artichokes and cook them in their marinade as directed. Toss the shallots with a splash of Champagne vinegar to draw out their color. Make the vinaigrette.

When the potatoes are cool enough to handle, cut them into halves or quarters and toss with the vinaigrette, shallots, and capers. Add the artichokes and toss everything together. Season with salt and pepper to taste. Garnish with the olives and serve.

SERVES FOUR TO SIX

Lemon-Tarragon Vinaigrette

½ teaspoon minced lemon zest
2 tablespoons fresh lemon juice
1 teaspoon Dijon mustard
1 garlic clove, finely chopped
½ teaspoon salt
A few pinches of pepper
5 tablespoons extra virgin olive oil
2 teaspoons coarsely chopped fresh tarragon

In a small bowl, combine the lemon zest and juice, mustard, garlic, salt, and pepper. Slowly whisk in the olive oil, then add the tarragon.

MAKES ½ CUP

Variation: In the spring, we often include blanched asparagus tips, even fava beans and wedges of Chioggia or golden beets. Toss the asparagus and peeled favas with the salad just before serving, or the acidity of the vinaigrette will discolor them.

POTATOES

We celebrate the first harvest of Green Gulch potatoes each year around Independence Day. We grill and toss them in salads or serve them with summer vegetables and a lemony aïoli. Potato soup with pesto is wonderful, but so are potatoes simply oven-roasted with fresh herbs and whole cloves of garlic. The cream of the crop are listed below.

Yellow Finns have a buttery yellow flesh that enriches soups and gratins. Bintjes have lighter yellow flesh than Yellow Finns, though they're just as flavorful. Rosefirs are truly a favorite—these tender, sweet fingerling potatoes with a rose-colored skin are delightful roasted or grilled. Red LaSotas have outstanding flavor—just 10 to 12 weeks after planting you'll enjoy them as new potatoes, wonderfully tender and pink.

When the ground has begun to warm, turn plenty of compost or other organic matter (not manure) into your soil and plant your seed potatoes in a 12-inch-deep trench. Cover with 4 inches of soil and, as they grow, fill them in with more soil, until the plant flowers. Sunlight is harmful to the tubers—they turn green and poisonous. When the plant flowers, it's setting tubers as well. You can dig around and steal a few potatoes; these "new" potatoes, picked before the plant dies and the sugars turn to starch, are sweet and delicious. One plant will produce 8 to 10 potatoes. Keep the soil evenly moist—you can't neglect them for a couple of weeks, or you'll weaken the plants.

You can have your own seed potatoes by saving good-looking potatoes without any cuts. Store them at 40°F in a dark place. They'll probably sprout, and if they do, leave the sprouts on. If they haven't sprouted when you're ready to plant, leave them outside for a couple of weeks until they begin to sprout and grow.

Grilled New Potato Salad with Cherry Tomatoes, Summer Beans, and Basil

Crispy grilled potatoes are tossed hot off the fire with colorful cherry tomatoes, tender beans, and salty black olives. It's the flavor of the grilled potatoes that makes this salad so exceptional, but if you don't have time to grill, skip the grilling and just use the roasted potatoes instead.

2 pounds new potatoes
Light olive oil
Salt and pepper
¼ pound fresh summer beans: green, yellow wax, green or yellow Romano
½ pint cherry tomatoes: Sweet 100 or pear tomatoes
1 handful of frisée or salad greens (optional)
Basil-Garlic Vinaigrette (recipe follows)
Champagne vinegar
12 Niçoise or Gaeta olives

Prepare the grill.

Preheat the oven to 400°F. Toss the potatoes in a baking dish with a little olive oil and sprinkle with a few pinches of salt and pepper. Cover and roast until tender, about 35 to 40 minutes. Set aside to cool. Cut the potatoes into halves, or quarters if large, then slide them onto skewers for grilling. (Skewers won't be necessary if the grill grates are close together.)

While the potatoes are roasting, remove the stem ends from the beans and cut them in half diagonally or leave whole if they're small. Bring a small pot of water to a boil and add ½ teaspoon salt. Drop the beans into the water and cook until just tender, about 3 to 4 minutes, depending on their size. Rinse under cold water and set aside to drain. Cut the cherry tomatoes into halves or leave whole if small. Wash the salad greens if you're using them and dry them in a spinner. Make the vinaigrette.

Place the potatoes on the grill, cut side down, and grill until they're golden and crisp and defined grill marks appear. Slide the grilled potatoes from the skewers and toss with the beans, cherry tomatoes, and vinaigrette. Adjust the seasoning, if needed, with a splash of Champagne vinegar and salt and pepper. Loosely arrange the greens on a platter, spoon the vegetables over, and garnish with the olives.

SERVES FOUR

Basil-Garlic Vinaigrette

2 tablespoons Champagne vinegar
6 tablespoons extra virgin olive oil
½ cup fresh basil leaves
½ teaspoon salt
1 garlic clove, coarsely chopped

Combine everything in a blender and blend until smooth.

MAKES ABOUT ½ CUP

LITTLE TOMATOES

Cherry tomatoes and their cousins grape, pear, and currant tomatoes come to us in all colors, sizes, and shapes throughout the summer, and we include them in many of our dishes. Here are a few of our favorites:

Sweet 100s are tiny red and yellow tomatoes that burst with juicy flavor. They're delicious in salads and simply warmed in a skillet with olive oil, shallots, and herbs. They're excellent marinated and tossed with pasta and Garlic Bread Crumbs. In a pinch, you can make them into a quick tomato sauce.

Mild-tasting Pear tomatoes are also fine in salads. Green Grapes are well named—these range in size and have a soft green hue. Tiny red and yellow Currant tomatoes are even smaller than Sweet 100s—they have an intensely sweet flavor and come to us still on the vine.

Little tomatoes like a sunny spot in the garden. They'll need a moist, deeply worked, well-drained soil with plenty of organic matter. Water low to the ground rather than overhead. As they grow, tie them loosely to stakes, wire cages, or trellises. Harvest any green tomatoes left on the vine for pickling before the first killing frost.

Spring Vegetables with Meyer Lemon Vinaigrette

We make this flavorful salad throughout the year, varying the vegetables with the seasons, and serve it warm or at room temperature. Rosefir or Yellow Finn potatoes, grown at Green Gulch Farm, add their own distinctive flavor. Tossed with the vinaigrette while still warm, the potatoes absorb the sweetness and the fragrance of the Meyer lemon juice and zest. If Meyer lemons aren't available, use ordinary lemons instead and whisk a little Dijon mustard into the vinaigrette to enrich its flavor.

½ pound small Rosefir, Yellow Finn, or new potatoes
Light olive oil
Salt and pepper
Meyer Lemon Vinaigrette (recipe follows)
2 shallots, thinly sliced
Champagne vinegar
½ medium-size red or yellow bell pepper, sliced into thin strips
1 medium-size carrot, cut in half lengthwise and sliced ½ inch thick on a diagonal
½ pound asparagus, woody ends removed, cut into 3-inch lengths on a diagonal
¼ pound snap peas, strings removed
½ pound English peas, shelled
¼ pound snow peas, strings removed
2 tablespoons pine nuts, toasted (page 263)
8 or 12 Niçoise olives

Preheat the oven to 400°F. Place the potatoes in a small baking dish; toss with a little olive oil and sprinkle with salt and pepper. Cover and bake until tender, 30 to 35 minutes. Make the vinaigrette. Sprinkle the shallots with a little Champagne vinegar to bring out their pink color. While the potatoes are still warm, cut them into halves or quarters and toss with the bell pepper, shallots, and ¼ cup of the vinaigrette.

The bright color and crisp texture of the vegetables are essential to the salad, so be sure to have all of the ingredients prepared before you begin. Bring a medium pot of water to a boil and add ½ teaspoon salt. Drop the carrot into the water, followed 30 seconds later by the asparagus, snap peas, and English peas. After 45 seconds, add the snow peas and cook together for 45 seconds. Pour the vegetables into a colander, rinse them under cold water, and drain. (To serve the salad warm, toss everything together with the vinaigrette as soon as you drain the vegetables.)

To keep the green vegetables from discoloring, toss the salad just before serving. Toss the vegetables together with the pine nuts and remaining vinaigrette. Garnish with 2 or 3 olives per serving.

SERVES FOUR

Meyer Lemon Vinaigrette

Zest of 1 Meyer lemon, minced
2 tablespoons Meyer lemon juice
1 tablespoon Champagne vinegar
½ teaspoon salt
⅛ teaspoon black pepper
6 tablespoons light olive oil

Combine everything but the oil in a small bowl, then whisk in the oil. Whisk in a little mustard if you're using ordinary lemons.

MAKES ABOUT ½ CUP

MEYER LEMONS

These fragrant orange-colored lemons with a delicate shape are a Bay Area backyard treasure. Because their skins are so soft, they can't be grown commercially, so they come to us from small farms, friends, and neighbors. The sweet juice and fragrant zest of Meyer lemons set them apart from others, like ordinary lemons (whose name is Eureka). They make the most delightful vinaigrettes and butter sauces. A Meyer Lemon Ice Cream, Pots de Crème, or mousse is unforgettable.

A dwarf Meyer lemon tree is happy to grow in a container in a protected spot on your deck or patio and can even be grown indoors. It needs airy, moist soil that drains quickly; be careful not to overwater. In the right climate (cool summer, relatively warm winter) this hardy tree will bear fruit year-round, beginning at an early age.

Three Tomato Salads

Tomato salads have a very special place on our summer menu. With the extraordinary varieties available, each salad is a delectable feast of color and bursting flavor. They're ripened on the vine, and often dry-cropped (grown with little water for intensity of flavor). We've chosen the following three salads as a sampling—similar in style, yet each has its own exceptional flavor and distinctive presentation. We hope they inspire your imagination; the possibilities are endlessly delicious.

TOMATOES

Late summer and early fall are the peak of tomato season, offering varieties in all tastes and colors. When tomatoes are in, we use them in every dish imaginable—knowing that they'll soon be gone.

We feature our favorite varieties—Golden Jubilee, Marvel Stripe, Zebra Stripe, and Golden Boy—on antipastos and in summer salads. The yellow and golden varieties are layered with alternating slices of red tomatoes on pizza or marinated together with olive oil and fresh herbs for pasta.

Not to be forgotten are the ripe red tomatoes, with a list of varieties that's almost endless. It's best to inquire at a nursery or speak with gardeners in your area to find out which strains will thrive and grow. All are delicious on open-face sandwiches or drizzled with olive oil and enjoyed on a thick slice of crusty bread.

A sunny southern slope is an ideal home for tomato plants; they need warmth and full sun as well as moist, well-drained soil with a good deal of humus to thrive. If you want to start from seed, sow in flats 6 or 7 weeks before the last frost, and keep them in a warm room. Transplant outdoors in late spring or early summer, when the nighttime temperature stays above 55°F. As they grow, tie them loosely to stakes, wire cages, or trellises. Keep them evenly moist, especially when the fruits begin to form, but don't water from overhead. Harvest any green tomatoes left on the vine before the first killing frost.

Tomato Salad with Avocado and Citrus-Chili Vinaigrette

Slices of creamy avocado alternate with wedges of red, Golden Jubilee, and Zebra or Marvel Stripe tomatoes. They're served on delicate leaves of mizuna, sprinkled with cherry tomatoes, then drizzled with a mildly spicy citrus vinaigrette.

> *2 cups mizuna, red mustard greens, or rocket (arugula)*
> *1 pound sweet, vine-ripened tomatoes, including Golden Jubilee and Zebra Stripe*
>   *tomatoes if available*
> *½ pint sweet cherry tomatoes: red or yellow Sweet 100 or pear tomatoes*
> *Citrus-Chili Vinaigrette (recipe follows)*
> *1 avocado*
> *Salt*

Remove the stems of the mizuna; wash and dry in a spinner. Wrap in a damp towel and refrigerate. Core the tomatoes and slice into wedges. Pluck the stems from the cherry tomatoes; cut in half if large. Make the vinaigrette.

Cut the avocado in half; peel and cut into thick slices on a slight diagonal. Toss the mizuna with a little of the vinaigrette and place on a serving platter. Arrange overlapping layers of tomato and avocado on top and sprinkle lightly with salt. Sprinkle with the cherry tomatoes and drizzle with the remaining vinaigrette.

SERVES FOUR

Citrus-Chili Vinaigrette

> *2 tablespoons fresh orange juice*
> *1 tablespoon fresh lime juice*
> *1 jalapeño chili, seeded and coarsely chopped*
> *¼ cup light olive oil*
> *¼ teaspoon salt*

Combine everything in a blender and blend until smooth. The vinaigrette should be lively and spicy. If it needs more heat, add another chili.

MAKES ABOUT ⅓ CUP

Vine-Ripened Tomatoes with Goat Cheese and Basil Vinaigrette

The tomatoes are drizzled with a vinaigrette of fruity extra virgin olive oil, Champagne vinegar, and pureed basil and nestled on a bed of peppery watercress with colorful cherry tomatoes, black Niçoise olives, and crumbled goat cheese.

1 pound vine-ripened tomatoes, including Golden Jubilee and Marvel Stripe if available
½ pint cherry tomatoes: Sweet 100, Green Grape or pear tomatoes
Basil Vinaigrette (recipe follows)
1 bunch of watercress
Salt and pepper
2 ounces mild, creamy goat cheese such as Montrachet
12 Niçoise or Gaeta olives

Core the tomatoes and cut into wedges or thick slices. Pluck the stems from the cherry tomatoes; leave whole if small and cut in half if large. Make the vinaigrette. Pluck the small sprigs of watercress, discarding the long stems; wash and dry in a spinner.

Spread the watercress on a serving platter and arrange the tomatoes over it. Sprinkle the tomatoes with salt and freshly ground black pepper, then drizzle on the vinaigrette. Sprinkle the cherry tomatoes over the salad, crumble on the goat cheese, and garnish with the olives.

SERVES FOUR

Basil Vinaigrette

1 tablespoon Champagne vinegar
¼ cup extra virgin olive oil
⅓ cup fresh basil leaves
¼ teaspoon salt

Combine everything in a blender and blend until smooth.

MAKES ⅓ CUP

Tomato Salad with Cucumbers, Feta Cheese, Oregano, and Mint

Half-rounds of crisp cucumbers mingle with juicy ripe tomatoes, crumbled feta cheese, salty Greek olives, and a sprinkling of oregano and mint. The spirited Lemon Vinaigrette accents the sweetness of the tomatoes and the crunch of the cucumbers. It's the unusual greens and the fresh mint that make this salad distinctive.

2 handfuls of mixed greens: watercress, mizuna, and red mustard greens
1 pound sweet, vine-ripened tomatoes
½ small cucumber
Lemon Vinaigrette (recipe follows)
Salt and pepper
2 ounces feta cheese, crumbled
½ teaspoon chopped fresh oregano
½ teaspoon chopped fresh mint
12 Kalamata olives

Remove the stems and any bruised leaves from the greens; wash and dry them in a spinner. Wrap the greens in a damp towel and refrigerate until needed. Core the tomato and slice into thick rounds or wedges. Peel and seed the cucumber and slice ¼ inch thick on a diagonal. Make the vinaigrette.

Spread the greens on a serving platter. Arrange the tomatoes and cucumbers on top, alternating and overlapping them slightly. Sprinkle with salt and freshly ground black pepper, then drizzle on the vinaigrette. Crumble the cheese over the salad, sprinkle on the oregano and mint, and garnish with the olives.

SERVES FOUR

Lemon Vinaigrette

½ teaspoon minced lemon zest
1 tablespoon fresh lemon juice
½ tablespoon Champagne vinegar
¼ teaspoon salt
¼ cup extra virgin olive oil

Combine everything but the oil in a small bowl, then whisk in the oil.

MAKES ABOUT ⅓ CUP

Baba Ghanouj

This traditional dish of roasted eggplant, lemon, and tahini holds its own as a mainstay of our Middle Eastern salad plates. The flavors are undoubtedly rich, and it's good to complement this with the refreshing flavor of Cucumbers with Yogurt and Mint (page 395). Serve Baba Ghanouj with grilled or warmed pita bread and salty black olives.

2 globe eggplants, about 2 pounds
3 tablespoons extra virgin olive oil
2 tablespoons roasted tahini (sesame paste)
1 garlic clove, finely chopped
½ teaspoon cumin seed, toasted and ground (page 89)
Juice of 1 lemon, about 2½ tablespoons
¾ teaspoon salt
Cayenne pepper
1 tablespoon chopped cilantro

Preheat the oven to 375°F. Cut the eggplant in half lengthwise and brush the cut sides lightly with olive oil. Place on a baking sheet, cut side down, and roast until very tender, about 35 minutes. Place the eggplant in a colander to drain for 15 minutes, then scoop the flesh out of the skin.

To make in the food processor: Combine the eggplant, remaining olive oil, tahini, garlic, cumin, 2 tablespoons of the lemon juice, the salt, and a few pinches of cayenne in the work bowl. Pulse until the eggplant is somewhat smooth but retains some of its texture.

To make by hand: Combine all of the ingredients except the eggplant and cilantro and whisk together. Chop the eggplant and add to the mixture.

Allow the Baba Ghanouj to sit for an hour at room temperature, then season to taste with additional lemon juice, salt, and cayenne. Toss in the cilantro and serve.

SERVES FOUR

Artichokes with Lemon and Mint

These tasty marinated artichokes make a frequent appearance on our antipasto and Middle Eastern salad plates. Make them a day or two in advance—just be sure to adjust the seasoning before serving. The bright flavor of the lemon can't be missed, and the mint is added at the last minute to give the artichokes a fresh, zesty finish. You can also include fresh marjoram or oregano or omit the herbs altogether. The serving possibilities are endless—tossed in a salad of roasted potatoes (page 251), for instance, or elegantly served alongside savory filo turnovers, roasted peppers, and flavorful black olives.

3 cups water
½ cup fresh lemon juice
3 tablespoons Champagne vinegar
¼ cup light olive oil
1 teaspoon salt
1 bay leaf
½ teaspoon whole peppercorns or whole coriander seeds
4 medium-size artichokes
1 teaspoon chopped fresh mint

Combine everything but the artichokes and mint in a large stainless-steel saucepan. Trim off the artichoke tops and stems and peel away all of the outer leaves, down to the pale green inner leaves. Cut the artichokes into quarters and remove the choke, adding the artichoke pieces to the saucepan as you go.

Bring the liquid to a boil, then reduce the heat and simmer until artichokes are tender, about 7 to 8 minutes. The artichokes should be tender but not too soft; they'll continue to cook a little as they cool. (If they're slightly overcooked, spread them out on a baking sheet to cool in the refrigerator.)

Pour the artichokes and their cooking liquid into a strainer (the marinade can be used again and will keep for up to 1 week in the refrigerator). Allow them to cool and toss with the mint just before serving.

SERVES FOUR TO SIX

Sicilian Salad with Roasted Eggplant, Peppers, and Garlic

The flavors of this salad grow rich and full if allowed to sit for a while. Japanese eggplant, thick slices of roasted red and yellow pepper, and roasted whole cloves of garlic are tossed together in their own juices, sweetly accented with balsamic vinegar, and nestled on a bed of peppery watercress. Serve with thin shavings of Parmesan cheese, croutons, and oil-cured olives.

2 medium-size red or yellow bell peppers
5 tablespoons extra virgin olive oil
16 garlic cloves, unpeeled
2 pounds Japanese eggplant
2 additional garlic cloves, finely chopped
Salt and pepper
2 tablespoons balsamic vinegar
Champagne vinegar
1 small bunch of watercress, about 2 cups sprigs
8 or 12 Gaeta or oil-cured olives

Preheat the oven to 500°F. Cut the peppers in half; remove the stems, seeds, and membrane. Place on a lightly oiled baking sheet, cut side down, and brush lightly with oil. Roast until their skins begin to blister and darken, about 15 minutes, then remove from the oven and place in a covered bowl to steam.

Lower the heat to 375°F to roast the garlic and eggplant. Toss the garlic cloves in a little olive oil and lightly oil the baking sheet. Cut the eggplant into ¾-inch-thick diagonal slices and toss with the remaining olive oil, the chopped garlic, ¼ teaspoon salt, and a few pinches of pepper. Place the eggplant and garlic on the baking sheet and roast until the garlic cloves are soft and the eggplant is quite tender, about 12 to 15 minutes. (If the garlic cloves are large, they may take longer to roast than the eggplant. They should be soft yet firm enough to hold their shape when peeled.) Remove from the oven and set aside to cool.

Peel the cooled peppers and cut lengthwise into ½-inch thick strips, saving their juice for the salad. Cut the stem end off the garlic cloves, then peel. Slice the eggplant into thick strips, similar in size to the peppers.

Combine the eggplant, peppers, and garlic cloves; toss with the balsamic vinegar. Add a splash or two of Champagne vinegar and season to taste with salt and pepper. Marinate the salad at room temperature for an hour to allow the flavors to develop. Arrange the watercress on the platter, spoon the salad over, and garnish each serving with 2 or 3 olives. Serve at room temperature.

SERVES FOUR TO SIX

Tip: For roasting the peppers, use parchment paper or aluminum foil to line the baking sheet instead of oiling it. You'll use less oil, and the pepper juices won't stick to the pan. If you're using foil, just wrap the roasted peppers in it to steam.

Variation: Fresh basil is a wonderful addition to this salad. Bundle whole leaves of green or opal basil together, cut into thin ribbons, and toss with the ingredients. The salad is also delicious marinated overnight with whole leaves of basil. The flavor and fragrance of the basil will permeate the salad.

ROASTING PEPPERS

Minus their tough skins, roasted peppers are supple and sweet—delicious tossed with olive oil and whole leaves of basil, layered into a gratin, or savored on a crusty end of sourdough. Roasting and skinning the peppers sounds like a lot of work, but in fact it's surprisingly easy. Peppers are wonderful roasted until blistered and charred over a stove-top flame or, even better, a bed of hot coals. Easiest of all is roasting them in a hot oven. Once roasted and skinned, they'll keep for 2 or 3 days in the refrigerator.

Preheat the oven to 500°F. Lightly oil a baking sheet or line it with foil or parchment paper. Slice each pepper in half lengthwise and remove the stems, seeds, and membranes. Lay the pepper halves cut side down on the baking sheet, brush lightly with oil, and roast until the skins darken and blister, about 15 minutes. (Oil is optional here, though it helps the peppers roast more evenly.) Remove the peppers from the oven, transfer to a bowl, and cover; the peppers will steam as they cool. After about 10 minutes, slip off the skins, dipping your hand in a little water if needed. (Do not dip the peppers in water—it will dilute their succulent flavor.) Slice or puree in a food processor or blender as directed and be sure to include the sweet juices.

Beets with Watercress and Orange

Serve this simple, refreshing salad by itself or alongside the more complex flavors of Baba Ghanouj (page 52) and Cucumbers with Yogurt and Mint (page 395). The orange juice and Champagne vinegar add brightness to the beets, and because there's no oil, their flavor is very light. We frequently use all red beets, but golden or striped Chioggia beets make this salad exceptionally beautiful.

1 pound beets, about 2 inches in diameter
3 tablespoons fresh orange juice
1 tablespoon Champagne vinegar
⅛ teaspoon salt
Pepper
1 bunch of watercress

Preheat the oven to 400°F. Trim away the beet greens and save them for pasta or a sauté. Rinse the beets under cold water and place them in a small baking dish with ½ inch water. Cover the dish and bake until the beets are tender, 35 to 40 minutes, depending on their size. Test them for doneness with a paring knife or a skewer. Cool and peel, then slice them into ¼-inch-thick rounds or wedges.

Combine the orange juice with the vinegar, the salt, and a few pinches of pepper; pour over the sliced beets. The color of red beets will run, so marinate them separately if you're using them with golden or Chioggia beets.

Pluck the small sprigs of watercress, discarding the long stems and bruised leaves; wash and dry in a spinner.

Place the watercress on a serving platter and arrange the sliced beets on top, alternating the colors if you're using more than one variety of beet. Sprinkle with freshly ground pepper.

SERVES FOUR TO SIX

Tip: To peel beets easily, dip them in a bowl of cool water as you peel them. The water helps to loosen the skin and makes the peeling fast and easy. (If the beets are difficult to peel, it's a sure sign they're undercooked.) Dip them a final time to remove any traces of skin, then set aside to drain. If you're using more than one variety of beet, be sure to peel the red ones last to keep them from discoloring the others.

Summer Beans with Cherry Tomatoes and Tarragon

At the peak of the season, fresh beans abound and we use three or four varieties—green and yellow Romano, Blue Lake, and yellow wax—along with red and yellow Sweet 100 cherry tomatoes or pear tomatoes.

The cooking time for the beans will vary, so cook them separately if you're using different varieties. Marinate the beans for an hour or two in advance if you like, but don't add the vinegar, or they'll quickly discolor. For an equally delicious variation on this exceptional summer salad, substitute opal or green basil for the tarragon.

2 shallots, thinly sliced
Champagne vinegar
Salt
1 pound fresh beans: any combination of Blue Lake green beans, yellow wax beans, and
    yellow or green Romano beans
3 tablespoons extra virgin olive oil
1 tablespoon coarsely chopped fresh tarragon or 2 tablespoons coarsely chopped fresh basil
Pepper
2 tablespoons sherry vinegar
½ pint cherry tomatoes, cut in half if large

In a medium-size bowl, toss the shallots with a few splashes of Champagne vinegar to draw out their pink color.

Bring a medium-size pot of water to a boil and add ½ teaspoon salt. Drop in the beans and cook until just tender—from one to two minutes for young green beans, up to six minutes or more for large Romano beans—then scoop them out of the water. Immediately toss the hot beans with the olive oil, shallots, tarragon, ½ teaspoon salt, and ⅛ teaspoon pepper. (The beans will soak up the flavors as they cool to room temperature.) Just before serving, add the vinegar and toss in the cherry tomatoes. Season with salt and pepper to taste.

SERVES FOUR TO SIX

Broccoli with Sun-Dried Tomatoes and Pine Nuts

The beauty of this versatile dish is in its simplicity. We serve it throughout the year, but it's best in the late spring and early summer, when the Green Gulch broccoli is in season. Grown with great care, the heads are slender, the florets closed and beautifully formed. Cut the florets from the stem at a slight angle and give them some length to show off their beauty. The robust vinaigrette is whisked to thicken slightly, then tossed with the salad just before serving.

1 head of broccoli, about 1 pound
3 tablespoons balsamic vinegar
1 small garlic clove, finely chopped
5 tablespoons extra virgin olive oil
Salt and pepper
2 sun-dried tomatoes packed in oil, drained and thinly sliced
1 tablespoon pine nuts, toasted (page 263)
Champagne vinegar

Cut the broccoli tops into florets about 1½ inches long. Peel the broccoli stems, cut in half lengthwise, and slice ½ inch thick on a diagonal.

In a small bowl, whisk together the balsamic vinegar, garlic, oil, ½ teaspoon salt, and a few pinches of pepper.

Bring a medium-size pot of water to a boil and add ½ teaspoon salt. Drop in the broccoli stems and cook for about 3 minutes, adding the florets for the last minute. The broccoli should be bright green and slightly crisp. Pour it into a colander, rinse under cold water, and drain thoroughly.

Toss the broccoli with the sun-dried tomatoes, pine nuts, and vinaigrette. Add salt and pepper to taste and a splash of Champagne vinegar to heighten the flavor.

SERVES FOUR TO SIX

Mushrooms and Roasted Pepper with Rocket

The sweet juices of the roasted pepper mingle with tart, salty capers and the highly seasoned Balsamic-Garlic Vinaigrette, while the mushrooms soak up the delicious flavors. Be sure to use firm, fresh mushrooms with closed caps. Serve with creamy young Asiago cheese, croutons, and Gaeta olives.

1 red or yellow bell pepper, roasted, peeled, and sliced into thick strips (page 55)
1 pound white mushrooms
Balsamic-Garlic Vinaigrette (recipe follows)
1 tablespoon drained capers, rinsed
2 handfuls of rocket (arugula)
Balsamic vinegar
Salt and pepper
8 or 12 Niçoise or Gaeta olives

While the pepper is roasting, quickly rinse the mushrooms under cool water and drain. Trim the base of the mushroom stems to even them, then cut them in half if large.

Make the vinaigrette, setting aside 2 tablespoons to toss with the rocket just before serving. Toss the pepper with the mushrooms, capers, and vinaigrette, being sure to include the sweet pepper juice in the salad. Marinate for 20 to 30 minutes to allow the flavors to develop.

While the vegetables are marinating, prepare the rocket. Remove and discard the stems; wash and dry in a spinner. When you're ready to serve the salad, toss the rocket with the reserved vinaigrette and arrange on a serving platter. Check the seasoning of the vegetables; add a splash of vinegar and a sprinkle of salt and pepper if needed. Arrange the vegetables over the rocket and garnish each serving with 2 or 3 olives.

SERVES FOUR TO SIX

Balsamic-Garlic Vinaigrette

¼ cup balsamic vinegar
1 garlic clove, finely chopped
¼ teaspoon salt
⅛ teaspoon pepper
¼ cup extra virgin olive oil

Combine everything but the oil in a small bowl, then gradually whisk in the oil.

MAKES ABOUT ½ CUP

Roasted Peppers with Cheese and Herbs

A delectable appetizer for entertaining—strips of roasted red and yellow sweet peppers sprinkled with fresh herbs and rolled with savory cheeses. We offer three variations here: crumbled feta cheese with oregano and mint, smoked mozzarella with whole basil leaves, and crumbled goat cheese with fresh herbs. The cheeses and herbs can be mixed in any number of ways; just be sure to roast the peppers until they're soft and supple, or they'll be difficult to roll.

2 large red or yellow bell peppers or a combination, roasted and peeled (page 55)
Extra virgin olive oil
Salt and pepper
¼ pound smoked mozzarella, feta, or mild, creamy goat cheese
24 to 36 whole fresh basil leaves or 1½ teaspoons each chopped fresh oregano and mint or
  1 tablespoon chopped fresh herbs: parsley, chives, marjoram, and thyme

Cut the roasted peppers into strips about 1½ inches wide. Lay the strips on a work surface; brush the inside of each strip with olive oil and sprinkle with salt and pepper.

Cut the smoked mozzarella into thin slices a little narrower than the peppers. Place 2 or 3 whole basil leaves along the length of each strip. Place a piece of mozzarella at the end of each strip, then roll the pepper over the cheese, continuing to roll the length of the pepper. Fasten with a toothpick, then repeat with the remaining strips.

If you're using crumbled feta or goat cheese, brush the strips with olive oil and sprinkle with salt and pepper. Sprinkle lightly with the chopped oregano and mint or the chopped herbs and place a generous crumbling of cheese at the end of each strip. Roll and fasten as directed. The flavors will develop as the peppers sit with the herbs and cheese, so they can be rolled in advance and refrigerated. Be sure to return them to room temperature before serving.

MAKES 12 FILLED PEPPERS

Chinese Cabbage with Lemon and Ginger

Crisp texture and clear, clean flavors—this lively salad adds a bright touch to sandwiches or grilled tofu drizzled with Dipping Sauce (page 344). The slightly sweet Chinese cabbage, thinly sliced, lends a distinctive character—remaining fresh and crunchy while absorbing the sparkling flavors of the chilies and ginger.

1 small head of Chinese cabbage, 1 pound, about 4 cups sliced
1 jalapeño chili, seeded and thinly sliced
1 scallion, white and green parts, thinly sliced on a diagonal
1 tablespoon coarsely chopped cilantro
2 tablespoons fresh lemon juice
½ tablespoon rice wine vinegar
1 teaspoon grated fresh ginger
2 tablespoons light olive oil or peanut oil
¼ teaspoon salt

Trim the base of the cabbage, cut it in half lengthwise, and remove the core. Cut the cabbage crosswise into ½-inch-thick slices. Toss with the chili, scallion, and cilantro. Whisk together the remaining ingredients. Toss the cabbage with the dressing, season with salt to taste, and serve.

SERVES FOUR TO SIX

Variation: Use ½ teaspoon hot pepper flakes in place of the fresh chili.

E*ggplant Caviar*

The beauty of this delectable roasted eggplant and garlic dish is that it gets better as the flavors develop, so let it sit for an hour or two before serving. It can even be made a day or two in advance, though it may need a splash of vinegar or a touch of salt to refresh it. Serve at room temperature with crisp croutons and salty black olives.

2 globe eggplants, about 2 pounds
3 tablespoons extra virgin olive oil
6 garlic cloves, unpeeled
2 sun-dried tomatoes packed in oil, drained and finely chopped
2 teaspoons balsamic vinegar
Salt and pepper
Red wine vinegar
1 tablespoon coarsely chopped Italian parsley

Preheat the oven to 375°F. Cut the eggplant in half lengthwise, brush the cut side lightly with olive oil, and place on a baking sheet, cut side down. Place the garlic on the baking sheet with the eggplant and brush lightly with oil. Bake until the eggplant is very tender and the garlic is soft, about 35 minutes. Set the eggplant in a colander to drain and, when cool, peel away the skin. Squeeze the roasted garlic from its skin and chop.

Chop the eggplant by hand or in a food processor and toss it with the remaining olive oil, the sun-dried tomatoes, garlic, balsamic vinegar, ¾ teaspoon salt, and a few pinches of pepper. The flavor of the caviar will develop as it sits, so set it aside for an hour before serving. Taste the caviar and adjust the seasoning with salt, pepper, and a splash of red wine vinegar. Sprinkle with the parsley just before serving.

SERVES FOUR

Jícama-Orange Salad

The original version of this refreshing salad appears in *The Greens Cookbook,* and we make it so often that we've included our current variation here. Cool and crisp, it's a great complement to Mexican and southwestern spices. The crunchy jícama picks up the sweet citrus flavor and the heat of the cayenne. You can include ruby grapefruit or even blood oranges. Serve with Spicy Black Beans with Chilies and Lime (page 31) and tortilla chips or alongside Enchiladas Rojas or Verdes (pages 244, 246).

1 small jícama, about 10 ounces
¾ cup fresh orange juice
1 or 2 tablespoons rice wine vinegar
Salt and cayenne pepper
3 navel oranges
3 or 4 large radishes, thinly sliced (optional)
Cilantro sprigs

Peel the jícama and cut it into thin slices. Cut the slices into thin strips, place them in a small bowl, and toss with the orange juice. Add the vinegar, ⅛ teaspoon salt, and a few pinches of cayenne.

With a sharp knife, trim the top and bottom from the orange and remove the peel and white pith down to the flesh. Remove each section from the inner membrane or cut the orange in half lengthwise and cut into half-moon slices. Toss the oranges with the jícama, then season to taste with salt and cayenne. Allow the salad to sit for a few minutes before serving. Garnish with the radish slices and sprigs of cilantro.

SERVES FOUR TO SIX

Hot Off the Grill

Grilling

Cooking over coals is such an integral part of our menu that it's hard to imagine a summer meal at Greens without grilled Green Gulch Farm potatoes or a crisp fall day without the smoky fragrance of fennel, succulent mushrooms, and tender sweet potatoes. We light our grill at midmorning each day—beginning with vegetables that we'll serve at room temperature for lunch, then on to grilling tofu for our bakery counter sandwiches. If the morning wind is gentle and coming in from the north off the Bay, the smoky essence of the grill will waft your way as you near Greens, awakening your appetite well before you open the restaurant's double wooden doors.

The choices of fuels are many, each with its own heat and smoky aroma. We use mesquite charcoal and like the quick intensity of its heat for grilling vegetables, tofu, polenta, and bread. Oak produces wonderful coals, though we actually prefer the lighter flavor that mesquite imparts. We don't recommend charcoal briquets, though they will certainly do, particularly if you add trimmings of fragrant wood or sprigs of fresh herbs or fennel.

Give yourself plenty of time to set up your grill so the coals have a chance to cool a bit before you begin grilling. Be sure to keep your fire going—have extra charcoal or wood at hand to add to the coals as needed, keeping the fresher coals to one side of the grill and moving them toward the center as they heat.

Have everything ready before you start to grill—we brush the vegetables lightly with olive oil to keep them from sticking, and then sprinkle them with salt and pepper. A pair of long metal tongs is indispensable, the best tool for handling most vegetables once they're on the grill. A metal spatula is handy for turning polenta and rounds of onions and helps keep the onion rings together. A bowl of olive oil and a pastry brush are useful for touching up mushrooms and vegetables that tend to dry out. Have a platter ready for family-style serving—there's nothing more beautiful than a rustic earthenware platter heaped with an array of grilled vegetables in all shapes, sizes, and colors.

For wonderful flavor, brush a seasoned butter or Reduced Balsamic Vinegar generously over the vegetables just before they're ready to come off the grill. Eggplant and zucchini really soak up the balsamic flavor and are particularly delicious grilled and marinated a day in advance. Layer the vegetables into a serving dish as you remove them from the grill, brushing them with more reduced vinegar if needed; sprinkle lightly with salt and pepper, finishing each layer with a sprinkling of fresh herbs or whole leaves of basil. Cover the dish and set the warm vegetables aside to marinate. Refrigerate overnight, but be sure to return to room temperature before serving.

Most of the summer vegetables are simply sliced and grilled—but potatoes, sweet potatoes, delicata squash, leeks, and green garlic will need to be precooked. Make the most of the hot coals by grilling onions, peppers, and potatoes to be served the next day, tossed into a pasta, layered on a pizza, or tossed together with a sharp vinaigrette for an absolutely delicious potato salad.

Mushrooms

Deliciously versatile and a snap to prepare, mushrooms are integral to our menu year-round, but particularly in the fall and winter. Brushed while still on the grill with Reduced Balsamic Vinegar (page 345), they can be served alongside a savory filo or as an elegant appetizer with other grilled vegetables—sliced fennel, sweet rounds of delicata squash, and leeks served with Port Beurre Rouge (page 330).

Cremini and White Mushrooms

Dark-skinned cremini have a deeper flavor than white mushrooms, though they are often harder to find. Whichever variety you choose, be sure they're firm and fresh, with closed caps.

Rinse the mushrooms quickly under cool water and pat them dry. Trim off the base of the stem, leaving most of the stem on. Slip them onto bamboo or metal skewers through the stem end, up through the cap, and place them snugly one above the other. Finely chop a clove of garlic and add it to enough olive oil to brush over the mushrooms. Brush them liberally, since they tend to dry out on the grill. Sprinkle with salt and pepper.

Grill the mushrooms until marks appear, turning to cook both sides. When they're soft and begin to shrivel they're ready to eat, though they may need a sprinkling of salt and pepper before serving.

Shiitake Mushrooms

Fresh shiitake mushrooms are a special treat brushed with Balsamic Vinaigrette (page 13) before grilling or served with Honey-Miso Sauce (page 342).

Select shiitake mushrooms with thick flesh and caps with closed clean edges. Trim the stem from the base of the cap and save for stock if you like. Brush the caps if they're sandy, but don't wash them, or they'll soak up the water like sponges. Place 3 or 4 shiitake caps on a work surface side by side with the gill side down; hold them in place with one hand and carefully run a skewer through them with the other, filling the skewer with mushrooms. Repeat until you've skewered all the mushrooms you'll need. Brush both sides of the caps with olive oil and sprinkle with salt and pepper.

Place the skewers on the grill, gill side down. Grill until the mushrooms are cooked through, about 5 minutes, then turn and grill the other side.

Porcini Mushrooms

Fall is the season for fresh porcini (also called *cèpes*), and the season is short—they're scarce in the markets and costly but worthy of a feast. They're indescribably sweet with an aroma that's pungent and earthy. The best way to serve them is simply so as not to disguise their flavor.

Trim off just the base of the stem, since it's often dirty and gritty, and wipe the mushroom with a damp cloth to remove dirt. Cut into thick slabs, making sure to include the tender

stem. Add a small shallot or chopped garlic clove to your best olive oil, brush it over, then
sprinkle with salt and pepper.

Grill on both sides until the tender flesh is cooked through. To serve, drizzle with olive oil,
and if you like, sprinkle with coarsely chopped Italian parsley.

Eggplant

One of our favorites. We grill Japanese and globe eggplant throughout the seasons. The
tender, sweet flesh is receptive to so many flavors—brushed while warm with Reduced
Balsamic Vinegar (page 345) and sprinkled with oregano and basil or served with Spicy
Peanut Sauce (page 343) alongside Chinese noodles.

We cut the small, slender Japanese eggplant in half lengthwise, leaving the stem end on, and
score the flesh with a crosshatch design to help them cook more quickly and evenly. The
globe eggplant is peeled first, then cut in thick slices irreverently known as "steaks." Both
are tossed or brushed before grilling with olive oil and chopped garlic, then sprinkled liberally with salt and pepper. Be judicious with the olive oil—eggplant will absorb every
drop that you give it.

Place the eggplant on the grill and leave it in place for 2 or 3 minutes, until grill marks appear. Reposition it so the grill marks form a crosshatch, then turn it over and grill the
other side until the flesh is soft and cooked through. Serve immediately or cool to room
temperature—it's delicious either way.

Potatoes

Crisp and hot off the grill, this has to be one of the most satisfying ways to enjoy potatoes.
By early summer, the Green Gulch crop is beginning to come in—Rosefir, Yellow Finn,
Bintje, and little red new potatoes. We roast them beforehand until tender, then cut them
into halves or quarters, to make bite-size pieces. Toss them with olive oil, garlic, salt, and
pepper—they're ready to grill. Slip them onto skewers and place on the grill cut side
down. The tender cut side of the potatoes will turn golden within a few minutes, sizzling
from the heat of the coals. Serve them alongside a savory tart or filo or on their own with
Basil or Chipotle Aïoli (page 340 or 341). To roast the potatoes, see page 251.

Fennel

In fall, when fennel is at its peak, its sweet, licoricelike flavor couldn't be better. Though it
comes in with late summer, we wait until the weather cools to grill it. For an elegant early
spring appetizer, include small red potatoes, grilled leeks or scallions, and serve with
Meyer Lemon Beurre Blanc (page 329). It's also delicious brushed with herb butter or
served alongside marinated cannellini beans and grilled peppers as an antipasto.

To prepare, trim a thin slice off the base of the fennel to loosen the tough outer leaves and peel them away, exposing the tender leaves. If the fennel is fresh and young, the bulb will be tightly formed and should yield 4 to 5 slices. With the base side up, grip the fennel firmly and cut down through the bulb in ¼-inch-thick slices. The end pieces will separate, and the inner pieces should hold together in a fingerlike formation connected by the base of the bulb.

Brush the slices on both sides with olive oil, salt, and pepper. Grill until marks appear, then turn over to grill the other side. The fennel should be a little soft when you take it from the grill. Serve immediately or cool to room temperature.

Corn

There's nothing more delicious than a tender, sweet ear of corn on the cob. Let the sweetness speak for itself and serve it unadorned or brush with Cinnamon-Chipotle Butter (page 332). There are a number of wonderful ways to grill corn in the husk, but we like to husk it and precook it (unless it's really tender), then grill it later. The corn is already tender, so it's grilled just long enough to heat it through and impart the smoky flavor of the coals.

Husk the corn and remove all the silk. Cook in a pot of boiling unsalted water until just heated through. Drain and rinse under cold water and set aside until you're ready to grill it. Grill the corn until marks appear and turn until the ears are heated through. Serve immediately.

Peppers

Thick slices of grilled peppers are delicious tossed with potatoes and a spicy chili vinaigrette or served with grilled eggplant, rounds of red onion, and Cilantro Pesto (page 338). When peppers are grilled this way, there's no need to peel them—the skin chars and blisters a bit, but it holds the shape of the pepper together. We most often use red and yellow sweet peppers, except in the early fall, when the markets are filled with the most extraordinary varieties—Corno di Toro, sweet red Italian, pimiento, Gypsy, and Anaheim, to name a few.

Cut the pepper in half lengthwise; remove the stem end, seeds, and membrane. Cut lengthwise into 1-inch-thick strips, then toss with olive oil, salt, and pepper. Grill for a minute or two, until grill marks appear and the pepper begins to soften. Serve right away or cool to room temperature.

Red Onions

We grill these onions all the time—however we use them, they add an unbelievably sweet, round flavor. Brush with Cinnamon-Chipotle Butter (page 332) and serve alongside a spicy polenta gratin (page 278). Or you can grill them ahead of time and toss with a pasta or layer on a pizza.

It's difficult to peel the onion whole, so we cut it into thick rings first, then peel the skin off the outermost layer. With a firm grip on the onion, slice across it in rounds about ½ inch thick, keeping the individual rings together as you go. Peel away the skin, then brush with olive oil and sprinkle with salt and pepper. Place the rounds on the grill; after a few minutes, turn them with a spatula and give the onions time to soften and cook all the way through. If you're using a flavored butter, brush it over the onions while they're still on the grill—over the heat of the coals, they'll soak up the wonderful flavors.

Leeks

Grilling leeks brings out the best of their flavor—they're delicious with new potatoes and the first spring asparagus or drizzled with a tangy mustard vinaigrette and served on their own. They come to us young and slender in the fall and early spring—in winter they're grown to full maturity. They'll need to be precooked before grilling, but the time involved is well worth the effort.

Take a thin slice at the base of each leek to trim off the root. Cut through the green top diagonally, leaving a few inches of green on the leek. Soak in cool water to loosen the sand that gets trapped in between the layers; wash again if the water is sandy. Drop the leeks into a wide pot of gently boiling salted water and cook until tender. The cooking time will vary depending on their size, so use a paring knife to test for tenderness. When it's inserted without resistance, drain and rinse under cold water. Set them aside until you're ready to grill.

If the leeks are large, cut them in half lengthwise before grilling. Brush with olive oil and sprinkle with salt and pepper. Grill until marks appear, then turn and grill the other side. Serve immediately or cool to room temperature.

Scallions

Easy to prepare and quick to grill, scallions add simple elegance to thinly sliced tofu with Dipping Sauce (page 344) or Chinese noodles with grilled Japanese eggplant. Trim off the root end and cut through the green top diagonally, leaving a few inches of green on each scallion. Brush with a light-flavored oil and sprinkle with salt and pepper. Grill until marks appear, then turn and grill the other side.

Green Garlic

It looks a bit like a young leek, but green garlic is the shoot of the garlic bulb, harvested before the bulb is formed. The strong, fresh garlic flavor holds up well on the grill. (It's also delicious made into a spring soup.) Prepare and grill as you would leeks, saving the tops for stock (page 79). The shoots can be fibrous, so be sure to precook them in boiling water until they're completely tender.

Summer Squash

Golden and green zucchini, yellow crookneck, and scallop-shaped sunburst and pattypan are a sampling of the summer squash we grill. Their taste is so sweet and simple, yet they readily take on the complex flavors of an herb butter or Reduced Balsamic Vinegar (page 345) while still warm on the grill.

Summer squash are almost effortless to prepare. Cut the zucchini or crookneck in half lengthwise, leaving the stem end on, and score the flesh with a crosshatch design to help it cook more quickly and evenly. If using sunburst or pattypan, cut them through the stem end in thick wedges. Toss the squash with olive oil and chopped garlic and sprinkle liberally with salt and pepper. For easiest grilling, slip the sunburst or pattypan onto metal or bamboo skewers. Grill until the flesh softens and marks appear, then turn and grill the other side. They may need another sprinkling of salt and pepper before serving.

Belgian Endive

The slightly bitter taste of fresh endive gives way to a smooth, soft flavor when grilled. Trim a thin slice off the base of the endive and discard any bruised or discolored outer leaves. Cut in half lengthwise, then brush with flavorful olive oil and sprinkle with salt and pepper. Place them on a cool spot on the grill and cook until tender and wilted from the heat. To serve, drizzle lightly with lemon juice and more olive oil if you like, then sprinkle with Italian parsley.

Radicchio

Its rich, deep red color is lost to the heat of the grill, but the radicchio is so delicious that you don't miss it. Peel away any bruised outer leaves and cut the radicchio into halves or quarters, leaving the core in place. Brush with extra virgin olive oil and sprinkle with salt and pepper. Find a cool spot on the grill and turn the radicchio as needed to wilt it. After grilling, drizzle generously with olive oil and flavorful red wine vinegar; sprinkle with salt and pepper and serve.

Delicata Squash

The delicate flavor of this winter squash is remarkably sweet, and its tender skin is edible. The small, slender striped squash cuts nicely into thick rings for the grill.

Before grilling, the squash needs to be roasted, which you can do earlier in the day. Preheat the oven to 375°F. Cut the squash into ½-inch-thick slices on a slight diagonal, then scoop out the seeds. Brush with olive oil (add some garlic if you like) and sprinkle with salt and pepper. Place on a baking sheet and roast for about 15 minutes or until tender.

Brush each side lightly with olive oil and grill until marks appear. It's so delicious that no other seasoning is needed, though you can brush it with butter mixed with a little thyme or sage. For an elegant appetizer, grill together with fennel, red onions, and shiitake mushrooms and serve with Port Beurre Rouge (page 330).

Sweet Potatoes

The irresistibly sweet, rich flavor of sweet potatoes (often called yams) makes them just right for grilling. Red Garnets are our favorites—we use them throughout the fall and winter on brochettes and serve them with grilled mushrooms and fennel as an appetizer. Like delicata squash, they need to be roasted beforehand. Preheat the oven to 375°F. Cut the sweet potatoes into diagonal slices about ½ inch thick. Toss with light olive oil and chopped garlic and sprinkle with salt and pepper. Roast for about 15 minutes, until just tender. Be careful not to overcook them, or they'll become soft and difficult to grill.

Brush the slices lightly with olive oil and place on the grill, leaving them in place until marks appear; turn and grill the other side.

Tofu

Grilled tofu has appeared on the menu since the day Greens opened. The tofu is marinated beforehand, then cut into cubes and grilled with seasonal vegetables for a brochette or sliced and made into a tofu sandwich. It's delicious grilled on its own, thinly sliced and served with Spicy Peanut Sauce (page 343) or Honey-Miso Sauce (page 342). Include grilled shiitake mushrooms and scallions and a sprinkling of toasted sesame seeds if you like.

Marinate the tofu beforehand (page 273), or it will stick to the grill. If the tofu is thick, cut the block in half. Grill until marks appear, then turn and grill the other side until the tofu is heated through. Serve immediately or later at room temperature.

Polenta

Grilled polenta is delicious served right off the grill with Salsa Roja (page 326) or simply brushed with Cinnamon-Chipotle Butter (page 332). The heat of the fire seals in the flavors, and the texture is just right—the edges crispy, the interior tender and moist. The recipe we use for grilling is slightly denser than our usual polenta (page 278).

Cut the polenta into squares or triangles and brush both sides lightly with olive oil. Place on the grill and leave in place until grill marks score the polenta. Turn with a spatula and grill the other side. It's best served right away but also holds well in a warm oven until you're ready for it.

Breads

Grilling bread over hot coals enlivens its flavor and lends a wonderful crisp texture that you can only approximate in the oven. It's a bit extravagant to light your grill just for bread, so include it in a meal that makes use of the grill elsewhere. Use flavorful extra virgin olive oil; it makes a real difference here. Have everything ready before grilling, so the bread is warm and moist when you serve it.

Pita Bread

Grilled pita bread is a favorite alongside Baba Ghanouj (page 52) or a trio of Middle Eastern salads. Brush lightly with olive oil and place on a cool section of the grill. Grill on both sides until the bread gets a little shiny, watching closely to keep it from burning. Stack the grilled pitas one on top of the other, cut into wedges, and serve.

Sourdough Bread

Grilled sourdough served with fresh mozzarella or Asiago is a welcome addition to any antipasto. Slice the sourdough as thick or thin as you like and brush with olive oil. (Chopped garlic is a delicious addition.) Grill the bread on both sides, then cut into wedges and serve.

*S*oups

Stocks

Stock is the flavorful broth that brings the elements of a soup together and makes the soup whole. There are three basic recipes here—each makes about 2 quarts of stock, plenty for the soups in this chapter. The recipes can easily be varied—you can use an onion in place of a leek top or two smaller potatoes when a large potato is called for—but stay away from vegetables in the brassica family, like broccoli and Brussels sprouts; the strong taste of cabbage will overpower the soup. Be sure to use the seeds and trimmings of winter squash if you're making stock for a winter squash soup. Fresh or canned tomatoes are a great addition to a stock for a brothy tomato soup. The tops and outer leaves of fennel bulbs, along with whole fennel or anise seeds, add subtle licorice flavor—delicious in a stock for Tomato-Fennel Soup.

Preparing the vegetables: Stock will taste just like the ingredients you use, so be sure they're flavorful and fresh. We wash vegetables before cutting them unless they need to be peeled. Leeks are often sandy, so we soak the sliced leeks in cold water before adding them. Always peel carrots and discard the skins unless they're very fresh or organic. Peel onions as well, because surprisingly their skins will make the stock bitter. With garlic it's different—crush the whole cloves with the side of a knife, leaving their papery skin on. Fresh herbs go right into the pot, stems and all—rinse them only if they're sandy. When cutting vegetables for stock, expose as much surface area as possible by slicing or cutting them on a diagonal.

Cooking the stock: Steaming the onions, leeks, and garlic in a little water is the first step in making a flavorful stock. Instead of steaming, you can sauté these foundation vegetables in a little oil if you like, though the oil tends to make the stock cloudy. A little salt is essential to draw out all the flavors. When the vegetables are wilted and aromatic, add the remaining ingredients and cover them with cold water. If you're short on time, you can skip this step—just combine all of the ingredients and begin with the full amount of water. Bring the pot to a boil, then reduce the heat to a gentle simmer and cook it uncovered—the stock will be ready in about an hour.

Garden treasures: Fresh herbs add flavor and dimension to stock—some of the more unusual herbs aren't included in the recipes, but they're worthy of mention. They can be strong and overpowering, so use them sparingly until you're familiar with their flavor.

A leaf or two of comfrey adds decided depth and richness—this Old World plant is well known for its healing qualities. A stalk or two of borage is always a welcome addition. Lovage, which looks a bit like Italian parsley, has a pungent, celerylike flavor that's wonderful with potatoes—a few small sprigs are all that's needed. Stinging nettles add a soothing flavor and make a delicious broth on their own. This garden volunteer has a strong sting and is best handled with gloves; once the nettles are submerged in water, though, the stinging is neutralized.

Reducing stocks: Reduced stock has an intensified flavor that adds depth and richness to a dish. These enriched flavors are essential to a delicious mushroom sauce or vegetable risotto. We sometimes reduce (or boil) a stock to half its original volume.

Keeping stocks: Stock will hold for a day or two in the refrigerator and will turn sour if kept much longer. It freezes indefinitely, so make a double recipe and freeze half to use later. You can freeze your leftover stock or add it to a soup or stew that needs thinning. Allow a frozen stock time to thaw and be sure to reheat it before adding it to a dish, or the cold stock will slow down the cooking process.

Soups

Soup making is a kind of ritual in the Greens kitchen—if you can make a delicious soup, you can make a good sauce or stew or almost any dish on the menu. Most soups have a humble beginning—it's the freshness and quality of the ingredients that make our soups sparkle.

There are a few essential techniques that we use throughout the recipes. Once you're familiar with them, your intuition and confidence will begin to take hold—and the pleasure of making soup really begins. Repetition is a wonderful teacher—find a favorite soup and make it a few times until you know it, then vary the herbs or vegetables or try white beans instead of chick-peas—the possibilities are only as limited as the ingredients you have on hand.

The foundation flavors: We begin most of our soups with onions or leeks sautéed in a little oil and at least a few cloves of chopped garlic. We always add salt at this point—to draw out the liquid in the vegetables and speed the cooking process. When the pan is moist, and not before, add the garlic along with dried herbs or spices—if added earlier, it will stick to the pan and burn. Add a little water or stock if the pan is sticking, just enough to loosen the pan juices. Be sure that the onions or leeks are perfectly tender before adding wine or tomatoes—the acidity will keep them from cooking further. Don't be in a hurry at this point, or the vegetables will remain unpleasantly crunchy.

Seasoning: Add the seasonings to the soup while it's cooking—don't put off seasoning to the last moment. Dried herbs and most spices need time to blend with other flavors, so we usually cook them along with the onions. We add salt a few times throughout the cooking and leave the final seasoning to your taste. We're always cautious with pepper and chilies—once they take over, their fiery heat is hard to disguise. Saffron has an exotic perfume and flavor—a pinch or two turns a tomato soup a rich, deep orange color. Saffron can be overpowering, so taste the soup before you add more. Chopped fresh herbs go into the soup right before serving, or we sprinkle them on as a garnish. Sometimes we use fresh and dried herbs together, particularly in slow-cooking bean soups.

Beneficial spirits: Wine, sherry, and port add depth and complexity to soup. White wine lends a crisp acidity, and we use it most often, while red wine has a deeper flavor, good in tomato soups. Sherry and port are smoother and much sweeter—port is the richer of the two. Cooking wine doesn't need to be fancy—a half cup is the most you'll need, so borrow it from a bottle you'll be drinking.

Adding stock: There's a rule here: add stock gradually. You can always add more, but once you've added too much, the soup will taste thin and the lost flavor will be hard to regain. Add the last of the stock when the soup is all together, but taste it before adding more—full flavor is more important than perfect texture. The starchier soups tend to thicken as they sit; leftover stock is great for thinning them.

Making the most of mushrooms: Plain white mushrooms are absolutely delicious sautéed over high heat with a generous amount of seasoning. Don't crowd them in the skillet, or they'll steam in their juices and their flavor will never develop. As the mushroom juices stick to the pan, add a little wine, stock, or dried mushroom–soaking liquid to loosen them. We often sauté (or sear) the mushrooms in two or three batches, so be sure to loosen all of the flavorful juices before adding the next batch, or they will burn onto the pan.

Beans, broth, and bundles of herbs: Bean soups can be hearty or wonderfully light, depending on the seasoning and the quantity of beans. Cook the beans in unsalted water until they're very tender—you can even let them fall apart completely. If the flavor of a brothy bean soup is a little thin, puree a cup of beans, then add the puree to the soup to enrich it. A bay leaf or two and leaves or sprigs of fresh herbs will transform the cooking water into a savory bean broth—we use it in place of stock, so be sure to save every ounce of it. You can bundle the herbs together or simply add them to the pot—a gift to the lucky finder.

Grains: Pasta, rice, and barley add hearty flavor and chewy texture. We precook pasta beforehand, but you can cook it in the broth if you like; just be careful not to use too much. This is also a good way to use leftover dried pasta. Add rice and barley to the soup while it's cooking—the starch will bind the broth ever so slightly. Like pasta, a little rice or barley really soaks up the broth, so we add them sparingly.

Butter and cream: We do most of our sautéing with olive oil or light vegetable oil, but occasionally a recipe for a potato, carrot, or winter squash soup calls for butter to enrich the flavors. A little butter will make a delicious difference here, but oil can always be used in its place. We use very little cream in our soups, but a tablespoon or two will magically transform a potato soup or winter squash soup into a silky, smooth consistency. Crème fraîche adds a slight tartness and smooths the texture just like cream—it's also an elegant garnish.

A few handy tools: A tall 8-quart pot is wonderful for making stocks and double recipes of soup. Invest in a good one and you'll have it for years. Be sure its surface is thick enough for soup making—never cook a soup in a pot with a thin bottom or sides—it's certain to burn. A large skillet with a close-fitting lid is invaluable, as is a 3½- or 4-quart saucepan. A food mill may sound like a fancy kitchen gadget, but we use ours all the time—it has a wonderful way of elegantly smoothing the texture of a soup and is a great alternative to a blender or food processor. Food mills are inexpensive, and you can find them at most hardware stores.

Vegetable Stock

Here is our basic stock, the foundation for many of our soups. Of course you can vary the vegetables or add more fresh herbs; just be sure the ingredients are flavorful and fresh and stay away from members of the cabbage family (broccoli, cauliflower, cabbage)—their strong flavor will quickly overpower the stock. We begin by steaming onions, leeks, and garlic with the salt, which breaks down their fiber to release more flavor. Then we add the remaining ingredients and simmer for a full hour to draw out all the vegetable flavor. You can easily double the recipe and freeze half the stock for later use.

1 yellow onion, thinly sliced
1 leek top, chopped and washed
4 garlic cloves, in their skin, crushed with the side of a knife blade
1 teaspoon salt
2 medium-size carrots, chopped
1 large potato, thinly sliced
¼ pound white mushrooms, sliced
2 celery ribs, sliced
6 parsley sprigs, coarsely chopped
6 fresh thyme sprigs
2 fresh marjoram or oregano sprigs
3 fresh sage leaves
2 bay leaves
½ teaspoon peppercorns
9 cups cold water

Pour just enough water into a stockpot to start the onion cooking. Add the onion, leek top, garlic, and salt. Stir the vegetables, then cover the pot, and cook them gently over medium heat for 15 minutes. Add the remaining ingredients and cover with 9 cups cold water. Bring to a boil, reduce the heat, and simmer, uncovered, for 1 hour. Pour the stock through a strainer, pressing as much liquid as possible from the vegetables, then discard them.

MAKES ABOUT 7 CUPS

Variation—Light Vegetable Stock: Lighter in flavor and color, this stock goes into potato soups to keep them from discoloring. Using the main recipe, add an extra potato, omit the carrots and mushrooms, and use the entire leek. The tops and outer leaves of fennel bulbs are excellent additions.

Mushroom Stock

We make this rich, intensely flavored stock for our mushroom soups, sauces, and ragouts. The dried shiitake mushrooms give the stock depth and tremendous flavor. They're readily available in the Asian section of most grocery stores, but if you can't find them, substitute another variety of dried mushrooms—fresh mushrooms alone will make a weak stock. This stock freezes well.

1 yellow onion, thinly sliced
1 leek top, chopped and washed
4 garlic cloves, in their skin, crushed with the side of a knife blade
1 ounce dried shiitake mushrooms
1 teaspoon salt
½ teaspoon peppercorns
½ pound white mushrooms, sliced
2 small carrots, chopped
6 parsley sprigs, coarsely chopped
3 fresh thyme sprigs
2 fresh marjoram or oregano sprigs
2 fresh sage leaves
2 bay leaves
9 cups cold water

Pour just enough water into the stockpot to start the onions cooking. Add the onion, leek top, garlic, shiitake mushrooms, and salt. Give the vegetables a stir, then cover the pot and cook gently over medium heat for 15 minutes. Add the remaining ingredients and cover with 9 cups cold water. Bring the stock to a boil, then simmer, uncovered, for 1 hour. Pour the stock through a strainer, pressing as much liquid as you can from the vegetables, then discard them.

MAKES 7 TO 8 CUPS

Corn Stock

Corn soup needs a light stock, one that won't discolor the soup as other vegetable stocks would or take away from the delicate, sweet flavor of the corn. Make this conservative stock with the shaved corn cobs after you've removed the kernels. Since our corn soup recipes vary, simply use the number of cobs the soup recipe calls for. Of course you can use whole ears of corn if you have an abundance.

Shaved corn cobs, broken into halves or thirds
1 yellow onion, thinly sliced
1 medium-size potato, sliced
1 celery rib, sliced
5 parsley sprigs, coarsely chopped
5 garlic cloves, in their skin, crushed with the side of a knife blade
1 teaspoon salt
½ teaspoon peppercorns
9 cups cold water

Combine all of the ingredients in a stockpot. Bring the stock to a boil, then reduce the heat to low and simmer, uncovered, for 1 hour. Pour the stock through a strainer, press as much liquid as you can from the vegetables, and discard them.

MAKES ABOUT 7 CUPS

Tomato, White Bean, and Sorrel Soup

The sorrel will lose its bright green color as soon as it's heated, but overlook the faded hue; it's the lemony sorrel flavor that makes this soup so distinctive.

1 cup dried white beans, about 6 ounces, sorted and soaked overnight
6 cups cold water
1 bay leaf
1 fresh marjoram sprig
2 fresh sage leaves
2 fresh thyme sprigs
1 tablespoon light olive oil
1 medium-size yellow onion, diced, about 2 cups
Salt and pepper
¼ teaspoon dried thyme
1 medium-size carrot, diced, about ¾ cup
6 garlic cloves, finely chopped
½ cup dry sherry
2 pounds fresh tomatoes, peeled, seeded, and pureed (page 95), about 3 cups, or 1 28-ounce can tomatoes with juice, pureed
30 fresh sorrel leaves, stems removed, bundled together and thinly sliced across the bundle, about 2 cups
Sugar
2 tablespoons chopped fresh herbs: parsley, marjoram, and thyme
Grated Parmesan, Gruyère, or Asiago cheese

Rinse and drain the beans. Place them in a medium-size saucepan with the water, bay leaf, and fresh herbs. Bring to a boil, then reduce the heat to medium and simmer, uncovered, until the beans are tender, 25 to 30 minutes. It's fine if they're soft and breaking down. Leave the cooked beans in their broth until you're ready to add them to the soup.

While the beans are cooking, heat the olive oil in a soup pot; add the onion, ½ teaspoon salt, a pinch of pepper, and the dried thyme. Sauté over medium heat until the onion begins to soften, about 5 to 7 minutes. Add the carrots and sauté until tender, about 5 minutes, then add the garlic and sauté for 1 to 2 minutes. Add the sherry and cook for 1 or 2 minutes, until the pan is almost dry.

Add the tomatoes to the onions and carrots with ½ teaspoon salt and cook for about 10 minutes. Add the beans and their broth, the sorrel, and ½ teaspoon salt. Cover and cook over low heat for 30 minutes. If the soup needs body, puree ½ cup of the cooked beans in some of their broth, then return into the soup. You may need to thin it with a little water or stock. Add more salt and pepper to taste, then add a few pinches of sugar to balance the flavors if the soup is acidic. Stir in the fresh herbs just before serving. Garnish each serving with a generous spoonful of cheese.

MAKES ABOUT 8 CUPS

Asparagus Soup with Orange Crème Fraîche

A simple, delicate soup to celebrate the early days of spring. The first asparagus hints at the change of season—away from the earthy taste of root vegetables, toward lighter, fresher flavors. For a beautiful variation, sprinkle each serving with chive blossoms. These little purple flowers add wonderful color and a very light licorice flavor.

5 cups Light Vegetable Stock (page 79); include the woody ends of asparagus
3 pounds asparagus, woody ends broken off
1 tablespoon light olive oil
2 cups thinly sliced onions, about 1 medium yellow onion
Salt and white pepper
1 medium-size potato, sliced, about 1 cup
¼ cup fresh orange juice
Orange Crème Fraîche (recipe follows)

Make the stock and keep it warm over low heat.

Cut the asparagus into 2-inch pieces. Set aside ½ cup 2-inch-long asparagus tips cut on the diagonal for garnish. Heat the olive oil in a soup pot and add the onions, ½ teaspoon salt, and a pinch of white pepper. Sauté over medium heat for about 5 minutes, until the onions are soft. Add the potatoes and 1 cup stock, cover the pot, and cook until the potatoes are soft, about 10 minutes. Add the asparagus, ½ teaspoon salt, and 1 quart stock; cook uncovered over medium heat until the asparagus is tender, about 15 minutes. Puree the soup in a blender or food processor, return it to the pot, and add the orange juice. Season to taste with salt and pepper.

Drop the asparagus tips into lightly salted boiling water and cook for 1½ minutes, until just tender. Rinse them under cold water unless the soup is going to be served immediately. Garnish each serving with a few asparagus tips and a swirl of Orange Crème Fraîche.

MAKES ABOUT 8 CUPS

Orange Crème Fraîche

½ cup Crème Fraîche (page 359)
2 tablespoons fresh orange juice
¼ teaspoon minced orange zest

Combine the ingredients.

Leek and Basmati Rice Soup

Make this elegant, brothy soup in the winter, when leeks are plentiful. The vegetables are sautéed in white wine, then simmered in leek stock with a bouquet of fresh herbs and fragrant basmati. The rice releases just enough starch to bind the broth, and the individual grains add their smooth, nutty flavor.

LEEK STOCK
1 yellow onion, sliced
10 garlic cloves, in their skin, crushed with the side of a knife blade
Salt
3 leek tops, coarsely chopped and washed
2 medium-size carrots, cut into large pieces
1 celery rib, cut into large pieces
1 large potato, sliced
1 bay leaf
2 fresh sage leaves
5 parsley sprigs
5 fresh thyme sprigs
2 fresh marjoram or oregano sprigs
9 cups cold water

Heat the onion and garlic in a soup pot or stockpot with 1 teaspoon salt and ¼ inch of water. Cover the pot and steam for 15 minutes over medium heat. Add the rest of the ingredients and bring the stock to a boil, then turn down the heat and simmer, uncovered, for 40 to 45 minutes. Pour through a strainer and discard the vegetables.

THE SOUP
1 tablespoon light olive oil
1 tablespoon unsalted butter
4 or 5 large leeks, white parts only, cut in half lengthwise, thinly sliced, and washed, about
*   9 cups*
Salt and white pepper
6 garlic cloves, finely chopped
½ cup dry white wine
1 medium-size carrot, diced, about ¾ cup
2 celery ribs, diced, about ¾ cup
¼ cup basmati rice
A fresh herb sachet: 1 bay leaf, 4 thyme sprigs, 5 parsley sprigs, 2 marjoram sprigs, and 1
*   sage leaf tied in cheesecloth or bundled and tied together*
1 tablespoon chopped fresh herbs: parsley, chives, and marjoram
Grated Parmesan cheese

Heat the olive oil and butter in a soup pot over medium heat; add the leeks, 1 teaspoon salt, and a few pinches of white pepper. Stir the leeks, coating them with butter and oil, then cover the pot, reduce the heat to low and cook for about 10 minutes, until the leeks are wilted. Add the garlic and sauté for another minute or two, then add the wine and cook for a minute or two, until the pan is dry. Add the carrots, celery, rice, ½ teaspoon salt, the sachet of herbs, and 1 quart stock. Bring the soup to a boil, then reduce the heat, cover, and simmer for 15 minutes. Add 3 cups stock and season the soup to taste with salt and pepper. Remove the herb sachet and add the chopped herbs just before serving. Garnish each serving with a sprinkle of Parmesan cheese.

MAKES 8 TO 9 CUPS

LEEKS

These beloved long bulbs come to us in all sizes—we never quite know what to expect. We do know that their mild, sweet flavor is a mouth-watering addition to savory tarts, pastry turnovers, all kinds of soups, and potato gratins. When slowly sautéed, they impart the rich, buttery texture essential to so many of our dishes. In spring we love to grill them.

Leeks need a nitrogen-rich bed of soil and plenty of moisture. They don't like hot sun, so plant them in a shady spot or plant a tall plant or a trellis of peas to the south or east. The trick with leeks is to "earth them up." Start the seeds indoors in early spring (or in early summer for a fall harvest or in November for "wintering over.") In midspring, transplant to a trench 6 inches deep. (If you're short on space and don't mind smaller leeks, you can plant them quite close together.) Cover the roots with an inch of soil, then gradually add soil as the plants grow. This way you'll have longer white stockings, the leeks will be tender, and the bugs will stay away. It's very important to keep them evenly and liberally moist, growing at an even steady rate. They'll take 6 months to reach full maturity but can be harvested at any time. Indeed young, tender leeks are all the rage.

Tomato-Fennel Soup with Garlic Croutons and Parmesan Cheese

A delicious soup for the early fall, made with late harvest tomatoes and the first fennel of the season. The acidity of the tomatoes will retard the cooking of the vegetables, so be sure they're very tender before adding them. Include the fennel trimmings in the stock; they'll enrich the flavor.

1 quart Vegetable Stock (page 79); add 2 cups canned tomatoes, ½ teaspoon fennel seed, and ½ teaspoon anise seed
1 tablespoon extra virgin olive oil
1 large yellow onion, diced, about 2 cups
Salt
1 teaspoon anise seed, ground
1 teaspoon fennel seed, ground
4 garlic cloves, finely chopped
2 medium-size carrots, diced, about 1 cup
2 medium-size fennel bulbs, quartered lengthwise, cored, and thinly sliced, about 2 cups
½ cup dry sherry
2 pounds fresh tomatoes, peeled, seeded, and pureed (page 95), about 3 cups, or 1 28-ounce can tomatoes with juice, pureed
Pepper
Sugar
Garlic Croutons (recipe follows)
Grated Parmesan cheese

Make the stock and keep it warm over low heat.

Heat the olive oil in a soup pot and add the onions, ¾ teaspoon salt, the anise, and the ground fennel. Sauté over medium heat until the onions are soft, then add the garlic, carrots, and sliced fennel. Cover the pan and cook the vegetables until very tender, about 5 minutes. Remove the lid, add the sherry, and cook for 1 or 2 minutes, until the pan is nearly dry. Add the tomato puree, 1 quart stock, and ¼ teaspoon salt; cover and cook over low heat for 30 minutes. Season to taste with salt and pepper. Add a few pinches of sugar if the soup tastes acidic. Serve with Garlic Croutons and freshly grated Parmesan cheese.

MAKES 8 CUPS

Garlic Croutons

1 to 2 tablespoons extra virgin olive oil, as needed
2 garlic cloves, finely chopped
¼ French baguette, thinly sliced

Preheat the oven to 375°F. Combine the olive oil and garlic. Lay the slices of baguette on a baking sheet and brush them lightly with the garlic oil. Bake for about 8 minutes, until the croutons are crisp and lightly browned.

RED GARLIC AND GREEN GARLIC

Red garlic is full of sweetness and good garlic flavor, and we await the fresh crop from Green Gulch each summer. Finely chopped, it adds depth to our savory dishes—it's never harsh. We roast the whole heads and spread the soft garlic on croutons or toss the roasted cloves with pasta. For a delightful surprise, tuck a few cloves with sprigs of fresh herbs into packets of parchment potatoes.

Green garlic is the early shoot from any garlic plant. It looks like a scallion, but its flavor is unmistakably that of young garlic. Grilled whole, it imparts a fresh tangy flavor to an antipasto—delicious with grilled new potatoes dipped in aïoli.

A head of garlic grows from one clove, and we recommend that you get the cloves from a nursery. In mild climates, plant in November—you'll be able to harvest fresh green garlic as early as May, and the remaining heads will be ready for drying in June. In colder climates, plant in early spring for a fall harvest. Turn plenty of compost or aged manure into the soil and plant the cloves a couple of inches down at 2- to 3-inch intervals, in a nice sunny spot in the garden. The key to garlic is to give it plenty of water for the first 4 to 5 months, then keep the soil somewhat moist—but don't water overhead. If the heads get too much moisture, they won't clove up. The garlic is ready to harvest when the tops turn brown; braid several heads together and store in a cool, dry, airy place—or as a reminder of the summer's harvest, hang the braid in your kitchen.

Spicy Corn and Chick-Pea Soup with Chilies

Make this delicious Mexican soup with sweet white corn and juicy, ripe tomatoes at the peak of summer. The chipotles are the star of this soup, but use them cautiously—their heat can easily overpower the other flavors.

½ cup dried chick-peas, about 3 ounces, sorted and soaked overnight
2 quarts cold water
1 bay leaf
2 fresh sage leaves
1 fresh marjoram sprig
1 tablespoon light olive oil
1 large yellow onion, diced, about 2 cups
Salt
1½ teaspoons cumin seed, toasted and ground (page 89)
½ teaspoon dried oregano, toasted
Cayenne pepper
6 garlic cloves, finely chopped
1 large red or yellow bell pepper, diced, about 1 cup
2 ears of corn, shaved, about 2 cups
½ cup canned hominy
2 pounds fresh tomatoes, peeled, seeded, and chopped (page 95), about 3 cups, or 1 28-
  ounce can tomatoes with juice, chopped
½ teaspoon Chipotle Puree (page 332)
2 green jalapeño chilies, seeded, coarsely chopped, and pureed with ½ cup water
2 teaspoons fresh lime juice
1 tablespoon chopped fresh sage
Sugar (optional)
3 tablespoons chopped cilantro

Drain and rinse the chick-peas; place them in a large saucepan with the water, bay leaf, sage leaves, and marjoram. Bring to a boil, then reduce the heat and simmer, uncovered, until the beans are very tender, 40 to 50 minutes. Remove the bay leaf and herb sprigs and leave the beans in their broth.

Heat the oil in a soup pot over medium heat and add the onions, ½ teaspoon salt, the toasted cumin and oregano, and a pinch of cayenne pepper. Sauté until the onions are soft, about 7 to 8 minutes, then add the garlic, peppers, corn, and hominy. Cook the vegetables for about 5 minutes, then add the tomatoes, 1 teaspoon salt, and the Chipotle Puree. Add the chick-peas and their broth.

Season the soup to taste with the jalapeño puree; if the jalapeños are mild, balance the heat with Chipotle Puree; just be careful not to make the soup too hot. Add the lime juice, sage, and ½ teaspoon salt. Add a few pinches of sugar if needed to balance the flavors. Cover and cook over low heat for 30 minutes. Season with salt to taste. Stir in the cilantro just before serving.

MAKES 10 TO 11 CUPS

TOASTING CUMIN, CORIANDER, AND OREGANO

Toasting dried herbs and seeds brings out unique, enticing flavors. Toasted cumin and oregano are essential in our kitchen, enhancing our sauces, spicy stews, and curries. Our black bean chili wouldn't be famous without them. Once toasted, they'll keep well in a small sealed container, so prepare extra to have on hand. A small heavy-bottomed skillet is indispensable here.

To toast cumin or coriander, place the whole seeds in a dry small skillet over low heat. Stir and shake until the seeds release their aroma and darken slightly, just a minute or two. Transfer to a bowl if you won't be grinding them right away—they'll continue to cook if left in the pan. Grind in a spice grinder or mortar and pestle.

Oregano can be toasted the same way; it will burn more easily, so watch it closely. It won't need to be ground.

P*alak Shorva*—*Curried Spinach Soup with Toasted Coconut*

Coconut milk and basmati rice lend rich, smooth flavor to this curried spinach soup. As the rice slowly simmers with the onions and spices, its starches break down to accept the exotic flavors. The quantity of spinach is essential—if the bunches are small, buy a third bunch to ensure that you'll have enough. For garnish, toast the coconut (be sure that it's unsweetened) until it turns light golden and releases its sweet fragrance.

Vegetable Stock (page 79), about 5 cups
1 tablespoon light olive oil
1 medium-size yellow onion, thinly sliced, about 2 cups
Salt and pepper
4 garlic cloves, finely chopped
2 teaspoons cumin seed, toasted and ground (page 89)
2¼ teaspoons coriander seed, toasted and ground (page 89)
1¼ teaspoons ground fenugreek
½ cup basmati rice or long-grain white rice
2 large bunches of spinach, stems removed and leaves washed, about 16 cups
1 cup canned coconut milk
1 tablespoon fresh lemon juice
¼ cup unsweetened shredded coconut

Make the stock and keep it warm over low heat.

Heat the oil in a soup pot and add the onions, ½ teaspoon salt, and a few pinches of pepper. Sauté the onions over medium heat until tender, 7 to 8 minutes, then add the garlic and spices. Sauté for 2 minutes, then add the rice and 3 cups stock; cover the pot and cook over medium heat for about 20 minutes, until the rice is tender.

Add the spinach, ½ teaspoon salt, and 2 cups stock; cook uncovered until the spinach is wilted and soft. Puree the soup in a blender or food processor and return it to the pot over low heat. Add the coconut milk. Add stock if necessary to reach the desired consistency. Add the lemon juice and season to taste with salt and pepper. Cook for 20 more minutes.

Toast the coconut in a dry sauté pan over medium-low heat until it begins to turn golden, about 2 minutes. Garnish each serving with a sprinkle of toasted coconut.

MAKES 8 TO 9 CUPS

Potato-Corn Chowder

Hearty and versatile, this staple of our summer menu is made without milk or cream. Instead, sweet corn and new potatoes are cooked together in Corn Stock, then pureed to make the soup base. Kernels of corn, cubes of new potatoes, and celery add the texture. The flavors are rich and full, even better on the second day. This soup loves fresh herbs—sprinkle with chopped basil, Italian parsley, marjoram, or chives. For a richer soup, garnish with grated cheddar cheese and sprinkle with parsley or chives.

Corn Stock (page 81), about 7 cups
5 ears of corn, shaved, about 5 cups
1 pound new or White Rose potatoes, cut into small cubes, about 3 cups
Salt and white pepper
2 bay leaves
1 tablespoon unsalted butter
½ tablespoon light olive oil
1 large yellow onion, diced, about 2 cups
¼ teaspoon dried basil
¼ teaspoon dried thyme
4 garlic cloves, finely chopped
1 celery rib, diced, ½ cup
¼ cup dry white wine
2 tablespoons chopped fresh basil

Make the stock and keep it warm over low heat.

Set aside 2 cups of shaved corn, then place the rest in a soup pot with half the potatoes; add 2 cups stock, ½ teaspoon salt, and a few pinches of white pepper. Bring the potatoes and corn to a boil, then reduce the heat, cover, and simmer until the potatoes begin to break apart, 20 to 25 minutes. Puree the corn and potatoes with 1 to 2 cups stock in a blender or food processor, then pass the puree through a food mill. Return the puree to the soup pot, add 3 cups stock and the bay leaves, and cook over low heat.

Heat the butter and olive oil in a sauté pan, add the onions, dried herbs, ½ teaspoon salt, and a pinch of white pepper. Sauté over medium heat for 5 to 7 minutes, until the onions are soft. Add the garlic, celery, reserved diced potatoes, and reserved corn. Sauté until the vegetables are tender, another 7 to 8 minutes, then add the wine and cook for 1 or 2 minutes, until the pan is almost dry.

Stir the sautéed vegetables into the corn and potato puree and add salt and pepper to taste. Cook the soup over low heat for 20 minutes. Stir in the basil just before serving.

MAKES 8 TO 9 CUPS

Green Corn Soup

One of our summer favorites, this lively soup brings a diversity of flavors together—the acidity of the tomatillos, the heat of the chilies, and the fresh flavor of cilantro perfectly balance the sweetness of the corn. The creamy base of pureed corn, tomatillos, and chilies is barely green, with kernels of corn adding texture. Be sure to use Corn Stock (save the corn cobs for it)—its light color will keep the soup bright. Serve with quesadillas (page 248) and a salad of Romaine Hearts with Avocado, Jícama, and Orange (page 20).

Corn Stock (page 81), about 5 cups
1 tablespoon light olive oil
1 large yellow onion, diced, about 2 cups
3 garlic cloves, chopped
Salt
6 ears of corn, shaved, about 6 cups
Cayenne pepper
¾ pound tomatillos, husked and coarsely chopped, about 2 cups
2 to 3 green jalapeño chilies, seeded and coarsely chopped
5 cilantro sprigs
2 tablespoons chopped cilantro

Make the stock and keep it warm over low heat.

Heat the olive oil in a soup pot and add the onion, garlic, and ½ teaspoon salt. Sauté over medium heat until the onion is soft, 5 to 7 minutes. Add the corn, a few pinches of cayenne, and 1 teaspoon salt; sauté until the corn is heated through, then add 2 cups stock, cover the pot, and simmer 20 to 25 minutes, until the corn is tender. Set aside 2 cups sautéed corn to add to the soup later. Add the tomatillos and 1 jalapeño and cook until the tomatillos are tender, about 5 minutes. Puree the remaining jalapeños with ¼ cup stock and set aside.

Add the cilantro sprigs and puree the soup with 1 cup stock in a blender or food processor. Pass it through a food mill to smooth the texture, then return it to the pot. Add the reserved corn and 1 to 2 cups stock, to reach the desired consistency. Season with salt and the jalapeño puree to taste. Cook over low heat for 25 minutes. Add the chopped cilantro just before serving or sprinkle over each serving.

MAKES 7 TO 8 CUPS

Tip: Passing the pureed corn through a food mill does wonders for the texture of the soup. It's definitely worth the time and extra effort.

Variation: Garnish each serving with a swirl of crème fraîche (page 359), then sprinkle with the chopped cilantro.

Pepper and Corn Soup with Basil

Flecks of red pepper and kernels of corn add color and texture to a creamy puree of corn, leeks, and sweet peppers. Make this beautiful, pastel soup at the beginning and end of summer, when leeks and corn are in the market (substitute yellow onions if leeks are not in season). The flavor of sweet peppers is essential—combine red and yellow peppers if you like, but don't use green peppers, because their strong flavor works against the sweetness of the corn.

Corn Stock (page 81), about 5 cups
1 tablespoon unsalted butter
1 tablespoon light olive oil
1 large leek, white part only, cut in half lengthwise, thinly sliced, and washed, about 2 cups
Salt and cayenne pepper
7 ears of corn, shaved, about 7 cups
3 medium-size red bell peppers, ½ cup diced and about 2 cups coarsely chopped
4 garlic cloves, finely chopped
2 tablespoons chopped fresh basil

Make the stock and keep it warm over low heat.

Heat the butter and ½ tablespoon olive oil in a soup pot. Add the leek, ½ teaspoon salt, and a few pinches of cayenne. Sauté over medium heat until the leek is heated through, about 2 minutes. Cover the pot and steam the leek for 5 to 6 minutes, until tender. Set aside 1 cup corn, along with the diced peppers, to be sautéed separately and added to the soup later. Add the remaining corn and the chopped peppers to the leek along with the garlic, ½ teaspoon salt, and a pinch of cayenne. Sauté for 2 to 3 minutes. Add 2 cups stock, cover, and cook over medium heat for 25 to 30 minutes, until the corn and peppers are tender. Add 1 cup stock, puree in a blender or food processor, then pass the puree through a food mill. Return the puree to the pot and cook over low heat.

Heat ½ tablespoon olive oil in a sauté pan. Add the remaining corn, the diced peppers, ½ teaspoon salt, and a pinch of cayenne; sauté until tender, 5 to 7 minutes. Add to the puree along with about 2 cups stock, to reach the desired consistency. Season to taste with salt and cayenne and cook over low heat for 10 to 15 minutes. Add the basil just before serving.

MAKES 7 TO 8 CUPS

*S*ummer *Minestrone*

Fresh, ripe tomatoes really make a difference here—their sweet juice works with the flavorful bean broth and the starch of the pasta to make a delicious base for this summer vegetable soup. Cook the red beans with a sprig of oregano and leaves of sage and bay; as the beans cook, they'll release their starch and take on the essence of the herbs. For a hearty winter minestrone, you can add white beans or chick-peas and substitute ribbons of chard or kale for the spinach. The flavors develop with time, and this soup is definitely at its best on the second day.

½ cup dried red beans, about 3 ounces, sorted and soaked overnight
6 cups cold water
2 bay leaves
2 fresh sage leaves
1 fresh oregano sprig
1 tablespoon extra virgin olive oil
1 medium-size red onion, diced, about 2 cups
Salt and pepper
¼ teaspoon dried basil
¼ teaspoon dried oregano
6 garlic cloves, finely chopped
1 small carrot, diced, about ¾ cup
1 small red bell pepper, diced, about ¾ cup
1 small zucchini, diced, about ¾ cup
¼ cup dry red wine
2 pounds fresh tomatoes, peeled, seeded, and coarsely chopped (page 95), about 3 cups, or
    1 28-ounce can tomatoes with juice, coarsely chopped
¼ cup small pasta, cooked al dente, drained, and rinsed
⅓ bunch of fresh spinach or chard, cut into thin ribbons and washed, about 2 cups packed
2 tablespoons chopped fresh basil
Grated Parmesan cheese

Drain and rinse the beans. Place them in a 2-quart saucepan with the water, 1 bay leaf, the sage leaves, and the oregano. Bring to a boil, reduce the heat, and simmer, uncovered, until the beans are tender, about 30 minutes. Remove the herbs.

While the beans are cooking, heat the olive oil in a soup pot. Add the onion, ½ teaspoon salt, the dried herbs, and a few pinches of pepper. Sauté the onion over medium heat until soft, 5 to 7 minutes. Add the garlic, carrots, peppers, and zucchini and sauté for 7 to 8 minutes. Add the wine and cook for 1 or 2 minutes, until the pan is almost dry. Add the tomatoes, 1 teaspoon salt, ⅛ teaspoon pepper, and the remaining bay leaf. Simmer for 15 minutes, then add the pasta, spinach or chard, and beans with their broth. Season with salt and pepper to taste. Add the fresh basil just before serving. Garnish each serving with a generous tablespoon of Parmesan cheese.

MAKES 8 TO 9 CUPS

PREPARING FRESH TOMATOES

We use sweet, plump, vine-ripened tomatoes whenever possible for pastas, sauces, soups, and stews. When you're cooking tomatoes for any length of time, you need to remove their skins and seeds beforehand. It's actually quite quick and easy, and it can be done in advance or even the day before—a good way to simplify the preparation of a complex lasagne or gratin.

Bring a large pot of water to boil and have ready a bowl of ice water and a metal basket or strainer for scooping the tomatoes from the pot. Drop two or three tomatoes at a time into the boiling water and count to 10; scoop them out, then plunge them into the ice water to cool. (The skins should be a little loose; if not, leave the tomatoes in the boiling water a few seconds longer.)

Core the tomatoes, slip off their skins, and slice them in half across the equator. If you're seeding a number of tomatoes, set a strainer over a bowl to catch the juice as you remove the seeds. (The delicious juice can be added to the seeded tomatoes or saved for another dish.) Gently squeeze the tomatoes, using your finger to loosen the seeds, then chop or puree in a food processor as directed.

Gazpacho

This delicious soup deserves the sweetest, juiciest tomatoes and a hot summer day to appreciate its cool, refreshing flavor. If yellow tomatoes are available, be sure to include a few and chop them for beautiful contrast. The seasoning depends on the flavor of the tomatoes, so remember not to add the Champagne vinegar and lime juice all at once. Allow the soup to chill for at least an hour, then adjust the seasoning to your taste just before you serve it.

1 medium-size cucumber
5 pounds vine-ripened tomatoes
½ medium-size red onion, diced, about 1 cup
1 or 2 jalapeño or serrano chilies, seeded and thinly sliced
¼ cup chopped fresh basil
Salt and pepper
2 or 3 tablespoons Champagne vinegar
2 or 3 teaspoons fresh lime juice

Peel the cucumber, cut it in half lengthwise, and scoop out the seeds; cut into small cubes and set aside.

Bring a medium-size pot of water to boil. Core the tomatoes and drop into the water a few at a time, for about 10 seconds, just long enough to loosen their skins. Scoop the tomatoes out of the water and continue with the rest. Rinse under cold water to cool them, then slip off their skins. Place a mesh strainer over a bowl. Cut the tomatoes in half crosswise and, over the strainer, squeeze out the juice and seeds. Save the juice to add to the soup and discard the seeds.

Puree half the tomatoes in a blender or food processor and coarsely chop the rest. Combine all of the tomatoes, the onion, cucumber, chilies, and basil in a large bowl. Season with 2 teaspoons salt, ¼ teaspoon pepper, 2 tablespoons vinegar, and 2 teaspoons lime juice. Refrigerate and let sit for at least 1 hour before serving, to allow the flavors to develop. Add salt, pepper, lime juice, and vinegar if needed. Serve chilled.

MAKES ABOUT 10 CUPS

Tip: If the soup is acidic, add a few pinches of sugar to balance the flavors before serving.

Chilled Beet Soup with Orange Crème Fraîche and Dill

Our cool San Francisco summer weather allows for a few sunny, windless days between long gray stretches of coastal fog. If we're quick enough, we'll slip in a chilled soup or two before the fog sweeps back through the Golden Gate.

This refreshing soup is easy to make and can be prepared a day in advance, then seasoned before you serve it. The flavor and sweetness of the beets will determine how much orange and lemon juice will be needed for seasoning. Chill the soup well before serving and garnish with a swirl of Orange Crème Fraîche and a sprinkling of fresh dill. It's equally delicious with crème fraîche and cubes of cucumber tossed with dill.

3 pounds beets
1 tablespoon light olive oil
½ yellow onion, coarsely chopped, about 1 cup
Salt and pepper
3 garlic cloves, finely chopped
½ cup fresh orange juice
2 or 3 teaspoons fresh lemon juice
Rice wine vinegar or Champagne vinegar
Orange Crème Fraîche (page 83)
2 teaspoons chopped fresh dill

Trim off the beet greens at the base of the beet. (If the greens are tender, save them for a sauté or to toss with pasta.) Bring a large pot of water to a boil and add the beets. Reduce the heat and cook, uncovered, at a low boil until tender, 30 to 40 minutes. Test the beets by inserting a paring knife or skewer. If there's no resistance, they're ready to be drained. Drain when tender and allow to cool or run them under cold water to cool them quickly. Peel, cut into large pieces, and set aside.

Heat the olive oil in a small sauté pan; add the onion and ¼ teaspoon salt. Sauté over medium heat until tender, about 7 minutes; add the garlic and sauté for 2 minutes more. Combine the onion and beets in a blender or food processor. Add 1 to 2 cups water and puree until smooth. Add 2 to 3 cups more water, to reach the desired consistency, being careful not to make the soup too thin. Add the orange juice, 2 teaspoons lemon juice, 2 teaspoons vinegar, 1 teaspoon salt, and a few pinches of pepper. Season if needed with lemon juice, vinegar, salt, and pepper.

Chill the soup, then ladle into bowls. Garnish each serving with a swirl of Orange Crème Fraîche and a sprinkle of dill.

MAKES 7 TO 8 CUPS

Butternut Squash Soup with Apple Confit

This is a delicious, satisfying soup for fall and winter. The squash puree is the smooth background flavor, with bits of apple throughout. Calvados (distilled from French cider) is the unusual ingredient here. We add it to the caramelized onions and again to the apples as they sauté. The buttery, tart confit adds a lively touch—you can even serve it as a relish alongside a potato or winter squash gratin. Remember to add the squash seeds and trimmings to the stock.

Light Vegetable Stock (page 79), about 3 cups
1 tablespoon light olive oil
1 medium-size yellow onion, thinly sliced, about 2 cups
Salt
Five-pepper mix or white pepper
3 tablespoons Calvados
4 pounds butternut squash, peeled, seeded, and cut into large cubes, about 6 cups
1 tablespoon unsalted butter
2 McIntosh or other flavorful, not too tart apples, peeled, cored, and sliced, about 2½ cups
½ cup apple juice
½ cup crème fraîche (page 359; optional)

Make the stock and keep it warm over low heat.

Heat the olive oil in a soup pot and add the onion, ½ teaspoon salt, and a pinch of pepper. Sauté over medium heat until the onions slightly caramelize, about 15 minutes, adding a little stock and using a wooden spoon to scrape them as they stick to the pan. Add 2 tablespoons of the Calvados and cook for 1 or 2 minutes, until the pan is almost dry.

Add the squash and 1 teaspoon of salt to the onions. Add just enough stock to barely cover the squash (about 2 cups); the squash breaks down quickly and releases its own liquid as it cooks. Cover the pot and cook over medium heat for 20 to 30 minutes, until the squash is very soft. Puree the soup in a blender or food processor, and thin it with stock to reach the desired consistency. Return the pureed soup to the pot, cover, and cook over low heat for 30 minutes.

While the soup is cooking, make the apple confit. Melt the butter in a medium-size sauté pan and add the apples; sauté over medium-high heat, stirring to coat them with the butter. When they're heated through, add the remaining Calvados and cook for 1 or 2 minutes, until the pan is almost dry. Add the apple juice, cover the pan, and cook over medium heat for 15 to 20 minutes, until soft; cook, uncovered, for 8 to 10 minutes to reduce the liquid. Mash the apples, making sure the confit retains some texture.

Stir half the confit into the soup, saving the rest to stir into each serving. Season the soup with salt and pepper to taste. Add a spoonful of apple confit and a swirl of crème fraîche to each serving.

MAKES 8 TO 9 CUPS

Serving Suggestion: To make a wonderful meal, serve this soup with crusty sourdough bread, nutty, well-aged Gruyère cheese, and a salad of bitter greens with toasted walnuts and walnut vinaigrette.

BORAGE

Borage is an Old World remedy for melancholy; it strengthens the heart and gives joy. The tiny star-shaped flowers range from pale lavender to a lovely deep blue, and we often use a sprig to decorate a platter of succulent grilled summer vegetables. Pluck the silky flowers from the prickly stems and toss them into a salad—save the stems and leaves to enrich a stock.

Borage is the heart of the Green Gulch garden. It seeds itself year after year, and is a favored plant of the honey bee. It's a large annual, about 2½ feet high, and looks ravishing at the back of the herb garden. Borage loves a sunny spot and thrives in any good garden soil.

Tomato, Saffron, and Roasted Garlic Soup

In this unusual soup the saffron gives the tomatoes a beautiful warm color and adds an enticing fragrance; the roasted garlic deepens the flavors, and the sherry brings all of the elements together.

Vegetable Stock (page 79), about 5 cups; add 2 cups chopped canned tomatoes
1 head of garlic brushed with olive oil
2 pounds fresh tomatoes, peeled and seeded (page 95), about 3 cups, or 1 28-ounce can of
*   tomatoes with juice*
1 tablespoon extra virgin olive oil
1 medium-size yellow onion, diced, about 2 cups
¼ teaspoon dried thyme
Salt and pepper
1 medium-size carrot, diced, about ¾ cup
1 celery rib, diced, about ½ cup
1 medium-size yellow or red bell pepper, diced, about ¾ cup
5 garlic cloves, finely chopped
½ cup dry sherry
2 to 3 pinches saffron threads, to taste
1 bay leaf
3 tablespoons chopped Italian parsley
Grated Parmesan cheese

Make the stock and keep it warm over low heat.

Preheat the oven to 350°F. Place the whole head of garlic in a small baking dish, and roast for 30 minutes, until the cloves are very soft. When the garlic cools, cut the top off, squeeze the garlic out of its skin, and puree with the tomatoes in a blender or food processor.

Heat the olive oil in a sauté pan and add the onion, dried thyme, ½ teaspoon salt, and a pinch of pepper. Sauté over medium heat for 5 minutes, then add the carrot, celery, peppers, and finely chopped garlic. Cook together until tender, then add the sherry and cook for 1 or 2 minutes, until the pan is almost dry. Add the tomato-garlic puree, ½ teaspoon salt, a pinch of pepper, the saffron, bay leaf, and 4 to 5 cups stock. Cover and cook over low heat for at least 30 minutes. Add salt and pepper to taste. Garnish each serving with a sprinkle of Italian parsley and Parmesan cheese.

MAKES 8 TO 9 CUPS

Tip: Add a few pinches of sugar to balance the flavors if the soup is acidic.

Mexican Lentil Soup with Roasted Garlic and Chilies

Roasted garlic adds a mellow richness to the smoky heat of the chipotle peppers and the deep flavor of the ancho chilies in this hearty soup. It improves as the flavors develop, so by all means make the soup a day or two ahead.

1 cup lentils, about 6 ounces
6 cups cold water
1 bay leaf
2 fresh sage leaves
1 fresh oregano or marjoram sprig
1 head of garlic
2 tablespoons light olive oil
1 pound fresh tomatoes, peeled and seeded (page 95), about 1½ cups, or 12 ounces canned
   tomatoes with juice
1 red onion, diced, about 2 cups
Salt
1 teaspoon cumin seed, toasted and ground (page 89)
½ teaspoon dried oregano, toasted (page 89)
1 small carrot, diced, about ½ cup
1 small red or yellow bell pepper, diced, about ½ cup
2 tablespoons Ancho Chili Puree (page 197)
½ teaspoon Chipotle Puree (page 332)
1 tablespoon chopped cilantro
1 tablespoon chopped fresh oregano

Sort and rinse the lentils and place them in a soup pot with the water, bay leaf, sage, and oregano sprig. Bring the water to a boil, reduce the heat, and cook, uncovered, at a gentle boil for 15 to 20 minutes, until the lentils are tender. Remove the herbs.

While the lentils are cooking, preheat the oven to 350°F. Rub the head of garlic with a little oil, place it on a baking sheet, and roast for about 30 minutes, until soft. When the garlic has cooled, slice off the top of the head and squeeze the garlic out of its skin. Puree with the tomatoes in a blender or food processor and set aside.

Heat the remaining oil in a large saucepan. Add the onion, ½ teaspoon salt, the cumin, and the dried oregano; sauté over medium heat until the onion is soft, about 7 to 8 minutes. Add the carrot and peppers and sauté until tender, about 5 minutes. Add the chili purees, the pureed tomatoes, and 1 teaspoon salt; simmer for 10 minutes.

Combine the beans and their broth with the vegetables, cover, and cook over low heat for 30 minutes. Add salt to taste. For more spice, add ancho or chipotle puree to taste. Sprinkle in the fresh cilantro and oregano just before serving.

MAKES 8 TO 9 CUPS

Potato Soup with Pesto

The pale yellow flesh of Yellow Finn potatoes lightly colors this summer soup; their flavor is deep and full. If they're not available, use White Rose or new potatoes. Small cubes of potatoes, carrots, and onions add texture, while the smooth potato base absorbs the rich taste of the pesto. Be sure to use Light Vegetable Stock—it will keep the color of the soup light.

Light Vegetable Stock (page 79), about 6 cups
2 pounds Yellow Finn or new potatoes, peeled and thinly sliced, about 7 cups
Salt and white pepper
1 tablespoon unsalted butter
1 tablespoon extra virgin olive oil
1 large yellow onion, diced, about 2 cups
4 garlic cloves, finely chopped
1 small carrot, diced, about ½ cup
1 medium-size potato, diced, about ½ cup
⅓ cup dry white wine
½ cup pesto (page 337)

Make the stock and keep it warm over low heat.

Place the sliced potatoes in a soup pot with 3 cups stock, ½ teaspoon salt, and a few pinches of white pepper; cook until they begin to break apart, about 15 minutes.

While the potatoes are cooking, heat the butter and olive oil in large sauté pan. Add the onion, ½ teaspoon salt, and a pinch of pepper and sauté over medium heat until soft, about 7 to 8 minutes. Add the garlic, carrot, and diced potatoes; cook until tender, then add the wine and cook for 1 or 2 minutes, until the pan is nearly dry.

Pass the potatoes and the cooking liquid through a food mill or quickly puree in a blender or food processor; combine with the vegetables and thin with 2 cups stock. Cover and cook over low heat for 15 minutes, adding stock to reach the desired consistency. The soup will continue to thicken as it cooks. Season to taste with salt and pepper.

Add a spoonful of pesto to each serving.

MAKES 8 TO 9 CUPS

Tip: For the best texture, pass the cooked potatoes through a food mill. If you puree the potatoes, do it ever so quickly; they'll become sticky if blended too long.

Winter Greens Soup

A hearty, nourishing winter soup, with full flavors and a smooth texture. The kale will take longer to cook than the spinach or chard, so be sure it's tender before you puree the soup. We often vary this recipe by adding a small handful of French sorrel leaves for their lemony flavor.

Vegetable Stock (page 79), about 4 cups; include the chard and kale stems
1 tablespoon light olive oil
1 large yellow onion, thinly sliced, about 3 cups
Salt and pepper
4 garlic cloves, finely chopped
1 cup chard stems, thinly sliced
1 medium-size potato, thinly sliced, about 1 cup
1 large carrot, thinly sliced, about 1 cup
¼ cup dry white wine
1 bunch of kale, stems removed and leaves washed, about 8 cups packed
1 bunch of green chard, stems removed and leaves washed, about 8 cups packed
1 bunch of spinach, stems removed and leaves washed, about 8 cups packed
1 tablespoon fresh lemon juice
1 recipe Garlic Croutons (page 87)
Grated Parmesan cheese

Make the stock and keep it warm over low heat.

Heat the olive oil in a soup pot and add the onions, ½ teaspoon salt, and several pinches of pepper. Sauté over medium heat until the onion is soft, 5 to 7 minutes. Then add the garlic, chard stems, potatoes, and carrot. Sauté until the vegetables are heated through, about 5 minutes. Add ½ cup stock, cover the pot, and cook for about 10 minutes. When the vegetables are tender, add the white wine and simmer for 1 to 2 minutes, until the pan is nearly dry. Stir in the kale, chard, 1 teaspoon salt, a few pinches of pepper, and 3 cups stock. Cover the pot and cook the soup for 10 to 15 minutes, until the chard and kale are tender. Add the spinach and cook for 3 to 5 minutes, until just wilted.

Puree the soup in a blender or food processor until it is smooth. Thin with a little more stock if it seems too thick. Season with lemon juice and salt and pepper to taste. Garnish each serving with Garlic Croutons and a sprinkle of Parmesan.

MAKES 9 TO 10 CUPS

Potato, Leek, and Celery Root Soup

We make this hearty soup throughout the fall and winter—a smooth background of potatoes and celery root cooked in a lightly colored stock, with sautéed leeks for added richness. We pass it through a food mill to smooth the texture, but for a more rustic soup you can let the potatoes and celery root cook until they fall apart or use a potato masher instead. A little cream is important here—it really pulls the starch of the potatoes and celery root together. An elegant swirl of Orange Crème Fraîche lightens the earthy flavors.

Light Vegetable Stock (page 79), about 6 cups
1 medium-size celery root bulb, about 1 pound
2 pounds large red or Yellow Finn potatoes, peeled and thinly sliced, about 7 cups
Salt and white pepper
1 bay leaf
4 garlic cloves, finely chopped
1 tablespoon light olive oil
1 tablespoon unsalted butter
2 medium-size leeks, cut in half lengthwise, thinly sliced, and washed, about 3 cups
¼ cup dry white wine
2 tablespoons cream
Orange Crème Fraîche (page 83)

Make the stock and keep it warm over low heat.

Peel, quarter, and thinly slice the celery root, discarding the inner core if it's soft and spongy.

Place the potatoes and celery root in a soup pot with 1 quart stock, 1 teaspoon salt, a few pinches of white pepper, the bay leaf, and the garlic. Bring to a boil, then reduce the heat, cover the pot, and simmer for 30 minutes, until the potatoes and celery root are very soft. Remove the bay leaf, then pass through a food mill or quickly mash with a potato masher. Return the potatoes and celery root to the pot, cover, and cook over low heat.

While the potatoes and celery root are cooking, heat the olive oil and butter in a sauté pan and add the leeks, ½ teaspoon salt, and a few pinches of pepper. Sauté over medium heat until the leeks begin to soften, about 3 to 4 minutes, then cover the pan and lightly steam them for about 10 minutes. Add the wine and simmer, uncovered, until the pan is almost dry.

Add the leeks to the potatoes and celery root along with 1 to 2 cups stock to reach the desired consistency. Cover and cook over low heat for 20 to 30 minutes. Season with salt and pepper to taste. Stir in the cream just before serving. Garnish each serving with a swirl of Orange Crème Fraîche.

MAKES 8 TO 9 CUPS

Tip: Celery root discolors if prepared in advance unless it's covered with acidulated water. If you're planning to prepare it ahead of time, add the juice of 1 lemon to 2 to 3 cups water. Place the sliced celery root in a bowl and cover with the lemon water; drain when you're ready to use it.

DILL

With its feathery fronds and sweet aromatic flavor, this graceful umbelifer has a way with spinach, cucumbers, beets, and potatoes. It originated in Scandinavia and is related to the wild fennel you see growing along country roadsides. The seeds add fresh flavor to pickled dishes—like the chopped leaves, their flavor is assertive and best used sparingly.

Fresh dill has a bright, refreshing quality. For a traditional potato salad with an unusual twist, toss the chopped leaves with purple Peruvian potatoes and diced celery. The lavender potatoes (their color lightens when boiled or steamed) are beautiful with pale green celery and the dark green flecks of chopped dill.

Dill likes a cooler climate, full sun, and well-drained soil. Sow the seeds thickly in a deserted side of the garden; dill grows like a weed. The tender leaves, sometimes called dill weed, *can be clipped to use anytime during the growing season. By the end of the season, dill raises its head like an umbrella. Let it go to seed and harvest the flower heads before they turn brown. Allow the flower heads to dry, then remove the seeds.*

Tuscan White Bean Soup
with Rosemary Croutons

This is a Greens classic, and we make it throughout the year. It's the flavor of the beans and their broth that makes this soup outstanding—we suggest Great Northern and small white beans, but cannellini and lima beans are also delicious. Cook the beans until they're thoroughly tender and be sure to include the fresh herbs and bay leaf. This rustic soup is even better on the second day.

1½ cups dried Great Northern beans, about 9 ounces, sorted and soaked overnight
1 cup dried small white beans, about 6 ounces, sorted and soaked overnight
2 quarts cold water
1 fresh rosemary sprig
2 fresh sage leaves
2 bay leaves
1 tablespoon extra virgin olive oil
1 medium-size yellow onion, diced, about 1½ cups
½ teaspoon dried basil
Salt and pepper
6 garlic cloves, finely chopped
¼ cup dry white wine
½ pound tomatoes, peeled, seeded, and chopped (page 95), about 1 cup, or 1 8-ounce can
*   tomatoes with juice, chopped*
Grated Parmesan cheese
Rosemary Croutons (recipe follows)

Drain and rinse the two types of beans. Place them in a soup pot and add the water, rosemary, sage, and bay leaves. Bring to a boil, then reduce the heat and simmer, uncovered, until the beans are very soft and beginning to break apart, 30 to 35 minutes. Remove the herbs and set aside 1 cup whole beans to add to the soup later. Pass the remaining beans through a food mill, adding their broth or water as needed, then return them to the soup pot and cook over low heat.

While the beans are cooking, heat the olive oil in a sauté pan and add the onion, basil, ½ teaspoon salt, and a few pinches of pepper. Sauté over medium heat until the onion is tender, about 7 minutes. Add the garlic and sauté for about 2 minutes, then add the wine and cook for 1 or 2 minutes, until the pan is nearly dry. Add the tomatoes and simmer for 10 minutes, then combine with the pureed beans. Add the cup of whole beans, ½ teaspoon salt, and a few pinches of pepper. Cover and cook over low heat for 30 minutes. Thin with a little water if needed and add salt and pepper to taste.

Garnish each serving with a spoonful of Parmesan cheese and the Rosemary Croutons.

MAKES 8 TO 9 CUPS

Rosemary Croutons

2 tablespoons olive oil
2 garlic cloves, finely chopped
¼ baguette, thinly sliced on a diagonal
¼ teaspoon finely chopped fresh rosemary

Preheat oven to 375°F. Combine the olive oil and garlic and brush it on the baguette slices; sprinkle with the rosemary. Bake on a baking sheet for 8 to 10 minutes, until the croutons are crisp and very lightly browned.

MAKES 8 TO 9 CUPS

ROSEMARY

This noble evergreen is highly aromatic. We toss whole sprigs of it with roasting potatoes and garlic and mix the finely chopped needles into moist focaccia dough—its woody, pinelike flavor is always invigorating. Be careful not to use too much—a pinch or two is all that's needed to add savor to a Tuscan White Bean Soup, a pizza with wilted spinach and feta cheese, or a simmering sauce of tomatoes. It's a beautiful herb and exceptionally so when in flower—we've used it to garnish our grilled vegetable brochettes since the day the restaurant opened.

Rosmarinus officinalis is an outstanding shrubby perennial that thrives in a marine environment. It needs a mild winter, but it's such a superb culinary plant that it can be grown in a container and brought indoors for cold winters. Start plants from stem cuttings; rosemary will tolerate poor soil if it's well drained and, once established, won't need much water. Rosemary does not like to be pruned heavily—don't cut into the old wood. This plant develops character slowly, season after season.

Spicy Black Bean Soup

This soup began as a variation of our popular black bean chili and evolved into its own recipe. The soup is garnished here with chopped tomatoes and cilantro, but delicious possibilities abound—fried strips of corn tortilla, thinly sliced avocado, or crème fraîche seasoned with orange juice, cumin, and cayenne.

2 cups dried black beans, about 12 ounces, sorted and soaked overnight
6 cups cold water
1 fresh oregano sprig
2 bay leaves
2 fresh sage leaves
1 tablespoon light olive oil
1 large yellow onion, thinly sliced, about 3 cups
Salt and cayenne pepper
½ teaspoon dried oregano, toasted (page 89)
8 garlic cloves, chopped
2 teaspoons Chipotle Puree (page 332)
1 heaped tablespoon Ancho Chili Puree (page 197)
¼ cup dry sherry
½ pound fresh tomatoes, peeled, seeded, and chopped (page 95), about 1 cup, or
  1 8-ounce can tomatoes with juice, chopped
½ cup fresh orange juice
½ pound fresh tomatoes, seeded and chopped, about 1 cup
1 tablespoon chopped cilantro

Rinse and drain the beans. Place them in a soup pot with the cold water, oregano, and bay and sage leaves. Bring to a boil, then reduce the heat and simmer, uncovered, until the beans are soft, 20 to 25 minutes.

Heat the olive oil in a sauté pan and add the onion, ½ teaspoon salt, ⅛ teaspoon cayenne, and the toasted oregano. Cook over medium heat until the onion is soft, 7 to 8 minutes. Add the garlic and the chili purees. Sauté for 3 to 4 minutes, add the sherry, and simmer until it is reduced it by half, a minute or two. Add the tomatoes and ½ teaspoon salt and cook for 10 minutes.

Set aside 1½ cups cooked beans and remove the fresh herbs and bay leaves. Combine the beans and their broth with the tomatoes and onions and puree in a blender or food processor. Pass through a food mill to remove the bean skins and return the puree to the soup pot; add the reserved beans, the orange juice, and ½ teaspoon salt. Season with salt and cayenne to taste. Cover and cook over low heat for 30 minutes.

Toss the tomatoes and cilantro together and garnish each serving with a spoonful.

MAKES 8 TO 9 CUPS

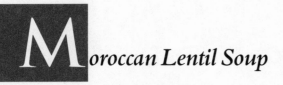oroccan Lentil Soup

The rich, complex flavors of this soup are satisfying on all levels—they become very full and round as the ginger, the pungent spices, and the vegetables slowly simmer with the lentils. The cilantro adds a fresh, light touch.

1 cup lentils, about 6 ounces
6 cups cold water
1 tablespoon extra virgin olive oil
1 medium-size yellow onion, diced, about 2 cups
Salt
Cayenne pepper
1 small carrot, diced, about ½ cup
1 celery rib, diced, about ½ cup
1 small red or yellow bell pepper, diced, about ½ cup
1 teaspoon cumin seed, toasted and ground (page 89)
½ teaspoon ground coriander
⅛ teaspoon turmeric
4 garlic cloves, finely chopped
1 tablespoon grated fresh ginger
½ pound fresh tomatoes, peeled, seeded, and chopped (page 95), about 1 cup, or
    1 8-ounce can tomatoes with juice, chopped
2 tablespoons chopped cilantro

Sort and rinse the lentils and place them in a soup pot with the cold water. Bring to a boil, then reduce the heat and simmer, uncovered, until tender, about 20 minutes.

While the lentils are cooking, heat the olive oil in a medium-size sauté pan and add the onion, ½ teaspoon salt, and a few pinches of cayenne. Cook over medium heat until the onions are soft, 7 to 8 minutes, then add the vegetables, another ½ teaspoon salt, and the spices. Cook for 5 minutes, then stir in the garlic and ginger and cook for another minute or two. Add the vegetables and tomatoes to the lentils and their broth. Cover and cook for 30 minutes, allowing the flavors to blend and deepen. Season to taste with salt and cayenne. Garnish each serving with a sprinkle of cilantro.

MAKES 8 TO 9 CUPS

M ushroom Soup with Caramelized Onions

Caramelized onions and dried porcini give this earthy soup complexity and depth. The mushroom essence comes from searing the mushrooms over high heat with garlic, sherry, and a touch of soy. All of the flavors come together in the rich mushroom broth, brightened with a splash of lemon.

Mushroom Stock (page 80), about 5½ cups
½ ounce dried porcini, soaked in ½ cup warm water for about 10 minutes
2 tablespoons extra virgin olive oil
2 medium-size yellow onions, thinly sliced, about 4 cups
Salt and pepper
6 garlic cloves, finely chopped
1 pound white mushrooms, thickly sliced, about 5 cups
¼ pound shiitake mushrooms, stems removed, sliced ¼ inch thick (save the stems for stock)
½ cup dry sherry
Soy sauce
1 medium-size potato, peeled and thinly sliced, about 1 cup
1 tablespoon chopped fresh herbs: parsley, thyme, and marjoram
Fresh lemon juice

Make the stock and keep it warm over low heat.

Pour the porcini through a fine strainer and save the liquid to use later. (If the liquid is sandy, let the sand settle, then pour off the liquid.) Finely chop the porcini, discarding any pieces that are gritty or hard. Set aside.

Heat 1 tablespoon olive oil in a soup pot and add the onions, ½ teaspoon salt, and a few pinches of pepper. Sauté the onions over medium heat until they begin to soften and release their juices, about 5 minutes, then add the porcini and half the garlic. Continue to cook over medium heat, gently scraping the pan with a wooden spoon to keep the onions from sticking as they caramelize. (Add a little stock if needed.) After about 25 minutes, the onions should be a rich golden brown.

While the onions are caramelizing, sauté the shiitake and white mushrooms together in 2 separate batches. Heat ½ tablespoon olive oil in the sauté pan, add half the white mushrooms, ¼ teaspoon salt, and a few pinches of pepper and sauté over high heat. As the mushrooms cook, they'll release their juices; then the juices will evaporate and the mushrooms will begin to sear. At this point they'll begin to stick to the pan, but don't stir them. Cook over high heat until they're golden, then stir once and continue to sear for 1 to 2 minutes. Add half the shiitake mushrooms, half the remaining garlic, 2 tablespoons of the sherry, and a splash of soy sauce. Cook for about 1 minute, stirring as needed, until the shiitake mushrooms are tender. The mushrooms will be very dark and flavorful. Add a little stock if necessary to loosen them from the pan, then transfer them to a bowl.

Sear the second batch of mushrooms in exactly the same way, being sure to save all of the flavorful pan juices.

Add ¼ cup of the remaining sherry and the porcini liquid to the onions to deglaze the pan. Add the potatoes and 1 cup of stock, then cover the pot and cook over medium heat until the potatoes are soft, about 15 minutes. Puree in a blender or food processor until smooth, then return to the pot. (This puree gives the soup its rich base.) Add the mushrooms and remaining stock and cook for 20 to 30 minutes.

Stir in the fresh herbs just before serving, then season to taste with salt, pepper, and a splash of lemon juice.

MAKES 8 CUPS

Mushroom-Barley Soup

Rich, dark mushroom stock is essential to this favorite winter soup. The mushrooms are seared over high heat with red wine and garlic to intensify their flavor, while the barley slowly simmers in the stock and soaks up all the good flavors. You can substitute dried shiitake mushrooms if porcini aren't available, or you can do without. Though the dried mushrooms will be missed, the depth and fullness of the other flavors will carry the soup.

Mushroom Stock (page 80), about 6½ cups
½ ounce dried porcini mushrooms, soaked in ½ cup warm water for about 10 minutes
1 tablespoon unsalted butter
1 medium-size yellow onion, diced, about 2 cups
Salt and pepper
6 garlic cloves, finely chopped
½ cup dry red wine
1 small carrot, diced, about ¾ cup
1 large celery rib, diced, about ¾ cup
⅓ cup pearl barley
1 bay leaf
1½ pounds white mushrooms, thinly sliced, about 8 cups
1½ tablespoons extra virgin olive oil
Soy sauce
1 tablespoon chopped fresh herbs: parsley, marjoram, thyme, and sage

Make the stock and keep it warm over low heat.

Pour the porcini through a fine strainer and save the liquid to use later. (If the liquid is sandy, let the sand settle, then pour off the liquid.) Finely chop the porcini, discarding any pieces that are gritty or hard. Set them aside.

Heat the butter in a soup pot and add the onion, ½ teaspoon salt, and a pinch of pepper. Sauté over medium heat until the onion softens and releases its juices, 5 to 7 minutes. Add the porcini and half of the garlic; sauté for 2 minutes, then add ¼ cup of the wine and the porcini soaking liquid; cook for 1 or 2 minutes, until the pan is nearly dry. Add the carrot, celery, barley, bay leaf, and 1 quart stock. Bring to a boil, cover the pot, and cook over medium heat for 30 to 40 minutes, until the barley is tender.

While the vegetables and barley are cooking, sear the mushrooms in 2 separate batches in a skillet over high heat, using ½ tablespoon olive oil, ¼ teaspoon salt, and a few pinches of pepper per batch. As the mushrooms cook, they'll release their juices; then the juices will evaporate and the mushrooms will begin to sear. At this point they'll begin to stick to the pan, but don't stir them. Cook over high heat until they're golden, then stir once and continue to stir for 1 to 2 minutes. Add half of the remaining garlic and stir again. Add a splash of soy sauce, 2 tablespoons of the remaining red wine, and stock to deglaze. Add the first panful of mushrooms to the soup, then repeat the process with a second batch of mushrooms. Be sure to include the flavorful pan juices; they add tremendous flavor to the soup.

When both batches of mushrooms have been added to the soup, add 2 cups stock and the fresh herbs. Season with salt and pepper to taste.

MAKES 8 TO 9 CUPS

Carrot Soup with North African Spices

Cumin and coriander are the smooth background flavors, but it's the fresh ginger, the orange juice, and a hint of cayenne that make this soup sparkle. A little potato adds silky texture; if your carrots aren't sweet, use a sweet potato instead.

Light Vegetable Stock (page 79) about 5 cups; add 10 thin coins of ginger
1 tablespoon light olive oil
1 medium-size yellow onion, thinly sliced, about 1½ cups
Salt
2 garlic cloves, finely chopped
1½ teaspoons cumin seed, toasted and ground (page 89)
1 teaspoon coriander seed, toasted and ground (page 89)
2 teaspoons grated fresh ginger
Cayenne pepper
2 pounds carrots, thinly sliced, about 7 cups
1 medium-size white potato or sweet potato, peeled and thinly sliced, about 1 cup
½ cup fresh orange juice
½ cup crème fraîche (page 359)
2 tablespoons coarsely chopped cilantro

Make the stock and keep it warm over low heat.

Heat the olive oil in a soup pot and add the onion and ½ teaspoon salt. Sauté over medium heat until it begins to release its juices, about 5 minutes, then add the garlic, cumin, coriander, ginger, and a few pinches of cayenne. Cook until the onion is very soft, about 10 minutes, adding a little stock if it sticks to the pan.

Add the carrots, the potato or sweet potato, 1 teaspoon salt, and 1 quart stock. Bring to a gentle boil, then reduce the heat, cover, and simmer until the carrots are very tender, about 15 minutes. Puree the soup in a blender or food processor until smooth, using a little extra stock if needed. Return to the pot, add the orange juice, and thin with stock to the desired consistency. Season with salt to taste and, for additional heat, a pinch or two of cayenne. Garnish each serving with a swirl of crème fraîche and sprinkle with cilantro.

MAKES 9 TO 10 CUPS

Carrot-Leek Soup with Thyme

Make this smooth, light soup in the spring with sweet carrots and tender, pale green leeks. It's the carrots that make this soup delicious, so use the most flavorful ones you can find.

> *6 cups Vegetable Stock (page 79)*
> *2 tablespoons light olive oil*
> *1 tablespoon unsalted butter*
> *1½ pounds carrots, sliced ¼ inch thick, about 3 cups*
> *Salt and white pepper*
> *½ pound potatoes, peeled and thinly sliced, about 1½ cups*
> *1 large leek, white part only, cut in half lengthwise, thinly sliced, and washed, about 2 cups*
> *2 garlic cloves, finely chopped*
> *½ teaspoon dried thyme*
> *2 tablespoons heavy cream (optional)*
> *Grated Gruyère cheese*
> *1 tablespoon chopped fresh thyme*

Make the stock and keep it warm over low heat.

Heat 1 tablespoon of the olive oil and butter in a soup pot; add the carrots, ½ teaspoon salt, and a pinch of pepper. Sauté over medium heat until the carrots begin to glisten and release their juices, about 10 minutes. Add 1 cup stock, stirring and scraping the bottom of the pot to loosen the sugars. Add 3 more cups of stock and the potatoes; bring the soup to a gentle boil, reduce the heat, and simmer, covered, for about 30 minutes, until the carrots are very tender. Add 2 more cups of stock and puree in a blender or food processor until smooth. Return to the pot and cook over low heat.

While the soup is cooking, heat 1 tablespoon olive oil in a sauté pan and add the leeks, garlic, ½ teaspoon salt, dried thyme, and a pinch of pepper. Cover and cook over medium heat until the leeks are tender, 5 to 7 minutes. (The water on the washed leeks will help to wilt them.)

Add the leeks to the carrot puree and cook, uncovered, over low heat for another 30 minutes. Add the cream if you're using it and season with salt and a few pinches of pepper to taste. Garnish each serving with Gruyère cheese and sprinkle with fresh thyme.

MAKES 9 TO 10 CUPS

Tip: If the flavor of the carrots is lacking, add a sweet potato to the soup to sweeten and bring out the flavors.

Roman Tomato-Lentil Soup with Mint

This is a simple soup, yet the flavor of the fresh mint, a typically Roman touch, makes it distinctive. Though we make it year-round, it's best in the summer, when tomatoes are sweet and ripe.

1 cup lentils, about 6 ounces
1 bay leaf
2 fresh oregano or marjoram sprigs
2 fresh sage leaves
6 cups cold water
1 tablespoon light olive oil
1 medium-size yellow onion, diced, about 1½ cups
1½ teaspoons salt
⅛ teaspoon pepper
½ teaspoon dried oregano
1 medium-size carrot, diced, about ¾ cup
1 medium-size red or yellow bell pepper, diced, about ¾ cup
4 garlic cloves, finely chopped
¼ cup dry sherry
1 pound fresh tomatoes, peeled, seeded, and pureed (page 95), about 1 cup, or 1 16-ounce
*   can tomatoes with juice, pureed*
2 tablespoons chopped fresh mint

Sort and rinse the lentils, then place them in a medium-size saucepan with the bay leaf, oregano sprigs, sage, and cold water. Bring to a boil, reduce the heat, and cook, uncovered, at a gentle boil until the lentils are tender, about 20 minutes.

While the lentils are cooking, heat the olive oil in a soup pot. Add the onion, ½ teaspoon salt, the pepper, and the dried oregano. Sauté over medium heat until the onion is soft, about 5 minutes. Add the carrot, peppers, and garlic; sauté until the vegetables are tender, about 10 minutes, then add the sherry and cook for 1 or 2 minutes, until the pan is nearly dry.

Remove the herbs and bay leaf from the beans, then add the lentils with their broth to the vegetables, along with the tomatoes and 1 teaspoon salt. Cover and cook over low heat for 30 minutes. Add the mint just before serving.

MAKES 8 CUPS

Tip: If the soup is acidic, add a few pinches of sugar to balance the flavors after the final cooking.

Pasta and Risotto

Pasta

Our pasta dishes have grown lighter as our cooking has evolved over the years—now it's extra virgin olive oil and fresh herbs that give our pastas their zesty flavor, but we still make a few special sauces with butter, cream or crème fraîche, and cheese.

We use a light hand with oil, but if even a little oil is a concern for you, try a rich Mushroom Stock or Vegetable Stock in place of olive oil or experiment by balancing the stock and oil until your palate adjusts to the lighter flavor. Fresh herbs, onions, garlic, and shallots will add complexity to the sauce.

At Greens we stopped making our own fresh pasta years ago. A good local pasta maker provides us with linguine, fettuccine, tagliatelle, pappardelle (wide noodles), and pasta sheets for lasagne, ravioli, and cannelloni. Homemade fresh pasta is wonderful, of course, but it's worth searching out a good commercial supplier if you simply can't manage it.

Dried pasta has its own characteristic taste and texture—you can count on it to be flavorful and what we call "toothy"—al dente. Dried pasta is very forgiving, as long as you don't overcook it. You can even cook it in advance for last-minute dishes—toss the cooked pasta with a little olive oil to keep it from sticking together and reheat it in a skillet before saucing and serving. The variety of sizes and shapes of dried pasta is remarkable—we like the way penne and fusilli catch the sauce and use them often in our dishes; little orecchiette (ear shapes) and shells are delicious in soups and stews. Find a good source of imported Italian dried pasta and stay with it, but have fun experimenting with the different sizes and shapes. We use De Cecco, a well-known brand found in specialty shops and in many supermarkets.

We buy fresh Chinese noodles in Chinatown for Asian noodle salads, but you can also use angel hair pasta if fresh Chinese noodles aren't available. Japanese soba (dried buckwheat noodles) work well with brown butter and Asian-inspired pasta dishes. You can find them in the Asian section of some grocery stores or in Japanese markets.

Whatever kind of pasta you're using, drop it into several quarts of salted boiling water. When it starts to soften, test a piece frequently so you catch it when it's perfectly done, when it still has just a little bite left. Drain it immediately and sauce it right away.

LASAGNE

Lasagne is such a satisfying dish—it's great for entertaining and make-ahead meals. Bake the layered pasta in an earthenware casserole and allow it to sit for a few minutes before serving—even the most devout meat-and-potato eaters will be won over by its inviting aroma and hearty, rich flavors.

Our lasagne recipes are lengthy, but if you start the day before, you can assemble the lasagne with ease on the day of serving. Make the sauce and refrigerate it overnight or take it from your freezer. The béchamel can be made ahead as well. Steep a bundle of fresh herbs in the béchamel as the sauce is cooking—the herbs' essence will flavor this surprisingly light sauce. Cut the vegetables or grate the cheese beforehand and store in sealed containers. You can even assemble the entire lasagne a day ahead, but return it to room temperature before baking, or it will be in the oven for hours.

You can use dried pasta if there isn't a pasta shop or specialty market in your area, but be sure to precook it, or the dried pasta will soak up all of the sauce. A good aged provolone, freshly grated Parmesan, or fresh mozzarella will greatly enhance all the flavors of the dish. If good fresh ricotta is available, it's worth the trip to a cheese store—*ricotta fresca* is sweet and light, superior to highly processed ricotta in every way. Season each element of the lasagne generously so the delicious flavors aren't lost to the pasta.

Risotto

This creamy Italian rice dish is wonderfully appealing—with wild mushrooms and leeks or juicy, sweet tomatoes, it's ethereal. Arborio rice is the essential ingredient here; with any other rice you'll make a pilaf or a fancy porridge, but it won't be risotto. Unlike any other, this Italian short-grain rice makes its own delectable sauce when gently cooked in stock.

A full-flavored stock makes all the difference to risotto. We use reduced Tomato-Mushroom Stock made with dried shiitake mushrooms—this rich, well-balanced stock works well with all of our risotto recipes. Mushroom Stock is a good choice for a hearty mushroom risotto. A little butter helps to bring the dish together—it coats the plump grains of rice and gives the sauce a silky texture.

Make risotto when you have plenty of patience. With your favorite spoon and a glass of wine in hand, devote yourself wholeheartedly to stirring the risotto. The rice will take about 20 to 25 minutes to cook once you add it to the pan. (We use a skillet, but you can also use a large heavy saucepan.) Cook it gently over low heat and add the stock gradually so the plump grains can slowly absorb the stock, releasing their starch to make the sauce. The risotto is ready to serve when the grains are tender but still toothy in the center—there should be a little resistance when you bite into the rice. You can always add a little stock and cook the rice longer if it isn't tender to your taste. If the taste is a little thin, stir a spoonful of crème fraîche or a sprinkling of Parmesan into the risotto just before you serve it to enrich the flavor. We like a saucy risotto, but if you like it drier, add less stock at the end. Serve the risotto immediately—it won't wait.

Risotto the easy way: If you haven't the patience for stirring risotto, here's a surefire alternative for making it in the oven. Bay Area food luminary Jim Nassikas passed this method along to Marion Cunningham, and she passed it along to us.

Preheat the oven to 375°F. In a large ovenproof skillet, sauté the onions or leeks and rice as directed in the recipe, then stir in 2 cups of stock. Place the skillet, uncovered, in the oven for 15 minutes, then remove it. Stir the rice mixture, then stir in 2 more cups of stock and return it to the oven for another 15 minutes. Remove the skillet from the oven and stir; if the risotto is a little dry, add up to 1 cup of stock and return to the oven for 5 minutes. If you're adding Parmesan or crème fraîche, stir it in just before serving the risotto.

Note: We've described the first stage of cooking the rice with onions or leeks, but the timing for adding the remaining ingredients varies with each recipe, so we haven't included the instructions here. Follow the risotto recipe as closely as possible to coordinate this method with the addition of those ingredients.

Fettuccine with Tomatoes, Fennel, Olives, and Walnuts

Early fall brings vine-ripened tomatoes at their peak as well as treats like freshly harvested walnuts. Here the new nuts and tasty black olives add flavor and texture to the tomatoes and fennel. If Golden Jubilee or yellow tomatoes are available, be sure to include them; they're a colorful addition to this flavorful pasta.

¼ cup walnut pieces, toasted (page 263)
1½ pounds tomatoes, cored and seeded
10 Niçoise or Gaeta olives, pitted and coarsely chopped
3 tablespoons extra virgin olive oil
Salt and pepper
1 medium-size or 2 small fennel bulbs, quartered lengthwise, cored, and sliced, about
    1½ cups
¾ teaspoon ground fennel seed
3 garlic cloves, finely chopped
½ pound fresh fettuccine
2 tablespoons chopped Italian parsley
Grated Parmesan cheese

Chop or break the toasted walnuts into small pieces with your hands. Set a large pot of water on the stove to boil.

Cut the tomatoes into large pieces and toss with the olives, 2 tablespoons of the olive oil, ½ teaspoon salt, and a few pinches of pepper. Set aside to marinate.

Heat the remaining tablespoon of olive oil in a large sauté pan and add the fennel slices, ground fennel, ¼ teaspoon salt, and a few pinches of pepper. Sauté over medium heat until tender, about 7 minutes, then add the garlic and the tomato mixture. Reduce the heat to very low and gently warm the tomatoes, being careful not to cook them too long, or they'll lose their skins.

When the water boils, add 1 teaspoon salt and the pasta. Cook until just tender; drain in a colander, shake off the excess water, and toss into the sauté pan along with the walnuts and parsley. Season to taste with salt and pepper. Serve with freshly grated Parmesan.

SERVES TWO TO FOUR

Linguine with Spring Vegetables and Orange-Saffron Butter

We make this celebratory pasta in the spring with fresh peas and tender young asparagus. To keep the butter from breaking, toss it with the pasta right before serving. It will coat the noodles and make a fragrant sauce. The chive blossoms are lovely with this dish; use them sparingly since they can be quite strong.

4 tablespoons unsalted butter, softened
1 generous pinch of saffron threads, soaked in 1 tablespoon hot water
Salt and pepper
½ pound asparagus, woody ends snapped off
½ pound English peas, shelled, about ¾ cup
1 tablespoon light olive oil
2 shallots, thinly sliced
½ red or yellow bell pepper, thinly sliced
¼ cup dry white wine
Juice of 1 orange, about ⅓ cup
Zest of 1 orange
½ pound fresh linguine
A sprinkling of chive blossoms (optional)
Grated Parmesan cheese

Set a large pot of water on the stove to boil. Cream the butter with the saffron, ⅛ teaspoon salt, and a few pinches of pepper. Set aside.

Slice the asparagus diagonally into 2-inch lengths. When the water boils, add 1 teaspoon salt. Drop the peas into the boiling water and cook until just tender, about 1½ minutes. Scoop them out and rinse under cold water. Drop the asparagus into the boiling water for 2 to 3 minutes, until just tender. Scoop them out and rinse under cold water. Set the peas and asparagus aside. Keep the water boiling.

Heat the olive oil in a large sauté pan and add the shallots, peppers, ¼ teaspoon salt, and a few pinches of pepper. Sauté over medium heat for 4 to 5 minutes, until the peppers are softened. Add the wine and orange juice; continue to cook over medium heat for about 3 minutes, until the liquid is reduced by half.

Meanwhile, cook the pasta in the boiling water until just tender. Just before you drain the pasta, reduce the heat under the sauté pan and add the asparagus, peas, ¼ teaspoon salt, and the orange zest to the peppers and shallots. Drain the linguine in a colander, shake off the excess water, and transfer the pasta to the pan. Quickly toss the vegetables and pasta together, then add the saffron butter. The butter will combine with the pan juices to make a light sauce. Sprinkle with the chive blossoms and serve with freshly grated Parmesan.

SERVES TWO TO FOUR

Linguine with Mushrooms, Red Onions, Capers, and Olives

The flavors of this year-round pasta are easily adapted to the changing seasons. In this recipe we use Italian parsley, but thyme, marjoram, basil, or chervil would be equally delicious. Be sure to choose fresh mushrooms with closed caps.

3 tablespoons extra virgin olive oil
½ pound white mushrooms or cremini, quickly rinsed and thickly sliced, about 3 cups
Salt and pepper
¼ cup dry sherry or dry white wine
½ medium-size red onion, thinly sliced, about 1 cup
3 garlic cloves, finely chopped
½ pound fresh linguine
6 Niçoise or Gaeta olives, pitted and coarsely chopped
2 teaspoons drained capers, rinsed
2 tablespoons chopped Italian parsley
Grated Parmesan or Romano cheese

Set a large pot of water on the stove to boil. Meanwhile, heat 1 tablespoon of the olive oil in a large sauté pan; sauté the mushrooms over medium-high heat with ¼ teaspoon salt and a few pinches of pepper. When the mushrooms are golden and almost crisp on the edges, add half the sherry and cook for about 1 minute, until the pan is nearly dry. (This small amount of liquid will loosen the flavorful pan juices.) Transfer the mushrooms to a bowl.

Heat the remaining 2 tablespoons oil in the same pan; add the onion, ¼ teaspoon salt, and a few pinches of pepper. Sauté over medium heat for 3 to 4 minutes, then add the garlic and remaining sherry; simmer for 1 or 2 minutes, until the pan is nearly dry.

When the water boils, add 1 teaspoon salt. Cook the pasta in the boiling water until just tender. Just before you drain the pasta, add ¼ cup pasta cooking water to the onions along with the mushrooms, olives, and capers. Drain the pasta in a colander, shake off the excess water, and add to the sauté pan. Toss with the vegetables and sprinkle with the parsley. Serve with freshly grated Parmesan or Romano.

SERVES TWO TO FOUR

Variation: You can include fresh or dried shiitake mushrooms as well as dried porcini. Soak 1 ounce dried shiitake or ½ ounce dried porcini in ½ cup warm water for 10 minutes. Pour the mushrooms through a strainer and save the soaking liquid. If it is sandy, let the sand settle, then pour off the liquid. If you're using shiitake, trim off the stems (save for stock) and thinly slice the caps. For porcini, discard any tough or gritty pieces and finely chop the rest. Sauté the soaked mushrooms with the onions and use the soaking liquid along with the sherry to deglaze the mushroom sauté pan.

ITALIAN PARSLEY

This versatile, shiny flat-leafed parsley is always in use somewhere in our kitchen. Grown in the rich, well-composted Green Gulch soil, its flavor is unbelievably delicious. Whole leaves or small sprigs freshen a salad of thinly sliced fennel, lemon juice, and olives. It's wonderful with potatoes, eggs, and pasta—or any dish when you're looking for fresh, clean flavor. A leafy parsley sprig is a simple edible garnish, a refreshing way to finish a meal. Save the crisp, green stems for soup stock; they're rich in iron and vitamin C.

Parsley is a biennial, growing in one season and flowering in the next—you can pluck it through both stages, harvesting the outer sprigs as you need them, keeping the smaller sprigs for next time. It has a long growing season and can withstand a moderately cold winter. Parsley needs rich, generously moist soil and does best in partial shade or filtered light; full sun may cause bitterness. Start the seeds indoors in the very early spring, soaking them in warm water for a full day before planting. You can set seedlings out four weeks before the last expected frost in your area. Pot up a plant in the early fall and set it on a sunny windowsill for the winter.

Pasta and White Bean Stew with Summer Vegetables

Our version of *pasta e fagioli* is more of a stew than a soup, and it features summer vegetables, tomatoes, and basil. As the cannellini beans cook, they begin to break down, and their starchy broth combines with the sweet juice of the tomatoes to make a wonderful sauce. A generous meal in itself, this delicious stew can be enjoyed over 2 to 3 days.

1 cup dried cannellini or Great Northern white beans, about 6 ounces, soaked overnight
6 cups cold water
1 bay leaf
2 fresh sage leaves
1 fresh marjoram or oregano sprig
2 fresh winter savory or thyme sprigs
Salt and pepper
¼ pound green beans, about 1½ cups, trimmed and cut into 3-inch lengths
2½ pounds fresh tomatoes, peeled and seeded (page 95), with their juice or 2 16-ounce
  cans tomatoes with juice
¼ pound fusilli or penne
3 tablespoons extra virgin olive oil
1 medium-size yellow onion, diced, about 2 cups
½ teaspoon dried basil
¼ teaspoon dried oregano or marjoram
5 garlic cloves, finely chopped
1 medium-size red or yellow bell pepper, thinly sliced, about 1 cup
½ pound sunburst squash or zucchini, cut into ½-inch-thick wedges or cut diagonally into
  ½-inch slices, about 2 cups
⅓ cup coarsely chopped fresh basil, about 20 leaves
Grated Parmesan cheese

Drain and rinse the soaked cannellini beans. Pour the beans into a medium-size saucepan, cover with the water, and add the bay leaf and fresh herbs. Bring to a boil, reduce the heat, and cook, uncovered, at a low boil until they are tender yet still retain their shape, about 30 to 35 minutes. Taste the beans to see that they are done. If their skins are still a little tough, cook them a little longer. Leave the beans in their broth and, when cool, remove the herbs and bay leaf.

While the dried beans are cooking, bring a large pot of water to a boil and add ½ teaspoon salt and the green beans. Cook them for 2 to 3 minutes, until tender yet still bright green. Scoop the beans out of the water with a strainer, rinse under cold water, drain, and set aside. Keep the water boiling.

Cut the tomatoes into large pieces and reserve their juice.

Cook the pasta in the boiling water for 7 to 8 minutes, until just tender. (It will continue to cook while it stews with the beans and vegetables.) Drain the pasta in a colander, rinse under cold water, and shake off the excess water. Toss with 1 tablespoon of the olive oil to keep it from sticking together.

Heat the remaining 2 tablespoons olive oil in a wide skillet; add the onion, ½ teaspoon salt, a few pinches of pepper, and the dried herbs. Sauté over medium heat for 5 minutes, until the onions begin to release their juices. Add the garlic and peppers and sauté until the onions and peppers are soft, another 5 to 6 minutes. Add the summer squash and sauté for 1 minute, just long enough to heat it through. Stir in the tomatoes, the beans and their broth, the fusilli, and the basil. Season with as much as 1 teaspoon salt, then add pepper to taste. Cook, uncovered, over medium-low heat for 20 minutes. This dish should be brothy, so add a little water or stock if more broth is needed. Add the green beans just before serving. Serve in warm bowls and pass the Parmesan cheese.

SERVES SIX GENEROUSLY

Tip: To make life easier, cook the pasta and beans a day in advance and refrigerate overnight. Cool the beans, then cover and store them in their cooking broth with the bay leaf and fresh herbs. Toss the pasta in a little olive oil to keep it from sticking together and keep it tightly covered.

Spinach Fettuccine with Artichokes, Sun-Dried Tomatoes, and Capers

The substantial flavors of this pasta make it a good main course for the fall and winter months. It's an especially pretty dish, the bright green fettuccine contrasting beautifully with the earthy colors of the artichokes and sun-dried tomatoes.

3 medium-size artichokes, trimmed and sliced (page 241)
3 tablespoons extra virgin olive oil
½ medium-size red onion, thinly sliced, about 1 cup
Salt and pepper
2 garlic cloves, finely chopped
1 teaspoon fresh lemon juice
¼ cup dry white wine
½ pound fresh spinach fettuccine
4 sun-dried tomatoes packed in oil, drained and sliced
1 tablespoon drained capers, rinsed
2 teaspoons chopped fresh thyme
½ cup Garlic Bread Crumbs (page 139)
Grated Parmesan or Romano cheese

Set a large pot of water on the stove to boil. Heat 2 tablespoons of the olive oil in a large sauté pan. Add the onion, ¼ teaspoon salt, and a few pinches of pepper. Sauté over medium heat for 2 to 3 minutes, until the onion is tender. Drain the artichokes and add to the onion with the garlic, the lemon juice, ¼ teaspoon salt, and a few pinches of pepper. Sauté until the artichokes are tender, 7 to 8 minutes, then add the white wine and simmer for 1 or 2 minutes, until the pan is nearly dry.

When the water is boiling, add 1 teaspoon salt and the fettuccine and cook until just tender. Before draining, add ¼ cup of the pasta cooking water to the artichokes along with the sun-dried tomatoes, capers, remaining tablespoon of oil, and thyme. Drain the pasta, shake off the excess water, and add to the artichokes and onions, tossing everything together. Season with salt and pepper to taste, sprinkle with the bread crumbs, and serve with freshly grated Parmesan or Romano.

SERVES TWO TO FOUR

Fettuccine with Broccoli, Roasted Peppers, and Olives

We make this simple pasta throughout the year, and the only time-consuming step is roasting the peppers, which can be done a day or two in advance. Chopped black olives, lemon juice, and plenty of garlic intensify the flavors.

1 medium-size red or yellow bell pepper, roasted and peeled (page 55)
1 stalk of broccoli, about 3 cups florets with stems
3 tablespoons extra virgin olive oil
3 garlic cloves, finely chopped
8 Niçoise or Gaeta olives, pitted and coarsely chopped
1 tablespoon fresh lemon juice
Salt and pepper
½ pound fresh fettuccine
2 tablespoons chopped fresh herbs: marjoram, parsley, and thyme
Grated Parmesan or Romano cheese

Set a large pot of water on the stove to boil. Slice the roasted pepper into thick strips, saving the juice, if any, to marinate it with. Cut the broccoli into florets about 1 inch long, slicing the stem diagonally as you cut. Trim away the tough outer skin of the broccoli stalk and thinly slice on the diagonal.

Heat 2 tablespoons of the olive oil in a large sauté pan, add the garlic, and sauté over medium-low heat for 2 minutes, being careful not to brown it. Reduce the heat and add the pepper strips, olives, lemon juice, and ¼ teaspoon salt.

When the water is boiling, add 1 teaspoon salt and the fettuccine. Cook the pasta for 30 seconds to 1 minute, then add the broccoli, allowing it about 1 minute to cook. Just before you drain the pasta, add ¼ cup of the cooking water to the sauté pan. Immediately drain the pasta and broccoli in a colander and shake off the excess water. Add to the sauté pan along with the remaining tablespoon of olive oil, ¼ teaspoon salt, and the fresh herbs. Season to taste with salt and pepper. Serve with freshly grated cheese.

SERVES TWO TO FOUR

Tip: Cook the broccoli and pasta separately if you prefer. Drop the broccoli into the boiling water for 45 to 60 seconds, then rinse under cold water and drain. Add the broccoli to the sauté pan just before you add the pasta; don't add it earlier, or the lemon juice will discolor it.

Spinach Fettuccine with Tomatoes, Crème Fraîche, and Basil

Save this pasta for late summer, when tomatoes are at their prime. The lightly tart crème fraîche blends nicely with the full, sweet flavors of the tomatoes and basil. The sauce is creamy but light—its pale pink color contrasts beautifully with the spinach pasta and the red flecks of tomato. If flavorful cherry tomatoes are available, include them here. To keep them from overcooking, warm them in the sauce just before adding the pasta, then gently toss together.

1½ pounds tomatoes, peeled and seeded (page 95)
2 tablespoons extra virgin olive oil
3 garlic cloves, finely chopped
⅓ cup coarsely chopped basil, about 20 to 25 leaves
1½ teaspoons salt
Pepper
1 cup crème fraîche (page 359)
½ pound fresh spinach fettuccine
2 ounces Parmesan cheese, grated, about ⅔ cup, plus more to serve at the table

Cut the tomatoes into large pieces and marinate with the olive oil, garlic, basil, ¼ teaspoon salt, and ⅛ teaspoon pepper. Bring a large pot of water to a boil and add 1 teaspoon salt. Warm the crème fraîche in a large skillet over medium heat until it thins. Add the tomatoes and cook for 3 to 4 minutes to infuse the flavors of the sauce. Add the pasta to the boiling water and cook until just tender. Drain in a colander and shake off the excess water. Add the pasta to the skillet along with the remaining ¼ teaspoon salt and a few pinches of pepper; toss together. Remove the skillet from the heat, add the ⅔ cup Parmesan, and toss again. Serve in warm bowls and pass more grated Parmesan at the table if you like.

SERVES TWO TO FOUR

Variation: To make a delicious creamy Gorgonzola pasta, substitute 1 cup heavy cream for the crème fraîche and include 2 or 3 ounces Gorgonzola cheese, crumbled. Heat the cream in the skillet and reduce it to ½ cup; lower the heat, add the tomatoes, and cook together for 3 to 4 minutes. Drain the pasta and add to the cream along with the crumbled Gorgonzola and the ⅔ cup Parmesan. Toss everything together and serve.

Buckwheat Noodles with Shiitake Mushrooms, Bok Choy, Ginger, and Scallions

On an early morning bike ride through the narrow streets of San Francisco's Chinatown, I'm amazed by the bustling activity of the outdoor market: bins brimming with beautiful heads of bok choy, fresh ginger, scallions, and cilantro, shoppers crowding to make their purchases. That is the vivid scene that inspired this unusual pasta. The light, crisp texture of the bok choy balances the earthy flavors of the mushrooms and the buckwheat noodles. We use *soba*—Japanese buckwheat noodles—available in Asian markets and natural food stores.

¼ pound fresh shiitake mushrooms
½ large or 2 small heads of bok choy
Salt
6 ounces thin dried buckwheat or soba noodles
2 tablespoons light vegetable oil or peanut oil
3 garlic cloves, finely chopped
1 tablespoon grated fresh ginger
1 to 2 jalapeño chilies, cut in half lengthwise and thinly sliced
1 scallion, thinly sliced on a diagonal
1 tablespoon dark sesame oil
2 tablespoons mirin (sweet cooking sake)
2 tablespoons soy sauce
2 tablespoons coarsely chopped cilantro
1 teaspoon sesame seed, toasted (page 263)

Set a large pot of water on the stove to boil. Remove the mushroom stems and cut the caps into ½-inch slices. (The stems can be saved for stock.) For small heads of bok choy, slice the stem lengthwise, leaving leaf and stem together. For a large head, slice the stems diagonally, ¾ inch thick, and slice the leaves into 2-inch-wide ribbons.

When the water boils, add 1 teaspoon salt. Add the noodles and cook as directed on the package, about 8 to 10 minutes. While the pasta is cooking, heat the vegetable oil in a large sauté pan; add the shiitake mushrooms and ¼ teaspoon salt. Sauté over medium heat for 3 to 4 minutes, then add the garlic, ginger, chilies, and bok choy and sauté for 2 minutes.

Drain the pasta in a colander when it is just tender. Reduce the heat under the sauté pan and add the scallion, sesame oil, mirin, and soy sauce. Quickly add the noodles, taking care not to overcook the bok choy. Remove from the heat, toss the noodles with the vegetables and cilantro, and season with salt to taste. Sprinkle with the sesame seed.

SERVES TWO TO FOUR

Fettuccine with Swiss Chard, Currants, Walnuts, and Brown Butter

This pasta is perfect for a midwinter meal. The flavors are full and rich—hearty sautéed chard, crunchy walnuts, and the sweetness of currants and golden raisins. The brown butter coats the pasta, and its warm, nutty flavor permeates the dish.

We use fresh fettuccine here, but penne is also a delicious pasta choice. It can be cooked in advance, tossed with a little olive oil, and reheated with the sauce, a make-ahead technique that works well for this dish.

⅓ cup brown butter (page 331)
1 tablespoon dried currants
2 tablespoons golden raisins
1 bunch of red or green Swiss chard, about 8 cups packed leaves
1 tablespoon light olive oil
½ medium-size red onion, thinly sliced, about 1 cup
Salt and pepper
2 garlic cloves, finely chopped
½ pound fresh fettuccine
⅓ cup walnut pieces, toasted (page 263)
Grated Parmesan cheese

Make the brown butter and keep it warm over very low heat. Set a large pot of water on the stove to boil. Plump the currants and golden raisins in a small bowl covered with ¼ cup hot water. Trim the stems from the chard and slice across the leaves to make 2-inch-wide ribbons.

Heat the olive oil in a large sauté pan; add the onion, ¼ teaspoon salt, and a few pinches of pepper. Sauté over medium heat for about 5 minutes, until the onion softens and begins to release its juices. Add the garlic, chard, and ¼ teaspoon salt. Sauté for 4 to 5 minutes, until the chard is just barely tender, then reduce the heat to low.

When the water boils, add 1 teaspoon salt. Add the fettuccine to the boiling water, timing it to finish cooking with the chard. (The chard should be very tender but not overcooked when the pasta is done.) When the pasta is just tender, drain it immediately in a colander, shake off excess water, and add it to the onions and chard, along with the plumped fruit, walnuts, and brown butter. Toss together and season with salt and pepper to taste. Serve with freshly grated Parmesan.

SERVES TWO TO FOUR

Variation: We often make this pasta with a mixture of winter greens—spinach, Swiss chard, and kale make a particularly satisfying combination. Kale is the slowest cooking of the greens, so add it to the onions 2 or 3 minutes before the chard. The spinach can be wilted quickly, so add it just before tossing with the cooked pasta.

KALE

Kale is a welcome winter green that's hearty, nutritious, and full of flavor. It's particularly tasty with Brussels sprouts and chestnuts sautéed in brown butter—the nutty, sweet flavor really comes through. With white beans it makes a wonderful soup—garnish with a rustic crouton and a sprinkling of Gruyère.

This cool climate plant is native to Russia; it will probably survive through the winter, its taste improving after the first frost. Kale is started easily from seed in early spring or fall—it needs plenty of organic matter, so turn in some compost or manure. Sow the seeds after the summer solstice in order to have plants ready for those fall and winter meals. You can get a good long harvest from even one plant, and the careful harvest of leaves is good for the plant. Don't let the leaves get any bigger than 8 to 10 inches, or they'll be tough.

Linguine with Onion Confit, Goat Cheese, and Walnuts

Although the flavors of this dish are very rich, there's actually very little oil and cheese. The sweetness of the onions is perfectly balanced by the creamy goat cheese and the texture of the walnuts. Gorgonzola is a delicious alternative to goat cheese.

1 tablespoon extra virgin olive oil
2 medium-size yellow onions, thinly sliced, about 4 cups
Salt and pepper
2 garlic cloves, finely chopped
¼ cup dry white wine
½ pound fresh linguine
⅓ cup chopped fresh basil, about 20 leaves
3 tablespoons walnut pieces, toasted (page 263)
1 ounce soft goat cheese or Gorgonzola

Heat the olive oil in a wide skillet. Add the onions and ½ teaspoon salt; sauté over medium heat for about 10 minutes, until the onions begin to soften and release their juices. Add the garlic and continue to cook over medium heat, gently scraping the pan with a wooden spoon to keep the onions from sticking as they caramelize. After 40 minutes, the onions should be a rich golden color and very sweet. At this point, add the wine to deglaze the pan and simmer over low heat.

Bring a large pot of water to a boil. Chop or break the toasted walnuts into pieces with your hands. When the water is boiling, add 1 teaspoon salt and the linguine and cook until tender, about 1 minute. Just before draining the pasta, add ¼ cup of the cooking water to the confit. (This will make the sauce juicier without using more oil.) Immediately drain the pasta, then add it to the confit along with the walnuts and basil. Season with ½ teaspoon salt and a few pinches of pepper. Crumble in the cheese and serve immediately.

SERVES TWO TO FOUR

Linguine with Chanterelles and Leeks

This elegant pasta is easy to prepare, and the flavors are so well suited to each other that it comes together quite effortlessly. If chanterelles are not to be found, you can use cremini or white mushrooms instead, though the sweet, earthy wild mushroom flavor will be missed.

½ pound chanterelles
1 leek, white part only, cut in half lengthwise, thinly sliced, and washed, about 1½ cups
2 tablespoons unsalted butter
Salt and pepper
3 garlic cloves, finely chopped
⅓ cup dry white wine
½ pound fresh linguine
2 teaspoons chopped fresh thyme
Grated Parmesan cheese

Use a brush or a damp cloth to clean the chanterelles carefully. Remove the dirt and bits of organic matter, but don't wash them, or they'll soak up the water and lose their delicate flavor. Trim off the base of the stem if it is particularly dirty. Cut the mushrooms into large pieces or thick slices and be sure to include the stem. Set a large pot of water on the stove to boil.

Melt the butter in a large sauté pan, then add the leeks, ½ teaspoon salt, and a few pinches of pepper. Sauté over medium heat for 3 to 4 minutes, until the leeks begin to wilt; add the garlic, cover the pan, and cook until the leeks are tender, about 5 minutes. Add the chanterelles and the white wine; gently simmer, uncovered, for about 10 minutes.

A minute or two before the chanterelles are finished cooking, add 1 teaspoon salt and the pasta to the pot of boiling water. Cook until just tender, 1 to 2 minutes, then drain in a colander and shake off the excess water; add to the sauté pan with ¼ teaspoon salt, a few pinches of pepper, and the thyme. Toss everything together and serve with the grated Parmesan.

SERVES TWO TO FOUR

Fettuccine with Spring Vegetables, Meyer Lemon, and Chive Blossoms

We make this lovely pasta when asparagus, fresh peas, and fava beans are in season. You can use any combination of spring vegetables, as long as they're flavorful and fresh. Meyer lemons are a rare treat, and their slightly sweet juice and fragrant zest are what make this pasta so exceptional. If Meyer lemons aren't available, ordinary lemons will do.

The fava beans are a little extra work, but their buttery flavor makes them well worth the effort. The thick outer pod looks intimidating at first, but it's easy to remove. Once the beans are out of the pods, blanch them for a minute, then slip them from their skins. The thin skin will be too bitter to eat unless the favas are very small.

¼ pound asparagus
¼ pound sugar snap peas, strings removed, about 1 cup
½ pound fresh fava beans
Salt and pepper
3 tablespoons extra virgin olive oil
3 shallots, cut in half lengthwise and thinly sliced
½ medium-size red or yellow bell pepper, thinly sliced, about ¾ cup
1 garlic clove, finely chopped
¼ cup white wine
½ pound fresh fettuccine
Juice and zest of 1 Meyer lemon
2 tablespoons coarsely chopped Italian parsley
A sprinkling of chive blossoms
Grated Parmesan cheese

Set a large pot of water on the stove to boil. Snap the woody ends off the asparagus and discard. Slice the asparagus diagonally into 2-inch lengths. If the snap peas are large, cut them in half. Remove the fava beans from their outer pods.

When the water is boiling, add 1 teaspoon salt. Drop the fava beans in and cook for about 1 minute. Scoop them out and rinse under cold water, then slip them out of their skins. Drop the remaining vegetables into the water and cook very briefly to make sure they retain their bright color and crisp texture. Allow 1 to 2 minutes for the asparagus and 3 to 4 minutes for the snap peas. Rinse the vegetables under cold water. Keep the pot of water at a low boil.

Heat 2 tablespoons of the olive oil in a large sauté pan; add the shallots and sauté over medium heat for 1 minute, then add the peppers, garlic, wine, ¼ teaspoon salt, and a few pinches of pepper.

Add the pasta to the boiling water and cook until just tender. Just before you drain the pasta, add the vegetables, lemon juice and zest, and remaining tablespoon of olive oil to the sauté pan. Immediately drain the pasta in a colander, shake off the excess water, and add to the skillet with ¼ teaspoon salt, ⅛ teaspoon pepper, and the chopped parsley. Sprinkle with the chive blossoms and serve with freshly grated Parmesan.

SERVES TWO TO FOUR

CHIVES

This subtle-tasting member of the onion family is essential in the herbal mix called fines herbes, *along with tarragon, chervil, and Italian parsley. It's a sprightly flavor in frittatas and potato gratins or tossed over a creamy goat cheese spread. The lovely lavender blossoms have a distinctively sharp flavor—they're beautiful sprinkled atop a spring pasta or a warm vegetable salad.*

Chives like a moist rich soil, and in our garden they grow year-round, though they do slow down in the cold season and surge in spring. Use them as a border plant in your rose garden and they'll help to prevent insect damage. Plant chives after the heaviest frosts are over; after the first year you can divide and replant.

Spinach Fettuccine with Shiitake Mushrooms, Spinach, and Sun-Dried Tomatoes

Spinach fettuccine is a good pasta choice for this boldly flavored dish. The deep, earthy taste of the shiitake mushrooms is heightened by the sun-dried tomatoes; the toasted pine nuts add nutty sweetness, and the quickly wilted spinach lightens all the flavors.

½ pound fresh shiitake mushrooms
3 tablespoons extra virgin olive oil
Salt and pepper
3 garlic cloves, finely chopped
¼ cup dry white wine
½ pound spinach fettuccine
1 small bunch of spinach, stems removed and leaves washed, 4 cups packed
3 oil-packed sun-dried tomatoes, drained and thinly sliced
1 tablespoon pine nuts, toasted (page 263)
2 tablespoons chopped fresh herbs: marjoram, chives, and thyme
Grated Parmesan cheese

Set a large pot of water on the stove to boil. Remove the mushroom stems and cut the caps into ½-inch slices.

Heat 2 tablespoons of the olive oil in a large sauté pan; add the mushrooms, ½ teaspoon salt, and a few pinches of pepper. Sauté over medium heat for 3 to 4 minutes, then add the garlic and wine. Cook for a minute or two to reduce the wine, but not completely; leave a little liquid in the pan to keep the mushrooms from sticking.

When the water boils, add 1 teaspoon salt. Add the pasta to the boiling water, and while it's cooking add the spinach to the mushrooms along with ¼ teaspoon salt and a few pinches of pepper. Sauté over medium heat for 1 minute, until the spinach is just wilted, then reduce the heat and add the sun-dried tomatoes, the remaining tablespoon of olive oil, and ¼ cup of the pasta cooking water to loosen the pan juices.

The pasta should be just tender at this point; drain it in a colander and add it to the sauté pan along with the pine nuts and herbs. Toss everything together and season with salt and pepper to taste. Serve with freshly grated Parmesan.

SERVES TWO TO FOUR

Tagliarini with Roasted Tomatoes, Golden Zucchini, and Basil

The roasted tomatoes and their juice bring sweetness and intensity to this summer pasta. We like the flavor of Roma (plum) tomatoes and use them for this recipe. The tomatoes hold well, so you can roast them a day in advance, but don't try to hurry the roasting if you're running late. Instead, substitute sun-dried tomatoes. Garlic Bread Crumbs are a delicious addition.

½ pound golden zucchini or summer squash
1 pound roasted tomatoes (page 258)
3 tablespoons extra virgin olive oil
3 garlic cloves, finely chopped
Salt and pepper
¼ cup dry white wine
½ teaspoon hot pepper flakes
½ pound fresh tagliarini
2 tablespoons pine nuts, toasted (page 263)
15 to 20 fresh basil leaves, bundled and thinly sliced, about ⅓ cup
Grated Parmesan cheese
½ cup Garlic Bread Crumbs (page 139)

Set a large pot of water on the stove to boil.

Cut the zucchini in half lengthwise and slice it diagonally into ½-inch-thick pieces. (If you're using scalloped summer squash, such as sunburst or pattypan, cut it in half through the stem end and slice into ½-inch-thick wedges.) Cut the roasted tomatoes in quarters or large pieces and reserve their juice for the sauce.

Heat 2 tablespoons of the olive oil in a large skillet and add the squash, garlic, ¼ teaspoon salt, and a few pinches of pepper. Sauté over medium-high heat for about 2 to 3 minutes, just long enough to heat the squash through, then add the wine and cook for another minute, until the pan is nearly dry. Add the remaining olive oil, the tomatoes and their juice, ¼ teaspoon salt, and the hot pepper flakes.

When the water is boiling, add 1 teaspoon salt. Add the tagliarini and cook until just tender. Before you drain the pasta, add ¼ cup of the cooking water to the sauté pan (this will make the sauce juicier). Immediately drain the pasta, then add it to the tomatoes and squash along with the pine nuts and basil. Reduce the heat, toss well, and add salt and pepper to taste. Sprinkle with Parmesan and bread crumbs and serve immediately.

SERVES TWO TO FOUR

Penne with Marinated Tomatoes, Basil, and Garlic Bread Crumbs

Penne is a favorite choice for this peak-of-summer pasta, when tomatoes and basil are at their best. The pasta tubes catch the olive oil and the juice of the tomatoes, and the crispy Garlic Bread Crumbs add just the right texture. For an equally delicious pasta, use fresh linguine or fettuccine. To ensure that the flavors are full and well developed, marinate the tomatoes for at least 30 minutes before cooking the pasta.

1 ½ pounds vine-ripened tomatoes, cored, cut in half crosswise, and seeded
¼ cup extra virgin olive oil
3 or 4 garlic cloves, finely chopped
⅓ cup coarsely chopped fresh basil, about 20 to 25 leaves
Salt and pepper
½ pound penne
½ cup Garlic Bread Crumbs (recipe follows)
Grated Parmesan cheese

Set a large pot of water on the stove to boil. Cut the tomatoes into large pieces and toss with the olive oil, garlic, basil, ½ teaspoon salt, and ⅛ teaspoon pepper. Set them aside to marinate for 30 minutes. (It's not necessary to peel the tomatoes for this pasta, because they're just heated through, not cooked long enough to lose their skins.)

When the water is boiling, add 1 teaspoon salt. Cook the penne in the boiling water until just tender, about 8 to 10 minutes. While the pasta is cooking, transfer the tomatoes to a large sauté pan and quickly warm them over medium heat, making sure not to cook them, or their skins will draw away.

Drain the penne in a colander. Shake off the excess water, then add the pasta to the sauté pan and toss with the tomatoes. Sprinkle generously with the bread crumbs and serve with freshly grated Parmesan cheese.

SERVES TWO TO FOUR

Garlic Bread Crumbs

Crispy bread crumbs add unexpected texture and garlic flavor to many of our favorite pastas. We make ours with French baguettes or sourdough bread, but almost any bread will do. We use about ½ cup bread crumbs for four servings of pasta or for a gratin. This simple recipe leaves the garlic decision to you, so use as much or as little as you like. Bread crumbs hold indefinitely in the freezer, though they will need to be crisped before using.

Garlic
Extra virgin olive oil
Sourdough bread or French baguette

Preheat the oven to 325°F. Peel and finely chop the garlic and add to the olive oil. Thinly slice the bread and brush it on one side with the garlic oil. Lay the brushed slices on a baking sheet and bake for about 10 minutes, until they are very crisp and golden. Set aside to cool. Break up the slices with your hands, then grind in a food processor or blender, leaving the texture a little coarse.

OPAL BASIL

This basil is distinctive with its wavy, purple leaves and pale pink flowers. The fragrant leaves add zest to a warm Bloomsdale spinach salad and are delightful nestled in a mix of leafy greens. Opal basil adds delicious flavor to dishes featuring summer favorites—shiny purple eggplant, sweet peppers, and juicy, ripe tomatoes. Bundled with sweet basil and sliced into thin ribbons, it's a beautiful accent to pasta or crusty sourdough bread mounded with tomatoes—with the essence of fruity olive oil and freshly chopped garlic.

Basil originated on the dry slopes around the Mediterranean, so it needs full sun and lean soil conditions—heat is its main love. Heavy fertilizer will produce luxuriant growth but not much flavor. Water it well to keep it succulent—otherwise it will be woody, almost bitter—and pluck the flowers as they bud to keep the plant from going to seed.

Chinese Noodle Salad with Citrus and Spicy Peanuts

Chinese Noodle Salad has been a favorite on the menu since the early days at Greens. In this newest version the lively flavors of ginger, orange, and rice wine vinegar work perfectly together to make a bright, distinctive noodle salad. The flavors will develop and become more balanced as the noodles marinate, so toss them with the marinade and let them sit for about 30 minutes before serving. The thinly sliced vegetables, along with the ginger and orange threads, make this a very beautiful salad.

THE MARINADE

This intensely flavored marinade is quite sharp, with two vinegars to lighten the taste of the sesame oil. The heat of chilies varies greatly, so take a small bite before you decide how much to add to the other ingredients.

Zest of 1 orange
½ cup fresh orange juice, about 1½ oranges
2½ tablespoons grated fresh ginger
3 tablespoons rice wine vinegar
5 tablespoons soy sauce
3 tablespoons sherry vinegar
½ cup dark sesame oil
1½ tablespoons sugar
¼ teaspoon salt
1 or 2 jalapeño or serrano chilies, seeds and stems removed

Using a citrus zester, remove the zest of one orange in long threads; or use a vegetable peeler and peel away long strips of the colored rind, then slice the strips into thin threads. Be sure to avoid the bitter white pith under the skin. Set aside to add to the salad later. Combine all of the remaining marinade ingredients in a blender and puree. Reserve ¼ cup of the marinade to toss with the vegetable garnish.

½ cup Spicy Peanuts (page 401)
½ ounce fresh ginger, about 2 inches in length
Salt
1 medium-size carrot, sliced into thin matchsticks
2 ounces snow peas, strings removed, sliced into thin matchsticks, about ½ cup
1 16-ounce package fresh thin Chinese noodles (thin mein), or angel hair pasta
2 scallions, both white and green parts, thinly sliced on a diagonal
½ cup thin matchsticks of daikon radish
3 tablespoons coarsely chopped cilantro
1 teaspoon hot pepper flakes
Cilantro sprigs for garnish

Set a large pot of water on the stove to boil. Prepare the peanuts and set them aside to cool. Peel the ginger, slice it into thin coins, and slice the coins into very fine threads. When the water comes to a boil, add 1 teaspoon salt. Drop the carrot and snow peas into the boiling water for 30 seconds, just long enough to cook them slightly and to draw out their color. Scoop them out of the water with a strainer, rinse under cold water, and set aside to drain. Keep the water boiling.

Separate and fluff the noodles so that they don't stick together while cooking. Drop them into the boiling water, give them a quick stir, and cook for 3 to 4 minutes. The high acidity of the citrus marinade will actually continue to cook the noodles, so be sure that they are just tender when you pull them from the water. Drain them in a colander and rinse with cold water. Shake off the excess water and put the noodles into a bowl.

Toss the snow peas, carrot, scallions, and daikon together in a small bowl. Add half the vegetables to the noodles and toss with the marinade, ginger, orange threads, cilantro, and hot pepper flakes. Toss the remaining vegetables with the reserved marinade and arrange on top of the noodles, garnishing the salad with cilantro sprigs and the Spicy Peanuts.

SERVES FOUR TO SIX

Chinese Noodles with Green Curry

The flavors of this Southeast Asian noodle salad are unique—the fresh green curry is poured over the lightly dressed noodles, then the vegetables and toasted cashews are sprinkled over. The recipe may look intimidating, but once the ingredients are prepared, it's easy to make. Take a small bite of the chilies before you decide how much to add to the curry. Remember, you can always add more.

THE CURRY
6 ounces canned coconut milk
3 scallions, both white and green parts, cut into 1-inch lengths
2 or 3 green jalapeño chilies, stems and seeds removed
2 garlic cloves, coarsely chopped
2 pinches of cayenne pepper
1 teaspoon cumin seed, lightly toasted and ground (page 89)
3 tablespoons fresh lemon juice, about 2 lemons
2 tablespoons peanut oil
½ teaspoon salt
2 tablespoons grated fresh ginger
½ to 1 bunch of watercress, long stems removed, about 1 cup packed short sprigs
½ bunch of cilantro, long stems removed, about 1 cup packed short sprigs
½ bunch of fresh mint, stems removed, about ½ cup packed leaves

Pour the coconut milk into a blender or food processor. Add the rest of the ingredients except the watercress, cilantro, and mint; puree until smooth. Add all of the greens and puree, adding a little water if the curry is thick. Don't overblend. Set aside.

THE VEGETABLES AND NOODLES
Salt
2 ounces snow peas, strings removed, thinly sliced, about ½ cup
2 scallions, both white and green parts, thinly sliced on a diagonal, about ¼ cup
½ cup thin daikon radish matchsticks
2 jalapeño chilies, seeded and thinly sliced
½ ounce fresh ginger, about 2 inches in length
1 16-ounce package fresh thin Chinese noodles (thin mein) or angel hair pasta
2 tablespoons peanut oil
Watercress or cilantro sprigs
1 tablespoon coarsely chopped cilantro
½ cup cashews, toasted (page 263), about 2 ounces

Set a large pot of water on the stove to boil. When the water boils, add 1 teaspoon salt. Add the snow peas and cook for about 30 seconds, so they're crisp and bright green. Scoop them from the water, rinse under cold water, and drain. Place them in a small bowl and toss with the scallions, daikon, and jalapeños. Keep the water boiling.

Slice the ginger into thin coins, then into thin strips to make ginger threads. Separate and fluff the noodles so that they don't stick together while cooking. Drop them into the boiling water, give them a quick stir, and cook for 3 to 4 minutes. Be sure they are just tender when you pull them from the water. Drain the noodles in a colander, rinse with cold water, and shake them to remove excess water. Toss with the peanut oil, ginger threads, and ½ teaspoon salt.

Pour the curry over the noodles and arrange the vegetables on top. If you're serving the salad on a platter, loosely arrange the watercress or cilantro sprigs on the platter. To serve in a bowl, arrange the greens around the sides of the bowl. Sprinkle with chopped cilantro and toasted cashews. Serve immediately; the noodles will soak up the curry over time.

SERVES FOUR TO SIX

Cannelloni with Spinach, Goat Cheese, Walnuts, and Roasted Garlic–Tomato Sauce

We make this cannelloni year-round, but it's particularly delicious in the summer, when we make the sauce with juicy, ripe tomatoes and freshly cropped red garlic from Green Gulch Farm. The spinach and mild goat cheese blend together to make the filling slightly creamy, and a touch of lemon zest enlivens the flavors.

ROASTED GARLIC–TOMATO SAUCE

1 head of garlic
1½ tablespoons extra virgin olive oil
2 pounds fresh tomatoes, peeled and seeded (page 95), about 3 cups, or 3 cups canned tomatoes with juice
½ small yellow onion, diced, about ½ cup
Salt and pepper
¼ cup dry sherry
1 bay leaf

Preheat the oven to 375°F. Rub the garlic with a little olive oil, place it on a baking sheet, and roast until very soft, 30 to 35 minutes. When the garlic is cool, slice off the top of the bulb and squeeze the cloves out of the skin. Puree them with the tomatoes in a blender or food processor.

Heat the remaining tablespoon of olive oil in a saucepan and add the onion, ½ teaspoon salt, and a few pinches of pepper; sauté over medium heat for 5 minutes. When the onion is soft, add the sherry and bay leaf and simmer for 1 or 2 minutes, until the pan is nearly dry. Add the tomato-garlic puree and ¼ teaspoon salt and simmer, uncovered, over low heat for 30 minutes.

THE FILLING

1½ tablespoons extra virgin olive oil
½ medium-size red onion, diced, about 1 cup
Salt and pepper
4 garlic cloves, finely chopped
2 large bunches of spinach, stems removed and leaves washed, about 16 cups
¾ teaspoon minced lemon zest
⅓ cup walnut pieces, toasted (page 263) and chopped
¼ cup chopped fresh herbs: marjoram, thyme, chives, and parsley
½ pound ricotta cheese, about 1 cup
1 egg, beaten
2 ounces Parmesan cheese, grated, about ⅔ cup
2 ounces Montrachet or other creamy, mild goat cheese

Heat 1 tablespoon of the olive oil in a large skillet. Add the onions, ½ teaspoon salt, and a few pinches of pepper; sauté over medium heat for about 5 minutes, until the onions begin to release their juices. Add half the garlic and sauté until the onions are soft, 2 to 3 minutes. Transfer the onions to a bowl.

Heat the remaining ½ tablespoon olive oil in a large skillet and quickly wilt the spinach over medium-high heat with ½ teaspoon salt, a few pinches of pepper, and the remaining garlic. Remove the spinach from the heat, drain, and cool. Squeeze out the excess moisture a handful at a time, then coarsely chop.

Add the spinach to the onions along with the lemon zest and walnuts. Set aside half of the fresh herbs to sprinkle on top after baking and add the rest to the spinach-onion mixture.

Place the ricotta in a bowl and stir in the egg. Set aside half of the Parmesan cheese to sprinkle over the cannelloni; add the rest to the ricotta with ¼ teaspoon salt and ⅛ teaspoon pepper. Combine the spinach and onions with the ricotta mixture, then crumble in the goat cheese. Season with salt and pepper to taste.

ASSEMBLING THE CANNELLONI
2 fresh pasta sheets, 10 ounces

Cut the pasta sheets into 12 4-inch squares (or comparable size to accommodate the size of the pasta sheets).

Preheat the oven to 350°F. Lay the pasta squares on a work surface and spread ¼ cup of the filling along the edge of each square. Roll loosely; the filling will expand during baking.

Ladle 1½ cups tomato sauce into the bottom of a 9- by 13-inch baking dish. Place the cannelloni close together in the dish, seam side down, and ladle the remaining sauce over them. Use a pastry brush to spread the sauce evenly, particularly on the ends, making sure all the pasta is covered with sauce.

Cover and bake for 20 to 25 minutes. Sprinkle the cannelloni with the reserved Parmesan and fresh herbs just before serving.

MAKES 12 CANNELLONI; SERVES SIX

Tip: Add up to 1 teaspoon sugar after simmering to balance the flavor if the Roasted Garlic–Tomato Sauce is acidic.

Cannelloni with Mushrooms and Fennel

Early fall is the time to make this cannelloni, with the last of the fresh tomatoes and the season's first fennel. Toasted pine nuts and Parmesan bring up the flavors of the filling and the Tomato-Fennel Sauce draws the elements of the dish together.

TOMATO-FENNEL SAUCE
1 tablespoon extra virgin olive oil
½ medium-size yellow onion, diced, about 1 cup
Salt and pepper
¾ teaspoon fennel seed, ground
4 garlic cloves, finely chopped
¼ cup dry red wine
2 pounds fresh tomatoes, peeled, seeded, and pureed (page 95), about 3 cups, or 3 cups
   canned tomatoes with juice, pureed
1 bay leaf

Heat the olive oil in a saucepan and add the onion, ½ teaspoon salt, a few pinches of pepper, and the fennel seed. Sauté over medium heat for 5 minutes, until the onion is soft, then add the garlic and red wine, and simmer for 1 or 2 minutes, until the pan is nearly dry. Reduce the heat to low and add the tomatoes, ¼ teaspoon salt, and the bay leaf. Simmer for 30 minutes. Season with salt and pepper to taste.

THE FILLING
2 tablespoons extra virgin olive oil
½ medium-size yellow onion, diced, about 1 cup
Salt and pepper
½ teaspoon fennel seed, ground
1 medium-size fennel bulb, quartered lengthwise, cored, and thinly sliced
4 garlic cloves, finely chopped
½ cup dry white wine
¾ pound white mushrooms, thickly sliced, about 4 cups
1 tablespoon pine nuts, toasted (page 263)
¼ cup chopped fresh herbs: Italian parsley, marjoram, and thyme
3 ounces Parmesan cheese, grated, about 1 cup
½ pound ricotta cheese, about 1 cup

Heat 1 tablespoon of the olive oil in a large skillet. Add the onions, ½ teaspoon salt, a few pinches of pepper, and the fennel seed; sauté over medium heat for 5 minutes, until the onions begin to soften. Add the fennel and half the garlic, and sauté until the fennel is tender, about 4 to 5 minutes. Add half the wine and simmer for 1 or 2 minutes, until the pan is nearly dry. Transfer the fennel and onions to a bowl.

Heat the remaining tablespoon of olive oil in the pan and sear the mushrooms over medium-high heat with ½ teaspoon salt and a few pinches of pepper. As the mushrooms cook, they'll release their juices; then the juices will evaporate and the mushrooms will begin to sear. At this point they'll begin to stick to the pan, but don't stir them. Cook over high heat until they're golden, then stir once and continue to sear for 1 to 2 minutes. Add the remaining garlic and stir again. Add the remaining wine and simmer for 1 or 2 minutes, until the pan is nearly dry.

Add the mushrooms to the fennel and onions and toss in the pine nuts. Set aside half the fresh herbs to sprinkle on the baked cannelloni and toss the rest with the mushroom-fennel mixture.

Set aside half the Parmesan cheese to sprinkle on top later and add the rest to the filling along with the ricotta cheese. Season with salt and pepper to taste.

ASSEMBLING THE CANNELLONI
2 fresh pasta sheets, 10 ounces

Cut the pasta sheets into 12 4-inch squares (or comparable size to accommodate the size of the pasta sheets).

Preheat the oven to 350°F. Lay the pasta squares on a work surface and spread ¼ cup of the filling along the edge of each square. Roll loosely; the filling will expand during baking. Ladle 1½ cups tomato sauce into the bottom of a a 9- by 13-inch baking dish. Place the cannelloni close together in the dish, seam side down, and ladle the remaining sauce over them. There will be just enough sauce to coat the pasta. Use a pastry brush to spread the sauce evenly, particularly on the ends, making sure all the pasta is covered with sauce.

Cover the dish and bake for 20 to 25 minutes. Sprinkle the cannelloni with the reserved Parmesan and herbs and serve.

MAKES 12 CANNELLONI; SERVES SIX

Tip: Add up to 1 teaspoon sugar after simmering to balance the flavor if the Tomato-Fennel Sauce is acidic.

Ravioli Filled with Eggplant, Roasted Garlic, and Romano Cheese

Roasted eggplant and garlic are tossed with toasted pine nuts, Romano, basil, and oregano to make a robust filling that works perfectly with the fresh, light tomato sauce. The salty Romano is delicious with the roasted flavors, but Parmesan works well too.

Ravioli are a labor of love, so give yourself plenty of time to enjoy the preparation. To cut down on the last-minute work, roast the eggplant and garlic in advance.

> 2 globe eggplants, about 2 pounds
> 4½ tablespoons extra virgin olive oil
> 15 garlic cloves, unpeeled
> ½ medium-size yellow onion, diced, about 1 cup
> Salt and pepper
> 5 garlic cloves, finely chopped
> ¼ cup dry white wine
> 2 tablespoons pine nuts, toasted (page 263) and coarsely chopped
> 2 tablespoons chopped fresh basil
> 1 tablespoon chopped fresh oregano or marjoram
> 3 ounces Romano cheese, grated, about 1 cup, plus more to pass at the table
> 1 pound fresh pasta sheets, rolled as thinly as possible
> 2 pounds tomatoes, peeled and seeded (page 95)
> 10 fresh basil leaves, bundled together and cut into very thin ribbons

Preheat the oven to 350°F. Cut the eggplant in half lengthwise; brush the cut side with 1 tablespoon olive oil and place cut side down on a lightly oiled baking sheet. Brush the cloves of garlic lightly with olive oil and place alongside the eggplant. Roast until the eggplant is very tender and the garlic is soft, about 25 to 30 minutes. Drain the eggplant in a colander and set the garlic cloves aside until cool, then peel them. Coarsely chop the eggplant and garlic by hand or in the bowl of a food processor and set aside.

While the eggplant and garlic are roasting, heat 1 tablespoon of the olive oil in a sauté pan; add the onion, ½ teaspoon salt, and a few pinches of pepper. Sauté over medium heat until it begins to release its juices, about 5 minutes, then add half the chopped garlic. Sauté for 5 more minutes, until the onion is soft; add the wine and cook for 1 or 2 minutes, until the pan is nearly dry. Transfer to a medium-size bowl and set aside to cool.

Add the eggplant and roasted garlic to the onions along with the pine nuts, chopped basil, oregano, ¾ teaspoon salt, a few pinches of pepper, and the cup of Romano. The flavor of the filling should be very bold.

Lightly flour a large work area. Cut the pasta sheets lengthwise into strips about 3½ to 4 inches wide, depending on the size of the sheets. Lay out a strip of pasta and cover the rest with a damp towel to keep them from drying out. Place tablespoon-size dollops of filling in the center of the strip, about 2 inches apart; spray the strip lightly with water and lay another strip on top. Gently press around the filling to force out all of the air and seal the pasta. Use a ravioli wheel to cut the ravioli and pinch them to make sure they're closed. Repeat until you've used all the pasta and filling. Place the ravioli on a floured baking sheet.

Bring a wide pot of water to a boil and add 1 teaspoon salt. Cut the tomatoes into medium-size pieces and toss with the remaining olive oil and chopped garlic, ¼ teaspoon salt, a few pinches of pepper, and half the basil ribbons.

Add the tomatoes to a large skillet and cook over medium heat for about 3 minutes, just long enough to heat the sauce.

While the sauce is heating, add the ravioli to the boiling water, lower the heat to a gentle boil, and cook until tender, 2 to 6 minutes, depending on the thickness of the pasta. Gently scoop the ravioli from the pot with a slotted spoon or a strainer, shake off the excess water, and immediately add to the sauce. Use a large spoon to gently coat the ravioli with the sauce. Add salt and pepper to taste. Serve the ravioli in warm pasta bowls, sprinkle with the remaining basil ribbons, and pass the Romano.

MAKES 20 TO 24 3½-INCH RAVIOLI; SERVES FOUR

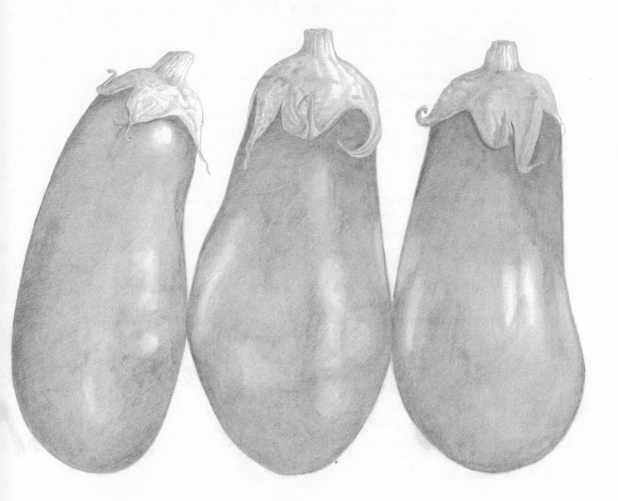

Eggplant Lasagne with Basil

Make this lasagne at the peak of the summer season, when the markets are filled with beautiful, deep purple Japanese eggplant, fragrant basil, and vine-ripened tomatoes. Use canned tomatoes if fresh tomatoes lack good flavor. The flavor and texture of the eggplant are essential, so season it generously and roast until it's tender and soft in the center. Make the sauce a day in advance if you like.

TOMATO SAUCE
1 tablespoon extra virgin olive oil
½ medium-size yellow onion, finely diced, about 1 cup
Salt and pepper
½ teaspoon dried basil
6 garlic cloves, finely chopped
¼ cup dry red wine
*2½ pounds fresh tomatoes, peeled, seeded, and pureed (page 95), about 4 cups, or 1 28-
    ounce can tomatoes with juice, pureed*
1 bay leaf

Heat the olive oil in a saucepan. Add the onion, ½ teaspoon salt, a pinch of pepper, and the basil; sauté over medium heat until soft, 5 to 7 minutes. Add the garlic and sauté for 5 minutes, then add the wine and simmer for 1 or 2 minutes, until the pan is nearly dry. Add the tomatoes, ¼ teaspoon salt, and the bay leaf; simmer, uncovered, for 30 minutes. Season with salt and pepper to taste.

THE EGGPLANT
2½ pounds Japanese eggplant, sliced ½ inch thick on a diagonal, about 7 cups
3 tablespoons extra virgin olive oil
2 garlic cloves, finely chopped
Salt and pepper

Preheat the oven to 375°F. Toss the eggplant with the olive oil, the garlic, ½ teaspoon salt, and a few pinches of pepper. Place the slices on a baking sheet and bake for 15 to 20 minutes, until the slices are soft in the center. Cool and slice into thick strips. Season to taste with salt and pepper. The eggplant should be very flavorful.

RICOTTA CUSTARD
1 pound ricotta cheese, about 2 cups
2 eggs, beaten
1 ounce Parmesan cheese, grated, about ⅓ cup
3 pinches of freshly grated nutmeg
½ teaspoon salt
⅛ teaspoon pepper

Place the ricotta in a mixing bowl and stir in the eggs; add the remaining ingredients and mix thoroughly.

HERB BÉCHAMEL
2½ cups milk
2 tablespoons unsalted butter
3 tablespoons unbleached white flour
Several fresh herb sprigs and leaves bundled together: parsley, sage, thyme, and marjoram
¼ teaspoon salt
⅛ teaspoon pepper

Heat the milk in a saucepan. Melt the butter in a separate pan, add the flour, and cook the resulting roux over low heat for 2 to 3 minutes, stirring constantly. When the milk is scalded, pour it into the roux a little at a time, whisking continuously. Add the bundled herbs, the salt, and pepper. Cook over low heat for 10 minutes. Remove the herbs just before assembling the lasagne.

ASSEMBLING THE LASAGNE
2 ounces Parmesan cheese, grated, about ⅔ cup
3 ounces provolone cheese, grated, about 1¼ cups
3 ounces mozzarella cheese, grated, about 1¼ cups
½ cup chopped fresh basil
1 pound fresh pasta sheets

Toss the cheeses together and set aside ⅓ cup to sprinkle on top during baking. Reserve 1 tablespoon of the basil to sprinkle on top after baking.

When you're ready to assemble the lasagne, preheat the oven to 350°F. In the bottom of a 9-by 13-inch baking pan, spread 1½ cups tomato sauce and cover it with a layer of pasta. Pour another cup of sauce over the pasta, followed by half the eggplant. Sprinkle with half the mixed cheeses, half the chopped basil, and another layer of pasta. Spread the ricotta custard evenly over the pasta and cover with another layer of pasta. Add a last cup of tomato sauce and then the rest of the eggplant and basil; follow with the rest of the cheese and a final layer of pasta. Top with the béchamel.

Cover and bake for 20 minutes. Sprinkle with the reserved ⅓ cup cheeses, and bake, uncovered, until the béchamel has set, 10 to 15 minutes. Remove from the oven and sprinkle with the reserved fresh basil.

SERVES SIX TO EIGHT

Variations: For more intense basil flavor, substitute pesto (page 337) for the basil. Spread the sauce over the layers of eggplant, then sprinkle with the cheese.

You can also make the lasagne without béchamel, using tomato sauce in its place. Double the sauce recipe; you'll need an extra cup of sauce to cover the top layer of pasta. You can freeze the leftover sauce or layer it on a pizza or toss with pasta.

Artichoke-Leek Lasagne

A lively tomato sauce and the strong-tasting Parmesan and provolone cheeses balance the subtle, fine flavor of the sautéed vegetables. The nutty flavor of the artichokes, combined with the richness of the leeks and a sprinkling of fresh herbs, makes this a distinctive lasagne.

TOMATO SAUCE
1 tablespoon extra virgin olive oil
½ medium-size yellow onion, diced, about 1 cup
Salt and pepper
¼ teaspoon dried marjoram
¼ teaspoon dried thyme
6 garlic cloves, finely chopped
¼ cup dry red wine
2½ pounds fresh tomatoes, peeled, seeded, and pureed (page 95), about 4 cups, or 2 16-ounce cans tomatoes with juice, pureed
1 bay leaf

Heat the olive oil in a medium-size saucepan. Add the onion, ½ teaspoon salt, a few pinches of pepper, and the dried herbs. Sauté the onion over medium heat until soft, 5 to 7 minutes. Add the garlic and sauté for 1 minute more, then add the wine and cook for 1 or 2 minutes, until the pan is nearly dry. Add the tomatoes, ¼ teaspoon salt, and the bay leaf. Simmer for 30 minutes. Season with salt and pepper to taste.

THE VEGETABLES
2 tablespoons extra virgin olive oil
2 large leeks, white parts only, sliced in half lengthwise, thinly sliced, and washed, about 4 cups
Salt and pepper
½ teaspoon dried thyme
4 medium-size artichokes, trimmed and sliced (page 241), about 4 cups
4 garlic cloves, finely chopped
½ tablespoon fresh lemon juice
¼ cup dry white wine
3 tablespoons chopped fresh herbs: marjoram, thyme, and parsley

Heat the olive oil in a wide skillet and add the leeks. Sauté over medium heat with ½ teaspoon salt, a few pinches of pepper, and the dried thyme until the leeks are wilted, about 3 minutes. Drain the artichokes and add to the leeks along with the garlic. Cover the pan and steam until tender, about 7 to 8 minutes. Add the lemon juice and deglaze the pan with the wine. Toss the herbs together and reserve 1 tablespoon to sprinkle on top after baking; stir the rest into the filling. Season with salt and pepper to taste.

ASSEMBLING THE LASAGNE

3 ounces Parmesan cheese, grated, about 1 cup
3 ounces provolone cheese, grated, about 1¼ cup
1 pound fresh pasta sheets
Ricotta Custard (page 150)
Herb Béchamel (page 151)

Set aside ⅓ cup Parmesan cheese to sprinkle on top during baking and toss the rest of the cheeses together.

When you're ready to assemble the lasagne, preheat the oven to 350°F. In the bottom of a 9-by 13-inch baking pan, spread 1½ cups of tomato sauce and cover it with a layer of pasta. Pour another 1½ cups sauce over the pasta, followed by the vegetables. Sprinkle with half the mixed cheeses, then lay down another layer of pasta. Spread the ricotta custard evenly over the pasta and cover with another layer of pasta. Add a last cup of tomato sauce, the rest of the cheese, and a final layer of pasta. Top with the béchamel.

Cover and bake for 20 minutes. Sprinkle on the remaining Parmesan cheese and bake, uncovered, until the béchamel has set, 10 to 15 minutes. Remove from the oven and sprinkle with the reserved fresh herbs.

SERVES SIX TO EIGHT

Tip: If the tomato sauce is acidic, add up to 1 teaspoon of sugar after simmering to balance the flavors.

Lasagne with Mushroom-Port Sauce

This elegant winter lasagne is truly a labor of love, and we save it for special occasions. The preparation is lengthy, but your efforts will be rewarded by the delicious flavor of this elegant dish.

The port lends the mushroom sauce a richness and complexity that sherry or red wine can't replicate. The sauce is layered into the lasagne with mushrooms, leeks, and Gruyère cheese; a creamy ricotta custard fills the center, and an herb béchamel covers the top layer of pasta.

MUSHROOM SAUCE
Mushroom Stock (page 80)
½ ounce dried porcini, soaked in warm water for 10 minutes
1 tablespoon light olive oil
½ medium-size yellow onion, diced, about 1 cup
½ teaspoon salt
Pepper
5 garlic cloves, finely chopped
½ cup Ficklin or good domestic port
3 tablespoons unsalted butter
¼ cup unbleached white flour

Make the stock and boil it over high heat until it is reduced to 3 cups. Keep it warm over low heat.

Strain the soaked porcini through a fine-mesh strainer, saving the soaking liquid. (If the soaking liquid is sandy, pour it through cheesecloth or pour off the liquid, avoiding the sand.) Finely chop the porcini, discarding any pieces that are gritty or hard.

Heat the olive oil in a medium-size saucepan; add the onion, the salt, and a few pinches of pepper. Sauté the onion over medium heat until it begins to release its juices, 5 to 7 minutes. Add the garlic and the porcini. Sauté until the onion is soft, 2 to 3 minutes, then add the port and the porcini liquid; simmer for 1 to 2 minutes, until the pan is nearly dry. Transfer to a bowl and set aside.

In the same saucepan, melt the butter and whisk in the flour. Cook the resulting roux over low heat for 2 to 3 minutes, stirring constantly to keep it from scorching. Whisk ½ cup mushroom stock into the roux to make a paste, then whisk in another ½ cup to thin it. Gradually add the remaining stock, and when all of the stock has been incorporated add the onion, making sure to include all of the pan juices. Cook the sauce over medium heat for 8 to 10 minutes, until it thickens slightly. It should be very flavorful.

2 tablespoons light olive oil

2 large leeks, white parts only, cut in half lengthwise, thinly sliced, and washed, about
*   4 cups*

½ teaspoon salt

Pepper

½ teaspoon dried thyme

5 garlic cloves, finely chopped

1 pound white mushrooms, thickly sliced, about 5 cups

¼ cup Ficklin or other good domestic port

¼ cup chopped fresh herbs: thyme, marjoram, and parsley

Heat 1 tablespoon of the olive oil in a wide skillet; add the leeks, ½ teaspoon salt, a few pinches of pepper, and the dried thyme. Sauté over medium heat for 2 minutes, add half the garlic, cover the pan, and steam the leeks until tender, 7 to 8 minutes. Transfer to a bowl.

Sear the mushrooms in 2 batches over high heat using ½ tablespoon olive oil, ¼ teaspoon salt, and a few pinches of pepper for each batch. As the mushrooms cook, they'll release their juices; then the juices will evaporate, and the mushrooms will begin to sear. At this point they'll begin to stick to the pan, but don't stir them. Cook over high heat until they're golden, then stir once and continue to sear for 1 to 2 minutes. Add half the remaining garlic, stir again, then add ⅛ cup port to deglaze. Add the mushrooms to the leeks. Sear the second batch and add it to the leeks.

Reserve 1 tablespoon chopped herbs and combine the rest with the mushrooms and leeks.

ASSEMBLING THE LASAGNE

3 ounces Parmesan cheese, grated, about 1 cup

¼ pound Gruyère cheese, grated, about 1½ cups

1 pound fresh pasta sheets

Ricotta Custard (page 150)

Herb Béchamel (page 151)

Set aside ⅓ cup of the Parmesan to sprinkle on top of the lasagne during baking and toss the rest of the cheeses together.

When you're ready to assemble the lasagne, preheat the oven to 350°F, and have a 9- by 13-inch baking dish ready. Spread 1 cup of the mushroom sauce on the bottom and cover it with one layer of pasta. Pour another cup of sauce over the pasta, followed by all of the leeks and mushrooms. Sprinkle with half of the mixed cheeses and add another layer of pasta. Spread the Ricotta Custard evenly over the pasta and cover with another layer of pasta. Add the last cup of sauce, the remaining cheese, and the final layer of pasta. Pour the béchamel over the lasagne, spreading it evenly to cover the corners.

Cover and bake for 20 minutes. Sprinkle with the reserved cheese and bake, uncovered, until the béchamel has set, 10 to 15 minutes. Remove from the oven and sprinkle with the reserved fresh herbs.

SERVES SIX TO EIGHT

Serving Suggestion: The flavors of this lasagne are very complex, so we like to balance it with clear flavors. Good winter accompaniments are roasted shallots and a sauté of winter greens with a touch of lemon, which can be prepared quickly while the lasagne is in the oven.

Tip: You can make the mushroom stock and reduce it a day or two in advance or freeze it ahead of time. You can also make the sauce a day in advance, though it will need to be reseasoned. The sauce is very intensely flavored, but its texture is light—thickened with just enough butter and flour to bind it—so don't be surprised if it appears to be thin.

Tomato-Mushroom Stock for Risotto

Tomato is the essence of this stock, with dried shiitake mushrooms to deepen the flavor. We use fresh tomatoes in the summer, but most of the year we use canned tomatoes. Fresh tomatoes make a sweet, light-tasting stock, while canned tomatoes make a more intensely flavored stock. Whether you use fresh or canned tomatoes is up to you—either will make a rich, flavorful stock, essential to delicious risotto.

2 quarts cold water
1 yellow onion, peeled and thinly sliced
1 leek top, sliced and washed
8 garlic cloves, in their skin, crushed with the side of a knife blade
1 teaspoon salt
1 ounce dried shiitake mushrooms
2 medium-size carrots, sliced
1 large unpeeled potato, sliced
¼ pound white mushrooms, sliced
2 celery ribs, sliced
1 28-ounce can tomatoes with juice or 2 pounds fresh tomatoes, coarsely chopped
6 parsley sprigs, coarsely chopped
6 fresh thyme sprigs
3 fresh sage leaves
2 fresh marjoram or oregano sprigs
½ teaspoon peppercorns

Pour ½ cup water into a stockpot and add the onion, leek top, garlic, and salt. Give them a stir, then cover the pot and cook the vegetables gently over medium heat for 15 minutes. Add the rest of the ingredients and cover with the remaining water.

Bring the stock to a boil, then reduce the heat and simmer, uncovered, for 1 hour. Pour the stock through a strainer, press as much liquid as you can from the vegetables, and discard them. Use immediately or cool and refrigerate or freeze. The stock will keep for 2 days in the refrigerator and indefinitely in the freezer.

MAKES ABOUT 7 CUPS

Spring Risotto with Asparagus and Peas

Tender asparagus, sugar snap peas, and English peas bring the light, fresh flavors of spring to this risotto. The reduced Tomato-Mushroom Stock makes a delicate tomato background to accent the vegetables. For a delicious variation, add a few pinches of saffron to the rice as you stir it into the onions—its enticing flavor and aroma will permeate the dish.

Tomato-Mushroom Stock (page 157)
Salt and pepper
¼ pound sugar snap peas, strings removed, about 1½ cups
½ pound English peas, shelled, about ½ cup
¼ pound asparagus, woody stems discarded, cut into 2-inch lengths on a diagonal, about
   1½ cups
1 tablespoon extra virgin olive oil
2 tablespoons unsalted butter
½ medium-size yellow onion, cut into ½-inch pieces
3 garlic cloves, finely chopped
1½ cups Arborio rice
1 medium-size carrot, diced, about ¾ cup
A generous pinch of saffron threads, soaked in 1 tablespoon hot water (optional)
½ cup dry white wine
1 ounce Parmesan cheese, grated, about ⅓ cup, plus more to serve at the table
2 tablespoons coarsely chopped Italian parsley

Pour the stock into a saucepan, bring it to a boil, and reduce it to 6 cups. Keep the stock warm over very low heat.

Bring a large pot of water to a boil and add ¼ teaspoon salt. Drop the snap peas into the boiling water for about 3 minutes; scoop them from the water with a strainer or slotted spoon and rinse under cool water. Drain and set aside. Repeating these steps, cook the English peas for about 2 minutes, followed by the asparagus, which will take 1½ to 2 minutes. Watch the vegetables closely as they cook to ensure that they're tender yet retain their bright green color.

Heat the olive oil and butter in a large skillet and add the onion, ¼ teaspoon salt, and a few pinches of pepper. Sauté over medium heat for 3 to 4 minutes, until it begins to soften, then add the garlic and sauté for another minute or two.

Add the rice and the carrot to the onion and sauté over medium heat for 2 to 3 minutes, stirring constantly. (If you're using saffron, add it now.) Begin adding the stock a cup at a time, allowing the rice to absorb each cup of stock completely before adding more. Keep stirring.

When the rice has absorbed 3 cups of stock, add the wine and ¼ teaspoon salt. Continue to add the stock, stirring constantly, until you have used 5 to 5½ cups. As you stir in the last of the stock, add the peas and the asparagus, ¼ teaspoon salt, and a few pinches of pepper. At this point the grains of rice will be a little toothy, the risotto will be quite saucy, and it should be ready to serve. To enrich the risotto, stir in ⅓ cup Parmesan cheese. Add the parsley and serve immediately with the remaining Parmesan.

SERVES FOUR TO SIX

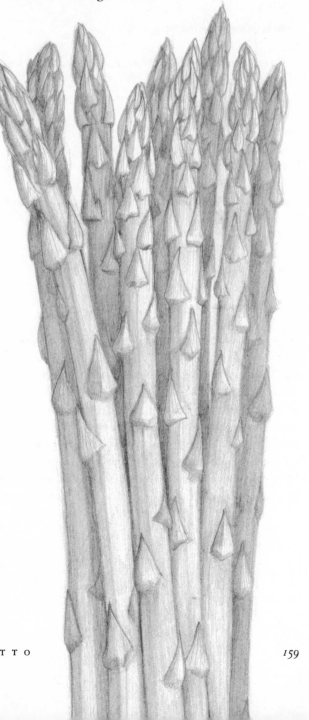

Risotto with Summer Beans, Tomatoes, Peppers, and Basil

The essential flavors of summer are here—tender young beans, juicy vine-ripened tomatoes, and the full fragrance of basil. Fresh tomatoes in the stock will enhance the delicate flavors of this summer risotto. A pinch of saffron will add extraordinary flavor and rich color. As the risotto cooks, its exotic perfume will fill the kitchen.

Tomato-Mushroom Stock (page 157)
Salt
¼ pound green beans, stem end removed, cut into 2-inch lengths on a diagonal or left
    whole if small
2 ounces yellow wax beans, cut into 2-inch lengths on a diagonal or left whole if small
1 tablespoon extra virgin olive oil
2 tablespoons unsalted butter
½ medium-size yellow onion, diced
Pepper
2 garlic cloves, finely chopped
A generous pinch of saffron threads, soaked in 1 tablespoon hot water (optional)
1½ cups Arborio rice
1 yellow or red bell pepper, diced, about 1 cup
¼ cup dry sherry
½ pound tomatoes, cored, seeded, and chopped
⅓ cup coarsely chopped fresh basil
Grated Parmesan cheese

Pour the stock into a saucepan, bring it to a boil, and reduce it to 6 cups. Keep the stock warm over very low heat.

Bring a small pot of water to a boil and add ¼ teaspoon salt. Drop the green beans into the boiling water for 2 to 4 minutes, until tender. Scoop them from the water with a strainer or slotted spoon and rinse under cold water. Drain and set aside. Cook the wax beans for 3 to 4 minutes or until tender; scoop from the water, rinse and drain as for the green beans, then add to the green beans. The cooking time of the beans will vary according to their variety and age, so watch them closely to see that they don't overcook and discolor.

Heat the olive oil and butter in a large skillet and add the onion, ¼ teaspoon salt, and a few pinches of pepper. Sauté over medium heat for 3 to 4 minutes, until it begins to soften, then add the garlic and sauté for another minute or two. (If you're using saffron, add it now.) Add the rice and sauté over medium heat for 2 to 3 minutes, stirring constantly. Begin adding stock a cup at a time, allowing the rice to absorb each cup of stock completely before adding more. Continue to stir.

When the rice has absorbed 3 cups of stock, add the peppers and sherry. Continue to stir and add stock until you have used 5 to 5½ cups. As you stir in the last cup of stock, add the beans, tomatoes, basil, and ¼ teaspoon salt. At this point the risotto should be ready to serve—the grains of rice will be a little toothy, and the risotto will be saucy. Serve immediately in warm bowls and pass the Parmesan.

SERVES FOUR TO SIX

Fall Risotto with Chanterelles and Late Harvest Tomatoes

Early fall is the time for this special risotto, as the tomatoes wind down and leeks and wild mushrooms begin to appear in the markets. The chanterelles are sautéed gently with butter and white wine and the creamy rice takes in their woodsy mushroom essence. If chanterelles are not available, use white mushrooms, cremini, or a combination of the two.

Tomato-Mushroom Stock (page 157)
½ pound fresh chanterelles
3 tablespoons unsalted butter
Salt and pepper
2 medium-size leeks, white parts only, cut in half lengthwise, thinly sliced, and washed,
    about 3 cups
4 garlic cloves, finely chopped
1½ cups Arborio rice
½ cup dry white wine
½ pound tomatoes, cored, seeded, and chopped
2 tablespoons coarsely chopped Italian parsley
Grated Parmesan cheese

Pour the stock into a saucepan, bring it to a boil, and reduce it to 6 cups. Keep the stock warm over very low heat.

Using a brush or a damp cloth, carefully clean the chanterelles. Remove the dirt and bits of organic matter, but don't wash them, or they'll soak up the water and lose their delicate flavor. Trim off the base of the stem if it is particularly dirty and discard. Cut the mushrooms into large pieces or thickly slice them, being sure to include the stem.

Heat 1 tablespoon of the butter in a large skillet; add the chanterelles, ¼ teaspoon salt, a few pinches of pepper, and ¼ cup stock. Gently sauté over medium heat until the mushrooms are barely tender. (The cooking time will depend on the moisture in the chanterelles.) Transfer to a bowl and set aside.

In the same skillet, heat the remaining 2 tablespoons butter; add the leeks, ½ teaspoon salt, and a few pinches of pepper. Sauté over medium-high heat until the leeks begin to wilt, about 3 minutes. Cover the pan and steam the leeks until tender, about 5 minutes. Add the garlic and cook for 2 minutes.

Add the rice to the leeks and sauté for 2 to 3 minutes, stirring constantly. Begin adding the stock a cup at a time, allowing the rice to absorb each cup of stock completely before adding more. Keep the pan over medium heat and continue to stir.

When the rice has absorbed 3 cups of stock, add the chanterelles and the wine. Continue to add the stock, stirring constantly, until you have used 5 cups. Add the tomatoes, ¼ teaspoon salt, a few pinches of pepper, and stock as needed. The grains of rice should be a little toothy and the risotto quite saucy. Stir in half of the parsley. Serve immediately in warm bowls. Sprinkle with the Parmesan and the remaining parsley.

SERVES FOUR TO SIX

Mushroom Risotto with Leeks and Fennel

We make this hearty risotto throughout the late fall and winter, when leeks and fennel are flavorful and abundant. Dried porcini add depth to the dish, so be sure to use them. For a delicious variation, include fresh wild mushrooms or substitute fresh thyme for the Italian parsley.

Tomato-Mushroom Stock (page 157)
¼ ounce dried porcini, soaked in ½ cup warm water for 10 minutes
2 tablespoons extra virgin olive oil
½ pound white mushrooms, washed and thickly sliced
Salt and pepper
4 garlic cloves, finely chopped
2 tablespoons unsalted butter
1 medium-size leek, white part only, cut in half lengthwise, thinly sliced, and washed,
    about 1½ cups
1 medium-size fennel bulb, quartered lengthwise, cored, and thinly sliced
1½ cups Arborio rice
½ cup dry white wine
2 tablespoons coarsely chopped Italian parsley
Grated Parmesan cheese

Pour the stock into a saucepan, bring it to a boil, and reduce it to 6 cups. Keep the stock warm over very low heat.

Drain the porcini and save the soaking liquid to add to the risotto later. (If the liquid is sandy, let the sand settle, then carefully pour off the liquid.) Finely chop the porcini, discarding any tough or gritty pieces. Set them aside.

Heat 1 tablespoon of the olive oil in a large skillet; add the white mushrooms, ¼ teaspoon salt, and a few pinches of pepper. Sauté over medium-high heat until the mushrooms are golden and crisp on the edges; add half the garlic, followed by the porcini soaking liquid to deglaze the pan. When the pan is almost dry, transfer the mushrooms to a bowl.

Heat the butter and remaining oil in the pan and add the leeks, ¼ teaspoon salt, and a few pinches of pepper. Sauté over medium heat for 3 to 4 minutes, until the leeks are wilted. Add the fennel, porcini, and remaining garlic; sauté for 1 to 2 minutes. Add the rice and sauté for 2 to 3 minutes, stirring constantly. Begin adding the stock a cup at a time, allowing the rice to absorb each cup of stock completely before adding more. Keep the pan on medium heat and continue to stir.

When the rice has absorbed 3 cups of stock, add the sautéed mushrooms and wine. Continue to add the stock, stirring constantly, until you have used 5 to 5½ cups. As you stir in the last cup of stock, add ¼ teaspoon salt and a few pinches of pepper. At this point the grains of rice will be a little toothy and the risotto quite saucy; it's ready to serve. Stir in half of the parsley. Serve immediately in warm bowls. Sprinkle with the Parmesan and the remaining parsley.

SERVES FOUR TO SIX

DRIED MUSHROOMS

We use dried mushrooms throughout the seasons, relying on their rich essence for depth and earthy flavor. The two we use most often are quite different in character.

Mellow shiitake mushrooms (also known as Chinese black mushrooms) *are an essential ingredient in our mushroom stocks and in many Asian-inspired dishes. These cultivated mushrooms can usually be found in the Asian section of your supermarket. They are more commonly available than fresh shiitake mushrooms and can be substituted for them in small quantities. Shiitake stems, dried or fresh, are too tough to eat but filled with mushroom flavor—we save them for stock.*

Rich porcini (Boletus edulis) are imported from Italy. In France they're known as cèpes—whatever their actual origin, we call them porcini. You can find them in gourmet shops or Italian specialty stores. Their sweet, luscious flavor enhances pastas, risottos, soups, and stews. We use these expensive fungi sparingly—a little of their rich flavor goes a long way. You can grind the dried mushrooms into a potent powder, breaking them into small pieces, then grinding them in a spice mill.

Porcini are truly wild, foraged in the wood—when plumped in warm water, the base of their tender stems is often studded with organic debris. Trim away the unusable parts, but do it carefully, saving as much of the stem as possible—the stems are as flavorful as the caps. The gills are sometimes unusable; if they're a little green, it's best to discard them.

Cover the dried shiitake or porcini with warm water and soak for about 10 minutes or until soft. Drain the mushrooms and save the flavorful soaking liquid to add to the dish. If the porcini liquid is sandy, carefully pour it through a fine strainer, avoiding the sand. Thinly slice the shiitake caps or finely chop the porcini and add to the dish as directed.

Risotto with Artichokes, Tomatoes, Spinach, and Thyme

The flavors of this risotto are full and smooth—the subtle, almost nutty taste of the artichokes works well with the fresh thyme and the acidity of the tomatoes. Add the tomatoes to the risotto at the last minute, allowing just enough time to heat them through, no longer. Otherwise, they'll overcook and lose their skins.

Tomato-Mushroom Stock (page 157)
2 packed cups spinach leaves
2 tablespoons unsalted butter
1 tablespoon extra virgin olive oil
½ medium-size red onion, diced, about 1 cup
Salt and pepper
3 medium-size artichokes, trimmed and sliced (page 241), about 3 cups
3 garlic cloves, finely chopped
2 or 3 teaspoons chopped fresh thyme
1½ cups Arborio rice
½ cup dry white wine
½ pound tomatoes, cored, seeded, and chopped
1 ounce Parmesan cheese, grated, about ⅓ cup, plus more to serve at the table
2 tablespoons coarsely chopped Italian parsley

Pour the stock into a saucepan, bring to a boil, and reduce it to 6 cups. Keep the stock warm over low heat.

Slice the spinach leaves into 1-inch ribbons and set aside.

Heat the butter and olive oil in a large skillet; add the onion, ¼ teaspoon salt, and a few pinches of pepper and sauté over medium heat for 2 to 3 minutes. Drain the artichokes, then add them to the onion with ¼ teaspoon salt, the garlic, and 2 teaspoons thyme. Sauté until the artichokes are tender, about 7 to 8 minutes.

Add the rice to the pan and sauté over medium heat for 2 to 3 minutes, stirring constantly. Begin adding the stock a cup at a time, allowing the rice to absorb each cup of stock completely before adding more. Keep the pan on medium heat and continue to stir.

When the rice has absorbed 3 cups of stock, add the wine; continue to add stock until you have used 5 cups. Add the tomatoes, spinach, and last cup of stock. The grains of rice will be a little toothy, and the risotto quite saucy. When the tomatoes have heated through and the spinach is wilted, taste the risotto; add the remaining thyme to taste. For richer flavor, stir in ⅓ cup Parmesan cheese. Add the parsley and serve immediately with the remaining Parmesan.

SERVES FOUR TO SIX

Pizza

Pizza

The simplest pizzas are often the best, provided the ingredients are flavorful and fresh. It's hard to set any rules for this well-loved food, though an essential point needs to be made: The seasoning must be lively. Tangy goat cheese or a sprinkling of Parmesan adds zest to a mild fresh mozzarella, while a splash of lemon juice will brighten a sauté of spinach or red chard for a Greek pizza. Olives, sun-dried tomatoes, capers, and fresh herbs add sharp contrast to more subtle flavors.

Our pizza dough recipe makes two 9-inch round pizzas or one 15-inch rectangular or round pizza. For those who prefer a dough without milk, we've included a variation made without it. Though all of the pizzas here are made with cheese, many are delicious without it, particularly if the recipe includes a sauce.

A word on baking pizzas: We make delicious, crusty pizzas daily in our makeshift "pizza ovens"—two temperamental ovens stacked one above the other, used for every kind of roasting and baking imaginable. Because we use them for everything, we've never installed baking stones in the ovens. So you can bake crisp pizzas in your home oven without fancy equipment, though a pizza stone and peel (wooden paddle) are wonderful to have on hand. The stone is also great for baking crusty sourdough breads or focaccia. Place the stone in the oven before preheating it to 500°F, allowing enough time for the stone to heat through. If you're not familiar with using a peel, prepare yourself for a few uneasy encounters with the dough until you're comfortable sliding it from the peel onto the stone. (Remember to dust the peel with flour or just a little cornmeal to keep the dough from sticking.) After you've practiced a few times, the dough will slide quite naturally onto the stone.

Pizza Dough

This basic dough is perfectly delicious made with all white flour, but we like the earthy flavor the cornmeal and rye flour add. Be sure to soak the cornmeal in the milk; it needs the moisture to soften it. The milk enriches the dough, but if you prefer to make the dough without it, use the variation at the end of the recipe.

1½ teaspoons active dry yeast
6 tablespoons warm (110°F) water
6 tablespoons milk
2 tablespoons extra virgin olive oil
1 tablespoon fine cornmeal
½ teaspoon salt
1 tablespoon rye flour
About 1¾ cups unbleached white flour
1 to 3 tablespoons additional flour for rolling the dough

Dissolve the yeast in the warm water and set aside in a warm place for 3 to 4 minutes. Meanwhile, combine the milk, oil, and cornmeal in a 1-quart bowl. Add the yeast mixture, then the salt and rye flour; mix well. Gradually add the white flour, making a soft, workable dough. Turn out onto a lightly floured work surface and knead for about 5 minutes, sprinkling in a little flour as necessary to keep the dough from sticking to the surface. Put the dough into an oiled bowl and turn it once so the surface is coated with oil. Cover the bowl with a kitchen towel or plastic wrap and let the dough rise in a warm place until it has doubled in bulk, about 35 to 40 minutes.

Prepare the topping.

Preheat the oven to 500°F and heat the pizza stone, if you're using one, for 20 minutes.

To shape the pizza, first form the dough into 1 round ball or 2 equal-size smaller balls. Roll out on a floured surface, turning it regularly to keep a round shape. It should be about ⅛ inch thick, slightly thicker at the edges. Lay the dough on an oiled pizza pan or a well-floured wooden peel. Cover with the topping you have chosen. Bake the pizza on its pan or slide it onto the heated pizza stone.

MAKES ONE 15-INCH PIZZA OR TWO 9-INCH PIZZAS

Variation made without milk: We've replaced the milk by increasing the water and doubling the olive oil, which the flour easily absorbs. The additional oil makes a very soft, easy-to-work dough.

1½ teaspoons active dry yeast
10 tablespoons warm (110°F) water
¼ cup extra virgin olive oil
1 tablespoon fine cornmeal
½ teaspoon salt

1 tablespoon rye flour
About 1¾ cups unbleached white flour
1 to 3 tablespoons additional flour for rolling dough

Prepare and roll out the dough as directed.

To freeze: Immediately after mixing the dough, form it into 1 or 2 balls and wrap tightly in 2 layers of plastic wrap. When you're ready to use the dough, thaw it in the refrigerator overnight, or set it in a warm place for 2 to 3 hours. Roll out as directed.

GARLIC OIL

We brush our rolled pizza dough with this garlic-infused oil before spreading on the topping—the garlic oil adds extra garlic flavor and forms a seal that helps protect the crust from moist toppings. To make it, finely chop a clove or two of garlic and cover generously with olive oil. Store garlic oil in a sealed container in the refrigerator and use it to sauté or season other dishes.

Pizza with Roasted Pepper Sauce, Leeks, and Olives

Our good friend Mark introduced this pizza to Greens a number of years ago, and we've served it ever since. It's easy to make—roasting and peeling the peppers is the most time-consuming step, but that can be done a day or two in advance. The deep orange color of the sauce contrasts beautifully with the leeks and the black olives.

1 tablespoon extra virgin olive oil
2 large leeks, white parts only, cut in half lengthwise, thinly sliced, and washed, about
*   3 cups*
¼ teaspoon salt
Pepper
1 garlic clove, finely chopped
Pizza Dough (page 169), ready to roll out
Garlic Oil (page 170)
Roasted Pepper Sauce (page 328)
8 Niçoise or Gaeta olives, pitted and coarsely chopped
3 ounces Fontina cheese, grated, about 1¼ cups
2 ounces provolone cheese, grated, about ¾ cup
½ ounce Parmesan cheese, grated, about 3 tablespoons
2 teaspoons chopped Italian parsley

Heat the olive oil in a skillet over medium heat and sauté the leeks with ¼ teaspoon salt, a few pinches of pepper, and the garlic until tender, about 7 to 8 minutes.

Preheat the oven to 500°F. Roll out the dough and place it on a lightly oiled pizza pan or a well-floured wooden peel; brush with the Garlic Oil. Spread about ⅔ cup pepper sauce over the dough. (You'll have a little sauce left over.) Cover with the leeks and sprinkle on the olives. Toss the Fontina and provolone together and spread on top.

Bake the pizza, in the pan or on a preheated pizza stone, for 8 to 12 minutes, until the crust is golden and crisp. Remove it from the oven and sprinkle with the Parmesan cheese and parsley.

MAKES ONE 15-INCH OR TWO 9-INCH PIZZAS

Mushroom-Leek Pizza

Dried porcini add depth and earthy flavor to this elegant winter pizza. The mushrooms are seared over high heat, then the pan is deglazed with the porcini-soaking liquid; every drop of the intense mushroom flavor is absorbed.

¼ ounce dried porcini, soaked in ½ cup warm water for about 10 minutes
2 tablespoons extra virgin olive oil
½ pound white mushrooms, thickly sliced, about 3 cups
Salt and pepper
2 large leeks, white parts only, cut in half lengthwise, thinly sliced, and washed, about
*   3 cups*
2 garlic cloves, finely chopped
¼ cup dry white wine
Pizza Dough (page 169), ready to roll out
Garlic Oil (page 170)
¼ pound Gruyère cheese, grated, about 1½ cups
1 ounce Parmesan cheese, grated, about ⅓ cup

Pour the porcini into a fine strainer and save the liquid to use later. (If the liquid is sandy, let the sand settle, then carefully pour off the liquid.) Finely chop the porcini, discarding any pieces that are gritty or hard. Set them aside.

Heat 1 tablespoon of the olive oil in a sauté pan and sear the white mushrooms over high heat with ¼ teaspoon salt and a few pinches of pepper. As the mushrooms cook, they'll release their juices; then the juices will evaporate and the mushrooms will begin to sear. At this point they'll begin to stick to the pan, but don't stir them. Cook over high heat until they're golden, then stir once and continue to sear for 1 to 2 minutes. Add the porcini soaking liquid to loosen the pan juices, then simmer for a minute or two, until the pan is nearly dry. Transfer to a bowl.

Heat the remaining tablespoon of oil in the sauté pan and add the leeks. Sauté over medium heat with ¼ teaspoon salt and a few pinches of pepper; when they begin to soften, in about 3 minutes, add the garlic and porcini. Cover the pan and steam for 5 to 6 minutes, until the leeks are tender. Add the wine to deglaze the pan, then simmer for a minute or two, until the pan is nearly dry. Add to the mushrooms, then set aside to cool. Season with salt and pepper to taste.

Preheat the oven to 500°F. Roll out the dough and place it on a lightly oiled pizza pan or well-floured wooden peel; brush with the Garlic Oil. Spread the mushroom-leek mixture over the dough. Save a little of the Parmesan cheese to sprinkle on top after baking, toss the rest of the cheeses together, and sprinkle on the pizza.

Bake the pizza, in the pan or on a preheated pizza stone, for 8 to 12 minutes, until the crust is golden and crisp. Remove it from the oven and sprinkle on the remaining Parmesan.

MAKES ONE 15-INCH OR TWO 9-INCH PIZZAS

Tomato-Fennel Pizza with Provolone Cheese

The flavors of this favorite winter pizza are classic—the tomato sauce is infused with fennel seed, and the fresh fennel adds crisp texture and light flavor. The assertive provolone cheese is a pungent surprise.

1 tablespoon extra virgin olive oil
¼ medium-size yellow onion, diced, about ½ cup
Salt and pepper
1 teaspoon ground fennel seed
2 garlic cloves, finely chopped
¾ pound fresh tomatoes, peeled, seeded (page 95), and pureed, about 1¼ cups, or 1 16-ounce can tomatoes with juice, pureed
1 medium-size fennel bulb, quartered lengthwise, cored, and thinly sliced
Pizza Dough (page 169), ready to roll out
Garlic Oil (page 170)
2 ounces mozzarella cheese, grated, about ¾ cup
2 ounces provolone cheese, grated, about ¾ cup
½ ounce Parmesan cheese, grated, about 3 tablespoons

Heat ½ tablespoon of the olive oil in a small saucepan over medium heat and add the onion, ¼ teaspoon salt, a pinch of pepper, and ½ teaspoon of the ground fennel. Sauté until the onion begins to release its juices, about 5 minutes, then add the garlic and cook for about 2 minutes. Add the tomatoes, ¼ teaspoon salt, and another pinch of pepper. Simmer gently, uncovered, for about 30 minutes, then season with salt and pepper to taste.

Heat the remaining ½ tablespoon olive oil in a sauté pan and sauté the sliced fennel over medium heat with the remaining ½ teaspoon ground fennel and a few pinches of salt and pepper until just tender, 4 to 5 minutes.

Preheat the oven to 500°F. Roll out the dough and place it on a lightly oiled pizza pan or well-floured wooden peel; brush with the Garlic Oil. Spread the sauce over the dough and lay the fennel on top. Toss the mozzarella and provolone cheeses together and sprinkle on the pizza.

Bake the pizza, in the pan or on a preheated pizza stone, for 8 to 12 minutes, until the crust is golden and crisp. Remove it from the oven and sprinkle with the Parmesan cheese.

MAKES ONE 15-INCH OR TWO 9-INCH PIZZAS

Variation: Sprinkle coarsely chopped pitted black olives over the pizza before adding the cheese.

Provençal Potato Pizza

Crisp, thinly sliced potatoes add unusual texture here, but it's the intensity of the smoked cheese, sun-dried tomatoes, and sage that makes the flavor of this pizza unique. You can use the oil from the tomatoes instead of Garlic Oil to brush on the dough; its concentrated flavor will add dimension. If Rosefir or Yellow Finn potatoes are available, use them instead of the new potatoes.

½ pound new potatoes
Garlic Oil (page 170)
Salt and pepper
Pizza Dough (page 169), ready to roll out
½ medium-size red onion, thinly sliced
4 sun-dried tomatoes packed in oil, drained and sliced
1 ounce Parmesan cheese, grated, about ⅓ cup
6 ounces smoked mozzarella cheese, grated, about 2¼ cups
1 tablespoon chopped fresh sage

Preheat the oven to 350°F. Thinly slice the potatoes, toss them with Garlic Oil, and sprinkle liberally with salt and pepper. Roast them on a baking sheet for 5 to 6 minutes, until tender and a little crisp.

Preheat oven to 500°F. Roll out the dough and place it on a lightly oiled pizza pan or well-floured wooden peel; brush with the Garlic Oil. Spread the onion on the dough and follow with the potatoes, then the sun-dried tomatoes. Set aside a little of the Parmesan cheese to sprinkle over the baked pizza, and toss the rest with the mozzarella cheese; sprinkle the cheeses on the pizza.

Bake the pizza, in the pan or on a preheated pizza stone, for 8 to 12 minutes, until the crust is golden and crisp. Remove it from the oven and sprinkle with the remaining Parmesan and the fresh sage.

MAKES ONE 15-INCH OR TWO 9-INCH PIZZAS

Greek Pizza with Spinach, Feta Cheese, and Rosemary

The flavors of this pizza are bold, and each ingredient adds its own distinctive taste. The spinach is quickly wilted, then feta cheese, Greek olives, and fresh rosemary are sprinkled over; a little lemon zest is added to lighten the intense flavors. You can substitute chard for the spinach; just be sure it's tender and well seasoned.

1 tablespoon extra virgin olive oil
½ medium-size red onion, thinly sliced
Salt and pepper
2 garlic cloves, finely chopped
1 large bunch of spinach, stems removed and leaves washed, 8 to 10 cups
1 teaspoon minced lemon zest
Pizza Dough (page 169), ready to roll out
Garlic Oil (page 170)
6 Kalamata olives, pitted and coarsely chopped
3 ounces feta cheese, crumbled, about 1½ cups
¼ pound mozzarella cheese, grated, about 1½ cups
½ ounce Parmesan cheese, grated, about 3 tablespoons
1 teaspoon chopped fresh rosemary

Heat 2 teaspoons of the olive oil in a sauté pan. Add the red onion, ¼ teaspoon salt, and a few pinches of pepper; sauté over medium heat for 4 to 5 minutes, until tender. Add half of the garlic and sauté for 1 minute. Transfer to a bowl.

Heat the remaining teaspoon of olive oil in the pan. Wilt the spinach over high heat with ¼ teaspoon salt, a few pinches of pepper, and the remaining garlic. When the spinach is wilted but still bright green, in about 1 minute, remove it from the pan and place it in a strainer to cool. Squeeze out the excess moisture with your hands, then coarsely chop and toss with the lemon zest.

Preheat oven to 500°F. Roll out the dough and place it on a lightly oiled pizza pan or well-floured wooden peel; brush with the Garlic Oil. Spread the onion on the dough, followed by the spinach. Sprinkle the olives over the spinach, follow with the crumbled feta, then add the mozzarella cheese.

Bake the pizza, in the pan or on a preheated pizza stone, for 8 to 12 minutes, until the crust is golden and crisp. Remove it from the oven and sprinkle with the Parmesan cheese and fresh rosemary.

MAKES ONE 15-INCH OR TWO 9-INCH PIZZAS

Eggplant and Sun-Dried Tomato Pizza

We make this delicious pizza year-round—this summer version features fresh basil. Season the eggplant liberally and roast it well—it should be soft in the center when you take it from the oven. If the sun-dried tomatoes are packed in oil, brush that over the dough in place of garlic oil; the dough will absorb its concentrated tomato flavor. You can also use fresh tomatoes or substitute marjoram or oregano for the basil.

2 medium-size Japanese eggplant, about ½ pound, sliced ½ inch thick on a diagonal
Garlic Oil (page 170)
Salt and pepper
Pizza Dough (page 169), ready to roll out
4 sun-dried tomatoes packed in oil, drained and thinly sliced
3 ounces provolone cheese, grated, about 1¼ cups
3 ounces mozzarella cheese, grated, about 1¼ cups
½ ounce Parmesan cheese, grated, about 3 tablespoons
10 fresh basil leaves, bundled and thinly sliced

Preheat the oven to 375°F. Toss the eggplant with 2 tablespoons Garlic Oil and sprinkle with salt and pepper. Place the slices on a baking sheet and roast for 15 to 20 minutes, until soft in the center. Cool and slice into thick strips.

Preheat oven to 500°F. Roll out the dough and place it on a lightly oiled pizza pan or well-floured wooden peel; brush it with the Garlic Oil. Lay the eggplant and sun-dried tomatoes on top. Toss the provolone and mozzarella cheeses together and sprinkle on the pizza.

Bake the pizza, in the pan or on a preheated pizza stone, for 8 to 12 minutes, until the crust is golden and crisp. Remove it from the oven and sprinkle with the Parmesan cheese and basil.

MAKES ONE 15-INCH OR TWO 9-INCH PIZZAS

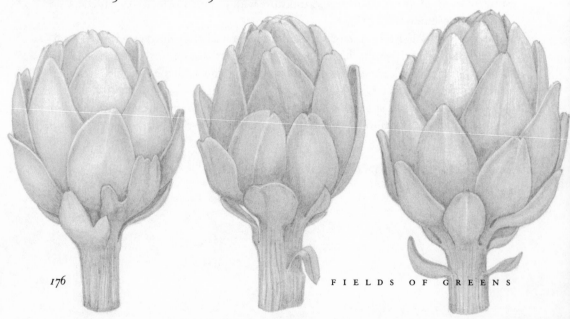

Artichoke and Red Onion Pizza with Thyme

The subtle, almost indescribable flavor of artichokes is well worth the time it takes to prepare them, especially for this delectable pizza. The artichokes and onions are sautéed together, then tossed with capers, fresh thyme, and lemon to accent the flavors. Season the artichokes well and make sure your Parmesan and Fontina are of good quality.

1 tablespoon extra virgin olive oil
1 medium-size red onion, thinly sliced, about 2 cups
Salt and pepper
3 medium-size artichokes, trimmed and sliced (page 241), about 3 cups
¼ cup dry white wine
1 teaspoon minced lemon zest
1 teaspoon fresh lemon juice
1 tablespoon chopped fresh thyme
Pizza Dough (page 169), ready to roll out
Garlic Oil (page 170)
1 tablespoon capers, rinsed and drained
1 ounce Parmesan cheese, grated, about ⅓ cup
5 ounces Fontina cheese, grated, about 2 cups

Heat the olive oil in a sauté pan and add the onion, ½ teaspoon salt, and a few pinches of pepper. Sauté over medium-high heat for 2 to 3 minutes, until it begins to release its juices. Drain the artichokes, then add to the onion with ¼ teaspoon salt and a few pinches of pepper. Sauté until tender, about 7 to 8 minutes. Add the white wine to deglaze; simmer for a minute or two, until the pan is nearly dry. Toss with the lemon juice, zest, and thyme, and set aside to cool. Season with salt and pepper to taste.

Preheat the oven to 500°F. Roll out the dough and place it on a lightly oiled pizza pan or well-floured peel; brush with the Garlic Oil. Lay the artichokes and onions on top and sprinkle on the capers. Set aside a little of the Parmesan to sprinkle on top after baking; toss the rest with the Fontina and spread over the pizza.

Bake the pizza, in the pan or on a preheated pizza stone, for 8 to 12 minutes, until the crust is golden and crisp. Sprinkle on the remaining Parmesan.

MAKES ONE 15-INCH OR TWO 9-INCH PIZZAS

Pizza with Onion Confit, Walnuts, and Gorgonzola Cheese

The flavor of the confit is full and rich—its sweetness is offset by the creamy Gorgonzola, the toasted walnuts, and the earthy sage. Fortunately you can make the confit in advance, because it does take time to cook the onions slowly to this reduced, almost jam-like stage. For a delicious variation, use basil instead of sage.

1 tablespoon extra virgin olive oil
2 medium-size yellow onions, thinly sliced
Salt and pepper
1 garlic clove, finely chopped
¼ cup dry white wine
Pizza Dough (page 169), ready to roll out
Garlic Oil (page 170)
⅓ cup walnut pieces, lightly toasted (page 263), coarsely chopped
3 ounces Gorgonzola cheese, crumbled
¼ pound mozzarella cheese, grated, about 1½ cups
½ ounce Parmesan cheese, grated, about 3 tablespoons
2 teaspoons chopped fresh sage

Heat the olive oil in a large sauté pan. Add the onions, ½ teaspoon salt, and a few pinches of pepper. Sauté over medium heat, gently scraping the pan with a wooden spoon to keep the onions from sticking as they caramelize. After about 35 minutes, the onions should be a rich golden color and very sweet. At this point, add the garlic and sauté for 5 minutes. Add the wine and deglaze the pan with it. Set the confit aside to cool.

Preheat the oven to 500°F. Roll out the dough and place it on a lightly oiled pizza pan or well-floured wooden peel; brush with the Garlic Oil. Spread the confit on the dough and sprinkle on the walnuts. Follow with the Gorgonzola cheese, then the mozzarella.

Bake the pizza, in the pan or on a preheated pizza stone, for 8 to 12 minutes, until the crust is golden and crisp. Remove it from the oven and sprinkle with the Parmesan cheese and sage.

MAKES ONE 15-INCH OR TWO 9-INCH PIZZAS

Pizza with Escarole, Roasted Peppers, and Olives

Escarole, a slightly bitter-tasting winter green, is the star ingredient of this pizza. With a splash of sherry vinegar to heighten its flavor, it works beautifully with succulent roasted peppers, salty black olives, and well-aged provolone cheese.

½ tablespoon extra virgin olive oil
½ medium-size head of escarole, washed and chopped, about 4 cups
Salt and pepper
Splash of sherry vinegar
1 roasted red bell pepper, peeled and thickly sliced (page 55)
Garlic Oil (page 170)
Pizza Dough (page 169), ready to roll out
½ medium-size red onion, thinly sliced
8 Niçoise or Gaeta olives, pitted and coarsely chopped
2 ounces Fontina cheese, grated, about 1 cup
3 ounces provolone cheese, grated, about 1 ¼ cups
½ ounce Parmesan cheese, grated, about 3 tablespoons
2 teaspoons chopped Italian parsley

Heat the olive oil in a sauté pan and add the escarole, ⅛ teaspoon salt, and a few pinches of pepper. Sauté over high heat for 1 to 2 minutes, until the escarole is wilted, then add a splash of sherry vinegar. Set aside to cool.

Toss the peppers with a little Garlic Oil and sprinkle with salt and pepper.

Preheat the oven to 500°F. Roll out the dough and place it on a lightly oiled pizza pan or well-floured wooden peel; brush with the Garlic Oil. Spread the red onions, then the escarole on top, following with the peppers and olives. Toss the Fontina and provolone cheeses together and sprinkle on the pizza.

Bake the pizza, in the pan or on a preheated pizza stone, for 8 to 12 minutes, until the crust is golden and crisp. Remove it from the oven and sprinkle with the Parmesan cheese and parsley.

MAKES ONE 15-INCH OR TWO 9-INCH PIZZAS

exican Pizza

Make the Salsa Roja a day in advance to simplify the preparation of this spicy Mexican-style pizza. Since you'll need only half the sauce, freeze the rest for polenta, grilled vegetables, or another Mexican pizza. The Cilantro Pesto is light and easy to make; it cuts through the heat of the Salsa Roja and the rich-tasting cheese.

6 tomatillos, outer husks removed
Salt and pepper
Pizza Dough (page 169), ready to roll out
Garlic Oil (page 170)
Salsa Roja with cinnamon variation (page 326)
3 ounces smoked cheese, grated, about 1¼ cups
¼ pound cheddar cheese, grated, about 1½ cups
Cilantro Pesto (page 338)

Cut the tomatillos into quarters and toss with a few pinches of salt and pepper.

Preheat the oven to 500°F. Roll out the dough and place it on a lightly oiled pizza pan or well-floured wooden peel; brush with the Garlic Oil. Spread the salsa over the dough and lay the tomatillos on top, skin sides down, to prevent burning. Toss the cheeses together and sprinkle over the pizza.

Bake the pizza, in the pan or on a preheated pizza stone, for 8 to 12 minutes, until the crust is golden and crisp. Remove it from the oven and brush on the Cilantro Pesto.

MAKES ONE 15-INCH OR TWO 9-INCH PIZZAS

Variation: For a simpler yet equally delicious pizza, substitute canned Anaheim chilies for the tomatillos and omit the Cilantro Pesto. Instead you can sprinkle the pizza with freshly chopped cilantro and sage leaves.

Pizza with Tomatoes, Gorgonzola, and Pine Nuts

The sweet flavor of plump vine-ripened tomatoes works wonderfully with the basil and the creamy Gorgonzola, while toasted pine nuts add little bites of nutty texture. If Golden Jubilee tomatoes are available, be sure to include them here, alternating the colors as you layer the tomatoes on the pizza.

Pizza Dough (page 169), ready to roll out
Garlic Oil (page 170)
½ medium-size red onion, thinly sliced, about 1 cup
¼ pound Fontina cheese, grated, about 1½ cups
1 tablespoon pine nuts, toasted (page 263)
2 ounces Gorgonzola cheese, crumbled
½ pound tomatoes, about 2 medium-size, thinly sliced
Salt and pepper
½ ounce Parmesan cheese, grated, about 3 tablespoons
10 fresh basil leaves, bundled and thinly sliced

Preheat the oven to 500°F. Roll out the dough and place it on a lightly oiled pizza pan or well-floured wooden peel; brush it with the Garlic Oil. Spread the sliced onion over the dough, followed by the Fontina, pine nuts, and Gorgonzola. Arrange the tomatoes over the cheese and sprinkle them lightly with salt and pepper.

Bake the pizza, in the pan or on a preheated pizza stone, for 8 to 12 minutes, until the crust is golden and crisp. Remove it from the oven and sprinkle with the Parmesan cheese and basil.

MAKES ONE 15-INCH OR TWO 9-INCH PIZZAS

Curries and Stews

Curries and Stews

There's much to be said about balanced flavors, depth, and complexity—so essential to a delicious and satisfying vegetable curry or stew. Sautéed onions are a foundation flavor and we often simmer them with sherry, wine, or port. Garlic and dried herbs, chilies, or spices and ginger are added as we sauté the vegetables, while fresh herbs are tossed in just before serving. A spoonful of crème fraîche is often all that's needed to smooth or enrich a southwestern or hearty mushroom stew.

There are so many wonderful vegetable combinations, and we always keep in mind how their colors, tastes, and textures work together. We cut the vegetables into large, uniformly sized shapes that are pleasing to the eye and maintain their texture while cooking. Sweet peppers, carrots, green beans, and fresh peas are always welcome—aside from adding flavor, their bright colors add sharp contrast to the dish. Potatoes, like cauliflower, work particularly well in curries. Pearl onions add a lovely touch, well worth the time it takes to peel them. Artichokes are wonderful; include the little ones if you can find them—they're easy to prepare, often harvested before the thistly choke develops inside.

Roasted vegetables are delicious in stews—this is a particularly nice way to include parsnips, rutabagas, and turnips, though tender spring turnips can also be sautéed along with carrots and peppers. Butternut and other creamy winter squashes are often sautéed, though we like the way they hold their shape when roasted. When tomatoes are abundant, we roast them and add them to stews—their soft, round flavor adds richness and depth.

At Greens we use fresh ripe tomatoes whenever possible, but most of the year we use canned tomatoes. Though plum tomatoes packed in tomato puree are delicious for soups and sauces, we prefer the lighter texture of tomatoes packed in juice for stews and curries. Organic canned tomatoes (available in natural food stores) are exceptionally flavorful. You can rely on canned tomatoes imported from Italy—Pomi, a brand of tomatoes packed in vacuum-sealed boxes, are also quite good.

The canned coconut milk in our curries is usually imported from Thailand. We find the flavor and sweetness to be quite variable, and we're careful not to overcook it, because it can become too thick.

You won't find a master recipe for curry powder—each curry recipe has its own blend of pungent or sweet spices, chilies, and fresh ginger. Remember that the heat of chilies is variable and can easily overpower the other flavors—take a very small taste before adding chilies to a stew or curry.

Lemongrass Stock for Curries

The zesty flavor of this exceptional stock cuts through the richness of coconut milk and adds an extra dimension to curries. This simple recipe makes enough stock for two curries. Use half and freeze the rest.

4 lemongrass stalks, dried outer leaves trimmed, cut into 3-inch lengths
1 yellow onion, thinly sliced
8 thin coins of fresh ginger
10 cilantro sprigs
½ teaspoon salt
1 teaspoon coriander seed
6 cups cold water

Place the ingredients in a medium-size saucepan. Bring the stock to a boil, reduce the heat, and simmer, uncovered, for 40 minutes. Pour the stock through a strainer, pressing as much liquid as possible from the vegetables, then discard them.

MAKES ABOUT 1 QUART

Spring Vegetable Curry with Sri Lankan Spices

A blend of sweet fragrant spices simmered with coconut milk, tomatoes, and ginger fills this curry with warm flavor and gentle heat. It's delicious made with peas as they come into season—sugar snap peas and shelled English peas add bright, fresh color.

You can make it in summer with tender green beans in place of the peas and include different varieties of summer squash, such as golden zucchini, scallop-shaped sunburst, or pale green pattypans. Serve with basmati rice tossed with toasted cashews and Mango-Papaya Chutney (page 393).

THE SPICES

1 teaspoon cumin seed
2 teaspoons coriander seed
1 teaspoon fennel seed
½ teaspoon fenugreek
½ teaspoon black mustard seed
½ teaspoon cinnamon, preferably freshly ground
¼ teaspoon ground cardamom
¼ teaspoon ground cloves
¼ teaspoon cayenne pepper

Toast the cumin, coriander, fennel, fenugreek, and black mustard seed over low heat in a dry small skillet, shaking or stirring often, until they become aromatic, a minute or two. Grind in a spice grinder or mortar and pestle and combine with the remaining ingredients.

SUGAR SNAP PEAS

These edible-pod peas are delectable in a spring pasta with asparagus and Meyer lemon butter, in a sauté with fresh ginger, or eaten right out of your hand.

Sugar snap peas need a humus-rich soil, full sun, and cool weather, so plant them outdoors as soon as the ground can be worked in the spring. Soak the seeds in water overnight to speed germination. You'll need to provide a trellis for them to twine themselves on. Mist the patch daily in the early morning until the seeds come up, but go easy on water until the plant begins to bloom. From bloom until final harvest, make sure the plants have a good deep watering about once a week. Harvesting the peas as soon as they're ready will encourage further growth.

1 pound fresh tomatoes, peeled, seeded, and chopped (page 95), about 2 cups, or 1 16-ounce can tomatoes with juice, chopped

1½ cups cold water

Salt

3 tablespoons grated fresh ginger

¼ pound sugar snap peas, strings removed, about 2 cups

¼ pound English peas, shelled, about ½ cup

1 tablespoon peanut oil

1 yellow onion, chopped, about 2 cups

4 garlic cloves, finely chopped

2 medium-size carrots, cut in half lengthwise and sliced ½ inch thick on a diagonal, about 2 cups

1 pound new potatoes, cut into halves, quarters, or 1-inch pieces if large, about 4 cups

½ small head of cauliflower, about 2 cups florets

1 medium-size zucchini, cut in half lengthwise, sliced ½ inch thick on a diagonal, about 1 cup

1½ cups canned coconut milk, stirred

Cayenne pepper

Combine the tomatoes, cold water, 1 teaspoon salt, 2 tablespoons of the ginger, and 1 tablespoon of the mixed spices in a medium-size saucepan. Simmer, uncovered, over low heat for 15 to 20 minutes while you cook the vegetables.

Bring a small pot of water to a boil and add ¼ teaspoon salt. Drop the snap peas into the water for about 2 minutes, until just tender. Scoop them out, rinse under cool water, and set aside. Repeat the procedure with the English peas. Set aside.

Heat the oil in a large skillet. Add the onion and ½ teaspoon salt; sauté until soft, about 7 to 8 minutes. Add the garlic, carrots, and potatoes; cook over medium heat for about 10 minutes. Add the cauliflower, zucchini, remaining spices and ginger, and ¼ teaspoon salt; sauté for about 5 minutes, until just heated through. Add the tomato mixture and the coconut milk; simmer, uncovered, for 30 minutes. Add the peas just before serving. Season with salt and cayenne to taste.

SERVES FOUR TO SIX

Summer Vegetables with Red Curry

Sweet red peppers are simmered with chilies, coconut milk, and Lemongrass Stock, then pureed to give the curry its creamy red color. The vegetables are stewed with fresh ginger, toasted caraway, and coriander, lending the stew a distinctive, unusual flavor. The Lemongrass Stock is essential to the dish, so be sure to make it. Serve with Mustard Seed Basmati Rice (page 274) and Apricot Chutney (page 394).

THE CURRY

1 tablespoon peanut oil or light vegetable oil
1 large red bell pepper, sliced, about 2 cups
2 or 3 red jalapeño chilies, seeded and sliced
Salt
Cayenne pepper
2 cups Lemongrass Stock (page 185)
1 tablespoon grated fresh ginger
3 garlic cloves, finely chopped
1 tablespoon coriander seed, toasted and ground (page 89)
1 teaspoon caraway seed, toasted and ground (page 263)
1 cup canned coconut milk, stirred

Heat the oil in a medium-size skillet; add the peppers, chilies, ½ teaspoon salt, and ⅛ teaspoon cayenne. Sauté over medium heat for 10 minutes. Add a little Lemongrass Stock to moisten the pan, then add the ginger, garlic, and spices. Sauté for about 5 minutes, then add the remaining Lemongrass Stock and simmer the curry until the peppers are very soft, about 10 minutes. Puree until smooth in a blender or food processor. (If there are flecks of tough pepper skins, you can pass the curry through a strainer, using a rubber spatula if needed to separate the pepper skins and push the liquid through.) Stir the coconut milk into the curry and set aside.

Salt

¼ pound green beans, stem ends trimmed, cut in half if large

1 tablespoon peanut oil or light vegetable oil

1 medium-size yellow onion, cut into ½-inch pieces, about 2 cups

⅛ teaspoon cayenne pepper

3 garlic cloves, finely chopped

2 medium-size carrots, cut in half lengthwise, then cut into ½-inch slices on a diagonal

1 pound new potatoes, cut into halves, quarters, or ½-inch pieces if large

1 yellow or red bell pepper, cut into thick slices and then triangles

2 medium-size zucchini, cut in half lengthwise, then cut into ½-inch slices on a diagonal

2 tablespoons grated fresh ginger

1 teaspoon coriander seed, toasted and ground (page 89)

½ teaspoon caraway seed, toasted and ground (page 263)

1 lemongrass stalk, dry outer leaves removed, cut into 3-inch lengths

2 tablespoons chopped cilantro

Bring a small pot of water to a boil and add ¼ teaspoon salt. Drop the beans into the water and cook for 2 to 3 minutes, until just tender. Rinse under cold water, drain, and set aside.

Heat the oil in a large skillet. Add the onion, ½ teaspoon salt, and ⅛ teaspoon cayenne; sauté over medium heat for about 5 minutes, until the onion begins to soften. Add the garlic, carrots, potatoes, and peppers; sauté for 10 minutes. Add the zucchini and sauté for 2 minutes. Add the curry, ginger, spices, and lemongrass; simmer, uncovered, over low heat for 30 minutes.

Remove the lemongrass stalks. Add salt and cayenne to taste. Stir in the green beans and cilantro just before serving.

SERVES FOUR TO SIX

Winter Vegetable Curry

We make this satisfying curry year-round, varying the vegetables with each season. In this winter version, pungent spices are stewed with tomatoes, ginger, coconut milk, and a mixture of earthy root vegetables. Fresh fennel is distinctive here—its sweet licoricelike flavor blends nicely with the smooth-tasting carrots and potatoes. You can also include celery root or turnips or use them in place of the potatoes. Serve with fragrant basmati rice and Fiery Pineapple Chutney (page 392).

THE SPICES

2 teaspoons yellow mustard seed
2 teaspoons cumin seed
2 teaspoons coriander seed
1 teaspoon fenugreek
½ teaspoon turmeric
¼ teaspoon cayenne pepper

In a small skillet, toast the mustard seed as described on page 191. Transfer to a bowl and set aside to add to the curry later. In the same skillet, toast the cumin and coriander seeds together over low heat until aromatic, a minute or two; combine with the fenugreek and grind in a spice grinder or with a mortar and pestle; add the turmeric and cayenne to the spice mixture.

THE STEW

1 pound fresh tomatoes, peeled, seeded, and chopped (page 95), about 2 cups, or 1 16-ounce can tomatoes with juice, chopped
1½ cups water
Salt
3 tablespoons grated fresh ginger
1 medium-size stalk broccoli, about 2 cups florets
2 tablespoons peanut oil or light vegetable oil
¾ pound white mushrooms, cut in half or left whole if small, about 4 cups
1 medium-size yellow onion, cut into ½-inch pieces, about 2 cups
4 garlic cloves, finely chopped
2 medium-size carrots, peeled, cut in half lengthwise, and sliced ½ inch thick on a diagonal, about 2 cups
1 pound new potatoes, cut into halves, quarters, or 1-inch cubes if large, about 4 cups
1 medium-size fennel bulb, the base trimmed, outer leaves discarded, cut into 1-inch pieces, about 2 cups
1 13½-ounce can coconut milk
Cayenne pepper
2 tablespoons chopped cilantro

In a medium-size saucepan, combine the tomatoes, water, 1 teaspoon salt, 1 tablespoon of the spice mixture, and 2 tablespoons of the ginger. Simmer, uncovered, over low heat for 15 to 20 minutes while you sauté the vegetables.

Bring a small pot of water to a boil and add ¼ teaspoon salt. Drop the broccoli into the water for about 1 minute, then rinse under cold water and drain. Set aside.

Heat 1 tablespoon of the oil in a large skillet over high heat. Sear the mushrooms in the oil with ¼ teaspoon salt until golden brown, about 7 minutes. Add a splash of water to loosen the pan juices. Transfer the mushrooms to a bowl.

Heat the remaining tablespoon of oil in the skillet over medium heat. Add the onions and ¼ teaspoon salt; sauté over medium heat for about 5 minutes, until soft. Add the garlic, carrots, potatoes, and fennel; cook for 10 minutes. Add the reserved mustard seed and remaining spices and ginger; sauté for 2 minutes. Add the mushrooms, tomatoes, and coconut milk; simmer, uncovered, over low heat for 30 minutes to allow the flavors to develop. Season with salt and cayenne to taste. Stir in the broccoli and cilantro just before serving.

SERVES FOUR TO SIX

TOASTING MUSTARD SEEDS

Toasting, or "popping," mustard seeds brings out their earthy sweetness—once toasted, ground mustard seeds are pungent and slightly bitter. You can toast them in ghee (clarified butter used in Indian cooking) or hot oil for seasoning curries and rice dishes—we like to toast them in a dry skillet. Either way, their flavor is delicious.

Place the mustard seeds in a small skillet and toast over medium heat until they begin to pop; remove from the heat and cover until the popping stops. The mustard seeds are now ready to be ground or can be left whole, then added to the dish.

A word on black and yellow mustard seeds: Whole black mustard seeds actually range in color from black to reddish brown. These tiny seeds are widely used in Indian seasonings—we add them to Indian curries, soups, and raitas. Yellow mustard seeds are commonly available in grocery stores, and we use them as well. They have a milder, less bitter flavor and can be substituted for black mustard seeds.

North African Vegetable Stew

We make this fragrant stew year-round, and the vegetables vary with the seasons. In the summer it's a mixture of sweet peppers, zucchini, and vine-ripened tomatoes. For fall and winter, try cubes of roasted winter squash, turnips, and potatoes. Cinnamon, saffron, and turmeric season the tomato and chick-pea broth, filling the stew with their rich aromatic flavor and giving the sauce a deep orange hue. Serve over a bed of Almond-Currant Couscous (page 277)—it will soak up all the delicious juices.

THE CHICK-PEAS
½ cup dried chick-peas, about 3 ounces, covered with cold water and soaked overnight
3 thin coins of fresh ginger
1 large bay leaf
1 1-inch cinnamon stick
1 quart cold water

Drain and rinse the chick-peas and place them in a medium-size saucepan with the ginger, bay leaf, cinnamon stick, and water. Bring the water to a boil, then lower the heat to medium; cook the chick-peas, uncovered, at a gentle boil until very tender, 50 to 60 minutes. Set aside and let the beans cool in their broth. Don't remove the flavorful spices or bay leaf until you add the beans and broth to the stew later.

THE SPICES
1½ teaspoons cinnamon, preferably freshly ground
¾ teaspoon turmeric
⅛ teaspoon cayenne pepper
1 large pinch of saffron threads
1 tablespoon hot water

In a small bowl, combine the cinnamon, turmeric, and cayenne. In a separate bowl, steep the saffron threads in the hot water. Set the spices and saffron aside.

2½ pounds fresh tomatoes, peeled, seeded, and chopped (page 95), about 4 cups, or
  2 16-ounce cans tomatoes with juice, chopped
Salt
1 medium-size broccoli stalk, about 2 cups florets
1 tablespoon light olive oil
1 medium-size yellow onion, cut into 1-inch pieces, about 2 cups
4 garlic cloves, finely chopped
2 tablespoons grated fresh ginger
1 pound new potatoes
3 medium-size carrots, cut in half lengthwise and then into ½-inch strips on a diagonal,
  about 3 cups
1 medium-size red or yellow bell pepper, cut into thick strips and then triangles, about
  1 cup
½ small head of cauliflower, about 2 cups florets
Cayenne pepper
1 tablespoon chopped fresh mint
2 tablespoons chopped cilantro

If you're using canned tomatoes, cook them in a medium-size saucepan with 1 teaspoon salt over low heat while you prepare the vegetables. (The extra cooking time will reduce their acidity.)

While the tomatoes are cooking, bring a small pot of water to a boil and add ¼ teaspoon salt. Drop the broccoli into the water for about 1 minute, until just tender. Drain and rinse under cool water. Set aside.

Heat the olive oil in a large skillet; add the onion and ½ teaspoon salt. Sauté over medium heat until the onion begins to release its juices, 7 to 8 minutes; add the garlic, ginger, and spices. Stir and cook for 1 minute. Add ½ cup chick-pea broth, the potatoes, and the carrots; cover the pan and simmer for about 10 minutes. Then add the peppers, cover, and cook for 5 minutes more. Add the cauliflower; stir and cook, uncovered, until just heated through.

Add the fresh or canned tomatoes, saffron, chick-peas, and all of their remaining broth. Stew, uncovered, over medium-low heat for 20 to 25 minutes, allowing the flavors to blend. Add salt and cayenne to taste. Add the broccoli a few minutes before serving, then stir in the mint and the cilantro.

SERVES FOUR TO SIX

Tip: Add a few pinches of sugar to the canned tomatoes while cooking them if they're quite acidic. Also add up to 1 teaspoon sugar after the final cooking if the sauce is acidic.

Creole Mushroom and Pepper Stew

This stew is at its best in the early fall, as tomato season is winding down and the markets are filled with sweet peppers. Earthy-tasting mushrooms and thyme mingle with the colorful peppers and sweet tomato juices, while fresh chilies add warmth and spicy flavor. For a richer stew, roast the tomatoes beforehand—their concentrated flavor will add depth and complexity. Serve on a bed of basmati rice tossed with toasted almonds or pistachios.

2 pounds fresh tomatoes, peeled, seeded, and chopped (page 95), about 3 cups, or 1 28-ounce can tomatoes with juice, chopped, or 3 pounds roasted tomatoes (page 258) without skins, chopped

2 tablespoons extra virgin olive oil

1 pound white mushrooms, cut in half or left whole if small, about 5 cups

Salt and pepper

5 garlic cloves, finely chopped

¼ cup dry red wine

1 medium-size red onion, cut into 1-inch pieces, about 2 cups

½ teaspoon dried thyme

1 red bell pepper, cut into thick strips and then triangles, about 1 cup

1 green bell pepper, cut into thick strips and then triangles, about 1 cup

1 yellow bell pepper, cut into thick strips and then triangles, about 1 cup

1 medium-size fennel bulb, quartered lengthwise, cored, and sliced ½ inch thick, about 2 cups

2 bay leaves

2 or 3 jalapeño or serrano chilies, seeded and finely diced

Cayenne pepper

2 medium-size zucchini, cut in half lengthwise and sliced ½ inch thick on a diagonal, about 2 cups

2 scallions, both white and green parts, thinly sliced on a diagonal

1 tablespoon chopped fresh thyme

½ teaspoon fresh lemon juice

If you're using canned tomatoes, simmer them in a medium-size saucepan over low heat while the vegetables are cooking. (The extra cooking time will reduce their acidity.)

Heat 1 tablespoon of the oil in a large skillet and add the mushrooms, ½ teaspoon salt, and a few pinches of pepper. Sear the mushrooms in the skillet over high heat until they're golden and browned, about 7 minutes, then add half the garlic and the wine and stir to loosen the flavorful pan juices. Reduce the wine until the pan is nearly dry and transfer the mushrooms to a bowl.

In the same skillet, heat the remaining tablespoon of olive oil. Add the onion, ½ teaspoon salt, and the dried thyme. Sauté over medium heat until the onion is soft, about 7 to 8 minutes. Add the remaining garlic, the peppers, fennel, bay leaves, chilies, and ⅛ teaspoon cayenne. Sauté over medium heat for 10 minutes, then add the zucchini and cook until just heated through, about 5 minutes.

Add the tomatoes and mushrooms; simmer, uncovered, over medium-low heat for 20 minutes to allow the flavors to come together. Season with a few pinches of salt and cayenne if needed. Add the scallions, fresh thyme, and lemon juice just before serving.

SERVES FOUR TO SIX

Tip: If the stew is acidic, add a few pinches of sugar to balance the flavors after the final stewing.

RED SCALLIONS

These beautiful Japanese scallions with a deep blush outer skin and a mild flavor turn sweet when grilled. Sliced on a graceful long diagonal and tossed with crisp Lemongrass Cucumbers, they're refreshing—beautiful tossed with mizuna and tat soi in a garnish of Asian greens.

Scallions are nothing more than the immature shoots of any onion; however, some varieties produce very fine immature shoots, and the lovely Purplette is a good example. They need even moisture, well-drained soil with some organic matter, and partial shade. Start seeds or sets early in the spring, 4 weeks before the last expected frost. (When buying sets, choose those ½ inch in diameter, which won't go to seed as rapidly.) Harvest when the greens are 10 to 12 inches long, a little more than 2 months after planting.

Southern Rio Stew

The flavors of this southwestern dish are warm, rich, and inviting—cubes of butternut squash are first roasted, then simmered in a stew of tomatoes, chilies, mushrooms, sweet peppers, and hominy. Ancho chilies can vary from mild to fiery, so be sure to taste them before adding to the stew. Serve with creamy soft polenta or basmati rice tossed with toasted pumpkin seeds. In summer, you can include fresh corn or substitute it for the hominy.

1 small butternut squash, about 1 pound, cut into ½-inch cubes, about 2 cups
2½ tablespoons light olive oil or vegetable oil
Salt and pepper
2 pounds fresh tomatoes, peeled, seeded, and chopped, (page 95), about 3 cups, or 1 28-ounce can tomatoes with juice, chopped
1 teaspoon cinnamon, preferably freshly ground
1½ teaspoons cumin seed, toasted and ground (page 89)
¾ pound white mushrooms, cut in half or left whole if small, about 4 cups
1 medium-size yellow onion, cut into ½-inch pieces, about 2 cups
5 garlic cloves, finely chopped
1 medium-size red or yellow bell pepper, cut into thick strips and then triangles, about 1 cup
2 medium-size zucchini, cut in half lengthwise and sliced into ½-inch slices on a diagonal, about 2 cups
1 cup canned hominy, drained and rinsed, or 1 ear of corn, shaved, about 1 cup kernels
½ teaspoon Chipotle Puree (page 332)
1 or 2 tablespoons Ancho Chile Puree (page 197)
1 tablespoon crème fraîche (page 359; optional)
2 tablespoons coarsely chopped cilantro
1 tablespoon chopped fresh mint

Preheat the oven to 400°F. Toss the squash with ½ tablespoon of the oil and sprinkle with salt and pepper. Bake in a covered dish until just tender, about 10 minutes. (The squash should still be firm so it holds its shape while it cooks with the stew.) If you're using canned tomatoes, cook them for 20 minutes in a medium-size saucepan over low heat with ½ teaspoon each of the cinnamon and cumin. The extra cooking time will reduce their acidity.

Heat 1 tablespoon of the oil in a large skillet. Sear the mushrooms over high heat with ¼ teaspoon salt and a few pinches of pepper, until golden, about 5 to 7 minutes. Transfer to a bowl and set aside.

Heat the remaining tablespoon of oil in the same skillet. Add the onion, ½ teaspoon salt, and the remaining cinnamon and cumin. Sauté over medium heat until the onion is tender, about 7 to 8 minutes. Add the garlic and peppers; sauté until peppers are almost tender, about 10 minutes, then add the zucchini and ¼ teaspoon salt. Sauté just long enough to heat the zucchini through, then add the tomatoes. (If you're using fresh tomatoes, add the cinnamon and cumin now.) Add the mushrooms, butternut squash, hominy, and chili purees. Cover and stew over medium-low heat for 20 to 25 minutes, stirring occasionally. Add salt and pepper to taste. Stir in the crème fraîche, if using it. Add the cilantro and mint just before serving.

SERVES FOUR TO SIX

Tip: If canned tomatoes are particularly acidic, add a pinch of sugar during the initial cooking time. You can also add a few pinches of sugar to balance the flavors if the stew seems acidic after the final cooking.

ANCHO CHILI PUREE

Ancho chilies are dried poblanos, available in Mexican specialty stores. These dark, wrinkled chilies range from rich reddish brown to nearly black. Ancho Chili Puree adds a particular depth and heat to our dishes, with its dark, almost musty flavor. The heat of the chilies varies greatly—they're mostly hot but can sometimes be quite mild.

To make the puree, pull the chilies apart at the stem end and remove the seeds. Place the chilies in a small bowl and cover with hot water, allowing them to soak for 15 to 20 minutes. Place them in a blender or food processor; add a small amount of the soaking liquid and process to a smooth puree, adding more liquid if needed.

The anchos can be roasted before soaking in a 350°F oven until they puff up and smell toasty, about 5 minutes—this will bring out even more flavor. The dry roasted chilies can also be seeded and ground into chili powder.

Ratatouille

Make this stew at the height of summer, when eggplant, peppers, and tomatoes couldn't be better. As the vegetables slowly simmer together, their sweet juices soak up the flavor of the fragrant fresh herbs. You can use Greek oregano in place of the marjoram, but taste it first—its strong, pungent flavor can overpower the delicate basil. Serve over creamy soft polenta (page 278) sprinkled with grated Parmesan. It's even better the next day, served at room temperature with crusty sourdough bread and salty black olives.

2 tablespoons extra virgin olive oil
1 medium-size red onion, cut into quarters and thickly sliced
Salt and pepper
6 garlic cloves, finely chopped
3 medium-size Japanese eggplants, cut in half lengthwise, then sliced ¾ inch thick on a
  diagonal, about 3 cups
2 medium-size bell peppers, cut into thick strips and then triangles, about 2 cups
1 pound summer squash, cut into thick slices or wedges
2 pounds vine-ripened tomatoes, peeled, seeded, and chopped (page 95), about 3 cups
1 bay leaf
3 tablespoons chopped fresh basil
½ tablespoon chopped fresh marjoram or Greek oregano

Heat the olive oil in a large skillet and add the onion, ½ teaspoon salt, and a few pinches of pepper. Sauté over medium heat until soft, about 5 minutes. Add the garlic, eggplant, peppers, ¼ teaspoon salt, and a few pinches of pepper; sauté for 8 to 10 minutes, until the eggplant and peppers are just tender. Add the summer squash, tomatoes, bay leaf, ½ teaspoon salt, and a few pinches of pepper. Stew over low heat for about 20 minutes, until everything is tender. Add the basil and marjoram just before serving. Season with salt and pepper to taste.

SERVES FOUR

Winter Vegetable Pie

This gratifying deep-dish pie is a treat for the senses. The winter vegetables take in the rich essence of the mushroom sauce as they simmer together—their steaming, earthy aromas are released as soon as you cut into the golden baked crust.

This is a time-consuming dish to prepare, but well worth the effort—if you plan ahead, a number of steps can be done in advance. The pastry dough can be made ahead and frozen or kept overnight in the refrigerator. Make the reduced Mushroom Stock a day in advance or take it from the freezer. Just be sure to reheat the stock and bring the dough up to room temperature before beginning to work with them. Though this dish is a meal in itself, a salad of bitter greens tossed with pears and toasted walnuts would add a touch of elegance.

Mushroom Stock (page 80)
Tart Dough (page 216)

Make the stock, and while it's cooking, prepare the dough. When the stock is finished, strain it and place in a saucepan. Bring to a boil to reduce to 3 cups. While the dough is resting in the refrigerator, make the sauce.

THE SAUCE

The salt in the Mushroom Stock intensifies as it reduces, and the soy sauce, added for flavor and color, also contains salt, so you should not need additional salt in this sauce.

3 cups reduced Mushroom Stock
3½ tablespoons unsalted butter
5 tablespoons unbleached white flour
⅛ teaspoon pepper
1 tablespoon soy sauce

Keep the stock warm over low heat. Melt the butter in a small saucepan, whisk in the flour, and cook the resulting roux over low heat for 2 to 3 minutes, whisking constantly. Whisk ½ cup stock into the roux, then whisk in the remaining stock over medium heat; the sauce should be smooth. Add the pepper and soy sauce and cook for 10 minutes, until the sauce thickens. Cook over low heat, stirring occasionally, while you prepare the vegetables.

THE VEGETABLES

2 tablespoons fresh lemon juice, about 1 lemon

2 cups water

1 medium-size celery root, about 1 pound

½ ounce dried porcini, soaked in ½ cup warm water for 10 minutes

2 tablespoons light olive oil

¾ pound white mushrooms, left whole or cut in half if large, about 4 cups

Salt and pepper

5 garlic cloves, finely chopped

½ cup dry sherry

1 medium-size yellow onion, cut into large pieces, about 2 cups

2 medium-size carrots, peeled, cut in half lengthwise, then cut into ½-inch slices on a
*   diagonal, about 2 cups*

1 medium-size fennel bulb, quartered lengthwise, cored, and sliced ½ inch thick, about
*   2 cups*

2 tablespoons chopped fresh herbs: marjoram, thyme, and parsley

1 egg, beaten

1 tablespoon water

Combine the lemon juice and water in a bowl. Peel the celery root and cut it into ¾-inch cubes. Immediately place them in the water as you prepare them, to prevent discoloration. Drain the celery root before adding it to the stew.

Strain the porcini through a fine-mesh strainer, saving the soaking liquid to add to the stew later. (If the porcini liquid is sandy, allow the sand to settle and pour off the liquid.) Finely chop the porcini, discarding any pieces that are hard or gritty. Remove the pastry from the refrigerator and allow it to come to room temperature.

Heat 1 tablespoon of the olive oil in a large skillet; add the white mushrooms, ¼ teaspoon salt, and a few pinches of pepper. Sear the mushrooms over high heat for 6 to 7 minutes, until golden. Add half the garlic and deglaze the pan with half the sherry. Simmer to reduce it. When the pan is almost dry, transfer the mushrooms to a bowl.

Heat the remaining tablespoon of olive oil in the skillet and add the onion, ½ teaspoon salt, and a few pinches of pepper; sauté over medium heat for 7 to 8 minutes. Add the remaining garlic, the porcini, celery root, carrots, and fennel; sauté for 10 minutes. Add the porcini soaking liquid; simmer for 5 minutes to reduce it.

Stir in the mushrooms, sauce, and fresh herbs. Season the stew with salt and pepper to taste. Pour it into a 9-inch round baking dish and allow it to cool.

Preheat the oven to 375°F. Roll out the pastry to 1 inch larger than the baking dish and lay it on top, turning the edges under and crimping them. Whisk the egg and water together and brush over the pastry. If there is leftover dough, you can make shapes and fasten them to the crust with the egg wash. Make 3 1-inch slits in the dough and bake the pie for about 40 minutes, until the crust is golden.

Variations: For a welcome addition, include some potatoes or use them in place of the celery root. Their smooth flavor and starchy texture are perfect for this dish. Turnips, parsnips, or rutabagas would also be delicious.

This also makes a comforting winter vegetable stew served over creamy soft polenta. Prepare the sauce and vegetables as directed and leave the vegetables in the skillet. Add the sauce, cover the pan, and simmer over low heat for 30 minutes, or until the vegetables are completely tender. Stir as needed, adding a little water to thin the sauce if necessary.

WINTER SAVORY

This beautiful evergreen is one of the oldest culinary herbs, considered beneficial for digestion. With its spicy peppery flavor, it's a wonderful addition to hearty dishes, particularly beans, both fresh and dried. In summer, toss it with tender green beans and a sprightly lemon vinaigrette. In winter, we mix it with chopped marjoram and thyme to season a hearty root vegetable stew. Add whole sprigs and a bay leaf or two to a simmering pot of cannellini beans—the starchy broth will be remarkably delicious.

Winter savory is a true perennial, a shrub that grows 12 to 18 inches high. With its tiny white flowers and fragrant foliage, this showy plant makes a lovely edging around the herb garden and is beautiful dried in herbal wreaths. It's easiest to propagate by cuttings or division and enjoys a fertile, moist position in the garden. When savory is sheared back heavily after flowering, it will produce a second cutting of succulent leaves.

Gratins

Gratins

There's nothing elegant about these hearty dishes—the flavors are full and deeply satisfying, and we serve them throughout the year. A gratin can be simple or complex, depending on the time and ingredients available. Fresh herbs and flavorful cheeses make a difference here—Gorgonzola, Parmesan, smoked mozzarella, and nutty Gruyère are just a few of the choices.

We vary the recipes each season with different vegetables, herbs, and cheeses—slicing root vegetables thinly to ensure that they cook evenly in a gratin of potatoes. In the fall and winter months, try celery root, sweet potatoes, turnips, or Belgian endive. In the summer, torn leaves of basil, pitted Niçoise olives, and seeded, chopped tomatoes are delicious. Nutty-tasting rocket (arugula) is a wonderful addition—the larger leaves are a bit peppery, just right for cutting through the richness of the cheese and cream. Potato gratins take a full hour to bake and sometimes more—the potatoes should be perfectly tender, with a crisp, golden top layer. For crunchy texture, sprinkle Garlic Bread Crumbs over the gratin, adding them along with the last of the cheese for the final minutes of baking.

A word on using cream in potato gratins: We use milk and cream together for their well-balanced flavor and richness. We've tried using all milk, but the flavor is a little light, and like half-and-half it tends to curdle when baked for over an hour at 375°F. Though our recipes don't include it, a light sprinkling of flour between the layers of potatoes will help keep milk or half-and-half from curdling. Heavy cream is very stable, even when combined with an equal portion of milk, and cooks perfectly into the potatoes.

Polenta gratins are always a favorite—particularly with tomatoes, olives, and creamy Fontina or with southwestern flavors. The seasoning is crucial here; these gratins can be heavy and uninspiring unless all the elements—the polenta, the sauce, and the vegetables—are alive with interesting flavors.

Gratins of eggplant and roasted vegetables can be a bit rich but often just what's needed for a main course. To lighten them, layer well-seasoned slices of zucchini in with the eggplant. Though we use cheese here, the gratin can be wonderful without it—here's where the taste of olives, fresh herbs, and roasted garlic really shines.

Gratin of Eggplant, Roasted Peppers, and Garlic

Save this gratin for late summer, when the markets are brimming with slender eggplant, colorful peppers, and fresh, sweet garlic. The vegetables are preroasted and layered with creamy Fontina cheese and a sprinkling of Parmesan and baked in a savory tomato sauce. For a simple variation, include a handful of chopped Niçoise or Gaeta olives. The gratin is beautiful baked in individual gratin dishes with Saffron Basmati Rice (page 274) or with wedges of grilled polenta served alongside.

4 pounds Japanese eggplant, sliced ¾ inch thick on a diagonal
4½ tablespoons extra virgin olive oil
3 garlic cloves, finely chopped
1 teaspoon salt
Pepper
24 unpeeled garlic cloves
2 medium-size red or yellow bell peppers, roasted, peeled, and sliced ½ inch thick (page 55)
2 tablespoons chopped fresh herbs: marjoram, Italian parsley, and thyme
Tomato Sauce (page 325), ½ teaspoon dried marjoram substituted for the basil
2 ounces Fontina cheese, grated, about ¾ cup
2 ounces Parmesan cheese, grated, about ⅔ cup

Preheat the oven to 350°F. Toss the eggplant with 3 tablespoons of the olive oil, the chopped garlic, ½ teaspoon of the salt, and a few pinches of pepper. Place on a baking sheet. Toss the whole garlic cloves with a little olive oil and place alongside the eggplant; bake for 20 to 25 minutes, until the eggplant is soft to the touch and the garlic is soft but still holds its shape. Set aside to cool. Carefully peel the garlic and toss it with the roasted pepper strips, the remaining olive oil and salt, a few pinches of pepper, and half the chopped herbs.

Pour the tomato sauce into the bottom of a 9- by 13-inch baking dish and layer the eggplant nearly upright (not flat) in rows across the width of the dish, overlapping the slices as you go. Continue to layer, packing the slices close together, until you've used all the eggplant. Tuck the pepper strips and garlic cloves in between the eggplant slices and sprinkle with the Fontina.

Cover and bake for 20 minutes, then sprinkle with the Parmesan. Bake, uncovered, for another 10 minutes, until bubbly. Sprinkle the remaining herbs over the gratin just before serving.

SERVES FOUR TO SIX

Tips: You can roast the peppers and make the sauce a day in advance. Once these steps are out of the way, the gratin can be assembled quite quickly.

There is a lot of eggplant here, but it will all fit in the dish if it's tightly packed, almost vertically stacked.

Polenta Baked with Tomatoes, Corn, and Basil

The sweet summer flavors of tender fresh corn, basil, and vine-ripened tomatoes work nicely with polenta. The delicious vegetable juices seep into the polenta, while fresh chilies add a hint of heat. A generous sprinkling of Parmesan brings all the flavors together.

Polenta (page 278)
Tomato Sauce (page 325)
1 tablespoon unsalted butter
3 ears of corn, shaved, about 2½ cups kernels
Salt
¾ pound tomatoes, cored and seeded
1 tablespoon extra virgin olive oil
Pepper
1 cup fresh basil leaves, chopped
1 or 2 jalapeño chilies, seeded and thinly sliced
2 ounces Parmesan cheese, grated, about ⅔ cup

Make the polenta, and while it's cooling, make the sauce; remove the bay leaf just before assembling the gratin.

Heat the butter in a large skillet and add the corn. Sauté over medium heat for 10 minutes, until the corn is tender; season with ¼ teaspoon salt. While the corn is cooking, cut the tomatoes into large pieces—you should have about 1½ cups. Marinate the tomatoes in the olive oil with ¼ teaspoon salt and a few pinches of pepper. Cool the corn and toss with the tomatoes, half the basil, and half the chilies. Add salt, pepper, and chilies to taste.

Preheat the oven to 375°F. Pour the sauce into the bottom of a 9- by 13-inch baking dish. Arrange the polenta triangles upright in rows across the width of the dish, overlapping the triangles slightly; use all of the polenta. Spoon the vegetables into the spaces between the polenta triangles, separating the rows as you go. Sprinkle with the cheese. Cover and bake for 25 minutes, then uncover and bake for 10 more minutes, until the gratin is bubbly. Sprinkle on the remaining basil and serve.

SERVES FOUR TO SIX

Tip: Taste the corn. If it's tough, add a little water to the skillet; cover and steam until the kernels are plump. If it lacks flavor, add a few pinches of sugar before steaming to sweeten it.

Polenta Baked with Artichokes, Tomatoes, and Olives

In this hearty gratin, sautéed artichokes mingle with tomatoes and fruity-tasting Niçoise olives. We use Roma (plum) tomatoes throughout the winter for this dish. Though they're not particularly sweet, they take on the essence of the olive and herb marinade. Season the artichokes well, or the polenta will overpower their fine subtle flavor.

Polenta (page 278)
Tomato Sauce (page 325)
4 medium-size artichokes, trimmed and sliced (page 241), about 4 cups
2 tablespoons extra virgin olive oil
Salt and pepper
¼ cup dry white wine
1 to 2 teaspoons fresh lemon juice
4 garlic cloves, finely chopped
¾ pound tomatoes, cored, seeded, and cut into large pieces, about 1½ cups
1 teaspoon chopped fresh marjoram
1 teaspoon chopped fresh thyme
12 Niçoise olives, pitted and coarsely chopped
2 ounces Fontina cheese, grated, about ¾ cup
1 ounce Parmesan cheese, grated, about ⅓ cup

Make the polenta, and while it's cooling, make the tomato sauce. Drain the artichokes.

Heat 1 tablespoon of the olive oil in a large sauté pan over medium heat; add the drained artichokes, ¼ teaspoon salt, and a few pinches of pepper. Sauté until the artichokes are tender, about 10 minutes. Add the wine, 1 teaspoon lemon juice, and half the garlic; simmer for about 2 minutes. Add salt, pepper, and more lemon juice if needed.

While the artichokes are sautéing, marinate the tomatoes with the remaining olive oil and garlic, the fresh herbs, ¼ teaspoon salt, and a few pinches of pepper. Toss the artichokes, tomatoes, and olives together.

Preheat the oven to 375°F. Pour the sauce into the bottom of a 9- by 13-inch baking dish. Arrange the polenta triangles upright in rows across the width of the dish, overlapping the triangles slightly; use all of the polenta. Spoon the vegetables and olives between the polenta triangles. Mix the cheeses together and sprinkle over the gratin. Cover and bake for 25 minutes, then remove the cover and bake for 10 minutes more, until the gratin is bubbly.

SERVES FOUR TO SIX

Potato Gratin with Artichokes and Smoked Mozzarella Cheese

Artichokes are sautéed with garlic and lemon to draw out their subtle flavor, then layered with thinly sliced potatoes and smoked mozzarella cheese. Hot cream, steeped with fresh herbs and bay, is poured over. As the gratin bakes, the potatoes take on the fragrance of the cream and bubble deliciously with the smoky flavor of the mozzarella. Serve the golden crisp gratin with a sauté of winter greens alongside.

1 tablespoon extra virgin olive oil
1 medium-size red onion, thinly sliced, about 2 cups
Salt and pepper
5 medium-size artichokes, trimmed and sliced (page 241), about 5 cups
6 garlic cloves, finely chopped
1 tablespoon fresh lemon juice
2 tablespoons chopped fresh herbs: parsley, marjoram, and thyme
1 cup heavy cream
1 cup milk
1 bay leaf
2 fresh sage leaves
2 fresh thyme sprigs
2 fresh marjoram or oregano sprigs
½ teaspoon peppercorns
1½ pounds large red, White Rose, or Yellow Finn potatoes
¼ pound smoked mozzarella cheese, grated, about 1½ cups

Heat the olive oil in a large skillet. Add the onion, ½ teaspoon salt, and a few pinches of pepper; sauté over medium heat for about 5 minutes. Drain the artichokes and add to the onion along with the garlic, ½ teaspoon salt, and a few pinches of pepper. Sauté for about 10 minutes, until the artichokes are tender, then add the tablespoon of lemon juice. When the artichokes and onion are cool, coarsely chop them and toss with half the chopped herbs.

While the onion and artichokes are sautéing, pour the cream and milk into a small saucepan; add the bay leaf and sage leaves, the herb sprigs, and the peppercorns. Steep over low heat for 20 minutes. Pour through a strainer and season with ¼ teaspoon salt.

Preheat the oven to 375°F and lightly oil a 9- by 13-inch baking dish. Slice the potatoes thinly and lay one-third of them in the bottom of the dish, overlapping the slices and rows as you go. Sprinkle generously with salt and pepper; spread half the onion-artichoke mixture over the potatoes. Sprinkle with one-third of the cheese, make another layer of potatoes, and sprinkle with salt and pepper. Follow with the remaining vegetables and one-third of the cheese. Top with a final layer of potatoes and pour the hot cream over.

Cover the dish and bake for 40 minutes. Sprinkle on the remaining cheese and bake, uncovered, for 15 minutes, until the potatoes are very tender. The gratin should be golden and a little crisp. Sprinkle with the remaining chopped herbs just before serving.

SERVES FOUR TO SIX

RED SWISS CHARD

This handsome plant strikes an elegant pose with its deep green leaves and brilliant ruby-red veins. The crisp stems are delectable thinly sliced and sautéed in olive oil with the leaves—with lemon and garlic, it couldn't be better. Swiss chard mixes well with kale and is terrific in winter cannelloni. Sliced into thick ribbons, it's delicious in a Summer Minestrone or a hearty vegetable stew.

Green and red chard have the same cultivation requirements—well-drained soil rich in nitrogen. Add some compost or aged manure when you plant. Sow a few seeds by the back door in early spring and late fall. You can harvest the outer leaves a few at a time, and the plants will keep producing all season. It will probably make it through the winter and come back at least one more season. Flea beetles may put a few holes in the leaves in the summer, but that won't hurt the plant. You can have a bed of chard plants 18 inches apart and plant a variety of lettuces in between.

Potato, Fennel, and Leek Gratin

This is a satisfying winter dish brimming with leeks, fragrant fennel, and fruity olives. Yellow Finn potatoes are our first choice here, but White Rose or red potatoes are delicious as well. We often serve the gratin on a bed of undressed mizuna, rocket, or frisée—the greens soak up the rich juices, and as they wilt, all the flavors melt together.

1 tablespoon extra virgin olive oil

3 large leeks, white parts only, halved lengthwise, thinly sliced, and washed, about 4½ cups

1 teaspoon ground fennel seed

Salt and pepper

2 large fennel bulbs, quartered lengthwise, cored, and thinly sliced, about 4 cups

5 garlic cloves, finely chopped

2 tablespoons chopped fresh herbs: Italian parsley, thyme, and marjoram

1 cup cream

1 cup milk

1 bay leaf

½ teaspoon peppercorns

½ teaspoon fennel seed

3 fresh thyme sprigs

3 parsley sprigs

2 ounces provolone cheese, grated, about ¾ cup

2 ounces Parmesan cheese, grated, about ⅔ cup

1½ pounds large Yellow Finn, White Rose, or red potatoes

12 Niçoise or Gaeta olives, pitted and coarsely chopped

Heat the olive oil in a large skillet; add the leeks, ground fennel, ½ teaspoon salt, and a few pinches of pepper. Sauté over medium heat until the leeks are heated through, then cover the pan and steam until wilted, about 5 minutes. Add the sliced fennel, garlic, and ½ teaspoon salt; sauté until the fennel is tender, about 5 minutes. Transfer the vegetables to a bowl and toss with half the chopped herbs.

While the leeks and fennel are sautéing, pour the cream and milk into a small saucepan; add the bay leaf, peppercorns, whole fennel seed, and herb sprigs. Steep the cream over low heat for 20 minutes. Pour through a strainer and season with ¼ teaspoon salt.

Preheat the oven to 375°F and lightly oil a 9- by 13-inch baking dish. Mix the cheeses. Thinly slice the potatoes and layer one-third of them in the bottom of the dish, overlapping the slices and rows as you go. Sprinkle the potatoes generously with salt and pepper, followed by the olives, half the leeks and fennel, and one-third of the cheese. Make another layer of potatoes, followed by salt and pepper, the remaining leeks and fennel, and one-third of the cheese. Top with a final layer of potatoes and pour the hot cream over. Cover the dish and bake for 40 minutes. Sprinkle with the remaining cheese and bake, uncovered, until the potatoes are very tender and the gratin turns golden and a little crisp, another 15 minutes. Sprinkle with the remaining chopped herbs just before serving.

SERVES FOUR TO SIX

ROCKET

The tender leaves have a nutty taste and grow more peppery by the day—when large, they have a pungent bite that smooths as it wilts deliciously under a savory potato gratin. It is known by many names—arugula, rocket salad, and roquette.

This tangy green is just about foolproof—it's quick to grow and needs little attention except continuous harvesting. Rocket is happiest when grown close together in rich, moist soil with filtered light. Harvest before the hot weather, while the plants are still tender, or the leaves will get bitter. You can take leaves two or three times, but we recommend harvesting the whole plant; it may go to seed if stressed. Sow seeds every month for a continuous supply of rocket. Rocket flowers are lovely in salads.

Polenta Gratin with Salsa Roja

A spicy dish that's rich and earthy, this gratin is one of our year-round favorites. Zucchini, mushrooms, and sweet peppers are layered with polenta, spiced with toasted cumin and dried chilies. The polenta takes in all the delicious flavors as it bakes with the Salsa Roja and the smoky cheese.

Polenta (page 278), 2 ounces smoked cheese, grated, substituted for the Parmesan and a
    few pinches of cayenne pepper added
Salsa Roja (page 326)
2 tablespoons light olive oil
¾ pound white mushrooms, thickly sliced, about 4 cups
¾ teaspoon salt
4 garlic cloves, finely chopped
1 medium-size zucchini, diced
½ medium-size red bell pepper, diced
1 teaspoon cumin seed, toasted and ground (page 89)
Cayenne pepper
1 tablespoon chopped cilantro
1 tablespoon chopped fresh marjoram or oregano
¼ pound smoked mozzarella cheese, grated, about 1½ cups

Make the polenta, and while it cools, make the Salsa Roja.

Heat 1 tablespoon of the olive oil in a large skillet. Sauté the mushrooms over high heat with ½ teaspoon of the salt until golden and crisp, about 5 minutes. Add half the garlic and sauté for 1 minute more. Transfer the mushrooms to a bowl and set aside.

Heat the remaining tablespoon of olive oil in the skillet; add the zucchini, peppers, cumin, remaining ¼ teaspoon salt, and a few pinches of cayenne. Sauté over medium heat for 7 to 8 minutes; add the remaining garlic and sauté for 2 minutes. Remove from the heat; toss with the mushrooms and half the fresh herbs.

Preheat the oven to 375°F. Pour the sauce into the bottom of a 9- by 13-inch baking dish. Arrange the polenta triangles upright in rows across the width of the dish, overlapping the triangles slightly; use all of the polenta. Sprinkle the vegetables between the polenta triangles, separating the rows as you go. Sprinkle the cheese over the gratin. Cover and bake for 30 to 40 minutes, until the sauce is bubbly and the polenta is heated through. Sprinkle the remaining cilantro and marjoram over the top just before serving.

SERVES FOUR TO SIX

Tarts, Fritters, and Savory Cakes

Tarts, Fritters, and Savory Cakes

Savory tarts can be elegant or rustic, the focus of a meal, a midafternoon snack, or a picnic. Thinly sliced, they're a delightful appetizer—served on a bed of peppery greens with a few salty black olives or simply passed on a lovely platter. They can be served warm or at room temperature, depending on the dough and the flavors of the filling. Tarts made with yeasted tart dough are best served warm from the oven, while our short crust tart dough is delicious either way. We fill our tarts with sparkling combinations of vegetables, herbs, and cheeses, then bake them in a light custard. Try using crème fraîche in the custard—its taste is smooth and tangy and rounds out the flavors of the filling.

Fritters and savory cakes are always satisfying and quite easy to prepare—served with a lively salad, they make a fine light meal. Some are tossed in a simple egg batter; others have beaten whites folded into the vegetable batter to lighten the cakes. We season the vegetables with citrus, fresh herbs, and chilies to sharpen and define their flavors. There's a beauty to these recipes—most will keep well in a warm oven until you're ready to serve them.

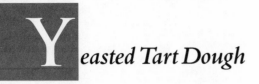Yeasted Tart Dough

This adaptation of Elizabeth David's recipe appears in *The Greens Cookbook,* and it's so essential to our kitchen that it's repeated here. Wonderful flavor aside, this dough is a joy to work with. You don't even have to roll it out. Like brioche dough, it's buttery and moist, but not quite so rich. The temperature of the ingredients is the key to light, tender dough—be sure the butter is very soft but not melted; it will incorporate easily. Have the egg at room temperature. If it's cold, it will slow the rising of the dough (to warm it quickly, place the egg in a bowl of warm water).

It's not necessary to prebake the shell. Once the dough is formed in the pan, it can be filled and baked immediately.

1 teaspoon active dry yeast, ½ package
Pinch of sugar
¼ cup warm (110°F) water
About 1 cup unbleached white flour
½ teaspoon salt
½ teaspoon minced lemon zest (optional)
1 large egg at room temperature
3 tablespoons soft unsalted butter
Unbleached white flour for shaping

Dissolve the yeast and sugar in the water and set it in a warm place while you gather the other ingredients. Combine 1 cup flour, the salt, and the minced lemon zest in a bowl and make a well. Break the egg into the middle of it; add the butter and pour in the yeast mixture, which should be foamy with bubbles. Mix with a wooden spoon to form a soft, smooth dough. Dust it with flour and gather into a ball; set it in a clean bowl and cover with plastic wrap or a kitchen towel. Let the dough rise in a warm place until it is doubled in bulk, 45 minutes to 1 hour. If you are not ready to shape the dough at this time, knead it down and let it rise again.

Use a 9-inch tart pan with a removable bottom. Flatten the dough, place it in the center of the pan, and press it out to the edge using either your knuckles or the heel of your hand. Add only enough flour to keep the dough from sticking. If the dough shrinks back while you're shaping it, cover with a towel and let it relax for 20 minutes before you finish pressing it out. It should be thin on the bottom and thicker at the sides, about ¼ inch higher than the rim of the pan. It can be filled immediately or refrigerated until needed. Once the tart is filled, bake in the middle of a 375°F oven for 35 to 45 minutes.

MAKES ONE 9-INCH TART SHELL

Tip: The dough can be made a day in advance and held in the refrigerator. Wrap it tightly in plastic wrap and allow the dough to return to room temperature before forming it. The dough can also be frozen, wrapped in foil.

Tart Dough

This is the classic Greens tart dough; we use this tender, buttery dough for savory turnovers as well as for tarts and appetizer-size tartlets. It can be made in advance and refrigerated overnight or frozen. For advance preparation, form the dough into a flattened round with the heel of your hand, firm up the edges, then seal tightly in plastic wrap. Allow it to return to room temperature before rolling out.

> *1 cup unbleached white flour*
> *3/8 teaspoon salt*
> *4 tablespoons cold unsalted butter, cut into small cubes*
> *1 1/2 tablespoons solid vegetable shortening*
> *2 1/2 to 3 tablespoons ice water*
> *Flour for rolling out*

To make the dough in an electric mixer: Use the paddle attachment and keep the machine on low speed throughout the mixing process. Combine the flour and salt in the bowl of the mixer. Add half of the cubed butter and mix until it is incorporated into the flour. Follow with the shortening and the remaining butter. Add 2 1/2 tablespoons water and work the dough until it holds together. Add the remaining 1/2 tablespoon of water if the dough is dry and doesn't hold together. Shape the dough into a disk, cover with wax paper or plastic wrap, and let rest in the refrigerator for at least 30 minutes before using.

To make the dough by hand: Combine the flour and salt in a bowl. Add the butter and shortening and work the fat and flour together, sliding it between your palms or between your thumbs and fingertips. When the butter and shortening are evenly distributed, add 2 1/2 tablespoons cold water and lightly work it into the flour, using a fork or your fingers. Gather the dough into a ball, sprinkling a few drops of water over any loose bits of flour and gathering them in. Shape the dough into a disk, cover with wax paper or plastic wrap, and let rest in the refrigerator for at least 30 minutes before using.

Rolling the dough: If the dough is stiff from cold, let it sit at room temperature for about 20 minutes before rolling. Lightly flour the work surface and the top of the dough. Roll it out with firm, even strokes, turning and sprinkling on flour as needed, until you have a round about 1/8 inch thick. Pick it up on the rolling pin, or fold it into quarters, and lay it on the tart or pie pan. Trim and crimp the edge.

Prebaking the crust: If the recipe calls for prebaking the crust, line it with buttered foil or parchment paper and fill with pie weights or 1 cup dried beans. Preheat the oven to 425°F and bake until the edges are set and slightly browned, about 8 to 10 minutes.

MAKES ONE 9-INCH TART SHELL

For pastry turnovers: You will need a double recipe of the tart dough to make 4 turnovers. Follow the instructions for making the dough. Divide it into 4 equal portions, shape into disks, cover with wax paper or plastic wrap, and let rest in the refrigerator for at least 30 minutes before using. Roll each disk into a circle about ⅛ inch thick. The pastries can be rolled in advance and stored in the refrigerator separated by pieces of wax paper or plastic wrap. Be sure to wrap and seal them tightly with plastic wrap.

Southwestern Corn Tart

We know that summer has finally arrived when this well-loved tart appears on the menu. Tender kernels of corn, thin slivers of fresh chilies, and good white cheddar cheese are the simple ingredients that make its flavor so exceptional. The heat of chilies is always uncertain, so try a tiny taste of one before tossing with the corn. Add more or less chilies to your taste; if they're mild, a few pinches of cayenne will add heat and spice. The cilantro and marjoram add a fresh, light taste.

1 recipe Yeasted Tart Dough (page 215)
1 tablespoon light olive oil
½ small red onion, diced, about ½ cup
Salt
2 ears of corn, shaved, about 2 cups kernels
Cayenne pepper
2 jalapeño chilies, seeded and thinly sliced
2 tablespoons chopped cilantro
1 tablespoon chopped fresh marjoram
3 eggs
1½ cups half-and-half or 1 cup half-and-half plus ½ cup crème fraîche (page 359)
1 ounce Vermont or other flavorful white cheddar cheese, grated, about ½ cup

Make the dough and follow the instructions for lining the tart pan.

Heat the olive oil in a large sauté pan and sauté the onion over medium heat with ¼ teaspoon salt until soft, 3 to 4 minutes. Add the corn, ¼ teaspoon salt, and ⅛ teaspoon cayenne; sauté until the corn is tender, about 5 minutes. Transfer to a bowl and toss with the jalapeños and herbs. Set aside to cool.

Preheat the oven to 375°F. In a separate bowl, beat the eggs. Add the half-and-half, ½ teaspoon salt, and a pinch of cayenne.

Spread the cheese on the bottom of the tart dough, followed by the corn and onion. Pour the custard over and bake for 35 to 40 minutes, until the top is golden and the custard is set.

MAKES ONE 9-INCH TART; SERVES SIX

Serving Suggestion: Serve with grilled red onions, summer squash, and thick strips of sweet pepper brushed with Cinnamon-Chipotle Butter (page 332). The smoky heat of the chipotle butter is a good balance to the fresh chilies in the tart.

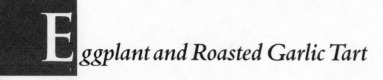

Eggplant and Roasted Garlic Tart

The custard is infused with the subtle flavor of roasted garlic, while thinly sliced sun-dried tomatoes and whole cloves of roasted garlic add intense flavor to every bite of this delicious eggplant tart. The taste and texture of the eggplant are essential—be sure to roast it until it's soft in the center. Otherwise the eggplant will be undercooked and the tart will be difficult to slice.

1 recipe Yeasted Tart Dough (page 215), 2 teaspoons chopped fresh marjoram added
1 head of garlic
2 tablespoons extra virgin olive oil
½ pound Japanese eggplant, sliced ¾ inch thick on a diagonal
Salt and pepper
1 tablespoon chopped fresh marjoram
3 large eggs
1½ cups half-and-half or 1 cup half-and-half plus ½ cup crème fraîche (page 359)
2 ounces provolone cheese, grated, about ¾ cup
2 sun-dried tomatoes packed in oil, drained and thinly sliced

Make the tart dough and follow the instructions for lining the tart pan.

Preheat the oven to 375°F. Brush the head of garlic with a little olive oil and roast it on a sheet pan until soft, about 30 minutes. When the garlic has cooled, cut the top off the bulb and squeeze the cloves out of the skin. Set aside half of the cloves (whole) for the tart and mash the remaining cloves for the custard.

The eggplant can be roasted in the same oven as the garlic. Brush both sides of the slices with the remaining olive oil, lay them on a sheet pan, and sprinkle with salt and pepper. Roast until the slices are soft, about 15 minutes. Cool, cut each slice into 2 or 3 strips, and toss with the marjoram.

Beat the eggs in a bowl and whisk in the mashed roasted garlic, followed by the half-and-half, ½ teaspoon salt, and ⅛ teaspoon pepper.

Spread the cheese on the bottom of the tart dough. Lay the eggplant slices on the cheese, followed by the roasted garlic cloves and sun-dried tomatoes. Pour the custard over the vegetables and bake for about 40 minutes, until the custard sets and the top turns golden.

MAKES ONE 9-INCH TART; SERVES SIX

Spring Tart with Asparagus and Red Onions

This elegant spring tart has subtle, refined flavors—early asparagus sweetened with an accent of orange, nutty-tasting Gruyère cheese, and a touch of chervil to flavor the custard. Serve with a salad of crunchy romaine hearts tossed with oranges and Niçoise olives.

1 recipe Yeasted Tart Dough (page 215)
1 tablespoon light olive oil
½ red onion, thinly sliced
Salt and white pepper
½ pound asparagus, tough ends discarded, sliced into 1-inch lengths on a diagonal, about 1½ cups
1 tablespoon chopped fresh chervil or Italian parsley
3 large eggs
1½ cups half-and-half or 1 cup half-and-half and ½ cup crème fraîche (page 359)
Zest of 1 orange, minced
2 ounces Gruyère cheese, grated, about 1 scant cup

Prepare the tart dough, following the instructions for lining the pan.

Heat the olive oil in a large sauté pan and add the onions, ¼ teaspoon salt, and a few pinches of pepper. Sauté over medium heat until the onions are soft, 7 to 8 minutes. Add the asparagus, ¼ teaspoon salt, and a few pinches of pepper and cook until the asparagus is tender, 7 to 8 minutes. Transfer the vegetables to a bowl, toss them with the herbs, and season to taste with salt and pepper. Set aside to cool.

Preheat the oven to 375°F. Beat the eggs in a bowl and add the half-and-half, orange zest, a generous ¼ teaspoon salt, and a few pinches of pepper.

Sprinkle the cheese on the bottom of the rolled dough and spread the asparagus and onions over it. Pour the custard over and bake for about 40 minutes, until the custard is golden and set.

MAKES ONE 9-INCH TART; SERVES SIX

Tomato-Basil Tart with Smoked Mozzarella Cheese

We make this summer tart at the height of the season with fully ripe tomatoes and fragrant basil. The tastes couldn't be better—the smoky cheese and the tasty black olives perfectly balance the sweetness of the tomatoes. It's important to remove the juice and seeds from the tomatoes; the juice will thin the custard. Delicious served warm or at room temperature, this tart is just the right dish for a picnic or a light evening meal.

1 recipe Tart Dough (page 216)
¾ pound fresh tomatoes, seeded, drained, and cut into ½-inch pieces, about 1½ cups
3 garlic cloves, finely chopped
1 loosely packed cup fresh basil leaves, coarsely chopped
8 to 10 Gaeta or Niçoise black olives, pitted and coarsely chopped
Salt and pepper
3 large eggs
1 cup half-and-half or ½ cup half-and-half plus ½ cup crème fraîche (page 359)
1 ounce smoked mozzarella cheese, grated, about ½ cup
1 ounce Parmesan cheese, grated, about ⅓ cup

Prepare the tart shell and follow the directions for prebaking it.

Toss the tomatoes with the garlic, basil, olives, ⅛ teaspoon salt, and a large pinch of pepper. Set them aside to marinate for 15 minutes, then drain off their juice.

Preheat the oven to 375°F. Beat the eggs in a bowl and add the half-and-half, a generous ¼ teaspoon salt, and a pinch of pepper.

Combine the mozzarella and Parmesan cheeses and sprinkle them on the bottom of the tart dough. Spread the tomatoes on the cheese, then pour the custard over. Bake for 35 to 40 minutes, until the custard is set and the top is golden.

MAKES ONE 9-INCH TART; SERVES SIX

Leek and Olive Tart

There is an elegance in the simplicity of this tart—the leeks are sautéed in fragrant olive oil until they're sweet, then tossed with good black olives and fresh thyme; a touch of lemon zest lifts the flavors. Serve in the spring with a sauté of asparagus; in fall with garden lettuces and late harvest tomatoes.

1 recipe Yeasted Tart Dough (page 215), ½ teaspoon grated lemon zest added
1 tablespoon extra virgin olive oil
3 medium-size leeks, white parts only, cut in half lengthwise, thinly sliced, and washed,
    about 3 cups
Salt and pepper
4 garlic cloves, finely chopped
8 to 10 Gaeta or Niçoise olives, pitted and chopped
2 teaspoons chopped fresh thyme
1 tablespoon coarsely chopped Italian parsley
3 eggs
1½ cups half-and-half or 1 cup half-and-half plus ½ cup crème fraîche (page 359)
½ teaspoon minced lemon zest
2 ounces Parmesan cheese, grated, about ⅔ cup

Make the tart dough and follow the instructions for lining the tart pan.

Heat the olive oil in a large sauté pan and sauté the leeks with ½ teaspoon salt and a few pinches of pepper over medium heat. When the leeks start to wilt, in about 3 minutes, add the garlic, cover the pan, and lightly steam until the leeks are tender, 7 to 8 minutes. Remove the lid and sauté, uncovered, for 2 more minutes. Transfer to a bowl and toss the leeks with the olives, thyme, and parsley. Set aside to cool.

Preheat the oven to 375°F. Beat the eggs in a bowl and mix in the half-and-half. Add ¼ teaspoon salt, a pinch of pepper, and the lemon zest.

Spread the cheese over the bottom of the tart dough, followed by the leeks and olives. Pour the custard over and bake for about 40 minutes, until the custard is golden and set.

MAKES ONE 9-INCH TART; SERVES SIX

Potato Cakes with Scallions and Smoked Mozzarella Cheese

Crisp and golden on the outside, moist and tender on the inside, these delicious griddle cakes couldn't be easier to make. The potatoes are precooked, so the cakes cook quickly, and the skillet or griddle top needs very little oil. Keep the first batch of cakes in a warming oven while you make the remaining cakes. Serve with a generous spoonful of crème fraîche.

2 pounds Russet potatoes
3 scallions, both white and green parts, thinly sliced
½ teaspoon salt
⅛ teaspoon pepper
1 egg, beaten
2 tablespoons crème fraîche (page 359) plus ½ cup to garnish
1 ounce smoked mozzarella cheese, grated, about ½ cup
Light vegetable oil for cooking the cakes

Boil the potatoes in their skins for about 20 minutes, until they're still a little firm and not completely cooked through. Cool and peel the potatoes, then grate on the largest hole of a grater or in a food processor. Toss the potatoes and the scallions together and add the salt and pepper. Beat the egg and crème fraîche together; mix into the potatoes. Add the cheese and mix together.

Form into little cakes about 3 to 4 inches in diameter and ½ inch thick. Cook in a lightly oiled skillet or on a griddle top over medium heat, allowing the first side to turn crisp and golden before turning the cakes over, about 4 to 5 minutes. Flip the cakes and cook for another 4 to 5 minutes.

MAKES 12 TO 15 CAKES; SERVES FOUR

*S*pinach and Mung Dal Fritters

These scrumptious fried dumplings are an adaptation of Spinach and Mung Bean Dumplings from Julie Sahni's *Classic Indian Cooking*. Their texture is surprisingly light, with ribbons of spinach, fresh chilies, cilantro, and a little lemon or lime to flavor the batter.

Mung dal, or yellow split mung beans, can be purchased at an Indian specialty food store. Use a food processor or blender to grind the beans and be sure to soak them beforehand as directed. An important point: find a warm place for the batter to rest; it needs to relax. (The resting time produces lighter fritters.) The fritters can be made an hour or two in advance and held in a warming oven. Serve as an appetizer with Mint-Cilantro Sauce (page 339).

1 cup dried yellow split mung beans (mung dal), about 6 ounces
½ cup water
¼ bunch of spinach, stems removed, washed and thinly sliced, about ½ cup packed
2 tablespoons chopped cilantro
2 jalapeño or other fresh green chilies, seeded and thinly sliced
⅛ teaspoon baking powder
¾ teaspoon salt
1 tablespoon fresh lemon or lime juice
½ teaspoon lemon or lime zest
Peanut or light vegetable oil for frying

Sort and rinse the beans. Place them in a bowl with enough water to cover the beans by at least 1½ inches and soak for 4 hours. Drain and rinse.

To use a food processor: Blend the beans with ½ cup water, stopping the machine every 20 seconds and scraping the sides regularly. It will take about 5 minutes to make a smooth paste.

To use a blender: Blend the beans with ½ cup water. You will have to stop the machine every few minutes to scrape down the sides and push the paste from the blades with a rubber spatula. Blend until the paste is perfectly smooth, about 5 minutes. It should be fairly thick, like muffin batter.

Cover the bowl and let the paste rest in a warm place for at least 2 hours. Resting the paste will allow it to ferment and cause it to rise, producing a lighter, fluffier texture.

When you're ready to fry the dumplings, stir in the spinach, cilantro, chilies, baking powder, salt, juice, and zest. Do not overmix.

Fill a skillet with 2 inches of oil and heat it until it is very hot but not smoking, 300°F to 325°F. Have a slotted spoon and paper towels ready. Drop a heaped teaspoon of the bean mixture into the oil. You can fry 8 to 12 dumplings at a time in a large skillet. Fry, stirring and turning, until the dumplings are light golden, 4 to 5 minutes, then remove them from the pan and drain them on the paper towels. Keep the first batch of dumplings in a warming oven while you fry the remaining dumplings.

MAKES 16 TO 18 FRITTERS; SERVES FOUR TO SIX

Serving Suggestion: Since the fritters can be made in advance and reheated, they're ideal for entertaining. For a satisfying Indian meal, follow the fritters with Summer Vegetables with Red Curry (page 188) or Spring Vegetable Curry with Sri Lankan Spices (page 186).

Spinach Cakes with Shiitake Mushrooms and Goat Cheese

These delectable cakes are a favorite winter dish. The tangy goat cheese works well with the flavors of the spinach, shiitake mushrooms, and fresh scallions. Be sure to use a light-tasting goat cheese such as Montrachet; a strong goaty flavor will overpower the cakes. Serve the cakes as an appetizer or make larger cakes and serve them as an entrée. Serve with room-temperature Salsa Verde (page 336) or simply garnish with crème fraîche (page 359).

2 tablespoons light olive oil
½ pound fresh shiitake mushrooms, stems removed, sliced ¼ inch thick (save the stems for stock)
Salt and pepper
3 garlic cloves, finely chopped
2 scallions, both white and green parts, thinly sliced
1 bunch of spinach, stems removed, thoroughly washed, about 8 cups packed
2 eggs, separated
½ pound ricotta cheese, about 1 cup
½ cup milk
½ cup unbleached white flour
1 teaspoon baking powder
2 ounces mild goat cheese, crumbled, about ½ cup
Vegetable oil for frying

Heat 1 tablespoon olive oil in a large skillet and add the mushrooms, ¼ teaspoon salt, and a few pinches of pepper. Sauté over medium heat for 3 to 5 minutes. Add the garlic and scallions and cook for 1 to 2 minutes more. Transfer the mushrooms to a bowl.

Wilt the spinach over medium heat with the remaining tablespoon olive oil, ⅛ teaspoon salt, and a few pinches of pepper. Allow the spinach to cool, then squeeze out the excess liquid in small handfuls and coarsely chop. Toss the spinach with the mushrooms.

Beat the egg whites to stiff peaks. In a medium-size bowl, combine the egg yolks, ricotta, and milk. Stir in the flour, baking powder, ¼ teaspoon salt, and a pinch of pepper. Stir the vegetables and goat cheese into the mixture; fold in the egg whites.

Spoon the batter into a lightly oiled skillet or griddle over medium-high heat, making 3-inch cakes. Cook each side for about 3 minutes, until browned, turning the cakes only once. Do not flatten them with the spatula.

MAKES TWENTY-FOUR 3-INCH PANCAKES; SERVES FOUR TO SIX

Spicy Corn Cakes with Smoked Cheese and Chilies

The flavors of sweet corn, smoky cheese, and fresh chilies make this dish a summer favorite. Serve with Tomatillo Sauce (page 327) or Salsa Fresca (page 335)—the acidity and fresh taste of either sauce will enhance the flavors of these savory griddle cakes. Use more or less jalapeño chilies, depending on their heat. For spicier cakes, increase the quantity of fresh chilies or add a few pinches of cayenne pepper.

½ tablespoon light vegetable oil
½ medium-size red onion, diced, about 1 cup
Salt
3 ears of corn, shaved, about 3 cups kernels
¼ teaspoon cayenne pepper
2 or 3 jalapeño chilies, seeded and thinly sliced
1 tablespoon fresh lemon juice
2 eggs, separated
½ pound ricotta cheese, about 1 cup
½ cup milk
½ cup unbleached white flour
1 teaspoon baking powder
2 ounces smoked cheese, grated, about ¾ cup
Light vegetable oil for the pan

Heat the olive oil in a large skillet; add the onion and ½ teaspoon salt. Sauté over medium heat until soft, about 5 minutes. Add the corn and the cayenne; sauté for about 5 minutes, until the corn is tender. Add the chilies and lemon juice to the warm corn, transfer to a bowl, and allow the mixture to cool.

Beat the egg whites to stiff peaks. In a medium-size bowl, combine the egg yolks, ricotta, and milk. Stir in the flour, ½ teaspoon salt, and the baking powder, then add the smoked cheese. Stir the corn into this mixture, then fold in the egg whites.

Spoon the batter into a lightly oiled skillet over medium-high heat, making 3-inch cakes. Cook for about 3 minutes on each side, until the cakes are lightly browned.

MAKES TWENTY-FOUR 3-INCH CAKES; SERVES FOUR TO SIX

Konomi Yaki—Savory Vegetable Cakes

The subtle, delicious flavor of these Japanese vegetable pancakes is in the seasoning of the vegetables—sesame, freshly grated ginger, and cilantro are the accent flavors. Shiitake mushrooms and crispy Chinese cabbage are key ingredients, but other vegetables can be added or varied. Mung bean sprouts, thinly sliced celery, and water chestnuts are some possibilities. The batter should be very light; you need just enough egg bound with flour to coat the vegetables. Serve with Dipping Sauce (page 344).

1 tablespoon dark sesame oil
1 small head of Chinese cabbage, thinly sliced, about 6 cups
Salt
1 medium-size carrot, thinly sliced on a diagonal and cut into thin matchsticks, about
    2 cups
2 tablespoons grated fresh ginger
2 tablespoons soy sauce
1 tablespoon mirin (sweet cooking sake; optional)
4 scallions, both white and green parts, thinly sliced on a diagonal
½ pound fresh shiitake mushrooms, stems removed, sliced ¼ inch thick (save the stems for
    stock)
¾ teaspoon hot pepper flakes
2 tablespoons unbleached white flour
2 eggs, beaten
2 tablespoons chopped cilantro
Light vegetable oil for cooking the cakes
1 tablespoon sesame seed, toasted (page 263)

Heat the sesame oil in a large skillet and add the Chinese cabbage and ¼ teaspoon salt. Sauté the cabbage over medium heat until it begins to wilt, 3 to 5 minutes, then add the carrots, ginger, soy sauce, and mirin. Sauté until the cabbage and carrot are tender, about 5 minutes. Add the scallions, mushrooms, and pepper flakes and cook off the excess liquid, about 2 to 3 minutes.

Transfer the cooked vegetables to a bowl and set aside to cool. Sprinkle the flour into the eggs and mix. Pour onto the vegetables along with the cilantro and toss.

Spoon the vegetable mixture into a lightly oiled skillet over medium-high heat, making 3-inch cakes. Cook for about 3 minutes and turn. Cook for another 2 to 3 minutes. Sprinkle with the sesame seeds.

MAKES SIXTEEN 3-INCH CAKES; SERVES FOUR

Turnovers, Filo, and Tortillas

Turnovers, Filo, and Tortillas

Filo is the perfect dish for a make-ahead meal, especially for entertaining. It's fairly easy to prepare—the hardest step may be finding good filo. The filo we use is exceptionally fresh and moist—made by hand at a local family-run bakery. Look for it in specialty markets or ethnic groceries or in the freezer case at the supermarket. We layer the delicate pastry with a savory filling or roll it into appetizer-size turnovers. Either way, the filo can be assembled up to a day in advance and refrigerated until you're ready to bake it.

We like the way filo crisps and browns when brushed with butter, but you can use olive oil just as well. If using butter, keep it warm—you'll use much less of it. Be sure that the filling is moist but not wet so the filo does not become soggy. Before baking a dish of filo, chill it until the top layer is firm; then score it into serving-size pieces and bake until golden brown. This extra step will keep the filo on top from flying away when you cut into it. Once baked, a casserole or turnover will hold well in a warming oven.

Frozen filo is often difficult to handle. Thaw it in the refrigerator overnight or set it in a warm spot to thaw for a few hours. Unroll the filo, then cover with a damp towel to keep it from drying out and becoming brittle. If you have thawed filo left over, wrap it tightly and refrigerate—it will keep for a few days. If the filo is fresh, it can be refrigerated for up to five days or frozen.

Quesadillas are the quickest tortilla dish I know of—these cheese pancakes really hit the spot with spicy salsa and good Mexican beer. The freshness of the tortillas makes all the difference—ours are made in the Mission District, and they're often still warm when delivered. Be sure to check for signs of spoilage or mold when purchasing them at the market.

Enchiladas are a well-loved dish, though they require some advance preparation. If you have everything ready, including the sauce, they will go together quite quickly. The Enchiladas Rojas and Enchiladas Verdes fillings and sauces (pages 244–246) can be used interchangeably—we vary them all the time. For a delicious Enchiladas Rojas variation, cook the sauce with a piece of stick cinnamon and a little chopped unsweetened chocolate.

Pastry turnovers can be filled in many ways—be sure the vegetable filling is highly seasoned and moist but not wet, or the turnovers will be soggy. These savory pastries can be the focus of a meal or made into bite-size servings. We like the little half-moon shapes, but you can also cut the pastry into small squares and serve them as little triangles. For a lovely touch, cut scraps of dough into decorative shapes and use egg wash—a beaten egg thinned with a little water—to paste them on the turnovers. You'll still need to cut a steam vent or two to release the moisture from the filling. Like filo, turnovers can be made in advance and refrigerated until you're ready to bake them. Once baked, they hold well in a warm oven.

Pastry Turnovers with Corn, Peppers, and Chilies

We serve these spicy summer turnovers as a main course, but they also work beautifully as appetizers. Simply divide your dough into smaller portions and fill. Remember, they'll take less time to bake than the larger turnovers. If you like, make them in advance and serve from a warming oven.

Double recipe Tart Dough (page 216)
1 tablespoon light olive oil
½ medium-size yellow onion, diced, about 1 cup
Salt and cayenne pepper
1 teaspoon cumin seed, toasted and ground (page 89)
3 to 4 ears of corn, shaved, about 3 cups kernels
½ red or yellow bell pepper, diced, about ½ cup
1 jalapeño chili, seeded and thinly sliced
½ teaspoon or more Chipotle Puree (page 332)
1 tablespoon chopped cilantro
1 tablespoon chopped fresh oregano
1 egg
2 tablespoons water
1 ounce cheddar cheese, grated, about ½ cup

Follow the instructions for making turnover pastry. Let it rest in the refrigerator while you prepare the filling.

Preheat the oven to 400°F. Heat the olive oil in a large skillet; add the onion, ½ teaspoon salt, ½ teaspoon of the cumin, and a few pinches of cayenne. Sauté over medium heat until soft, about 5 minutes, then add the corn, peppers, and ¼ teaspoon salt. Sauté for 8 to 10 minutes, until the corn is tender, then add the jalapeño and Chipotle Puree. Toss in the cilantro and oregano. Add salt and cayenne or Chipotle Puree to taste.

Follow the instructions for rolling out the dough for turnovers. Make an egg wash by whisking the egg and water together. Place ⅔ cup filling in the center of each pastry circle and sprinkle with 2 tablespoons grated cheese. Brush the edge of the turnover lightly with water, then fold the dough over the filling and gently press the edges together. Crimp the edges and lay the turnover on a baking sheet. Brush lightly with the egg wash, being sure to brush the edges. Cut 3 1-inch slits in the top of the turnover. Bake for 25 to 30 minutes, until the pastry turns golden brown.

MAKES 4 TURNOVERS

Pastry Turnovers with Butternut Squash, Leeks, and Thyme

The roasted butternut squash and pleasant nutty flavor of the Gruyère cheese make this an elegant autumn dish. The squash—which can be any winter squash—is roasted with sprigs of fresh thyme until just tender, then gently tossed with the leeks. The pastry dough for these turnovers can be made several days in advance and stored in the freezer. Serve with a salad of bitter greens, pears, and toasted walnuts, tossed in a walnut vinaigrette.

Double recipe Tart Dough (page 216)
5 garlic cloves, finely chopped
2 tablespoons light olive oil
1½ pounds butternut squash, peeled, seeded, and cut into ½- inch cubes, about 3 cups
Salt and pepper
A few fresh thyme sprigs
*2 large leeks, white parts only, cut in half lengthwise, thinly sliced, and washed, about
    3 cups*
½ teaspoon dried thyme
¼ cup dry white wine
1 tablespoon chopped fresh thyme
1 egg
2 tablespoons water
2 ounces Gruyère cheese, grated, about ¾ cup

Make the tart dough, following the instructions for turnover pastry. Let it rest in the refrigerator while you prepare the filling.

Preheat the oven to 400°F. Combine 2 cloves of chopped garlic with 1 tablespoon of the oil. Place the cubed squash in a baking dish and toss with the garlic oil, ½ teaspoon salt, and a few pinches of pepper. Add the thyme sprigs, cover, and bake until the squash is tender but still holds its shape, 25 to 30 minutes. Do not overcook. Remove the thyme sprigs.

Heat the remaining tablespoon of oil in a large skillet; add the leeks, ½ teaspoon salt, a few pinches of pepper, and the dried thyme. Sauté over medium heat for about 2 minutes, until the leeks begin to soften. Add the remaining garlic and cover the pan, allowing the leeks to steam. When tender, after about 8 minutes, add the wine and cook until the pan is nearly dry.

Gently toss the squash and leeks together with the fresh thyme. Season with salt and pepper to taste. The filling should be well seasoned so its flavor comes through the pastry.

Follow the instructions for rolling out the dough for turnovers. Make an egg wash by whisking the egg and water together. Place ⅔ cup filling in the center of each pastry circle and sprinkle with 2 tablespoons grated cheese. Brush the edge of the turnovers lightly with water, then fold the dough over the filling and gently press the edges together. Crimp the edge and place the turnovers on a lightly oiled baking sheet. Brush lightly with egg wash, being sure to brush the edges. Cut 3 1-inch slits in the top of each turnover. Bake for 25 to 30 minutes, until the pastry turns golden brown.

MAKES 4 TURNOVERS

WINTER SQUASH

This noble vegetable gets us through the fall and winter each year. The names alone are wonderfully appetizing—each has its own taste and texture. Here are a few favorites.

Sweet dumpling is a small globe-shaped squash that's truly sweet, like sweet potatoes—you can roast it and eat the tender flesh right out of the skin. Butternut has a creamy flavor and a soft skin that's easy to peel, a favorite in soups and savory stews. Kabocha is a round Japanese variety that's flaky and sweet, ideal for baking. Red Kuri has a rich red-orange flesh and, like sugar pumpkins, is excellent for pies and soups. Delicata is deliciously sweet—its edible skin makes this slender squash perfect for roasting or grilling.

Winter squashes need a deep, rich, well-drained soil with plenty of organic matter. Plant the large seeds as soon as the ground temperature reaches 50°F to 60°F and keep them evenly moist. Once you have 6 to 8 fruits on a plant, remove all further blossoms so the plant will devote itself to the fruit already set. Harvest after the vines have died back or after the first light frost.

Filo Turnovers with Mushrooms and Pine Nuts

The sherry in these delicate pastries gives them a subtle sweetness, and the full, rich flavor of the mushrooms really comes through. They are wonderful served as appetizers and can be assembled ahead of time. Garnish with sprigs of watercress.

8 frozen filo pastry sheets
1 tablespoon olive oil
¾ pound white mushrooms, sliced, about 4 cups
Salt and pepper
3 garlic cloves, finely chopped
¼ cup dry sherry
1 ounce Parmesan cheese, grated, about ⅓ cup
1 tablespoon chopped parsley
⅓ cup pine nuts, toasted and coarsely chopped (page 263)
½ cup melted unsalted butter or olive oil

Remove the filo pastry from the freezer and let it come to room temperature while you make the filling. Preheat the oven to 375°F.

Heat the olive oil in a large skillet and sear the mushrooms with ¼ teaspoon salt and a few pinches of pepper over high heat until golden brown, about 7 minutes. Add the garlic and sauté for a few more minutes. The pan will be brown with mushroom juices. Add the sherry to deglaze the pan and simmer for a minute or two, until the pan is nearly dry. Transfer the mushrooms to a bowl and cool. Toss them with the Parmesan cheese, the parsley, and half the pine nuts. Season with salt and pepper to taste.

Assembling the turnovers: Unroll the pastry, remove 8 sheets, and return the package to the freezer. Keep the filo covered with a damp cloth to prevent it from becoming dry and brittle.

Preheat the oven to 375°F. If you're using butter, melt it in a small pan and set it over hot water to keep it warm as you prepare the turnovers. Lay 4 sheets of filo on the counter and place a second sheet of filo on top of each, making 4 double layers. Brush the top sheets lightly with butter and sprinkle with the rest of the pine nuts. Cut each double sheet of filo lengthwise into 3 strips.

Roll the turnovers into triangles loosely, so the filling will have room to expand during baking. Think of folding a flag. Once the ingredients are assembled, this can be done rather quickly. Place 1 heaped tablespoon of filling at the end of each filo strip, then fold over at a 45° angle to form a triangle. Repeat this step 4 or 5 times, folding on the angle until you reach the end of the filo strip. Fold under any excess filo. Brush the turnovers lightly with butter and place on a lightly oiled baking sheet. The turnovers can be refrigerated at this point for later baking.

Bake at 375°F until golden, about 15 minutes.

MAKES 12 TURNOVERS

Filo Turnovers with Spinach, Feta Cheese, and Rosemary

We serve these savory turnovers as appetizers with roasted peppers and Greek olives. The individual turnovers take time to roll, but they can be prepared in advance and refrigerated for later baking. They also hold well in a warming oven until you're ready to serve them.

8 frozen filo pastry sheets
1 tablespoon extra virgin olive oil
¼ medium-size red onion, diced, about ½ cup
Salt and pepper
3 garlic cloves, finely chopped
2 bunches of spinach, stems removed and leaves washed, about 16 cups packed
½ teaspoon finely chopped lemon zest
½ teaspoon finely chopped fresh rosemary
3 ounces feta cheese, crumbled, 1 scant cup
½ cup melted unsalted butter or olive oil
⅓ cup walnut pieces, toasted and chopped (page 263)

Remove the filo pastry from the freezer and let it come to room temperature while you make the filling.

Preheat the oven to 375°F. Heat ½ tablespoon of the olive oil in a large skillet and add the onion, ¼ teaspoon salt, and a few pinches of pepper. Sauté over medium heat until the onion begins to release its juices, about 5 minutes. Add the garlic and sauté until the onions are soft, 2 to 3 minutes more. Transfer to a bowl.

In the same pan, heat the remaining ½ tablespoon olive oil and add the spinach with ¼ teaspoon salt and a few pinches of pepper. Wilt the spinach over high heat, using a pair of tongs to toss it. Cool, then squeeze out the extra moisture a small handful at a time; it should be moist but not wet. Coarsely chop the spinach and toss it with the onions, lemon zest, rosemary, and feta cheese. Add salt and pepper to taste.

Assembling the turnovers: Unroll the pastry, remove 8 sheets, and return the package to the freezer. Keep the filo covered with a damp cloth to prevent it from becoming dry and brittle.

If you're using butter, melt it in a small pan and set it over hot water to keep it warm as you prepare the turnovers. Lay out 4 sheets of filo on the counter and place a second sheet of filo on top of each, making 4 double layers. Brush the top sheets lightly with butter and sprinkle with the walnuts. Cut each double sheet of filo lengthwise into 3 strips.

Roll the turnovers into triangles loosely, so the filling will have room to expand during baking. Think of folding a flag. Once the ingredients are assembled, this can be done rather quickly. Place 1 heaped tablespoon of filling at the end of each filo strip, then fold over at a 45° angle to form a triangle. Repeat this step 4 or 5 times, folding on the angle until you reach the end of the filo strip. Fold under any excess dough. Brush the turnovers lightly with butter and place on a lightly oiled baking sheet. The turnovers can be refrigerated at this point for later baking.

Bake at 375°F until golden, about 15 minutes.

MAKES 12 TURNOVERS

BLOOMSDALE SPINACH

There's ordinary garden spinach, and then there's Winter Bloomsdale Long-Standing, an extraordinary variety that takes spinach to another level. The distinctive flavor of its crinkly dark green leaves makes Bloomsdale a favorite for salads, soups, pizzas, pasta, or a simple dish of wilted spinach in a little olive oil with lemon and garlic.

Bloomsdale is a cool weather crop that thrives on the coast, so it flourishes in the misty fog of Green Gulch Farm. Each spring we await its arrival and are rewarded throughout the early summer months with the exceptionally delicious crop. Start from seed in the early spring and plant in rich fertile soil—keep it moist. It wants shade in summer, and by the time the big summer heat has arrived, Bloomsdale is gone.

Mushroom-Leek Filo with Gruyère Cheese and Thyme

The smooth, almost buttery flavor of leeks provides the background for rich, earthy-tasting mushrooms and fresh thyme. Sauté the fresh mushrooms over high heat, using the porcini-soaking liquid to loosen the delicious pan juices, so that the full mushroom flavor is used. Dried shiitakes will do nicely if porcini aren't available. For an elegant winter meal, serve with roasted Delicata Squash and a sauté of hearty kale.

16 frozen filo pastry sheets
2 tablespoons light olive oil
2 large leeks, white parts only, cut in half lengthwise, sliced, and washed, about 3 cups
¼ teaspoon dried thyme
Salt and pepper
5 garlic cloves, finely chopped
¼ cup dry white wine
¼ ounce dried porcini, soaked in ½ cup warm water for 10 minutes
¾ pound white mushrooms, sliced, about 4 cups
1 tablespoon chopped fresh thyme
1 pound ricotta cheese, about 2 cups
2 eggs, beaten
2 ounces Parmesan cheese, grated, about ⅔ cup
6 tablespoons unsalted butter or light olive oil
½ cup almonds, toasted (page 263) and finely chopped
2 ounces Gruyère cheese, grated, about ¾ cup

Remove the filo pastry from the freezer and let it come to room temperature while you make the filling. Heat 1 tablespoon of the olive oil in a large skillet and add the leeks, dried thyme, ½ teaspoon salt, and a few pinches of pepper. Cover the pan and steam the leeks over medium heat for 4 to 5 minutes. Add half the garlic and cook for 2 minutes. Add the white wine to deglaze the pan and simmer for a minute or two, until the pan is nearly dry. Transfer the leeks to a bowl.

Pour the porcini into a fine strainer and save the liquid to use later. (If the liquid is sandy, let the sand settle and carefully pour off the liquid.) Chop the porcini, discarding any pieces that are gritty or hard.

Heat the remaining tablespoon of oil in the skillet and sauté the fresh mushrooms and porcini over high heat with ¼ teaspoon salt and a few pinches of pepper. When the mushrooms are golden, in about 6 to 8 minutes, add the remaining garlic and sauté for 1 minute. The pan will be browned; use the porcini-soaking liquid to loosen the mushroom juices. Toss the leeks and mushrooms together with the fresh thyme. Season to taste with salt and pepper.

Place the ricotta in a bowl; add the eggs, ½ teaspoon salt, ⅛ teaspoon pepper, and half the Parmesan cheese. Mix thoroughly.

Preheat the oven to 375°F. If you're using butter, melt it in a small pan and set it over hot water to keep it warm as you layer the filo. Unfold the dough, lay it on the counter, and cover with a damp towel to keep it from becoming dry and brittle. Butter the bottom of a 9- by 13-inch baking dish and lay down a sheet of filo, brushing it lightly with butter and sprinkling with some of the nuts. Continue layering this way with 7 more sheets of filo, using half the nuts. Spread the ricotta custard on the filo, followed by the vegetables. Toss the Gruyère and remaining Parmesan cheese together and sprinkle over the vegetables. Layer on 8 more sheets of filo, lightly brushing each with butter and sprinkling with the remaining nuts. Brush the top layer thoroughly with butter.

Refrigerate the filo for 10 minutes to chill the top layer. If necessary, cut around the edges of the pan to remove any excess dough. Cut the filo into 6 squares and cut each square into 2 triangles. (It's best to cut the portions before baking, because the filo will be flaky and difficult to cut afterward.) Bake for 35 to 40 minutes, until golden.

MAKES ONE 9- BY 13-INCH FILO PASTRY; SERVES SIX

THYME

This abundant herb has an Old World association with happiness and courage. We use it year-round, both fresh and dried. Its deep earthy flavor blends subtly with mushrooms, domestic and wild. Thyme adds rich complexity to potatoes and leeks, brothy soups, and bubbling gratins. For a bit of savor, sprinkle it over crusty croutons spread with goat cheese and heat them under the broiler until golden. Bundle a few sprigs together and simmer in a hearty mushroom stew with butternut squash, pearl onions, and red-veined ribbons of chard.

There are many species and varieties of this semi-woody perennial herb, with foliage ranging from dark to gray green, golden to silver. A mixture of varieties makes a lovely aromatic ground cover. Lemon thyme really is lemony; the silver thymes are not only tasty but especially beautiful. English thyme is most commonly used in our kitchen—its profusion of delicate pink flowers is not to be missed—delicious tossed into a spring pasta, simply beautiful in an herbal bouquet.

More than any other Mediterranean herb, thyme loves full sun and fast-draining soil. It'll need plenty of heat to give it a strong flavor. Keep it well pinched back so it will keep producing.

Filo with Spinach, Mushrooms, Goat Cheese, and Pine Nuts

Creamy, mild goat cheese and sweet, toasted pine nuts give this winter pastry its distinctive flavor. Serve with a salad of winter greens and marinated beets tossed with a sharp sherry-shallot vinaigrette.

16 frozen filo pastry sheets
2½ tablespoons extra virgin olive oil
½ medium-size red onion, sliced, about 1 cup
Salt and pepper
6 garlic cloves, finely chopped
¾ pound white mushrooms, sliced, about 4 cups
¼ cup dry white wine
2 bunches of spinach, stems removed and leaves washed, about 16 cups packed
2 tablespoons chopped fresh herbs: parsley, marjoram, and thyme
1 pound ricotta cheese, about 2 cups
2 eggs, beaten
1 ounce Parmesan cheese, grated, about ⅓ cup
6 tablespoons unsalted butter or light olive oil
⅓ cup pine nuts, toasted and coarsely chopped (page 263)
¼ pound goat cheese, crumbled, about ⅔ cup

Remove the filo pastry from the freezer and let it come to room temperature while you make the filling. Heat 1 tablespoon of the olive oil in a large skillet; add the onion, ¼ teaspoon salt, and a few pinches of pepper. Sauté over medium heat until the onion begins to soften and release its juices, about 5 minutes; add half the garlic and cook for 3 to 4 minutes, until tender. Transfer to a bowl.

Heat 1 tablespoon of the remaining oil in the skillet and sear the mushrooms over high heat with ¼ teaspoon salt and a few pinches of pepper. Cook until the mushrooms are golden brown, about 7 minutes, then add the remaining garlic; sauté for 1 minute more. The pan will be browned with the mushroom juices. Add the wine to deglaze the pan and cook for a minute or two, until the pan is nearly dry. Add the mushrooms to the sautéed onions.

Heat the remaining oil in the skillet. Add the spinach, ½ teaspoon salt, and a few pinches of pepper. Wilt the spinach quickly over high heat, then cool and drain it. Squeeze the moisture out of the spinach a handful at a time; it should be moist but not wet. Coarsely chop the spinach and add it to the onions and mushrooms along with the fresh herbs. Season with salt and pepper to taste.

Place the ricotta in a bowl; add the eggs, ½ teaspoon salt, ⅛ teaspoon pepper, and the Parmesan cheese. Mix thoroughly.

Preheat the oven to 375°F. If you're using butter, melt it in a small pan and set it over hot water to keep it warm as you layer the filo. Unfold the filo dough, lay it on the counter, and cover with a damp towel to keep the dough from becoming dry and brittle. Butter the bottom of a 9- by 13-inch baking dish and lay down a sheet of filo, brushing it lightly with butter and sprinkling with some of the nuts. Continue layering this way with 7 more layers of filo, using half the chopped nuts. Spread the ricotta custard on the filo, followed by the vegetables. Sprinkle the goat cheese over the vegetables. Layer on 8 more sheets of filo, lightly brushing each with butter and sprinkling with the remaining nuts. Brush the top layer thoroughly with butter.

Refrigerate the filo for 10 minutes to chill the top layer. If necessary, cut around the sides of the pan to remove excess dough. Cut the filo into 6 squares and cut each square into 2 triangles. (It's best to cut the portions before baking, because the filo will be flaky and difficult to cut afterward.)

Bake at 375°F for 35 to 40 minutes, until golden.

MAKES ONE 9- BY 13-INCH FILO PASTRY; SERVES 6

PREPARING ARTICHOKES

The heart and inner leaves of artichokes are wonderfully tender once you peel away the dark outer leaves. Even the smallest artichokes have an armor of tough outer leaves to protect the nutty, sweet treasure inside. Include the stems if you like; you'll need to peel them before slicing. The stems can be sweet, like the hearts, but they're also sometimes bitter. Be sure to use a nonreactive knife to keep the cut surfaces from turning dark.

Artichokes will discolor if prepared ahead of time, unless you cover them with lemon water. To make lemon water, add the juice of 1 lemon to 2 to 3 cups water in a medium-size bowl. You can also add a few cut wedges of the squeezed lemon to the water if you like.

Trim off the tops and stem ends of the artichokes. Peel away the outer leaves, down to the tender light green inner leaves. Cut the artichokes into quarters and trim away the choke. Cut the quarters into 3 or 4 slices (or as directed in the recipe) and immediately place in the lemon water. They'll even keep overnight in the refrigerator this way, just be sure to cover the bowl. When you're ready to use the artichokes, drain them, then proceed with the recipe.

Artichoke and Sun-Dried Tomato Filo

This remarkably flavorful dish is particularly welcome in late winter, when you need a bit of inspiration and fresh spring produce is a month or two away. The delicate flavor of the artichokes mingles with the robust sun-dried tomatoes, giving the dish a fresh-from-the-garden appeal. If good Asiago cheese isn't available, you can use Parmesan instead.

16 frozen filo pastry sheets
4 medium-size artichokes, trimmed and sliced, about 4 cups (see page 241)
1 tablespoon extra virgin olive oil
1 medium-size red onion, thinly sliced, about 2 cups
Salt and pepper
5 garlic cloves, finely chopped
½ tablespoon fresh lemon juice
¼ cup dry white wine
3 sun-dried tomatoes packed in oil, drained and chopped, about ¼ cup
3 tablespoons chopped fresh herbs: parsley, oregano, and thyme
1 pound ricotta cheese, about 2 cups
2 eggs, beaten
1 ounce Parmesan cheese, grated, about ⅓ cup
6 tablespoons butter or light olive oil
½ cup almonds, toasted and finely chopped (page 263)
2 ounces Asiago cheese, grated, about 1 cup

Remove the filo pastry from the freezer and let it come to room temperature while you make the filling. Drain the artichokes.

Heat the olive oil in a large skillet. Add the onion, ½ teaspoon salt, and a pinch of pepper. Sauté over medium heat until the onion is soft, 4 to 5 minutes. Add the artichokes, garlic, ¼ teaspoon salt, and lemon juice. Sauté over medium heat until the artichokes are tender, 7 to 8 minutes. Add the wine and cook for a minute or two, until the pan is nearly dry. Transfer the vegetables to a bowl, cool, and toss with the sun-dried tomatoes and herbs. Season with salt and pepper to taste.

Place the ricotta in a mixing bowl; add the eggs, ½ teaspoon salt, ⅛ teaspoon pepper, and the Parmesan cheese. Mix thoroughly.

Preheat the oven to 375°F. If you're using butter, melt it in a small pan and set it over hot water to keep it warm as you layer the filo. Unfold the dough, lay it on the counter, and cover it with a damp towel to keep it from becoming dry and brittle.

Butter the bottom of a 9- by 13-inch baking dish and lay down a sheet of filo, brushing it lightly with butter and sprinkling with some of the nuts. Continue layering this way with 7 more sheets of filo, using half the nuts. Spread the ricotta custard on the filo, followed by the vegetables. Sprinkle with the Asiago cheese. Layer on 8 more sheets of filo, lightly brushing each with butter and sprinkling with the remaining nuts. Brush the top layer thoroughly with butter.

Refrigerate for 10 minutes to chill the top layer. If necessary, cut around the sides of the pan to remove excess dough. Cut the filo into 6 squares and cut each square into 2 triangles. (It's best to cut the portions before baking, because the filo will be flaky and difficult to cut afterward.) Bake for 35 to 40 minutes, until golden.

MAKES ONE 9- BY 13-INCH FILO PASTRY; SERVES SIX

Enchiladas Rojas

An appetizing, warming dish for a winter night. The distinctive flavors of toasted oregano and ancho chilies combined with cumin, chipotle peppers, and cheddar cheese give these hearty enchiladas a rustic character with deep, smoky undertones. Serve with fragrant basmati rice tossed with toasted pumpkin seeds or chopped almonds.

THE SAUCE

1 tablespoon light olive oil
1 medium-size yellow onion, diced, about 2 cups
Salt
2 teaspoons cumin seed, toasted and ground (page 89)
2 teaspoons dried oregano, toasted (page 89)
8 garlic cloves, finely chopped
2½ pounds fresh tomatoes, peeled, seeded, and pureed (page 95), about 4 cups, or 1 28-ounce can tomatoes with their juice, pureed
2 tablespoons Ancho Chile Puree (page 197)
1 teaspoon Chipotle Puree (page 332)

Heat the oil in a large saucepan; add the onion, ½ teaspoon salt, the cumin, and the oregano. Sauté over medium heat until the onion begins to release its juices, 3 to 4 minutes; add the garlic and sauté until the onion is soft, about 5 minutes. Add the tomatoes, chili purees, and ¼ teaspoon salt. Reduce the heat and cook the sauce, uncovered, over low heat for 15 to 20 minutes. Add salt to taste.

MAKES 1 QUART

THE FILLING

2 tablespoons vegetable oil
1 medium-size yellow onion, diced, about 2 cups
Salt
1 teaspoon cumin seed, toasted and ground (page 89)
1 red bell pepper, diced, about 1 cup
4 or 5 medium-size zucchini, diced, about 4 cups
5 garlic cloves, finely chopped
¾ pound white mushrooms, thickly sliced, about 4 cups
½ teaspoon or more Chipotle Puree (page 332)
1 tablespoon chopped fresh marjoram
1 tablespoon chopped fresh sage

Heat 1 tablespoon of the oil in a large skillet. Add the onions, ½ teaspoon salt, and half the cumin; sauté over medium heat for 5 to 7 minutes, until the onions are soft. Add the peppers, zucchini, ½ teaspoon salt, half the garlic, and the remaining cumin. Stir the vegetables together and cook for about 10 minutes, until the zucchini is soft but not over-cooked. Transfer the vegetables to a bowl.

In the same skillet, heat the remaining tablespoon of oil; sear the mushrooms over high heat with ¼ teaspoon salt. When they're golden brown, add the remaining garlic and stir. Add a little water to deglaze the pan and cook for a minute or two until the pan is nearly dry. Toss the mushrooms with the other vegetables along with the Chipotle Puree, mar-joram, and sage. Season with salt and chipotle to taste. The filling should be spicy and intensely flavored, but not too hot, unless that's your preference.

ASSEMBLING THE ENCHILADAS
Peanut or vegetable oil for frying
12 corn tortillas
6 to 8 ounces grated cheddar cheese, about 3 cups

Preheat the oven to 375°F. Fill a heavy-bottomed medium-size skillet with ¼ inch of oil; heat to just below the smoking point—the tortilla should sizzle when it touches the hot oil. While the oil is heating, lay out paper toweling on a work surface. Using a pair of tongs, dip a tortilla in the oil just long enough to heat it through, 2 to 3 seconds. The tor-tilla should still be very soft. Lay it on the paper toweling to absorb the excess oil. Repeat with the rest of the tortillas, making sure they don't overlap on the toweling. You can also layer the tortillas on top of each other, with paper towels in between.

Lay the tortillas out on a work surface. Set aside ½ cup of the cheese to sprinkle on top. Place a generous ⅓ cup of the vegetables in the center of each tortilla and sprinkle with 2 ta-blespoons of cheese. Roll the tortillas, making sure that the filling extends to the edges.

Pour 2 cups of the sauce into the bottom of a 9- by 13-inch baking dish and lay the enchiladas on the sauce. Ladle the remaining sauce over the enchiladas, and bake, covered, for 20 to 25 minutes, until they're hot and the sauce is bubbling. Sprinkle with the remaining cheese and serve.

MAKES 12 ENCHILADAS; SERVES SIX

Tip: If the sauce is acidic, add up to 2 teaspoons sugar at the end of the cooking to balance the flavors.

Enchiladas Verdes

Toasted cumin, sweet corn, chilies, and smoky cheese make this a spirited summer dish—well worth the effort. Make sure your filling is well seasoned, because the tortillas will soak up some of the flavors. For a richer finish to the tangy Tomatillo Sauce, add a spoonful of crème fraîche prior to serving. Serve with a salad of romaine hearts, avocado, and tangelos tossed with citrus vinaigrette.

THE FILLING
1 tablespoon vegetable oil
½ medium-size red onion, diced, about ¾ cup
Salt and cayenne pepper
3 ears of corn, shaved, about 3 cups kernels
2½ teaspoons cumin seed, toasted and ground (page 89)
5 garlic cloves, finely chopped
3 jalapeño or serrano chilies, seeded and thinly sliced
3 medium-size zucchini, diced, about 2 cups
3 tablespoons chopped cilantro

Heat the oil in a large skillet and add the onion, ¼ teaspoon salt, and 3 pinches of cayenne. Sauté over medium heat until the onion is soft, about 5 to 7 minutes. Add the corn, ½ teaspoon salt, the cumin, garlic, and chilies. Sauté until the corn is just tender, about 5 minutes. Add the zucchini and cook for 4 to 5 minutes, until the zucchini is tender but not soft. Set aside 1 tablespoon of the cilantro for garnish and toss the rest into the cooked filling. Add salt and cayenne pepper to taste.

ASSEMBLING THE ENCHILADAS
Double recipe Tomatillo Sauce (page 327)
Peanut or vegetable oil for frying
12 corn tortillas
6 ounces smoked cheddar cheese, grated, about 2 cups

Make the Tomatillo Sauce and set it aside.

Fill a heavy-bottomed medium-size skillet with ¼ inch of oil; heat to just below the smoking point—the tortilla should sizzle when it touches the hot oil. While the oil is heating, lay out paper toweling on a work surface. Using a pair of tongs, dip a tortilla into the oil just long enough to heat it through, 2 to 3 seconds. The tortilla should still be very soft. Lay it on the paper toweling to absorb the excess oil. Repeat with the rest of the tortillas, making sure that they don't overlap on the toweling. You can also layer the tortillas on top of each other, with paper towels in between.

Lay the tortillas out on a work surface. Set aside ½ cup of cheese to sprinkle on top. Place

⅓ cup vegetables in the center of each tortilla and sprinkle with 2 tablespoons cheese. Roll the tortillas, making sure that the filling and cheese extends to the edges.

Ladle 2 cups of the sauce into the bottom of a 9- by 13-inch baking dish and place the enchiladas in the dish. Ladle the remaining 2 cups of sauce over the enchiladas and bake, covered, for 20 to 25 minutes, until they're hot and the sauce is bubbling. Sprinkle with the remaining cheese. Sprinkle with the reserved cilantro just before serving.

MAKES 12 ENCHILADAS; SERVES SIX

Tip: Though it may seem like an extra step, quickly dipping the tortillas in the hot oil makes the tortillas softer and less likely to fall apart during baking. Be sure to have plenty of paper towels available to absorb the excess oil.

SERRANOS

These slender little chilies are usually green and sometimes tinged with orange—they're much hotter than jalapeños, though not as fiery as tiny red or green Thai chilies. Their heat has a spicy flavor—delicious in salsas, enchiladas, and eggs. We use them interchangeably with jalapeños but, because of their more intense heat, more sparingly. You may want to wear gloves while preparing serranos and other fresh chilies; they can leave your fingers stinging.

Quesadillas

These filled tortillas can be made on a moment's notice. Make them simply for a quick meal on the run or a bit more elaborately and serve them as an appetizer with Spicy Black Beans with Chilies and Lime (page 31), Jícama-Orange Salad (page 63), and Pickled Red Onions (page 399).

There's really no specific recipe for quesadillas, though a few ingredients are essential in our kitchen—fresh corn or flour tortillas, a flavorful cheddar, jack, or smoked cheese, spicy salsa, and lots of cilantro. We often brush them lightly with a puree of chipotle peppers—the heat and smoky flavor of the chipotles couldn't be better with the melted cheese and fragrant warm tortilla. Sliced avocado, tomatoes, scallions, and fresh chilies are also welcome additions. A few chopped or thinly sliced sage leaves will add an earthy dimension—on its own or combined with cilantro.

Here are just two suggestions for quesadillas—the possibilities are endless. They're both delicious with Salsa Fresca (page 335) or Tomatillo Salsa (page 334).

Flour tortillas brushed with Chipotle Puree (page 332) and filled with smoked, cheddar, or jack cheese, cilantro or sage

Corn or flour tortillas filled with sliced avocado, thinly sliced scallions and fresh chilies, cilantro, and smoked or cheddar cheese

If you're making a number of quesadillas, it's a good idea to have your ingredients all together before warming the tortillas.

Heat the tortillas in a dry skillet (cast iron is a favorite here) or brush them lightly with oil if you like, but oil is not necessary. Stack a few tortillas in the skillet, cover, and soften them over medium heat, removing the lid and turning to warm them through, being careful not to crisp them. Turn the heat off under the skillet.

Place the tortillas on a work surface and quickly fill them with grated or thinly sliced cheese, the herbs, and other ingredients. (If you're using Chipotle Puree, brush it lightly over the warm tortillas before adding the other ingredients.) Place the filling on the lower half of the tortilla, keeping the cheese close to the center, and don't use too much, or it will melt onto the skillet. Fold the tortillas over the filling and place them in the skillet. Cover the pan and cook them over medium-low heat, turning them when the first side is golden. Serve whole or cut into wedges for appetizers.

Companion Dishes:

Warm Vegetables,

Beans, and Grains

Companion Dishes: Warm Vegetables, Beans, and Grains

The vegetables in this chapter are roasted, sautéed, and filled. Many of the dishes are seasonal and reflect a particular time of year. You can vary the ingredients—using red chard or kale in place of wilted spinach or outer leaves of escarole if radicchio isn't available. When the new-crop potatoes are in, try Yellow Finn or Rosefir potatoes instead of little redskins. Buttery, smooth Calvados is just right with a sauté of apples and fennel, but if you don't have it in your cupboard, try apple cider or a splash of flavorful cider vinegar instead.

When filling vegetables, be sure to roast and season them well. You can switch the stuffed zucchini and roasted pepper fillings—we do it all the time. When peppers are at their peak in early fall, try stuffing pimientos, Corno di Toro, or Gypsy peppers instead of sweet bell peppers. For crunchy texture and extra garlic flavor, sprinkle Garlic Bread Crumbs over the filled eggplant, peppers, and zucchini.

For simple rice dishes, basmati is our hands-down favorite—this nutty, aromatic long-grain rice is grown in the Himalayan foothills and literally means "queen of fragrance." Its flavor is so rich that it barely needs to be seasoned, though butter, fresh herbs, and toasted nuts are always delicious additions. We like to cook the rice in a pot of rapidly boiling water (this technique is called free boiling), but it's also wonderful as a pilaf—sautéed in a skillet with onions and garlic, then covered in water or stock and simmered until the grains are plump and tender.

Couscous and bulgur (or cracked wheat) are quick and easy to prepare—they're precooked, so we simply cover them with boiling water or stock. Couscous is a kind of hard wheat semolina that has been ground, then moistened and rolled in flour; the little wheat grains are sometimes described as pasta. Bulgur is a whole wheat that has been boiled until tender, then dried and ground. Both are wonderfully light and distinctive in flavor.

The flavorful broth that's produced when dried beans are cooked with fresh herbs and bay leaves is what keeps the dish saucy, so don't discard it. Black and White Runner Beans, large white lima beans, and pale green flageolets are a few of the beans we use—these exceptional heirloom varieties are organically grown at Phipps Ranch in Pescadero, on the coast just south of San Francisco. Even the most flavorful beans take more seasoning than you might imagine—an extra sprinkling of salt, a dab of Chipotle Puree, or a handful of fresh herbs may be all that's needed to make their flavor transcendent.

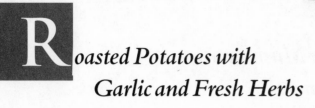

Roasted Potatoes with Garlic and Fresh Herbs

Served at room temperature as potato salad, grilled for an appetizer, or twice roasted and served alongside a savory tart or filo, these delicious potatoes are a mainstay of our menu. In the summer months we serve unusual varieties grown at Green Gulch Farm—Rosefir, Bintje, and Yellow Finn, also known as Yellow Finnish. Whole cloves of garlic and sprigs of fresh herbs add aroma, but it's the remarkable flavor of the potatoes that really comes through.

2 pounds small Rosefir, Yellow Finn, or new potatoes
Extra virgin olive oil
Salt and pepper
10 unpeeled garlic cloves
Fresh herb sprigs: rosemary, thyme, sage leaves, and oregano

Preheat the oven to 400°F. Leave the potatoes whole if small; cut into halves or quarters if large. Toss them in a baking dish with just enough oil to coat them and sprinkle with salt and pepper. Add the garlic and a few sprigs of fresh herbs; cover and roast for 35 to 40 minutes, until tender. If serving immediately, remove the herbs and season with salt and pepper to taste; or set them aside to use later.

SERVES FOUR TO SIX

Variations

Sibella's Firecracker Potatoes: For a spicy variation, toss the potatoes and garlic with a few whole dried chilies and include a bay leaf or two. As the potatoes roast, they'll take on the heat of the chilies and the pungent, earthy flavor of the bay leaf. Discard the bay leaf and chilies after roasting or include the chilies for those who dare.

Twice Roasted Potatoes: This is a great way to use leftover roasted potatoes. Preheat the oven to 450°F. If the potatoes are whole, cut them into halves, quarters, or large pieces. Toss with a little olive oil, salt, and pepper; bake in an uncovered dish until the potatoes are crisp and golden, about 20 to 25 minutes. Toss with chopped parsley or thyme and serve.

Potatoes and Shiitake Mushrooms Baked in Parchment

The summer harvest of potatoes and red garlic at Green Gulch inspired this recipe, but potatoes and garlic baked in parchment are delicious year-round. Shiitake mushrooms add their rich essence to these fragrant potato packets, though artichokes, leeks, or scallions would be wonderful as well. We've suggested a selection of herbs here, but almost any combination of Mediterranean herbs will do; if the sprigs are small, they won't overpower the delicate flavor of the potatoes.

This recipe makes one parchment package. Plan on serving one packet per person and make a few extras. For all its simplicity, this dish is always popular.

2 fresh shiitake mushrooms, about 1½ ounces
4 to 5 small Rosefir, Yellow Finn, or new potatoes, about ¼ pound
1 sheet of kitchen parchment paper, approximately 11 by 16 inches
3 or 4 unpeeled garlic cloves
1 fresh thyme sprig
1 fresh marjoram sprig, or 1 small rosemary branch
1 fresh sage leaf
½ tablespoon extra virgin olive oil
Dry white wine
Salt and black pepper

Preheat the oven to 400°F. Remove the stems from the mushrooms and save for stock. Cut the potatoes into halves, quarters, or 1-inch pieces. If the potatoes are quite small, leave them whole. Lay the parchment on a work surface and place the mushrooms, potatoes, garlic, and fresh herbs in the center. Drizzle the oil over the vegetables, add a splash or two of wine, and sprinkle generously with salt and freshly ground black pepper.

Fold the parchment over the vegetables so the edges of the paper meet. Roll the parchment tightly along the edges, forming a semicircle as you go. When you reach the end, tuck the last corner snugly under itself to seal the packet. Place the packet on a baking sheet and bake for 20 minutes. Serve immediately, while the packet is hot and filled with the fragrance of the garlic and herbs.

MAKES I PARCHMENT PACKET; SERVES ONE

Variation: Include artichoke hearts or short lengths of leeks or scallions. Leeks or scallions can be assembled on the parchment and seasoned with the vegetables, but artichokes will need to be seasoned separately. (If the leeks are large, they'll need to be cut in half lengthwise.)

Allow 2 to 3 pieces of artichoke per packet. Trim the artichokes down to the hearts; cut the hearts into quarters, or halves if small, and remove the choke. Toss with a little olive oil, salt, pepper, and a splash or two each of Champagne vinegar and dry white wine. Place the artichokes on the parchment along with the vegetables. Seal and bake as directed.

SWEET MARJORAM

This cousin of oregano has a soft, sweet flavor that's actually quite heady. Sweet marjoram grows profusely at Green Gulch, arriving at Greens' back door bursting out of recycled tomato cans from our kitchen. It's milder than Greek oregano, but don't underestimate its strength. This favorite herb gives depth and fragrant dimension to marinated beans, brothy tomato soups, and succulent eggplant dishes. Tossed into a mixture of freshly chopped herbs, its flavor is outstanding. The whole sprigs are a graceful garnish, particularly when the pale green buds are in flower.

A true Mediterranean plant, this tender perennial likes lean chalky soil sweetened with lime and full hot sun. Start your plant from a cutting or root division. Marjoram loves to be cut back hard in the height of the growing season—otherwise the soft stems will turn woody. Keep the flowers trimmed and you'll get more luxuriant growth.

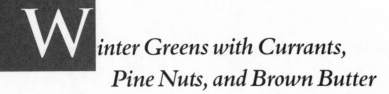

Winter Greens with Currants, Pine Nuts, and Brown Butter

The flavors of this dish are warm and soothing—it's just the right accompaniment to a hearty winter meal. The nutty sweetness of brown butter coats the leaves of spinach, chard, and kale. Plump currants and toasted pine nuts are hidden in the wilted leaves, adding little bites of sweet richness and crunchy texture.

2 to 3 tablespoons brown butter (page 331)
1 tablespoon dried currants
¼ cup hot water
6 cups kale leaves
6 cups red or green chard leaves, plus a few chard stems
6 cups spinach leaves
1 tablespoon light olive oil
1 garlic clove, finely chopped
¼ cup water
Salt and pepper
1 tablespoon pine nuts, toasted (page 263)

While the brown butter is cooking, cover the currants with the hot water to plump them. Set the brown butter and currants aside.

Prepare the greens. Tear the kale leaves away from the stems, tearing along the length of each stem. Discard the stems and cut the leaves into thick ribbons 2 to 3 inches wide. Separate the chard leaves and stems in the same way, saving a few of the stems to slice and sauté with the greens. Sort through the spinach; discard the stems and bruised or yellow leaves. Keeping the greens separate, wash and dry them in a spinner. Thinly slice the chard stems on a slight diagonal until you've sliced ¾ cup. Wash the stems.

Have everything ready before you sauté the greens. Heat the oil in a large sauté pan. Add the chard stems, garlic, water, and a pinch each of salt and pepper. Sauté over medium heat for about 1 minute. Add the kale and, using metal tongs to toss, sauté for 1 minute more. Add the chard, ¼ teaspoon salt, and a few pinches of pepper; toss over medium-high heat for 2 to 3 minutes or until the kale and chard are just tender. (The pan will be overfull when you first add the kale, but the greens will quickly cook down.) Lower the heat and add the brown butter, spinach, currants, and pine nuts; cook until the spinach is just wilted. Season with salt and pepper to taste. Serve immediately, being sure to include the sweet pan juices.

SERVES FOUR

Sautéed Apples, Fennel, and Radicchio with Calvados

The flavorful bite of radicchio and escarole blends well with the tart crispness of apples and thinly sliced fennel. A lovely sauce of reduced apple juice, Calvados (distilled apple cider), and butter coats the wilted greens and softens all the flavors. This elegant sauté is just right for fall and winter, served with Pastry Turnovers with Butternut Squash, Leeks, and Thyme (page 232). You can use dry sherry in place of Calvados, though their flavors are quite different.

1 cup flavorful apple juice
1 small head of radicchio, about 2 cups leaves
2 cups inner escarole leaves
1 tablespoon light olive oil
1 medium-size fennel bulb, quartered lengthwise, cored, and thinly sliced, about 2 cups
Salt
Five-pepper mixture or black pepper
1 medium-size crisp, tart apple, cored and thinly sliced
1 tablespoon Calvados or dry sherry
1 tablespoon unsalted butter

Pour the apple juice into a small saucepan set over medium-high heat and reduce the volume to about ⅓ cup. Set aside.

Prepare the radicchio and escarole leaves. Trim off the base and separate the leaves; keep the small leaves whole and cut the larger leaves into pieces. Wash and spin them dry.

Heat the oil in a medium-size sauté pan; add the fennel, ¼ teaspoon salt, and a few pinches of pepper. Sauté over medium heat for about 2 minutes, then add the radicchio and escarole along with ¼ teaspoon salt and a pinch of pepper. Cook for about 1 minute, until the greens are just wilted. Add the apples, juice, and Calvados; sauté for 1 minute more, until the greens are completely wilted. Turn off the heat to cool the pan. (This will keep the butter from melting and breaking.) Add the butter and toss everything together. Serve immediately.

SERVES FOUR

Wilted Spinach with Lemon and Pine Nuts

The beauty of this dish is its simplicity—we serve it throughout the year. Fruity hot olive oil coats the leaves, with a splash of lemon to brighten the flavors. For a special treat, use crinkly Bloomsdale spinach or combine with tender chard, young mustard, and beet greens. Just remember to wilt the spinach quickly, and don't overcook it.

1 large bunch of spinach, about 12 cups leaves
1 tablespoon extra virgin olive oil
1 or 2 garlic cloves, finely chopped
2 teaspoons fresh lemon juice
Salt and pepper
1 tablespoon pine nuts, toasted (page 263)

Sort through the spinach, discarding the stems and bruised or yellow leaves. Wash the spinach in plenty of cold water; if it's sandy, wash a second time, then spin dry.

Heat the oil in a large sauté pan over medium-high heat. Add the garlic and lemon juice and sauté for 1 minute. Turn the heat to high and add the spinach, ¼ teaspoon salt, and a few pinches of pepper. Wilt the spinach, tossing with tongs to coat the leaves with the hot oil and garlic. (The water left on the leaves after washing will help it to wilt quickly.) Toss in the pine nuts and add salt and pepper to taste. Serve immediately.

SERVES FOUR

Tip: Spinach wilts quickly, so if you're using a combination of greens, add the spinach at the last minute, just before serving. Add a little water to the pan to braise the greens; when they're just tender, toss in the spinach.

Sautéed Summer Beans and Cherry Tomatoes

The keys to this simple summer sauté are the freshness of the beans and the sweetness of the cherry tomatoes. Use any variety of beans you like, just as long as they're tender. For wonderful color and texture, combine two or three varieties with red and yellow cherry tomatoes. Toss with fresh marjoram, basil, or tarragon to highlight the delicious flavors.

Salt and pepper
1 pound green beans, yellow wax beans, Romano beans, or any combination of fresh beans, about 4 cups
1 tablespoon extra virgin olive oil
1 shallot, diced
1 garlic clove, finely chopped
1 to 1½ teaspoons fresh lemon juice
2 tablespoons dry white wine
½ pint cherry tomatoes, halved, about 1 cup
1 tablespoon chopped fresh tarragon, marjoram, or basil

Bring a large pot of water to a boil and add ½ teaspoon salt. Trim the stems from the beans, leaving the tail ends on. Cut them in half on a diagonal or leave whole if small. Drop the beans into the water and cook until tender, 4 to 5 minutes, depending on their size. (If you're using different varieties of beans, cook them separately, because their cooking time will vary.) Rinse under cold water and set aside to drain.

Heat the olive oil in a medium-size sauté pan; add the shallots, garlic, 1 teaspoon of the lemon juice, and the white wine; cook over medium heat for 1 minute, until the pan is nearly dry. Add the beans, ¼ teaspoon salt, and a few pinches of pepper; sauté for 2 to 3 minutes. Add the cherry tomatoes and herbs; sauté for 1 to 2 minutes, just long enough so that the tomatoes heat through without losing their shape. Season with salt, pepper, and lemon juice to taste. Serve immediately.

SERVES FOUR

Roasted Tomatoes

Roma (plum) tomatoes roast particularly well because their flesh is dense and they're not very juicy. This recipe requires very little effort, and the full, intense flavor of the tomatoes is well worth the slow roasting time. They're a truly delicious addition to pasta, soups, stews, or cannellini beans; be sure to use every drop of their sweet juice. Since they hold well for up to a week, you may want to double the recipe and use the tomatoes in a variety of dishes.

1 pound Roma (plum) tomatoes
Extra virgin olive oil

Preheat the oven to 250°F. Core the tomatoes and cut them in half crosswise. Squeeze them gently to drain their juice and remove the seeds. Place the tomatoes cut side down on a lightly oiled baking sheet. Roast for 2 hours, until the tomatoes are very shrunken. As they slowly roast, their flesh will shrink and the skin will shrivel, but they should not brown or burn. Use them immediately or refrigerate in a sealed container.

MAKES 1 CUP

Tip: Line the baking sheet with parchment paper to keep the juice of the tomatoes from cooking onto the pan. We use this technique for roasting peppers as well; it makes cleaning the pan very easy.

Brussels Sprouts and Chestnuts with Maple Butter

Roasted chestnuts, tender Brussels sprouts, and sautéed red onions absorb the rich sweetness of maple butter in this warming winter dish. Perfect for a holiday meal, this festive dish is simple to make and even easier if you roast the chestnuts in advance and freeze them.

6 chestnuts
4 tablespoons unsalted butter, softened
2 or 3 tablespoons maple syrup
1½ pounds Brussels sprouts, about 4 cups
Salt and pepper
Light olive oil
½ medium-size red onion, thinly sliced, about 1 cup
¼ cup water

Preheat the oven to 400°F.

Using a paring knife, score the tops of the chestnuts with an X. Place them in a baking dish, brush them with a little oil, and roast, uncovered for 10 minutes. Remove from the oven and cover the dish, allowing the chestnuts to steam. Let sit for 5 minutes, then peel and coarsely chop or break the chestnuts apart with your hands; you should have about ⅓ cup. Set aside.

Cream the butter with 2 tablespoons of the maple syrup. (The butter will be a little wet from the moisture of the maple syrup.) Add the remaining maple syrup to taste. Set aside.

Trim the base off the Brussels sprouts and discard any discolored outer leaves. Cut them in half or leave whole if small. If leaving whole, score the bottom with an X.

Bring a large saucepan of water to a boil and add ½ teaspoon salt. Drop the Brussels sprouts into the water and cook for 6 to 8 minutes, until tender. Their color should be bright when you take them from the water. Drain and rinse under cold water.

While the Brussels sprouts are cooking, heat 1 tablespoon olive oil in a medium-size sauté pan. Add the onions, ¼ teaspoon salt, and a few pinches of pepper. Sauté over medium heat until the onions are tender, about 5 minutes. Add the Brussels sprouts, chestnuts, ¼ teaspoon salt, a few pinches of pepper, and the water; sauté for 2 minutes, until the Brussels sprouts are heated through. Remove the pan from the heat to cool it a little. (This will help to keep the butter from melting and separating when tossed into the pan.) Add the maple butter and toss together. Add salt and pepper to taste and serve immediately.

SERVES FOUR

Roasted Shallots

Slightly sweetened with balsamic vinegar and roasted with sprigs of fresh thyme, these shallots offer a delightful accent to an antipasto, a savory filo, or an elegant pastry turnover. They're delicious served warm or at room temperature and can be roasted a day or two in advance. Peeling the shallots is a bit of work, but once that step is out of the way, the rest is effortless. Substitute a flavorful red wine vinegar for the balsamic if you like.

1 pound shallots, 3 or 4 per person, depending on size
Extra virgin olive oil
Balsamic vinegar
Salt and pepper
5 or 6 fresh thyme sprigs

Preheat the oven to 400°F. Trim off both ends of the shallots and peel them. Place in a baking dish and toss with just enough olive oil to coat them, 1 tablespoon balsamic vinegar, ¼ teaspoon salt, and a few pinches of pepper. Add the thyme sprigs; cover and bake for 30 to 35 minutes, until tender. Season with salt and pepper to taste and a splash of balsamic vinegar if needed.

SERVES FOUR

Variation: Omit the vinegar if you like or, for a stronger acidic flavor, toss the shallots with 2 tablespoons balsamic vinegar before roasting.

Balsamic Roasted Red Onions

These dark, rich onions lend a savory touch to any meal. Served warm or at room temperature, they're delicious alongside a lasagne or filo, as an element of an antipasto, or simply placed on a colorful platter. The onions are roasted whole, then brushed with reduced balsamic vinegar to enhance their natural sweetness. The roasting time will vary with their size; cook them until they're absolutely tender.

3 medium-size red onions
Extra virgin olive oil
Salt and pepper
¼ cup water
⅓ cup balsamic vinegar

Preheat the oven to 375°F. Remove the outermost layer of onion skin, rub the onions all over with olive oil, and sprinkle them with salt and pepper. Place the onions close together in a baking dish and roast, uncovered, for about 1½ hours, until tender when pricked with a fork. (The onions will release their juices while roasting and should be soft but not mushy.) Remove the onions from the pan and set aside. Add the water to the baking dish and stir to loosen and collect the pan juices; transfer to a small saucepan. Add the vinegar and cook over medium heat for 2 to 3 minutes, reducing the mixture to about ¼ cup syrup.

Cut the onions in half lengthwise and brush the cut surface generously with the syrup, allowing it to sink down into the layers. Sprinkle with salt and pepper to taste and serve.

SERVES FOUR TO SIX

Sweet Dumpling Squash Filled with Wild Rice, Golden Raisins, and Pine Nuts

This savory winter dish fills the kitchen with fragrance—sweet dumpling squash is roasted, then baked with a nutty wild rice filling. If sweet dumpling squash isn't available, use another rich-flavored winter squash, such as delicata, kabocha, or butternut. If you can't find fennel, use two celery ribs instead. Serve with Roasted Shallots (page 260) and a hearty soup of winter greens.

THE SQUASH

4 medium-size sweet dumpling, delicata, or other flavorful winter squash, about 2 pounds each
Light olive oil
Salt and pepper

Preheat the oven to 375°F. Rinse the squash, cut it in half lengthwise, and scoop out the seeds. Lightly brush the flesh with olive oil and place the squash halves cavity side down on a baking sheet. Bake for about 20 minutes, until just barely tender. The squash will finish cooking after it's filled. Remove the squash from the oven, turn it cavity side up, and sprinkle lightly with salt and pepper. While the squash is baking, prepare the filling.

THE FILLING

⅓ cup golden raisins
⅓ cup dried currants
½ cup hot water
1 quart water
Salt and pepper
1 cup wild rice
1 tablespoon light olive oil
½ medium-size red onion, diced, about 1 cup
1 garlic clove, finely chopped
1 fennel bulb, quartered lengthwise, cored, and diced, about 1 cup
¼ cup dry white wine
2 tablespoons pine nuts, toasted (page 263)
Zest of 1 orange, cut into thin threads

Preheat the oven to 375°F. In a small bowl, combine the golden raisins and currants; cover them with the hot water and set aside to plump. Bring the quart of water to a boil in a medium-size saucepan. When it boils, add ½ teaspoon salt and the wild rice. Lower the heat to a gentle boil; cover and cook until the grains are tender but still chewy, about 30 to 35 minutes. Drain the rice if necessary.

Meanwhile, heat the olive oil in a sauté pan; add the onions and ½ teaspoon salt. Sauté over medium heat until the onions are soft, about 5 minutes, then add the garlic and fennel. Heat the fennel through, then add the wine and simmer until the pan is nearly dry.

In a medium-size bowl, toss the rice with the sautéed onions and fennel; add the plumped fruit, pine nuts, and orange zest and season with salt and pepper to taste. The filling should be well seasoned.

Divide the filling among the 8 squash halves and place in a baking dish with ¼ inch water. Cover and bake until the filled squash is hot and steamy, about 30 to 40 minutes.

SERVES EIGHT

TOASTING NUTS AND SEEDS

Toasting nuts draws out their rich flavor—perfectly toasted, they release their nutty fragrance, and their color deepens to a beautiful golden brown. Walnut pieces, almonds, hazelnuts, pumpkin seeds, and pecans are easily toasted in the oven, while pine nuts and sesame and caraway seeds can be toasted in a dry skillet quite quickly. If the nuts or seeds are overly toasted, transfer them immediately to a cool surface to keep them from burning.

In the oven: Place the nuts in an ovenproof dish or on a baking sheet and toast for 8 to 10 minutes in a preheated 350°F oven. The cooking time varies from nut to nut—when they smell nutty (and they will), they're done.

Toasted hazelnuts will need to be peeled. Wrap the hot toasted nuts in a dish towel and rub them between your hands to remove the skins.

In a small skillet: This stove-top method allows you to keep an eye on quick-toasting pine nuts or sesame or caraway seeds, which can burn in the blink of an eye. Place the nuts or seeds in the dry skillet and toast them over very low heat, stirring or shaking the pan as needed, until they're golden and fragrant—about 5 minutes for pine nuts and just a minute or two for the seeds.

Eggplant Filled with Mushrooms, Sun-Dried Tomatoes, and Pine Nuts

The eggplant for this flavorful dish is brushed lightly with olive oil and garlic, seasoned, and preroasted. The overall richness of the eggplant is balanced with a complex and intensely flavored filling. Serve with tomato sauce (page 325) and grilled polenta triangles (page 278).

THE EGGPLANT

6 medium-size Japanese eggplant or 1 globe eggplant, about 1½ pounds
2 tablespoons olive oil
1 garlic clove, finely chopped
Salt and pepper

Preheat the oven to 375°F. Cut the eggplant in half lengthwise and scoop out the center, leaving a shell about ¼ inch thick. Leave the stem end on. Save enough scooped eggplant for 1 cup diced.

Combine the oil and garlic and brush the insides of the eggplant shells; sprinkle with salt and pepper. Bake cut side down on a baking sheet until the eggplant is tender, 10 to 12 minutes for Japanese or about 15 minutes for globe eggplant.

THE FILLING

2 tablespoons light olive oil
½ medium-size yellow onion, diced, about 1 cup
Salt and pepper
1 cup diced eggplant scooped from the eggplant shells
4 garlic cloves, finely chopped
¾ pound white mushrooms, thinly sliced, about 4 cups
¼ cup dry white wine
2 sun-dried tomatoes packed in oil, drained and diced, about 2 tablespoons
2 tablespoons pine nuts, toasted and coarsely chopped (page 263)
1 ounce Parmesan cheese, grated, about ⅓ cup
2 tablespoons chopped Italian parsley

Preheat the oven to 375°F. Heat 1 tablespoon of the olive oil in a large skillet; add the onions, ¼ teaspoon salt, and a few pinches of pepper. Sauté over medium heat until the onions are soft, about 5 minutes, then add the eggplant and half the garlic. Sauté until the eggplant is tender, 4 to 5 more minutes. Transfer to a bowl.

In the same skillet, sear the mushrooms over high heat with the remaining tablespoon of olive oil, ½ teaspoon salt, and a few pinches of pepper. When the mushrooms are golden brown, about 7 minutes, add the remaining garlic and cook for 1 to 2 more minutes. Add the wine to deglaze the pan and simmer for a minute or two, until the pan is nearly dry.

Chop the mushrooms and toss with the onions and eggplant. Add the sun-dried tomatoes and pine nuts. Set aside 2 tablespoons of the Parmesan to sprinkle on top and add the rest to the filling. Set aside half the parsley and combine the rest with the filling.

Mound the filling into the eggplant halves. Place the filled eggplant in a lightly oiled baking dish. Cover and bake for 20 minutes for Japanese eggplant, 25 to 30 minutes for globe eggplant. Sprinkle with the reserved Parmesan and bake for 5 more minutes, uncovered. Sprinkle with the remaining parsley just before serving.

SERVES FOUR TO SIX

JAPANESE EGGPLANT

These long, slender purple fruits can be halved lengthwise and grilled to perfection or sliced at an angle, roasted, and layered into lasagne or a tart or onto a pizza. Grilled and brushed with balsamic vinegar, they make a delectable relish with olives, roasted sweet peppers, and garlic.

Eggplant needs warm weather and a long growing season, so start seeds indoors in northern climates about 8 weeks before the last expected frost or plant purchased seedlings at the beginning of summer, when the ground is really warm. They need a rich, well-drained soil and even moisture. When the first fruits begin to appear, spread leaves around the plants and cover with black plastic to help retain moisture and warmth. Once you have several fruits going on a plant, pinch off any new flowers to speed the maturation of the fruits. Harvest when the fruits are 3 or 4 inches in diameter. Strikingly beautiful, Japanese eggplant makes a nice potted plant. If you live in an area where there's no frost all year, the plant will grow for a number of years and will need to be staked.

Zucchini Filled with Corn, Chilies, and Smoked Cheese

This pleasing summer dish is light yet wonderfully satisfying. The sweet corn and zucchini are tossed with a savory blend of toasted cumin, fresh chilies, cilantro, and smoked cheese—lively flavors to enhance the simple taste of the zucchini. Serve with Tomatillo Sauce (page 327) and grilled red onions brushed with Cinnamon-Chipotle Butter (page 332).

THE ZUCCHINI
6 medium-size zucchini, about 6 inches long
1 garlic clove, finely chopped
1 tablespoon light olive oil
Salt

Preheat the oven to 375°F. Cut the zucchini in half lengthwise, leaving the ends on. Scoop out the centers of the zucchini, leaving about a ¼-inch shell. Save the scooped flesh to add to the filling. Mix the garlic and olive oil and brush the inside of the zucchini. Sprinkle with salt, place on a baking sheet cut side down, and bake until just tender, about 20 minutes. The zucchini will finish cooking after they're filled.

THE FILLING
1 tablespoon light olive oil
½ medium-size red onion, chopped, about 1 cup
1 teaspoon cumin seed, toasted and ground (page 89)
Salt and cayenne pepper
3 or 4 ears of corn, shaved, about 3 cups kernels
3 garlic cloves, finely chopped
1 cup diced zucchini, either the scooped zucchini flesh or a new zucchini so green skin will show in filling
2 jalapeño or serrano chilies, seeded and thinly sliced
2 tablespoons chopped cilantro
1 tablespoon chopped fresh marjoram
2 ounces smoked cheddar cheese, grated, about ¾ cup

Preheat the oven to 375°F. Heat the olive oil in a medium-size skillet. Add the onion, the cumin, ¼ teaspoon salt, and a few pinches of cayenne. Sauté over medium heat until the onion is soft, about 5 minutes, then add the corn, garlic, and ½ teaspoon salt. Sauté until the corn is tender, about 10 minutes. Add the zucchini and sauté for 2 more minutes, until just tender. Transfer the vegetables to a bowl.

Toss the chilies, cilantro, marjoram, and cheese with the filling. Season to taste with salt and cayenne.

Mound the filling into the zucchini, place in a lightly oiled baking dish, cover, and bake for 25 to 30 minutes.

SERVES FOUR TO SIX

SUMMER SQUASH

This summer staple has a simple flavor that's deliciously sweet, particularly when grilled over coals or sautéed in fruity olive oil with plenty of garlic. The colors and shapes are sensational—golden zucchini and golden and green scallop squash, known to us as pattypan and sunburst, are among the most flavorful.

Summer squash needs a rich humus soil, and loves water—water goes right into the fruit. The plants are prolific, so harvest the squash while it's still young, tender, and flavorful; one rule of thumb is to harvest when the blossom has just withered. Keep a sharp eye out; a squash may be hiding under a leaf and growing into a monster. A single plant can produce enough to feed an entire family.

Roasted Peppers Filled with Eggplant, Summer Squash, and Basil

Freshly roasted peppers permeate this summer dish, balancing the eggplant and zucchini filling with their rich, sweet flavor.

The preparation of the peppers makes all the difference here—choose peppers that are firm and large enough to make 2 servings each. They're preroasted until their shape softens and relaxes. The skins will blister slightly, but don't peel them; the peppers need their skins to support the weight of the filling. Serve with Tomato Sauce (page 325) and Saffron Basmati Rice (page 274).

THE PEPPERS
3 medium-size red bell peppers
1 tablespoon extra virgin olive oil
Salt and pepper

Preheat the oven to 400°F. Cut the peppers in half lengthwise and remove the stem, seeds, and membrane. Brush the inside lightly with olive oil and sprinkle with salt and pepper. Place cut side down on a lightly oiled baking sheet. Bake until the flesh of the peppers is soft but still supports itself, about 10 minutes.

THE FILLING
1 tablespoon extra virgin olive oil
½ medium-size yellow onion, chopped, about 1 cup
Salt and pepper
5 garlic cloves, finely chopped
3 medium-size Japanese eggplant, diced, about 2 cups
3 medium-size zucchini, diced, about 2 cups
8 Gaeta olives, pitted and coarsely chopped
2 ounces Fontina cheese, grated, about ¾ cup
1 ounce Parmesan cheese, grated, about ⅓ cup
3 tablespoons chopped fresh basil

Preheat the oven to 375°F. Heat the olive oil in a medium-size skillet; add the onion, ¼ teaspoon salt, and a few pinches of pepper. Sauté over medium heat until soft, about 5 minutes. Add the garlic and eggplant and sauté for about 5 minutes, until the eggplant is just tender. Add the zucchini, ½ teaspoon salt, and a pinch of pepper and cook for 7 to 8 minutes, until the zucchini is tender. Transfer the vegetables to a bowl.

Add the olives and Fontina to the filling. Set aside 2 tablespoons Parmesan to sprinkle on top and add the rest to the filling. Set aside half the basil and combine the rest with the filling. Season to taste with salt and pepper.

Lightly oil a baking dish. Fill the roasted pepper halves with a generous ½ cup filling. Place them in the baking dish, cover, and bake for 25 to 30 minutes. Sprinkle with the reserved Parmesan cheese and bake, uncovered, for 5 minutes to melt the cheese. Sprinkle with the reserved basil and serve.

SERVES FOUR

Variation: For added crunch and texture, sprinkle Garlic Bread Crumbs (page 139) over the filled peppers along with the last of the Parmesan after baking for 25 to 30 minutes. Return the peppers to the oven and bake for 5 minutes more, until the cheese is melted.

GREEK OREGANO

Oregano, sometimes called wild marjoram, *is at the heart of Mediterranean dishes—a loving companion to eggplant, summer squash, tomatoes, sweet peppers, and basil. This pungent variety of oregano is especially prolific. Strip the flowers and leaves from the stems and chop them. For a wonderful, earthy aroma when you're grilling, throw the woody stems over a bed of hot coals. The dried leaves are delicious in a tomato sauce for lasagne or toasted and combined with ground cumin seeds for spicy Mexican dishes.*

This sun-worshiping perennial can grow 2½ feet tall in the right conditions—full sun and fast-draining soil. It spreads by underground stems and tends to colonize a whole bed. It reproduces massively and gives, gives, gives. Start plants from cuttings or division rather than seed; you'll get a stronger plant. Trim back your oregano when it flowers, then bundle the stems and hang them upside down in a warm spot to dry.

arm Cannellini Beans with Sage

Cannellini beans make their own rich sauce as they slowly simmer in their broth with onions, fruity olive oil, and sage. If cannellini aren't available, you can use Great Northern
beans instead—but creamy Pueblo or large White Runner beans are even more delicious
here. For a simple, satisfying meal, serve with crusty sourdough bread and thin shavings
of Parmesan cheese.

2 cups dried cannellini beans, about 12 ounces, sorted and soaked overnight
6 cups water
1 bay leaf
2 fresh winter savory or thyme sprigs
10 fresh sage leaves
2 tablespoons extra virgin olive oil
1 medium-size yellow onion, cut into ½-inch pieces
Salt and pepper
3 garlic cloves, finely chopped
⅓ cup dry white wine
½ tablespoon chopped Italian parsley

Drain the soaked beans and rinse them well. Pour into a large saucepan with the water, bay
leaf, savory, and 2 of the sage leaves. Bring to a boil, then reduce the heat and simmer,
uncovered, until tender, about 35 to 40 minutes. Watch them closely during the last 5 to
10 minutes to make sure the skins have softened and the beans have opened but still hold
their shape. Remove the herbs and bay leaf. Leave the beans in their broth.

While the beans are cooking, chop the remaining sage leaves. Heat the oil in a large skillet;
add the onion, ½ teaspoon salt, and a few pinches of pepper. Sauté over medium heat until the onion begins to release its juices. Add the garlic and sage; sauté for about 10 minutes, then add the wine and cook for a minute or two, until the pan is nearly dry.

Add the beans and their broth to the onions along with ½ teaspoon salt and a few pinches
of pepper. Lower the heat and cook for 20 minutes, adding a little water if needed to keep
the beans saucy. Add salt and pepper to taste. Add the parsley just before serving.

SERVES FOUR TO SIX

Warm Black Beans with Chilies and Cilantro

Black beans lend themselves to pungent spices and sweet citrus flavors. In this rustic, saucy dish, both are used to balance the heat and smoky taste of dried chilies. The bean broth is important here, so be sure to use all of it. Serve with warm tortillas and Salsa Fresca (page 335) or alongside a spicy polenta gratin (page 212).

2 cups dried black beans, about 12 ounces, sorted and soaked overnight
5 cups cold water
1 fresh oregano or marjoram sprig
3 fresh sage leaves
1 bay leaf
1 tablespoon light olive oil or vegetable oil
½ medium-size yellow onion, diced, about 1 cup
Salt
3 garlic cloves, finely chopped
1½ teaspoons cumin seed, toasted and ground (page 89)
1 teaspoon dried oregano
1 or 2 tablespoons Ancho Chili Puree (page 197)
½ teaspoon Chipotle Puree (page 332)
¼ cup fresh orange juice
Rice wine vinegar
2 tablespoons coarsely chopped cilantro
Crème fraîche (page 359; optional)

Drain and rinse the soaked beans; place them in a large saucepan with the water, oregano, sage, and bay leaf. Bring to a boil, then reduce the heat and cook, uncovered, at a gentle boil until tender, 30 to 35 minutes.

While the beans are cooking, heat the oil in a large skillet; add the onion and ½ teaspoon salt. Sauté over medium heat until the onion softens, about 5 minutes, then add the garlic, cumin, and oregano. Keep the onion on very low heat.

Add the beans and their broth to the onion with ½ teaspoon salt and the chili purees. Cook, uncovered, over medium-low heat for 20 to 30 minutes. If the beans need more liquid, add a little water to keep the dish saucy. Add the orange juice, 1 teaspoon of vinegar, and the cilantro just before serving. Add salt to taste and a splash of vinegar if needed. For spicier beans, add more of the Ancho and Chipotle purees. Garnish with crème fraîche or save a little of the cilantro to sprinkle on top.

SERVES FOUR

Pinto Beans with New Mexican Chilies

The warmth of chilies and fragrant, earthy sage flavor these saucy beans. Though this dish is meant to be spicy, it's best to check the heat of the chili purees before adding them to the beans. If New Mexican chilies aren't available, use ancho chilies. Serve with enchiladas or quesadillas (pages 244–248) or simply with warm corn tortillas.

2 cups dried pinto beans, about 12 ounces, sorted and soaked overnight
6 cups cold water
1 bay leaf
3 fresh sage leaves
1 or 2 dried New Mexican chilies, seeded
½ cup hot water
1 tablespoon light olive oil or vegetable oil
½ medium-size yellow onion, chopped, about 1 cup
Salt
1¾ teaspoons cumin seed, toasted and ground (page 89)
3 garlic cloves, finely chopped
½ teaspoon Chipotle Puree (page 332)
2 teaspoons chopped fresh sage, 5 to 10 leaves

Drain the beans and rinse them well. Place them in a large saucepan with the cold water, bay leaf, and whole sage leaves. Bring to a boil, reduce the heat, and cook, uncovered, at a gentle boil until tender, about 30 minutes. Remove the herbs and set the beans aside.

Meanwhile, cover the chilies with the hot water, soak for about 20 minutes, and puree in a blender. Heat the oil in a large skillet; add the onion, 1 teaspoon salt, and 1 teaspoon of the cumin. Sauté over medium heat until tender, 5 to 7 minutes. Add the garlic and sauté for 1 to 2 minutes more.

Add the beans and their broth to the onion along with ½ teaspoon salt, the remaining cumin, and the chili purees. Cook over medium heat for 20 to 25 minutes, stirring as needed. The beans should be saucy and soft but not mushy. If they need more liquid, add a little water. Add the chopped sage and salt to taste.

SERVES FOUR

Tofu with Sweet Ginger Marinade

A variation of Tofu Teriyaki from *The Tassajara Recipe Book*, this marinated tofu is delicious fresh or grilled with Honey-Miso Sauce (page 342) or Spicy Peanut Sauce (page 343) or served alongside Chinese noodles. The dried shiitake mushrooms are optional, but they do enrich the flavor. Be sure to use firm tofu, because it can be handled easily without breaking and holds up well on the grill. For the best results, marinate the tofu for a full day before using.

1 package of firm tofu, about 1 pound
½ cup soy sauce or tamari
¾ cup water
½ cup dry white wine or mirin (sweet cooking sake)
⅓ cup sugar
¼ cup dark sesame oil
½ ounce dried shiitake mushrooms (optional)
1½ teaspoons dry mustard
2 tablespoons grated fresh ginger
4 garlic cloves, crushed with the side of a knife

Slice the block of tofu in half horizontally or cut into slabs 1 inch thick. Place in a colander and drain for 10 to 15 minutes. While the tofu is draining, prepare the marinade. Combine all the ingredients in a small saucepan. Bring to a boil, then reduce the heat and simmer for 10 minutes.

Place the tofu in a square or rectangular nonreactive pan. If the tofu is sliced, arrange the slices close together in the bottom of the pan or on top of one another in a double layer. Pour the hot marinade over the tofu, being sure to cover it with the marinade. Cool, then cover with a lid or seal tightly with plastic and refrigerate.

The tofu will hold for a week or two in the refrigerator, as long as it's sitting in the marinade in a well-sealed container.

MAKES 1 POUND; SERVES FOUR TO SIX

*S*imple Basmati Rice

Its nutty flavor and rich aroma make basmati a favorite companion to savory stews and spicy curries. Simply seasoned or tossed with spices, fresh herbs, or toasted nuts, it lends itself to endless variations. We add a little butter, but the flavor is so full that it's fine without it. It's so easy to overcook rice—to be sure that it's done, taste it during the last minute or two of cooking.

6 to 8 cups water
Salt and pepper
1 cup basmati rice
1 tablespoon unsalted butter

Place the rice in a strainer and rinse under cool water until the water runs clear. Set aside to drain. Pour the water into a large saucepan and bring to a boil; add ½ teaspoon salt and the rice, then give it a stir. Cook the rice, uncovered, at a vigorous boil, stirring occasionally, until tender, 10 to 12 minutes. When the rice is perfectly tender, drain and immediately transfer to a bowl.

Gently toss with the butter, ¼ teaspoon salt, and ⅛ teaspoon pepper. Add more salt and pepper to taste. Serve immediately or hold in a warm oven.

MAKES 3 CUPS; SERVES THREE TO FOUR

Variations
Mustard Seed Basmati Rice: Toast ½ teaspoon yellow mustard seed (page 191) and toss with the cooked rice along with the butter, salt, and pepper.
Orange-Scented Cumin Rice: Drain the cooked rice, toss in 1 tablespoon unsalted butter, then toss with ½ teaspoon chopped orange zest, ¼ cup fresh orange juice, ½ teaspoon toasted and ground cumin seed (page 89), ¼ teaspoon salt, and ⅛ teaspoon pepper.
Saffron Basmati Rice: While the rice is cooking, steep a generous pinch or two of saffron threads in 1 tablespoon hot water. Toss into the cooked rice along with the butter, salt, and pepper. You can also season the rice with 2 or 3 tablespoons of fresh orange juice to bring out the saffron flavor.
Rice with Toasted Nuts: Toss the cooked rice with butter, salt, and pepper. Add ¼ cup toasted pine nuts or chopped toasted cashews, peanuts, or pumpkin seeds.
Herb Rice: Toss the cooked rice with butter, salt, and pepper. Add 1 to 2 tablespoons chopped parsley, chives, scallions, or cilantro. For stronger herbs, such as marjoram, oregano, or thyme, a teaspoon or two should do.

S*weet Pepper Rice*

This recipe was introduced to the restaurant by Greg, a Greens dinner chef who has a wonderful way with peppers and chilies. This colorful rice dish is ideal for a Mexican meal. The rice takes on the warm essence of sweet peppers, onions, and paprika as they slowly simmer together. Be sure your paprika is fresh so its delicious flavor comes through. Cayenne pepper adds a bit of heat, but for a spicier version, include a diced jalapeño chili or two.

1 cup basmati rice
1 tablespoon light olive oil or vegetable oil
1 tablespoon unsalted butter
½ medium-size yellow onion, diced, about 1 cup
1 teaspoon salt
1 garlic clove, finely chopped
¼ cup dry white wine
1 medium-size red or yellow bell pepper, diced, about 1 cup
1 or 2 jalapeño chilies, seeded and diced (optional)
1 teaspoon paprika
Cayenne pepper
⅛ teaspoon black pepper
2 cups boiling water
2 or 3 tablespoons coarsely chopped cilantro

Rinse the rice well and set it aside to drain.

Heat the oil and butter in a large skillet that has a tight-fitting lid. Add the onion and ½ teaspoon salt; sauté over medium heat for about 5 minutes, until the onion is soft. Add the garlic and wine and cook for 1 to 2 minutes, until the pan is nearly dry. Follow with the peppers (and the chilies if you're using them), ½ teaspoon salt, the paprika, a few pinches of cayenne, and the black pepper. Stir in the drained rice and sauté with the onions and peppers until it is heated through, about 3 minutes. Pour the boiling water over, making sure that all the rice is covered. When the water returns to a boil, reduce the heat to low, cover the pan, and cook until the rice is tender, just under 20 minutes. Gently stir in the cilantro and serve.

MAKES 3 CUPS; SERVES FOUR

Basmati and Wild Rice Pilaf

This delicious pilaf is nutty and light, infused with the subtle sweetness of fennel and a hint of lemon. Basmati rice is gently simmered with fennel, white wine, and lemon threads, then tossed with wild rice and toasted pine nuts. The rice is cooked with a minimum of water, so make sure your skillet has a tight-fitting lid and cook it slowly.

6 cups water
Salt and pepper
½ cup wild rice, rinsed and drained
1 tablespoon unsalted butter
1 tablespoon light olive oil
½ medium-size onion, diced, about 1 cup
1 medium-size fennel bulb, quartered lengthwise, cored, and diced, about ¾ cup
1 teaspoon ground fennel
1 garlic clove, finely chopped
¼ cup dry white wine
1 cup basmati rice, rinsed well and drained
Zest of 1 lemon
2 tablespoons pine nuts, toasted (page 263)
2 tablespoons chopped Italian parsley

Bring 1 quart water to a boil in a large saucepan and add ½ teaspoon salt and the wild rice. Lower the heat to a gentle boil; cover and cook until the grains are tender but still chewy, about 30 to 35 minutes. Remove from the heat and set aside, leaving the cover on the pan to keep the rice warm.

Heat the butter and oil in a large skillet. Add the onion and ½ teaspoon salt; sauté over medium heat until tender, about 5 minutes. Add the fresh fennel, ground fennel, garlic, wine, and a few pinches of pepper. Cook over medium heat for about 5 minutes, until the pan is nearly dry.

Bring the remaining 2 cups water to a boil in a small saucepan. Meanwhile, add the basmati rice to the skillet and sauté gently for 5 minutes, stirring as needed. Add the zest, then pour in the boiling water, stirring once or twice to moisten all the rice. When the water returns to a boil, cover the skillet and lower the heat. Cook over low heat for about 20 minutes, until the rice is tender. Turn off the heat. Gently mix the wild rice into the basmati-onion mixture, along with the pine nuts and the parsley. Add salt and pepper to taste. Serve immediately or hold in a warm oven until ready to serve.

MAKES ABOUT 5 CUPS; SERVES FOUR TO SIX

Almond-Currant Couscous

This nutty, aromatic couscous is quick and easy to prepare. Served under a spicy North African Vegetable Stew (page 192), it soaks up the delicious juices and adds a sweetness of its own.

¼ cup whole almonds, unskinned, toasted (page 263)
2 tablespoons unsalted butter
1½ cups instant couscous
1½ cups water
Salt
½ teaspoon cinnamon, preferably freshly ground
¼ cup dried currants

Chop the toasted almonds when they have cooled.

In a medium-size skillet with a tight-fitting lid, melt the butter. Add the couscous grains and nuts and stir over medium heat for 4 to 5 minutes, until the grains are fragrant and heated through. Turn off the heat.

While toasting the couscous, bring the water to a boil in a small saucepan. Add ¼ teaspoon salt, the cinnamon, and the currants; give it a quick stir and pour over the couscous. Cover the skillet and let sit for 20 minutes. Fluff the couscous with a fork and season with salt if needed. Serve immediately or hold in a warm oven until you're ready to serve it.

MAKES 4 CUPS; SERVES FOUR TO SIX

Variation: Use ¼ cup chopped dried apricots in place of the currants or substitute pine nuts for the almonds. You can use cumin in place of the cinnamon or omit the spices altogether.

Polenta

We feature polenta so many ways—served soft with crumbled Gorgonzola, walnuts, and basil; simply for breakfast with a pitcher of warm maple syrup; grilled; or as the primary ingredient in a complex gratin. The light texture and delicious flavor of this basic recipe make it ideal for baking or cooking on a griddle. Though the recipe calls for Parmesan, you can use other cheeses—provolone, cheddar, or smoked cheese are all good choices, depending on the flavors of the dish you're preparing.

6 cups water
1½ teaspoons salt
1½ cups coarse cornmeal
¼ teaspoon pepper
Cayenne pepper (optional)
2 tablespoons unsalted butter
½ cup grated Parmesan cheese, about 1½ ounces

Lightly oil a 9- by 13-inch baking dish and set aside. Bring the water to a rapid boil in a large saucepan. Add the salt, then vigorously whisk in the cornmeal. Reduce the heat and cook at a low boil for about 20 to 25 minutes, stirring frequently, until the grains have opened up and the polenta is smooth.

Remove the pan from the heat; stir in the pepper, a few pinches of cayenne if you're using it, the butter, and the cheese. Pour the hot polenta into the baking dish and set aside to cool. For polenta gratin, cut it into 12 squares, then cut each square into two triangles.

MAKES 24 POLENTA TRIANGLES; SERVES SIX

Tip: If you're making grilled polenta (see Variations) or a polenta gratin (page 212), you can make the polenta in advance. Allow it to cool, then cover tightly with plastic wrap. It will hold well for a day or two in the refrigerator.

Variations
To Grill Over Coals: To make a dense polenta that holds up well on the grill, decrease the water to 5½ cups. Decrease the salt to 1 teaspoon and make the polenta as directed. It does

get thick, so if you need to, add a little water, but not more than a tablespoon or two. Pour into an oiled baking dish. For grilling directions, see page 72.

Spicy Soft Polenta: Add Cinnamon-Chipotle Butter (page 332) to the polenta and serve in bowls sprinkled with smoked cheese and chopped cilantro.

Breakfast Polenta: Decrease the salt to ½ teaspoon and omit the pepper and cheese. To enrich the flavor and smooth the texture, increase the butter to 3 or 4 tablespoons. Serve the soft polenta in bowls with maple butter (page 259) or warm maple syrup.

Crisp Polenta: To serve in crisp squares or triangles, pour the soft polenta into a lightly oiled 9- by 13-inch baking dish. Allow to cool, then cut into shapes. Cook on a lightly oiled griddle or in a skillet until the edges are crisp and golden. Serve immediately.

Frittatas, Omelets, and Scrambled Eggs

Frittatas, Omelets, and Scrambled Eggs

Egg dishes are satisfying and uncomplicated, delicious any time of day. Frittatas are particularly versatile—they're great for breakfast with crispy pan-fried potatoes, for lunch or a simple supper with roasted Yellow Finn potatoes tossed with escarole hearts and a sharp vinaigrette, or savored as a leftover. These open-face omelets can be served warm or at room temperature—either way, we like to glaze them with Reduced Balsamic Vinegar when we take them from the pan—the warm frittata glistens as it soaks up the dark balsamic syrup.

We feature omelets and scrambled eggs each week for Sunday brunch and feed an enormous crowd. The menu always features an egg dish with a name that's slightly eccentric—Winds of Winter, Uprising at the Gate, Forest of Light, or Clement Street Scramble. We vary the omelets with savory and spicy fillings of vegetables, herbs, cheeses, and chilies. If you can't find an ingredient at the market, try something different in its place. Each of the recipes will fill two omelets quite generously.

Scrambled eggs are usually prepared more simply—with a sprinkling of fresh herbs and Parmesan or Gruyère, or wilted tat soi with fresh ginger and thinly sliced scallions. Scrambled eggs are often at their best with a spicy salsa. Try Salsa Fresca or Tomatillo Salsa—both have the clean, fresh taste of chilies and cilantro.

TAT SOI

This little green plant with crisp, spoon-shaped leaves and sweet, crunchy stalks comes to us from Star Route Farms in Bolinas. We also know it as Chinese flat cabbage. *The whole leaves and stems are delicious in salads and we love it sautéed with garlic, fresh ginger, and a splash of soy. In scrambled eggs with chilies and cilantro, its flavor is crisp and clean.*

Tat Soi is a hardy plant that grows well in the early spring or fall; it's so tolerant of cold temperature that it can even be harvested from under the snow. Harvest the young plants when you thin them, leaving the rest to mature to full open heads.

*S*pinach and Roasted Pepper Frittata

Roasted peppers add a lively twist to this savory Greek frittata. A hint of fresh rosemary permeates the eggs and wilted spinach, while the tangy feta cheese picks up all the flavors. Take it on a picnic or serve for a light supper with a salad of vine-ripened tomatoes tossed with fruity olive oil, red wine vinegar, Kalamata olives, and chopped garden mint.

1½ tablespoons light olive oil
2 bunches of spinach, stems removed and leaves washed, about 16 cups packed
Salt and pepper
4 garlic cloves, finely chopped
1 yellow or red bell pepper, roasted, peeled (page 55), and diced
2 scallions, both white and green parts, thinly sliced on a diagonal
1 ounce Parmesan cheese, grated, about ⅓ cup
3 ounces feta cheese, crumbled, about ¾ cup
1 teaspoon finely chopped fresh rosemary
2 teaspoons fresh lemon juice
8 eggs, beaten
3 tablespoons Reduced Balsamic Vinegar (page 345; optional)

Preheat the oven to 325°F.

Heat ½ tablespoon of the olive oil in a large skillet. Wilt the spinach over high heat with ¼ teaspoon salt, a few pinches of pepper, and the garlic. Drain and cool the spinach. Squeeze out the excess moisture a handful at a time and coarsely chop. Place the spinach in a bowl with the peppers, scallions, Parmesan, feta, rosemary, and lemon juice. Stir the eggs into the mixture and add ¼ teaspoon salt and a few pinches of pepper.

In a 9-inch sauté pan with an ovenproof handle, heat the remaining tablespoon of oil to just below the smoking point. Swirl the oil around the sides of the pan to coat it, turn the heat down to low, then immediately pour the frittata mixture into the pan. The pan should be hot enough so that the eggs sizzle when they touch the oil. Cook the frittata over low heat for 1 to 2 minutes, until the sides begin to set; transfer to the oven and bake, uncovered, for 20 to 25 minutes, until the frittata is golden and firm.

Loosen the frittata gently with a rubber spatula; the bottom will tend to stick to the pan. Place a plate over the pan, flip it over, and turn the frittata out. Brush with the vinegar if you like. Serve warm or cool to room temperature. Cut into wedges and serve.

The frittata can also be cooked entirely in the oven. Pour into a lightly oiled baking dish and bake for about 25 minutes, until the eggs are golden and set.

MAKES ONE 9-INCH FRITTATA; SERVES EIGHT TO TEN

Frittata with Caramelized Onions, Goat Cheese, and Sage

The flavors of this frittata are wonderfully appealing—the richness of the caramelized on-ions is just right with the tangy goat cheese and the pungent, earthy sage. A glaze of Re-duced Balsamic Vinegar is the final touch—brushed over the warm frittata, its sweet acidity highlights the unusual flavors.

You can caramelize the onions a day in advance, but don't be in a hurry. They'll need plenty of time to release their sugars and cook down to that wonderful jamlike consistency.

2 tablespoons light olive oil
3 large onions, about 2 pounds, quartered and thinly sliced
Salt and pepper
3 garlic cloves, finely chopped
8 eggs
1 ounce Parmesan cheese, grated, about ⅓ cup
1 tablespoon chopped fresh sage
3 ounces mild, creamy goat cheese, crumbled
3 tablespoons Reduced Balsamic Vinegar (page 345)

Preheat the oven to 325°F. Heat 1 tablespoon of the olive oil in a large skillet; add the onions, ½ teaspoon salt, and ⅛ teaspoon pepper. Sauté the onions over medium heat for about 10 minutes to release their juices. Add the garlic; continue to cook over medium heat for about 40 minutes, gently scraping the pan with a wooden spoon to keep the onions from sticking as they caramelize. (Add a little water if needed to loosen the sugars from the pan.) Transfer the onions to a bowl and set aside to cool.

Beat the eggs in a medium-size bowl. Stir in the onions along with the Parmesan and sage. In a 9-inch sauté pan with an ovenproof handle, heat the remaining tablespoon of oil to just below the smoking point. Swirl the oil around the sides of the pan to coat it. Turn the heat down to low, then immediately pour the frittata mixture into the pan. The eggs will sizzle from the heat. Crumble in the goat cheese and cook over low heat for 5 minutes, until the sides begin to set; transfer to the oven and bake, uncovered, for 20 to 25 minutes, until the frittata is golden and firm.

Loosen the frittata gently with a rubber spatula; the bottom will tend to stick to the pan. Place a plate over the pan, flip it over, and turn the frittata out. Brush the bottom and sides with the vinegar and cut into wedges. Serve warm or at room temperature.

MAKES ONE 9-INCH FRITTATA; SERVES EIGHT

Tip: We always begin cooking our frittatas on the stove, but they can also be cooked entirely in the oven. Combine the vegetables and eggs as directed, but don't add the cheese. Pour the egg-vegetable mixture into an oiled baking dish, then sprinkle or crumble on the cheese. (Adding the cheese at this point keeps it from settling and sticking to the bottom of the baking dish.) Bake for about 25 minutes.

SAGE

Often called "the herb of the heart," this silver-leafed perennial strengthens the circulatory system. The freshly chopped leaves are pungent and robust—a flavor we prefer to the strong, slightly musty taste of dried sage. Stew this savory herb with onions as they melt into a confit or roll it into focaccia dough. Whole leaves impart their earthy fragrance to a steamy packet of parchment potatoes or a simmering pot of pinto beans with spicy New Mexican chilies. The flowers are beautiful in salads.

Sage needs a hot environment, full sun, and perfect drainage. It's easily propagated by seed or cuttings and likes a lean soil. Prune it back once or twice during the growing season to keep it from getting woody. In areas of frost, trim it in early spring. Be sure not to trim it too early in the winter; new growth is prone to frostbite.

*S*weet Pepper and Basil Frittata

This delicate frittata is filled with the warmth and fragrance of summer. Red and yellow peppers are gently stewed together, then tossed with basil and creamy Fontina cheese. The eggs take on the sweetness of the peppers and their rich, rosy color. The frittata is ideal for a light meal served with roasted or grilled potatoes and a salad of garden greens.

2 tablespoons light olive oil
1 medium-size yellow onion, thinly sliced, about 2 cups
Salt and pepper
4 medium-size sweet peppers, preferably a combination of red and yellow, thinly sliced,
    about 4 cups
4 garlic cloves, finely chopped
1 bay leaf
8 eggs
1 ounce Fontina cheese, grated, about ½ cup
2 ounces Parmesan cheese, grated, about ⅔ cup
¼ cup fresh basil leaves, bundled and thinly sliced
3 tablespoons Reduced Balsamic Vinegar (page 345)

Preheat the oven to 325°F. Heat 1 tablespoon of the olive oil in a large skillet; add the onion, ½ teaspoon salt, and a few pinches of pepper. Sauté the onion over medium heat until it begins to release its juices, about 4 to 5 minutes. Add the peppers, garlic, and bay leaf; stew the onion and peppers together for about 15 minutes, until the peppers are juicy and soft. Set the vegetables aside to cool. Remove the bay leaf.

Beat the eggs in a bowl and add the onion-pepper mixture, cheeses, and basil. Season with ¼ teaspoon salt and ⅛ teaspoon pepper.

In a 9-inch sauté pan with an ovenproof handle, heat the remaining tablespoon of olive oil to just below the smoking point. Swirl the oil around the sides of the pan to coat it. Turn the heat down to low, then immediately pour the frittata mixture into the pan. The pan should be hot enough so that the eggs sizzle when they touch the oil. Cook the frittata over low heat for 1 to 2 minutes, until the sides begin to set; transfer to the oven and bake, uncovered, for 20 to 25 minutes, until the frittata is golden and firm.

Loosen the frittata gently with a rubber spatula; the bottom will tend to stick to the pan. Place a plate over the pan, flip it over, and turn the frittata out. Brush the bottom and sides with the vinegar and cut into wedges. Serve warm or at room temperature.

MAKES ONE 9-INCH FRITTATA; SERVES EIGHT TO TEN

Greek Omelet with Spinach, Feta Cheese, and Dill

Creamy warm feta is tucked into a savory spinach filling lightened with lemon and a hint of fresh dill. Delicious for breakfast, this omelet is also ideal for a light lunch or dinner, served with roasted potatoes, warmed bread, or simply served alone.

1 tablespoon light olive oil
¼ red onion, thinly sliced
Salt and pepper
1 garlic clove, finely chopped
1 bunch of spinach, stems removed and leaves washed, about 8 cups packed
Zest of 1 lemon, minced
2 teaspoons chopped fresh dill
6 eggs, beaten
¼ cup water
Butter for the pan
1 ounce feta cheese, crumbled, about ½ cup

Heat ½ tablespoon of the oil in a medium-size skillet; add the onion, ⅛ teaspoon salt, and a pinch of pepper. Sauté over medium heat for 4 to 5 minutes, until the onion is tender, then add the garlic and sauté for 1 minute. Transfer to a bowl and set aside.

Heat the remaining ½ tablespoon oil in the skillet and quickly wilt the spinach with ¼ teaspoon salt over high heat. Transfer to a colander, drain, and cool. Using your hands, squeeze out the excess moisture and coarsely chop. Add the spinach to the onions along with the lemon zest and dill. Add salt and pepper to taste. The filling should be well seasoned.

Season the eggs with ¼ teaspoon salt and a few pinches of pepper; add the water and whisk. Melt the butter in a seasoned omelet pan. When the butter is hot, add half the egg mixture. With a spatula, move the eggs toward the center of the pan as they begin to set on the edges. Tilt the pan so that the entire surface is covered again with wet eggs. As the eggs begin to set, place half the vegetable mixture in the center, then sprinkle with half the feta. Gently fold the omelet over and turn it out onto a plate. Repeat with the second omelet.

MAKES 2 GENEROUSLY FILLED OMELETS

Ratatouille Omelet

Eggplant, zucchini, and sweet peppers are sautéed in fruity olive oil, then tossed with tomatoes and basil for this traditional omelet filling. The assertive provolone and the delicately seasoned eggs work beautifully with the rich, sweet flavors of the summer vegetables.

1 tablespoon extra virgin olive oil
½ medium-size red onion, thinly sliced
Salt and pepper
½ red bell pepper, diced
1 small zucchini, diced
1 small Japanese eggplant, diced
2 garlic cloves, finely chopped
2 tablespoons coarsely chopped fresh basil
¼ pound tomatoes, cored, seeded, and chopped, about ½ cup
6 eggs, beaten
¼ cup water
Butter for the pan
1 ounce provolone or Parmesan cheese, grated, about ½ cup

Heat the oil in a large skillet; add the onion, ¼ teaspoon salt, and a large pinch of pepper. Sauté over medium heat until the onion releases its juices, about 4 minutes, then add the peppers, zucchini, eggplant, garlic, and ¼ teaspoon salt. Sauté for about 15 minutes, stirring occasionally, until the vegetables are quite tender but not overcooked. Remove the pan from the heat and stir the basil and tomatoes into the warm mixture.

Season the eggs with ⅛ teaspoon salt and a few pinches of pepper; add the water and whisk. Melt the butter in a seasoned omelet pan. When the butter is hot, add half the egg mixture. With a spatula, move the eggs toward the center of the pan as they begin to set around the edges. Tilt the pan so that the entire surface is covered again with wet eggs. As the eggs begin to set, place half the vegetable mixture in the center, then sprinkle with half the cheese. Gently fold the omelet over and turn it out onto a plate. Repeat with the second omelet.

MAKES 2 GENEROUSLY FILLED OMELETS

Cajun Omelet

The spicy filling of mushrooms, peppers, and celery is heightened by the heat of cayenne and the fresh taste of basil and thyme. The smoky cheese brings the omelet together, blending the lightness of the eggs with the intensely flavored filling.

1 tablespoon light olive oil
¼ pound white mushrooms, thickly sliced, about 1½ cups
Salt and cayenne pepper
Dry white wine
¼ medium-size yellow onion, thinly sliced
1 celery rib, thinly sliced
½ green bell pepper, thinly sliced
2 garlic cloves, finely chopped
2 tablespoons chopped fresh basil
1 teaspoon chopped fresh thyme
6 eggs, beaten
¼ cup water
Butter for the pan
1 ounce smoked cheese, grated, about ½ cup

Heat ½ tablespoon of the oil in a medium-size sauté pan; add the mushrooms and ⅛ teaspoon salt. Sear the mushrooms over high heat until golden, then add a few splashes of wine to the pan and cook for 1 or 2 minutes, until the pan is nearly dry. Transfer the mushrooms to a bowl and set aside.

Heat the remaining ½ tablespoon oil in the pan and add the onion; sauté over medium heat until it begins to release its juices, 3 to 4 minutes, then add the celery, peppers, ¼ teaspoon salt, ⅛ teaspoon cayenne, and the garlic. Sauté for about 15 minutes, until the vegetables are tender. Combine the vegetables, mushrooms, basil, and thyme; add salt and cayenne to taste.

Season the eggs with ¼ teaspoon salt and a few pinches of pepper; add the water and whisk. Melt the butter in a seasoned omelet pan. When the butter is hot, add half the egg mixture. With a spatula, move the eggs toward the center of the pan as they begin to set on the edges. Tilt the pan so that the entire surface is covered again with wet eggs. As the eggs begin to set, place half the vegetable mixture in the center, then sprinkle with half the cheese. Gently fold the omelet over and turn it out onto a plate. Repeat with the second omelet.

MAKES 2 LARGE OMELETS

Five-Vegetable Omelet with Sesame and Ginger

This surprising omelet is full of wonderfully contrasting tastes and textures. Crisp celery and napa cabbage play off the silky shiitake mushrooms and delicate eggs, while spicy ginger and hot pepper flakes bring out the clear, fresh flavors of the vegetable filling.

1 tablespoon light vegetable oil
1 large celery rib, thinly sliced on a diagonal
Salt and pepper
¼ pound shiitake mushrooms, stems removed, sliced ¼ inch thick
2 garlic cloves, finely chopped
2 teaspoons grated fresh ginger
1 tablespoon soy sauce
A handful of mung bean sprouts
2 cups thinly sliced napa cabbage
1 scallion, both white and green parts, thinly sliced on a diagonal
Hot pepper flakes
1 teaspoon dark sesame oil
1 tablespoon chopped cilantro
6 eggs, beaten
¼ cup water
Butter for the pan

Heat the oil in a large skillet; add the celery and ⅛ teaspoon salt. Sauté over medium heat for 5 to 6 minutes, then add the shiitake mushrooms and sauté for 1 to 2 minutes. Add the garlic, ginger, soy sauce, bean sprouts, cabbage, and scallions; sauté for 2 to 3 minutes, until the cabbage is wilted. Add ¼ teaspoon hot pepper flakes, the sesame oil, and the cilantro. The filling will be wet; drain off the excess liquid before you fill the omelet. Season to taste with additional hot pepper if you like.

Season the eggs with ⅛ teaspoon salt and a few pinches of pepper; add the water and whisk. Melt the butter in a seasoned omelet pan. When the butter is hot, add half the egg mixture. With a spatula, move the eggs toward the center of the pan as they begin to set around the edges. Tilt the pan so that the entire surface is covered again with wet eggs. As the eggs begin to set, place half the vegetable mixture in the center. Gently fold the omelet over and turn it out onto a plate. Repeat with the second omelet.

MAKES 2 GENEROUSLY FILLED OMELETS

Green Gulch Special

These delightful scrambled eggs are filled with rich and varied flavors—shiitake mushrooms, tofu, and peppery watercress are seasoned with cilantro, fresh ginger, sesame, and soy sauce. We grill the tofu beforehand, so use a savory smoked tofu if you can find it in a natural food store.

1 tablespoon light olive oil or vegetable oil
¼ pound shiitake mushrooms, stems removed, sliced ¼ inch thick
Salt and pepper
1 tablespoon soy sauce
1 teaspoon dark sesame oil
2 garlic cloves, finely chopped
2 teaspoons grated fresh ginger
1 large scallion, both white and green parts, thinly sliced on a diagonal
2 ounces tofu, cut into small cubes, about ½ cup
6 eggs, beaten
2 tablespoons coarsely chopped cilantro
½ bunch of watercress, long stems removed, about 1 cup sprigs
Toasted sesame seeds (page 263; optional)

Heat the olive or vegetable oil in a medium-size skillet; add the mushrooms and a few pinches of salt. Sauté the mushrooms over medium heat for 2 to 3 minutes, then add the soy sauce, sesame oil, garlic, ginger, scallions, and tofu. Sauté for a minute or two more, until the tofu is heated through.

Season the eggs with ⅛ teaspoon salt and a few pinches of pepper; pour them into the pan. Scramble the eggs over medium heat, stirring as needed to keep them from sticking to the pan. Add the cilantro and watercress for the last moments of cooking so the watercress is just wilted by the heat of the moist eggs. Sprinkle with the sesame seeds (if using) and serve.

SERVES TWO TO THREE

BOK CHOY

This Oriental cabbage has silky green leaves and a crunchy white stem. With its fine fresh flavor, bok choy is perfect sautéed with fresh ginger, chilies, garlic, and sesame oil. The broad leaves are delicious, but it's the crisp sweetness of the stems that's so outstanding.

Set out seedlings after the last expected frost. Seeds or plants can be started again in midsummer for a fall crop. Turn in a good amount of compost at planting time to help the soil hold the needed moisture.

Mexican Scrambled Eggs with Tortillas and Smoked Cheese

This Sunday brunch favorite is always a sellout—we can never prepare enough. The eggs take on the essence of warmed corn tortillas, peppers, and the spicy heat of chilies. Fresh corn is a wonderful addition, so when it's in season, try including it here. Serve with Salsa Fresca (page 335) or Tomatillo Salsa (page 334).

1 tablespoon light olive oil or vegetable oil
½ red bell pepper, thinly sliced
1 jalapeño chili, seeded and thinly sliced
Salt and cayenne pepper
1 or 2 soft corn tortillas, cut into small wedges
1 scallion, both white and green parts, thinly sliced on a diagonal
6 eggs, beaten
1 ounce smoked cheese, grated, about ½ cup
2 teaspoons chopped cilantro

Heat the oil in a medium-size skillet and add the peppers, jalapeño, ¼ teaspoon salt, and a few pinches of cayenne; sauté over medium heat for 4 to 5 minutes. Add the tortilla pieces and the scallions and sauté for 1 minute. Season the eggs with ⅛ teaspoon salt and a few pinches of cayenne; pour them into the pan. Scramble the eggs over medium heat, stirring as needed to keep the eggs from sticking. Add the cheese and cilantro for the last moments of cooking and season with salt if necessary.

SERVES TWO TO THREE

Scrambled Eggs with Fines Herbes

This classic combination of fresh herbs brings a distinctive, light flavor to the eggs, while nutty Gruyère cheese adds a touch of elegance. If your chives are blossoming, sprinkle the lavender chive blossoms over the eggs just before serving.

6 eggs
Salt and pepper
Butter for the pan
1 ounce Gruyère cheese, grated, about ½ cup
1 tablespoon chopped fresh herbs: tarragon, chervil, Italian parsley, and chives
A sprinkling of chive blossoms (optional)

Beat the eggs, then add ¼ teaspoon salt and a few pinches of pepper. Melt the butter in a sauté pan over medium heat. When the butter is hot, pour the eggs into the pan; gently stir as needed to keep the eggs from sticking. When the eggs are still a little wet, add the cheese and herbs; cook until the eggs are just set and serve, garnished with a sprinkle of chive blossoms.

SERVES TWO TO THREE

CHERVIL

The lacy leaves and mild anise flavor of this delicate herb are wonderful in egg dishes and add an elegant finish to a potato soup swirled with crème fraîche. The whole sprigs are delightful tossed into a mix of tender spring greens.

Chervil is so essential in French kitchen gardens that it's called "French parsley." Plant this feathery annual in a container inside or on the patio with cilantro and rocket. Or sow the seeds in early spring or late fall in a protected area with partial shade or filtered light. Chervil prefers cool weather and rich soil that's moist but well drained. This lovely herb reseeds itself quite readily.

Sandwiches

Sandwiches

Stock your kitchen with crusty fresh bread, a few fine cheeses, roasted peppers or juicy vine-ripened tomatoes, and a pot of basil growing on your windowsill. Then combine these simple ingredients any time of day or night and you have the makings of a fantastic sandwich. A humble slice of sourdough can make the most inspiring open-face sandwich: toast or grill it, add a thick slice of garden tomato and a leaf or two of basil, then drizzle with fruity olive oil—these fresh summer flavors are hard to beat.

Open-face sandwiches are great for entertaining—cut the bread into small slices, toast them like croutons, and finish these bite-size servings with a creamy goat cheese or Stilton, thinly sliced cucumber, and a sprig of watercress or a sprinkling of olives or chives. Little Focaccia Sandwiches are mouth-watering—they're always a hit at parties, but be prepared for an involved preparation.

At Greens we feature these sandwiches throughout the year and vary the ingredients as new ideas come our way. We hope they spark your imagination and add to your sandwich-making repertoire.

Grilled Sandwich with Mushrooms, Fontina, and Dijon Mustard

Savory mushrooms and tangy Dijon mustard make this the ultimate grilled cheese sandwich. Creamy melted Fontina is just right with these flavors, but you can use Gruyère or omit the cheese altogether. Sourdough or nutty Cracked Wheat Bread is a good choice for this sandwich. For a light supper, serve with Winter Greens with Apples, Pecans, and Stilton Cheese (page 16).

1 tablespoon extra virgin olive oil
½ medium-size red onion, thinly sliced
Salt and pepper
½ pound white mushrooms, sliced, about 3 cups
2 teaspoons chopped Italian parsley
4 slices of sourdough or Cracked Wheat Bread (page 318)
Dijon mustard
1 or 2 ounces Fontina cheese, grated, ½ to 1 cup
Unsalted butter, softened or melted

Heat ½ tablespoon of the olive oil in a medium-size sauté pan; add the onion and a sprinkling of salt and pepper. Sauté over medium heat for about 5 minutes, until soft. Transfer the onion to a bowl. Heat the remaining oil in the pan; add the mushrooms, ¼ teaspoon salt, and a few pinches of pepper. Sear the mushrooms over high heat until golden and a little crisp on the edges, adding a little water to the pan as they finish cooking, to loosen the delicious pan juices. Add the mushrooms to the onions and toss together with the parsley.

Place the sliced bread on the work surface and brush each slice lightly with the mustard. Pile the mushrooms and onions on 2 of the slices, using the palm of your hand to press them onto the bread, then sprinkle on the cheese. Press the other 2 slices on top of the sandwiches, then brush or spread the top with the butter.

Place the sandwiches buttered side down in a heated skillet or on a griddle, then brush or spread the top side with the butter. Cover and cook over medium heat until golden, about 4 to 5 minutes, then turn and cook the other side. Serve immediately.

MAKES 2 SANDWICHES; SERVES TWO

B aguette Sandwich with Roasted Eggplant, Tomatoes, and Pesto

This favorite summer baguette sandwich features vine-ripened tomatoes and pesto. There are two cheese possibilities here, both equally delicious—provolone is strong and assertive; Fontina has a mild, creamy, smooth character. Be sure to roast the eggplant until it's completely tender and season it generously with balsamic vinegar.

¾ pound Japanese eggplant, sliced ½ inch thick on a diagonal
1½ tablespoons extra virgin olive oil
1 garlic clove, finely chopped
Salt and pepper
1 tablespoon balsamic vinegar or Reduced Balsamic Vinegar (page 345)
1 French baguette
⅓ to ½ cup pesto (page 337)
½ pound tomatoes, sliced
¼ pound provolone or Fontina cheese, thinly sliced
A few lettuce leaves

Preheat the oven to 350°F. Toss the eggplant slices with the olive oil, garlic, ¼ teaspoon salt, and a few pinches of pepper. Lay the eggplant on a baking sheet and bake for 15 to 20 minutes, until soft in the center. Remove from the oven and brush the warm eggplant with the vinegar.

Cut the baguette in half lengthwise and hollow out the center. Brush both sides generously with the pesto, then lay the eggplant on the bottom in overlapping slices. Follow with an overlapping layer of tomatoes and sprinkle them lightly with salt and pepper. Place the cheese on top and follow with the lettuce. Place the top of the baguette on the sandwich and slice diagonally into 4 sandwiches.

SERVES FOUR

Variations
Using the roasted eggplant, try the sandwich with any combination of these inspiring ingredients: Basil Aïoli (page 340), rocket (arugula), watercress, roasted peppers, smoked mozzarella cheese, and pitted Niçoise or Gaeta olives.

Focaccia Sandwich: We often use the baguette sandwich ingredients to make focaccia sandwiches. They're delicious for lunch or dinner or cut into small squares or wedges and served as appetizers.

To make the sandwich from start to finish, use the Focaccia recipe on page 320. (Half of the Focaccia recipe will make 4 large sandwiches.) To make 4 sandwiches, double the quantity of all the ingredients in this recipe.

When the focaccia cools, cut it in half horizontally and lay the 2 pieces cut side up on the work surface. Brush both pieces with the pesto. Layer the eggplant on the bottom piece and follow with the tomatoes, cheese, and lettuce. Place the top on the sandwich and cut into squares, then cut each square into 2 triangles.

MAKES 4 GENEROUS FOCACCIA SANDWICHES

MUSTARD GREENS

The mottled leaves of Giant Red Mustard are best when young and tender—their appealing peppery bite becomes sharp and pungent as the leaves grow larger. Tossed with mizuna and frisée, they're delicious under a warm potato salad with capers and a tangy lemon vinaigrette. Their mustardy flavor is delightful in sandwiches.

This quick-growing plant is not fussy and needs little thinning. It's frost hardy and does well in early spring and late fall. Red mustard is not particular about soil and will thrive in a shady, cool spot. You can harvest leaves or entire plants, picking the tender young leaves for salads and letting some grow a bit longer for braising.

Baguette Sandwich with Marinated Mushrooms, Roasted Peppers, and Smoked Mozzarella Cheese

The seasoning of the vegetables is sharp and clear, with smoked cheese and nutty-tasting rocket—better known in some areas as arugula—to enhance the flavors. Use a fresh, crusty baguette and allow the vegetables plenty of time to marinate in the garlicky Balsamic Vinaigrette before you assemble the sandwich. It's perfect to take on a hike, a bicycle ride, or for a row on the Bay.

1 red bell pepper, roasted and peeled (page 55)
½ pound white mushrooms, thickly sliced, about 3 cups
1 teaspoon drained capers
8 to 10 pitted Niçoise or Gaeta olives, chopped
Balsamic Vinaigrette (recipe follows)
Salt and pepper
1 French baguette
¼ pound smoked mozzarella cheese, thinly sliced
1 cup rocket leaves or lettuce leaves

Cut the roasted pepper into slices and place in a bowl with the mushrooms, capers, and olives; toss with the vinaigrette. Add salt and pepper to taste and set aside to marinate for 30 minutes.

Slice the baguette in half lengthwise and use your fingers to hollow out the center. When the vegetables are ready, spread them on the bottom half of the baguette, drizzling the vinaigrette over both halves of the sandwich. Lay the sliced cheese over the vegetables and follow with the rocket. Replace the top of the baguette and slice diagonally into 4 sandwiches.

SERVES FOUR

Balsamic Vinaigrette

2 tablespoons balsamic vinegar
1 tablespoon sherry vinegar
5 tablespoons extra virgin olive oil
2 garlic cloves, finely chopped
½ teaspoon salt
A pinch of pepper

Combine the ingredients in a small bowl and whisk together.

MAKES ½ CUP

Variation: For something a little different, try chunks of seeded tomato in place of the roasted pepper.

SWEET BELL PEPPERS

Plump, sweet peppers are wonderfully versatile—roasted and pureed for a colorful sauce or a sweet summer soup, simply sautéed, or cut into thick slices and grilled, skins and all—we use them throughout the year. Come early fall, when the harvest is in, the markets are filled with the most extraordinary varieties.

Corno di Toro ("The Bull's Horn") have a long, curved hornlike shape that makes them perfect for roasting and stuffing. Italian sweet peppers are long and slender—their sweet flesh is just right for a sauce or a sauté. Gypsy peppers are a plump version of Italian sweets and, like Corno di Toro, can be roasted or filled. Pimientos are our favorite for stuffing. This small, late harvest pepper has a graceful taper. Its thick red flesh is deliciously sweet, but beware of its unusually tough skin—we roast them lightly and remove the skin before we stuff them.

Pepper plants like a rich, well-drained soil, some full sun, and warmth, but not too much. Transplant seedlings with care, trying not to disturb the roots. They like to be planted close together in the garden, about 12 inches apart, or in large pots. Keep them evenly moist and fertilize with fish emulsion when the fruits first appear.

Toasted Sourdough Bread with Roasted Peppers, Fontina, and Rocket

This great little sandwich is easy to prepare, particularly if the peppers are already roasted. We like to pretoast the bread so the sandwich will be crisp, since the cheese will melt quite quickly. The sharp rocket (arugula) wilts under the creamy Fontina, blending perfectly with all of the flavors.

1 red bell pepper, roasted and peeled (page 55)
Salt and pepper
1 small garlic clove, finely chopped
Extra virgin olive oil
2 slices of sourdough bread
Dijon mustard
A small handful of rocket, stems trimmed and leaves washed
2 ounces Fontina cheese, sliced or grated

Slice the pepper into strips and sprinkle with salt and pepper. Add the garlic to a little olive oil and brush it lightly over the top of the bread slices. Toast the bread under the broiler or in a toaster oven until it begins to crisp. Remove from the heat and brush with the mustard. Place a few rocket leaves and half the peppers on each slice, then cover with the cheese. Broil or toast until the cheese is just melted. Sprinkle with pepper and serve immediately.

MAKES 2 OPEN-FACE SANDWICHES; SERVES ONE OR TWO

Variation: Use Italian parsley in place of the rocket. Place small sprigs of it on the sandwich after melting the cheese, just before serving.

Goat Cheese, Pears, and Walnuts on Toasted Sourdough Bread

Perfectly ripe pears, tangy goat cheese, and new-crop walnuts are just right together on crusty sourdough bread. We serve this simple, elegant sandwich in the fall and winter with Beets with Watercress and Orange (page 56). If Red Bartlett pears are available, use them here.

⅓ cup walnut pieces, toasted (page 263)
¼ pound mild, creamy goat cheese
2 tablespoons milk or cream
Salt and pepper
1 ripe Bosc, Comice, or Bartlett pear
4 slices of sourdough bread

Coarsely chop or break the toasted walnuts into pieces with your hands.

Cream the goat cheese with the milk or cream to get a smooth, spreadable consistency. Season with salt and pepper to taste. Just before you toast the bread, halve, core, and thinly slice the pear. Lightly toast the bread and spread the cheese over the warm slices. Arrange a fan of pear slices on the cheese and sprinkle on the walnuts. Serve immediately to keep the pears from discoloring.

MAKES 4 OPEN-FACE SANDWICHES; SERVES TWO OR FOUR

Tip: If the goat cheese is very mild and creamy, the milk or cream will not be necessary. If the flavor of the goat cheese is strong, make a milder spread by creaming it with 2 ounces fresh cream cheese and 1 tablespoon milk.

Open-Face Sandwich with Gorgonzola Cheese, Tomatoes, and Basil

The delicious flavors of this summer sandwich are hard to beat. If golden or yellow tomatoes are available, use them here, alternating the colors as you lay the slices over the cheese, then sprinkle with opal or green basil. For a wonderful light meal, serve with Rosefir potato salad with fresh beans, Niçoise olives, and Balsamic Vinaigrette (page 301).

¼ pound Gorgonzola cheese
2 ounces natural cream cheese
Salt and pepper
4 slices of sourdough bread
1 pound tomatoes, cored, cut in half if large, then sliced
10 to 12 opal or green basil leaves, bundled and cut into very thin ribbons

Cream the Gorgonzola with the cream cheese and a few pinches of salt and pepper to make a soft spread. Toast the bread and spread each slice with cheese. Layer the tomatoes over the cheese, overlapping them slightly, then sprinkle lightly with salt and pepper. Garnish with the basil and serve.

MAKES 4 OPEN-FACE SANDWICHES; SERVES TWO OR FOUR

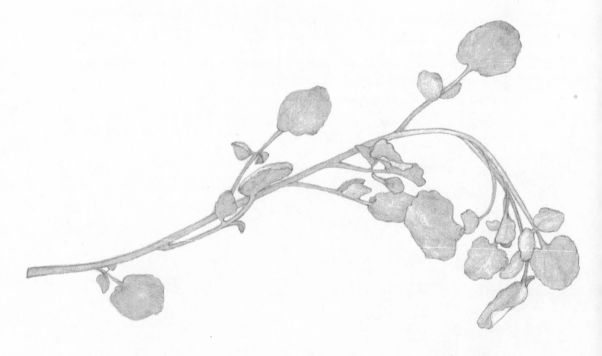

Polenta Open-Face Sandwiches

These little bites of warm polenta are actually more like croutons than sandwiches. They're great for parties—they can be prepared ahead of time, and the polenta can be made a day or two in advance. This is a delicious way to combine leftover polenta with odds and ends in your refrigerator. We've included a few of our favorite toppings here. They're not really recipes but suggestions to kindle your imagination and excite your palate.

Mexican style: Brush lightly with Chipotle Puree (page 332) or Ancho Chili Puree (page 197) and sprinkle with smoked or cheddar cheese and cilantro or sage. You can also include chopped seeded tomatoes or thinly sliced fresh chilies. Cilantro Pesto (page 338) is delicious here.

Crumbled goat cheese or Gorgonzola with toasted chopped walnuts, basil, scallions, or chives.

Crumbled goat cheese or grated Fontina with sun-dried tomatoes and basil, thyme, or small sprigs of Italian parsley. Drizzle a little sun-dried tomato oil on top.

Strips of roasted pepper, grated Fontina, and basil or a dab of pesto (page 337). Rocket (arugula) is a nice variation here—place a leaf under the cheese so it wilts as the cheese melts.

Marinated tomatoes with olives, Parmesan, or smoked mozzarella cheese and basil or other fresh herbs.

Use the polenta recipe on page 278 and pour into a 9- by 13-inch baking dish. When the polenta has cooled and set, use a paring knife or a cookie cutter to cut into rounds, triangles, or almost any shape, about 2 to 3 inches in size. Place a little topping on each, keeping it close to the center. (Save the herbs to sprinkle on after baking.) A light crumbling or grating of cheese will be plenty; more than that will make the polenta difficult to serve. Place the polenta pieces on a lightly oiled baking sheet and bake in a 400°F oven for 8 to 10 minutes, until bubbly and hot. Sprinkle with the herbs and freshly ground pepper. Serve immediately.

MAKES 20 TO 24 SMALL POLENTA SANDWICHES

Tapenade Toasts

A crusty sourdough or French baguette is best for these intensely flavored toasts. We grill
the bread whenever possible, but for the perfect make-ahead appetizer we toast the bread
instead. Remember to use the tapenade sparingly—a little taste of this olive paste is all
you'll need.

We often include these in an assortment of crostini—marinated tomatoes and basil, caramelized onions and goat cheese, sprinkled with thyme and warmed under the broiler,
and roasted Japanese eggplant with a thin slice or two of sun-dried tomato. There's a
beauty to this appetizer—the ingredients can be prepared in advance and assembled just
before you serve them.

THE TAPENADE

We make our tapenade with two or three types of olives, including Kalamata,
oil-cured, and Gaeta or Niçoise—they're tossed with capers and coarsely
chopped, then marinated with fruity olive oil, lemon or orange zest, and crunchy
fennel. Once the olives are marinated, they'll keep indefinitely in the refrigerator,
though it's best to add fresh herbs and seasonings on the day you serve the tapenade.

3 tablespoons extra virgin olive oil
¼ cup diced red onion —1/2 cup if fresh fennel isn't available
¼ fennel bulb, quartered lengthwise, cored, and diced, about ⅓ cup
¼ teaspoon ground fennel seed
1½ cups olives, pitted: Kalamata, Gaeta, green or black Niçoise, and oil-cured
1 tablespoon drained capers, rinsed
¼ to ½ teaspoon minced lemon or orange zest
1 tablespoon chopped Italian parsley
Pepper

Heat a little olive oil in a small sauté pan and add the onion, fennel, and ground fennel seed.
Sauté over medium heat until just tender, about 5 minutes.

Coarsely chop the olives and capers or pulse in a food processor, being sure to leave some
texture. Place the chopped olives in a bowl; add the onion-fennel mixture, the remaining
olive oil, ¼ teaspoon zest, the parsley, and a few generous pinches of pepper. Set aside to
marinate for an hour or more before serving. (The longer it sits, the more the flavors will
develop.) Add more zest and pepper if you like.

THE TOASTS

1 garlic clove, finely chopped
¼ cup extra virgin olive oil
16 thin slices of baguette or 4 thin slices of sourdough bread, cut into wedges or quarters
Italian parsley sprigs

Preheat the oven to 375°F. Add the garlic to the olive oil and brush the garlic oil on the bread. Place on a baking sheet and toast until crisp and lightly golden, about 8 minutes.

Spread ½ tablespoon tapenade on each of the toasts or place a small dollop on one end or corner. Place a small sprig of Italian parsley on top just before serving.

MAKES 16 TOASTS

Variation: Omit the zest and fennel. Use diced seeded tomatoes or peeled roasted peppers instead and include a mixture of chopped fresh herbs. You can also marinate the olives with whole leaves of basil or sage and small sprigs of fresh marjoram, oregano, thyme, or rosemary.

CITRUS ZEST

Zest is an accurate description of the exhilarating essence found in the colored rind of citrus fruits—we add it to pastas, vinaigrettes, tapenade, and salads of all kinds to make their flavors sparkle. A zester is a handy tool, indispensable in my home kitchen—it instantly removes the zest in long, thin ribbons. If you don't have a zester, use a fine grater instead. In a pinch, you can remove the zest with a vegetable peeler. Most of our recipes call for finely chopping the zest after it's removed from the fruit. Whatever your method, be sure to avoid the bitter white pith underneath the peel. We recommend using organic fruit whenever possible—conventionally grown citrus is heavily waxed and colored and should be well scrubbed with a vegetable brush before you zest it.

Breads

Breads

Greg Tompkins, the head baker at Tassajara Bread Bakery, wrote the recipes and the introduction to this chapter. With the help of his staff, he scaled down the large bakery recipes for home kitchen use and tested them again and again and again; they really do work. These breads are among our Tassajara favorites, and with the exception of the Sourdough Corn Rye, we serve them daily at Greens.

Bread making is a craft requiring practice, intuition, and hand skills. If you're a novice baker, we suggest you follow the recipe directions to the letter. If you've been baking bread most of your life, read the recipes, then go ahead and do what you've always done. Here are a few key bread baking tips.

Kneading: Kneading is the rhythmic motion of working the dough with the heels of your hands—it creates a home for the yeast by developing a protein structure that traps the gas the yeast produces. Make sure it's a warm home—bread will rise very slowly in the refrigerator but prefers temperatures that range from the 70s to the mid-80s. Kneading comes quite naturally once you've made a few batches of bread. Always pay close attention to the kneading time—rub the dough along the work surface, fold it back on itself, turn it 90°, repeat, and continue for 10 to 15 minutes, even though your arms may grow tired. You're far more likely to underdevelop the dough when kneading by hand than to overdevelop it.

Flour and dough: Flours vary from brand to brand, and a single brand will vary from week to week, depending on how you store it. The same dough will rise leisurely across the space of a cool morning, then spring up like a science fiction monster on a warm, humid afternoon. Whole grain doughs may leave your arms rubbery at the end of kneading, while sourdough becomes silky and elastic seemingly without effort.

Storing bread: Each of these recipes will make two loaves. Once the bread has cooled, store it at room temperature in a plastic bag or wrapped in plastic film. Sourdough will remain crustier if you store it in a paper bag, but it tends to dry out when stored this way—you may want to transfer it to a plastic bag or wrap it tightly and freeze it if you're keeping it for more than a day. Refrigerator temperatures hasten the staling process, so never store bread in the refrigerator; even a tightly wrapped loaf will stale overnight. (Staling is the result of the starch in the bread giving up its moisture—it isn't the same as drying out.) You can always simply enjoy the bread as it changes day by day—toast it for breakfast and save the last slices to make into Garlic Bread Crumbs or croutons.

Sourdough Corn Rye

This light rye bread is full of great tastes and textures. A touch of honey softens the tangy sourdough, while coarse cornmeal adds crunch to the chewy, moist dough. The rye sourdough starter is used here for flavor, but not for leavening, so the bread can be made in the space of an afternoon.

1 envelope of active dry yeast, 2¼ to 2½ teaspoons
1½ cups warm (110°F) water
½ cup rye or white sourdough starter (page 314)
1¼ cups dark rye flour
⅓ cup coarse cornmeal
2 teaspoons whole caraway seed
2 teaspoons ground caraway seed
2 tablespoons honey
2 teaspoons fine sea salt
3 cups unbleached white flour
1 egg beaten with 1 teaspoon of water

Combine the yeast and water in a medium-size bowl and stir until the yeast is dissolved. Allow the mixture to stand for 10 minutes to activate the yeast.

Stir in the starter until it is well blended. Stir in the rye flour, cornmeal, whole and ground caraway, and honey. Add the salt and 2½ cups of the unbleached flour; stir until the dough comes together enough to be kneaded by hand. Sprinkle the work surface with the remaining ½ cup flour, turn the dough out on top of it, and knead for about 12 minutes, until a firm, elastic dough has formed. Resist the temptation to add more flour than is called for. The dough should feel tacky at the end of kneading. Place the dough in an oiled bowl, turning to coat its entire surface with oil. Cover with a damp towel or plastic wrap and let rise until doubled in size.

Turn the dough out of the bowl and punch it down. Divide into 2 equal pieces and form each piece into a ball by rolling it against the work surface with your hands. Each ball should feel firm and have a small dimple where it has been worked against the work surface. Place the rounds, dimple down and well spaced, on a lightly oiled baking sheet. Cover loosely and allow to rise until doubled.

Preheat the oven to 400°F. With a single-edged razor blade or a sharp knife, lightly score the surface of the loaves. We traditionally decorate this bread with the "sunray slash": score the rounds straight across the center, then, from the starting point of the first cut, score two lines radiating outward on each side. It should look like the rays of the rising sun.

Brush the rounds with the egg wash and bake for about 25 minutes, until the loaves sound hollow when tapped on the bottom. Transfer to a rack to cool.

MAKES TWO 1-POUND LOAVES

*S*ourdough Bâtard

This chewy sourdough is the star of Tassajara's repertoire—a favorite for sandwiches, croutons, and grilling. We form the bread into a thick oval the French call a *bâtard*. The word translates as "bastard" and may have something to do with the loaves' shape belonging neither to the rounded bread family (*boules*) nor to the stick-shaped bread family (*baguettes*).

This bread is leavened entirely with wild yeast, the natural yeasts that are present in any kitchen. It has a very slow rise and is one of the most capricious breads you'll ever work with. (The dough rises overnight, then there's a second lengthy rising the following day.) The key to success is beginning with a well-aged and well-maintained starter.

> *1¼ cups sourdough starter (page 314)*
> *2¾ cups warm (110°F) water*
> *6¾ to 7 cups unbleached bread flour*
> *1½ tablespoons fine sea salt*

Stir the starter to remove any gas that may be trapped in it before measuring for this recipe. Combine the starter and water in a large bowl and stir to blend. Add 4 cups of the flour, 1 cup at a time, stirring between additions.

Add the salt and 2 more cups of flour, again 1 cup at a time. At this point the dough should be cohesive enough to turn by hand. Turn the dough out onto a lightly floured surface and knead for 10 minutes, incorporating the remaining flour as needed to form a smooth, elastic dough. Place in an oiled bowl, turn to coat the surface, cover with plastic wrap, and let rise overnight (11 to 12 hours) at room temperature.

The dough will be a little sticky after it has risen. Turn it out onto a lightly floured surface and knead briefly to make it more manageable. Divide into 2 equal pieces.

To form a *bâtard*, take one of the pieces and stretch it between your hands until it is about a foot long. Fold each end back into the middle. Press the ends into the center so that they stick. The dough should have a roughly rectangular shape at this point. Starting with the closest corners of the rectangle, roll them into the center. Continue rolling, forcing the outside into the center, until you wind up with a loaf that resembles a fat football. Find the loaf's seam and seal it by pinching the edges of the dough together. Finally, roll the *bâtard* back and forth on the work surface with your hands at the ends of the loaf to taper and smooth it. Repeat with the second loaf.

Place the *bâtards* on a floured surface, cover with a damp towel, and let rise at room temperature for 2½ to 3 hours, until doubled in size.

Preheat the oven to 450°F. Place 2 cups of water in a shallow pan or pie plate on the lowest rack of the oven while it preheats. Transfer the *bâtards* to a baking sheet, being careful to space them adequately. With a single-edged razor (or a sharp knife), score each loaf ¼ inch deep along its length. Brush with water and bake for 15 minutes. Using a spray bottle, mist the oven with water every 5 minutes during this period.

At the end of 15 minutes, remove the pan of water from the oven, brush the loaves with water, and lower the oven temperature to 375°F. Return to the oven and bake for about 40 minutes, until the loaves sound hollow when tapped on the bottom. Transfer to a rack to cool.

MAKES TWO 1½-POUND LOAVES

Sourdough French Variation: We make another sourdough that is similar to the preceding recipe but contains a small amount of whole wheat flour. We call it Sourdough French because the addition of whole wheat flour mimics the darker bread flours available to European bakers. This recipe uses a whole wheat sourdough starter but is put together in exactly the same way with unbleached white flour. You can also use sourdough starter (page 314) made with unbleached white flour.

1 cup whole wheat sourdough starter (page 315)
3 cups warm (110°F) water
1 cup stone-ground whole wheat flour
6¼ to 7¼ cups unbleached white flour
2 tablespoons fine sea salt

*S*ourdough Starter

A starter is a perpetual colony of leavening. The sponges used in the other recipes in this chapter are created and consumed each time the bread is made. A starter can be something as elaborate and painstakingly maintained as a bubbling crock of sourdough starter or as simple as a portion of each day's dough held back and added to the following day's baking.

A true sourdough starter is made by encouraging the growth of wild yeast and benign bacteria in a simple flour and water dough. It is these bacteria that produce the acid, or combinations of acids, that sours the starter.

To make sourdough bread, a portion of the starter is added when the dough is made. The yeasts and bacteria in the starter leaven and sour the finished product. Wild yeasts are ubiquitous, but the bacteria that produce the acids are different from region to region. A Des Moines sourdough won't taste like a San Francisco sourdough for just that reason. And because a sourdough starter must be refreshed periodically, a San Francisco starter taken to Des Moines quickly becomes a Des Moines starter as local ingredients are used to feed it.

There are two main issues in the production of any sourdough starter: how to get the wild yeast and bacteria into it in the first place and how to maintain a starter of constant strength.

The yeast and bacteria necessary to produce a sourdough starter are naturally present in the flour you use every day. Encouraging their growth from a mixture of that flour is tricky, however, and requires careful attention to the water content of the starter as well as the temperature of its environment. A simpler way of getting started is to take advantage of the yeasts that are naturally present on the skin of grapes or, as in the recipe below, the raisins made from those grapes. Begin with:

½ pound organic raisins
3 cups water

It's important to use organic raisins, which will not have been treated with any preservatives or antifungal chemicals. Combine the raisins and water in a bowl and squeeze the raisins until the water turns a muddy brown. This releases sugars that will act as food for the wild yeast over the next few days.

Cover the bowl loosely and set aside at room temperature for 2 or 3 days. At this point the liquid in the bowl should be foamy or will effervesce slightly when the bowl is shaken; this is carbonation caused by the yeast. There may also be some patches of mold floating on top of the raisins, because the conditions for growing yeast are also ideal for mold growth. The mold will be on the surface only and can easily be scooped off with a spoon. Drain and discard the raisins, reserving the raisin water. Combine:

2 cups raisin water
1½ pounds unbleached white flour, about 6 cups

Beat the raisin water and the flour together in a bowl until a soft, sticky dough has formed. Transfer to a container at least 3 times its volume and cover lightly. Let the dough ferment at room temperature for 24 hours, then refrigerate for 24 hours. The dough will swell and bubble; if it looks like it will overflow the container, punch it down and allow it to continue to ferment. After 24 hours in the refrigerator, refresh the starter as follows:

1 pound starter, about 2 cups (discard any remaining starter)
2 cups water
1½ pounds unbleached flour, about 6 cups

Combine the ingredients in a bowl and beat until a soft, sticky dough forms. Allow to ferment at room temperature for 24 hours, then refrigerate for at least 3 days. At this point the starter is ready to use.

Initially the starter and the bread made from it won't be very sour. It takes several refreshings, over a period of about a year, for the starter to begin to resemble (and smell like) what you would expect a sourdough starter to be. It is because of this lengthy initial start-up period that existing starters are so lovingly maintained and passed on from baker to baker. To use and maintain your starter, follow these simple guidelines:

Keep the starter refrigerated. Allow it to come to room temperature before using.
Use unrefreshed starter when making a batch of sourdough bread.
Refresh the starter after every use, but at least once every three weeks.

To refresh, or feed, a starter, you add flour and water to the existing starter. To maintain a starter of constant strength, use these porportions (by weight):

1 part starter
1 part water
1½ parts unbleached white flour

Combine the starter, water, and flour and proceed as directed. Let the refreshed starter ferment at room temperature overnight, then refrigerate for at least 3 days before using.

Variations: At Tassajara, we have three different sourdough starters—white, wheat, and rye. This recipe produces a white starter. To produce a wheat starter, follow the preceding directions, but use fine whole wheat flour in place of the unbleached white to refresh the starter. The starter will not rise as much and will be much pastier when properly fermented. It will also be a bit more sour than the white.

To produce our rye starter, refresh the starter with a half-and-half mixture of rye and fine whole wheat flours.

Viennese Five-Grain Bread

A great bread for sandwiches, filled with hearty grains and seeds. The dough is a joy to work with—its texture is surprisingly light. This is actually a four-grain/three-seed bread and perhaps unknown in Vienna, but we like the sound of Viennese Five-Grain Bread. Whatever you decide to call it, it makes some of the best toast you'll ever have.

There are some unusual seeds and grains here, so a trip to a natural food store is likely. Gluten flour helps to lighten the dough, so be sure to remember it. Buy enough of these ingredients to have on hand, because you'll surely be making this delicious bread again.

THE SPONGE
4½ teaspoons active dry yeast, 2 packages
¾ cup warm (110°F) water
1 cup unbleached white flour

Combine the yeast and water in a medium-size bowl. Stir to dissolve the yeast and let sit for 10 minutes. Stir in the flour until well incorporated and let sit for 1 hour.

THE DOUGH
2 cups warm (110°F) water
1½ cups dark rye flour
1½ teaspoons gluten flour*
½ cup rye flakes
3 tablespoons flax seed
3 tablespoons sesame seed
3 tablespoons sunflower seed
3 tablespoons rolled oats
3 tablespoons millet
4½ tablespoons dark unsulphured molasses
2 teaspoons sea salt
About 4 cups unbleached white flour

THE TOPPING
1 egg white beaten with 1 teaspoon water
1 tablespoon each rolled oats, sesame seed, flax seed, and hulled sunflower seed

Combine the sponge and the warm water in a large bowl and stir to break up the sponge. Stir in all of the ingredients except for the salt and unbleached white flour. Add the salt and 1 cup unbleached white flour. Stir until the ingredients are moistened, then continue adding the flour 1 cup at a time. (It may be necessary to knead in the last of the flour by hand.)

Turn the dough out onto a lightly floured work surface and knead it for 10 to 15 minutes,

*Also known as vital wheat gluten, available at natural food stores.

adding more flour as needed to keep the dough from sticking, until the dough is smooth and elastic. The dough should feel tacky and moist throughout the kneading. Keep track of how much flour you're adding as you knead the dough; try not to use more than a total of 4½ cups.

Place the dough in an oiled bowl, turning to coat the surface with oil. Cover with a damp towel or plastic wrap and let rise at room temperature for about 1 hour, until doubled in size.

Lightly oil 2 8½- by 4-inch loaf pans. (The bread can be baked in standard 9- by 5-inch loaf pans, but the smaller pans will yield a loftier loaf.) Turn the dough onto the work surface, punch it down, and divide in half. Form into 2 loaves and place in the oiled pans. Cover the pans loosely with a damp towel and allow to rise for 1 hour, until doubled in size.

Preheat the oven to 350°F. Combine the topping ingredients. Brush the loaves with the egg white and water and sprinkle with the topping. Bake for 40 to 45 minutes, until the loaves sound hollow when tapped on the bottom. Remove from the pans and transfer to a rack to cool.

MAKES 2 LOAVES

Cracked Wheat Bread

This is an exceptional whole grain bread, delicious for sandwiches or simply toasted and eaten first thing in the morning with fresh fruit preserves. The cracked wheat adds just the right texture, bringing the nutty whole wheat flavor and the sweet taste of honey together.

Gluten flour (available at natural food stores) is an essential ingredient—it allows the bread to be made entirely with whole wheat flour without producing a dense, heavy loaf. In addition to the gluten flour, a lengthy kneading time is necessary to develop the gluten in the whole wheat flour. Your efforts will be rewarded with lofty, fragrant loaves.

THE SPONGE AND CRACKED WHEAT

4½ teaspoons active dry yeast, 2 packages
¾ cup warm (110°F) water
1 cup whole wheat flour
½ cup cracked wheat
½ cup boiling water

Combine the yeast and water in a medium-size bowl and let sit for 10 minutes. Stir in the flour, cover with plastic wrap, and let sit for 1 hour. While the sponge is rising, place the cracked wheat in a small bowl; pour the boiling water over, cover, and let sit for 20 to 30 minutes.

THE DOUGH

1½ cups warm (110°F) water
4½ cups whole wheat flour
½ cup gluten flour*
2½ tablespoons vegetable oil
⅓ cup honey
1 tablespoon sea salt
1 egg white beaten with 1 teaspoon water
2 tablespoons sesame seed

Combine the sponge and water in a large bowl and stir to break up the sponge. Combine the flours and stir about half this mixture into the sponge. When the flour is moistened, add the soaked cracked wheat, oil, honey, and salt. Stir until the ingredients are well incorporated. Add half the remaining flour and stir, then add the rest of the flour. (It may be necessary to knead in the last of the flour by hand.) Turn the dough out onto a lightly floured work surface and knead for 10 to 15 minutes to form a smooth, firm dough. (The long kneading time is necessary to develop the gluten in the dough.)

Transfer to an oiled bowl and turn the dough to coat the entire surface with oil. Cover with

*Also known as vital wheat gluten, available at natural food stores.

a damp towel or plastic wrap and let rise at room temperature for 1 to 1½ hours, until doubled in size.

Lightly oil 2 8½- by 4-inch loaf pans. (The bread can be baked in standard 9- by 5-inch pans, but the smaller pans will yield a loftier loaf.) Turn the dough out onto the work surface, punch it down, divide it in half, and shape into 2 loaves. Place the loaves in the oiled pans, cover loosely with a damp towel or plastic wrap, and let rise until doubled, about 1 hour.

Preheat the oven to 350°F. Brush the loaves with the egg wash and sprinkle on the sesame seed. Bake for 40 to 45 minutes, until the loaves sound hollow when tapped on the bottom. Remove from the baking pans and transfer to a rack to cool.

MAKES 2 LOAVES

Variation: For a nuttier bread, include some sunflower seeds and sesame seeds, with the following changes: Mix ¼ cup hulled sunflower seed and 3 tablespoons sesame seed into the dough when you add the honey and the oil. To make up for the added dry ingredients, decrease the cracked wheat and boiling water to ¼ cup each. Brush the dough with the egg wash and sprinkle with 2 tablespoons each sunflower and sesame seed before baking.

F*ocaccia*

The Latin root for focaccia is *focus*—meaning fireplace or hearth, the center of the home. This simple olive oil bread has a special place each weekend on our dinner menu. We call it by different names, depending on the dishes we're serving—focaccia, fougasse, or simply hearth bread. The basic dough remains the same, but nuts, fresh herbs, or olives are added to highlight the flavors of the meal. This tender, moist bread also makes an exceptional sandwich (page 299).

4½ teaspoons yeast, 2 packages
2 cups warm (110°F) water
1 tablespoon sugar
½ cup extra virgin olive oil
5½ cups unbleached white flour
2 teaspoons salt
2 tablespoons chopped fresh rosemary, 3 tablespoons chopped fresh sage, or 3 tablespoons chopped mixed herbs (optional)
Extra virgin olive oil for brushing the focaccia
Coarse sea salt

Combine the yeast, ½ cup of the warm water, and the sugar in a large bowl. Let it sit for about 10 minutes, until foamy. Add the olive oil, remaining water, and herbs (if you're using them). In a separate bowl, combine the flour and salt; add it to the wet mixture 1 cup at a time. (It may be necessary to knead the last cup of flour into the dough.) Turn the dough out onto a lightly floured work surface and knead vigorously for 5 to 10 minutes, adding a little more flour if necessary to keep it from sticking. The dough will be very sticky at the beginning but will become more cohesive as you knead it. Place the dough in an oiled bowl, turn it to coat the surface, cover with plastic wrap or a damp towel, and allow it to rise in a warm place for 1½ hours.

Preheat the oven to 450°F and lightly oil 2 9- by 13-inch baking dishes. Turn the dough out onto the counter, divide it in half, and press each piece into an oiled baking dish. Cover and let rise for 30 minutes. Dimple the dough with your fingertips, brush with oil, and sprinkle with coarse sea salt. Place in the oven, reduce the temperature to 375°F, and bake for 20 to 25 minutes, until light golden. Transfer to a rack to cool.

MAKES TWO 9- BY 13-INCH SHEETS

Variations

Our standard focaccia is usually quite simple for sandwiches, but we use a number of variations when we serve it at the table for a meal. The following are a few of our favorite variations:

Nuts: We sometimes knead toasted chopped nuts into the dough, but most often we sprinkle untoasted nuts over the dough and gently press them into the surface. Toasted pine nuts are always delicious—you'll need about ½ cup chopped. We use chopped pumpkin seeds when we're serving a southwestern meal, about ¾ cup.

Sun-Dried Tomatoes: Add ⅓ to ½ cup chopped drained sun-dried tomatoes to the wet ingredients before you add the flour. The beautiful red flecks of dried tomato will permeate the dough with their intense tomato flavor. For even more tomato flavor, brush the dough with sun-dried tomato oil.

Olives: Add ½ cup chopped pitted olives to the dough or sprinkle them over the top and gently press them in. Use a combination of olives if you like.

Sautéed Red Onions: While the dough is rising, thinly slice 1 medium-size red onion and sauté in a skillet with 1 tablespoon extra virgin olive oil, ¼ teaspoon salt, and a few pinches of pepper. (Add a clove or two of chopped garlic if you like.) Sauté over medium heat for about 5 minutes, until the onion is tender but not completely soft. Set aside to cool, then season to taste with salt and pepper. Add a few splashes of balsamic vinegar and make sure the onion is well seasoned. Place the dough in the baking dishes as directed and brush with olive oil. Spread the onion over the dough, gently press them into the surface, then bake.

Roasted Garlic: The sweet flavor of the garlic really comes through here. You can also roast the garlic and serve it with the bread instead of adding it to the dough.

Rub an entire head of garlic with olive oil and place in a small baking dish or wrap in aluminum foil to bake. Bake in a 375°F oven for about 30 minutes or until the garlic is quite soft. When the garlic is cool, slice off the top of the bulb and squeeze out the garlic. If the cloves still have some shape, you can leave them that way or mash with a spoon. Add to the wet ingredients before adding the flour, then proceed with the bread.

Chili-Infused Oil: This is a wonderful way to enjoy this hearth bread with a southwestern meal. Stir 1 teaspoon Ancho Chili Puree (page 197) or Chipotle Puree (page 332) into ¼ cup light olive oil. Taste the oil; if you like it hotter, add more puree. Brush the oil over the dough before baking. For a lively combination, press toasted pumpkin seeds onto the surface of the dough after brushing with the chili oil. For an earthier flavor, add chopped fresh sage to the dough.

Sauces

Sauces

A sprightly sauce is a sure way to draw the elements of a dish together. Whether you're making a rich mushroom lasagne, a smoky polenta gratin, or grilled potatoes, be sure the sauce enhances the flavors of the dish and doesn't overpower them. Freshness is always important here—your own garden basil, cilantro, parsley, or mint can make all the difference in Mint-Cilantro Sauce, Salsa Verde, or Cilantro Pesto.

Tomato sauce is an essential ingredient in so many of our dishes—we vary the seasoning of Tomato Sauce with fresh and dried chilies, herbs, and spices each time we make it. If you have an abundance of tomatoes, make a double recipe and freeze it in small containers—you can adjust the seasoning later. For a spicy southwestern tomato sauce, add toasted cumin and a little Chipotle Puree. A spoonful of pesto from your freezer will make a midwinter lasagne sauce shine. Dried porcini lend their rich earthy essence to tomato sauce—¼ ounce is all you'll need, and be sure to include the flavorful soaking liquid.

Flavored butters are easy to make—great for brushing over grilled or roasted vegetables or for tossing with a summer squash sauté. Herb butter is good to have on hand for a simple pasta sauce or for last-minute dishes. To make it, add a tablespoon or two of chopped fresh herbs to softened butter and season with salt and pepper. For more complex flavor, you can always add a diced shallot.

Tomato Sauce

We make tomato sauces year-round, using fresh or canned tomatoes, depending on the season. In late summer and early autumn the sauces are fresh and sweet. In the winter and spring a sauce of canned tomatoes is the base of a hearty winter stew, a lasagne, or a gratin. This sauce is easy to make and freezes well, so it's a good idea to double it when tomatoes are abundant. The red wine is not necessary if you're using flavorful tomatoes, but it brings out the best in canned tomatoes, balancing the acidity while adding a depth and complexity of its own to the sauce. Note that the basil is dried, not fresh; the fragrance of fresh basil wouldn't survive the extended cooking of the sauce.

1 tablespoon light olive oil
½ medium-size yellow onion, diced, about 1 cup
½ teaspoon dried basil
Salt and pepper
3 garlic cloves, finely chopped
¼ cup dry red wine
*1½ pounds fresh tomatoes, peeled, seeded, and chopped (page 95), about 2 cups, or 1 16-
    ounce can tomatoes with their juice, chopped*
1 bay leaf

Heat the oil in a medium-size saucepan; add the onion, basil, ½ teaspoon salt, and a few pinches of pepper. Sauté over medium heat until the onion is soft, about 7 to 8 minutes, then add the garlic and sauté for 1 to 2 minutes. Add the wine and simmer a minute or two to reduce; when the pan is almost dry, add the tomatoes and the bay leaf. Reduce the heat to low and cook for 30 minutes. Add salt and pepper to taste.

MAKES ABOUT 2 CUPS

Variation: For a spicy tomato sauce seasoned with fresh chilies, add ½ teaspoon toasted cumin seed (page 89) and a few pinches of cayenne to the onion; omit the wine. Puree 2 or 3 seeded jalapeño or serrano chilies and cook with the tomatoes. This sauce is delicious served with Spicy Corn Cakes with Smoked Cheese and Chilies (page 227) or stuffed zucchini or peppers.

Tip: If the sauce is acidic, add a little sugar.

Salsa Roja

We serve this spicy, satisfying sauce throughout the year. In summer fresh sweet tomatoes make up its base and require minimal seasoning. In the winter months even the best of canned tomatoes tend to be acidic. Here they're balanced with the earthy flavor of toasted cumin and the smoky heat of pureed chipotle and ancho chilies. The sauce is delicious baked with polenta and summer vegetables for a southwestern gratin, with enchiladas, or spread over a pizza. Make it ahead of time and store in the freezer.

1 tablespoon light vegetable or olive oil
½ medium-size yellow onion, chopped, about 1 cup
1 teaspoon cumin seed, toasted and ground (page 89)
Salt
5 garlic cloves, finely chopped
1½ pounds fresh tomatoes, peeled, seeded, and chopped (page 95), about 2 cups, or 1 16-ounce can tomatoes with juice, chopped
1 tablespoon Ancho Chili Puree (page 197)
Chipotle Puree (page 332)

Heat the olive oil in a medium-size saucepan; add the onion, cumin, and ½ teaspoon salt. Sauté over medium heat until the onion begins to release its juices, about 5 minutes; add the garlic and sauté until the onion is soft, about 5 minutes. Add the tomatoes, the Ancho Chili Puree, ½ teaspoon Chipotle Puree, and simmer over medium-low heat for 30 minutes. Add salt and Chipotle Puree to taste.

MAKES ABOUT 2 CUPS

Tip: If the sauce is acidic, add a little sugar to balance the flavors.

Variations: To add another level of warmth to the flavor, cook the sauce with a 2-inch length of cinnamon stick or add ¼ teaspoon freshly ground cinnamon to the onion along with the cumin.

Add half a head of roasted garlic to the sauce. Roast the garlic (page 100) and peel when cool; chop or puree with a little of the tomato, then add to the sauce along with the tomatoes.

Tomatillo Sauce

We serve this tangy, pale green sauce so many ways—baked with Enchiladas Verdes (page 246), with Spicy Corn Cakes with Smoked Cheese and Chilies (page 227), or with grilled summer vegetables brushed with Cinnamon-Chipotle Butter (page 332). The sauce is made without oil, so the clear taste of the tomatillos really comes through—a little green pepper deepens the flavors, while fresh chilies add spicy heat. A tablespoon of crème fraîche will round out the flavors, but the sauce is perfectly delicious without it.

½ medium-size yellow onion, thinly sliced, about 1 cup
Salt and cayenne pepper
½ medium-size green bell pepper, coarsely chopped, about ½ cup
1 pound fresh tomatillos, husked
1 or 2 jalapeño or serrano chilies, seeded and chopped
2 tablespoons chopped cilantro
1 tablespoon crème fraîche (page 359; optional)

Pour a little water into a medium-size saucepan; add the onion, ½ teaspoon salt, and a pinch of cayenne. Cover and cook the onion without stirring, over medium heat until soft, about 5 minutes. Add the bell pepper, tomatillos, and chilies. Cover again and cook until the tomatillos are very soft and have released their juices, about 15 to 20 minutes.

Puree in a blender or food processor until the sauce is smooth; season with ¼ teaspoon salt and more chilies or cayenne to taste. Add the cilantro and crème fraîche (if you're using it) just before serving.

MAKES ABOUT 2 CUPS

To save a little time, soak the tomatillos in warm water for a few minutes before husking them. The warm water softens the husk and loosens it from the slightly sticky skin of the tomatillo.

Tips: If the sauce is acidic, add a little sugar to balance the flavors.

Roasted Pepper Sauce

This sweet, flavorful sauce works well with roasted or grilled vegetables or spread on a pizza. It's also an elegant garnish swirled into a potato or summer squash soup. If the peppers aren't full of natural sweetness, an extra splash of balsamic vinegar will heighten their flavor. Or, for a spicier sauce, use a little Chipotle Puree (page 332); it will deepen the color and give the finished sauce a smoky, subtle heat.

3 medium-size red bell peppers, roasted and peeled (page 55)
Balsamic vinegar or Chipotle Puree (page 332)
Salt and pepper

Place the peppers in a blender or food processor. Add a splash of balsamic vinegar or Chipotle Puree, ¼ teaspoon salt, and a few pinches of pepper. Blend until smooth. Season to taste with salt and another splash or two of balsamic or chipotle.

MAKES ABOUT I CUP

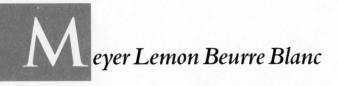

Meyer Lemon Beurre Blanc

Save this exceptional sauce for the first spring asparagus and serve with grilled new potatoes. The butter is whisked into a delicate reduction, enhanced by the sweet juice and fragrant zest of Meyer lemons. The flavor of the sauce is light yet wonderfully complex.

2 tablespoons Meyer lemon juice or 1 tablespoon each fresh lemon and orange juices
1½ tablespoons Champagne vinegar
3 tablespoons dry white wine
2 large shallots, finely diced, about ¼ cup
½ pound cold unsalted butter, cut into small cubes
½ tablespoon minced Meyer lemon or orange zest
Salt and white pepper

Place the Meyer lemon or citrus juices, vinegar, wine, and shallots in a small saucepan. Reduce over high heat until the liquid is almost gone. Turn the heat to low and whisk in the butter, a small handful at a time, making sure each addition is incorporated before adding the next. Keep whisking as you add the butter. Add the zest, ¼ teaspoon salt, and a few pinches of pepper. Taste and add salt and pepper if needed.

MAKES ABOUT I CUP

Tip: Unless you or a friend has a backyard tree, Meyer lemons can be difficult to find. To substitute, use 1 tablespoon each of lemon and orange juices and ½ teaspoon minced orange zest.

BUTTER SAUCES

A few tips for making beurre blanc or beurre rouge: Butter sauces have a reputation for being difficult to make, but they're actually quite quick and easy. The key is to incorporate the butter without melting it, or the sauce will separate. You can add the butter over high or low heat—we prefer moderately low heat—but you need to keep it moving by whisking constantly until all of the butter has been incorporated.

Once the sauce is made, it needs to be kept at a steady, warm temperature until served, or it will cool and the butter will thicken. It's best to make the sauce shortly before serving and keep it warm over a pan of barely simmering water. To help stabilize the sauce, add a tablespoon of heavy cream to the reduction before whisking in the butter.

P ort Beurre Rouge

The rich, sweet flavor of this sauce works beautifully with grilled fall and winter vegetables. Butter is whisked into a fragrant reduction of port, balsamic vinegar, and shallots, giving the sauce a creamy purple hue. For a classic combination, serve with grilled shiitake mushrooms, sliced fennel, and tender slices of delicata squash. You don't need a great aged port here; we usually use Ficklin.

⅓ cup port
⅓ cup balsamic vinegar
2 large shallots, finely diced, about ¼ cup
½ pound cold unsalted butter, cut into small cubes
Salt and pepper

Place the port, vinegar, and shallots in a small saucepan. Over high heat, reduce the volume of the liquid to a thin syrup. Turn the heat to low and whisk the butter into the reduction, a small handful at a time, making sure each batch of butter is incorporated before adding the next. Keep whisking as you add the butter. Add ½ teaspoon salt and a few pinches of pepper. You may need to balance the flavor with a splash of balsamic.

MAKES ABOUT 1 CUP

B rown Butter

Brown butter has a rich aroma and a distinctive nutty, sweet flavor. We use it year-round, but it's particularly delicious as a fall and winter seasoning—tossed with pasta or added to a hearty sauté of escarole, red chard, and kale. The time and attention needed to make it are minimal—just be sure to use unsalted butter and remove it from the heat before its warm amber color begins to darken. The butter will hold indefinitely in the refrigerator, so make enough to have on hand when you need it.

½ pound unsalted butter

Melt the butter in a small saucepan over low heat. As the butter gently simmers, the butter fat and milk solids will separate from each other. The solids will settle to the bottom of the pan, coloring the butter as it cooks. When it turns a rich amber color, in about 8 to 10 minutes, remove from the heat. Line a fine-mesh strainer with a paper towel or cheese-cloth and pour the butter through it, straining out the solids. The butter can be used immediately or cooled and refrigerated in a sealed container.

MAKES ABOUT ¾ CUP

Cinnamon-Chipotle Butter

Enjoy this spicy butter brushed over grilled potatoes, summer squash, and thick rounds of red onions. The smoky heat of the chipotle peppers is just right with the sweet flavor of freshly ground cinnamon, brightened with the sharp taste of lime.

¼ pound unsalted butter, softened
1 teaspoon Chipotle Puree (see below)
¼ teaspoon cinnamon, preferably freshly ground
¼ teaspoon salt
Fresh lime juice

Cream the butter with the Chipotle Puree, cinnamon, and salt. Add lime juice, starting with ½ teaspoon, then adding more to taste. For a spicier butter, add more Chipotle Puree. The vegetables will really soak up the heat of the butter, so it should be fairly hot but not overpowering.

MAKES ½ CUP

CHIPOTLE PUREE

Chipotles are jalapeño chilies that have been smoked and dried—a favorite Greens seasoning. Their smoky heat is delicious brushed over tortillas and pizzas and carefully added to soups and stews. Chipotles can be found in Mexican specialty stores, as whole dried chilies or in small cans. We use canned chipotles packed in adobo sauce—a puree of smoked jalapeños and vinegar, though the chilies are so fiery hot that you'd hardly know the vinegar was there. Take care in handling chipotles, remembering that a little of this smoky chili puree will go a long way. Puree a whole can at a time in the blender or food processor and store in the refrigerator until needed. The puree will keep almost indefinitely; if you know you'll be storing it for a long period of time, cover the puree with a thin layer of oil.

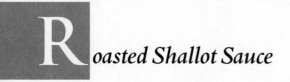R oasted Shallot Sauce

Laura, one of our dinner chefs, introduced us to this elegant sauce. It's easy to make and delicious with grilled or roasted vegetables. The shallots are roasted and pureed, then seasoned with a tangy hint of Dijon mustard, a touch of honey, and a splash of sherry vinegar to sharpen the flavors.

1 pound shallots
Light olive oil
Salt and pepper
½ cup water or Light Vegetable Stock (page 79)
Honey
2 teaspoons Dijon mustard
Sherry vinegar

Preheat the oven to 375°F. Trim both ends off the shallots, cut them in half lengthwise, and
peel them. Toss the shallots in just enough olive oil to coat them and sprinkle with salt
and pepper. Roast in a covered baking dish for 30 to 35 minutes, until soft. Puree the
warm shallots in a blender or food processor with the water or stock. Transfer to a bowl
and season with 1 tablespoon honey, the mustard, ½ teaspoon salt, a few pinches of pepper, and a splash of sherry vinegar. For a sweeter, sharper flavor add a little more honey
and another splash of vinegar. Serve warm or at room temperature.

MAKES I CUP

Tomatillo Salsa

Raw tomatillos give this salsa a bright, fresh flavor, and crisp, clean texture. It's best made a good hour before serving. The salsa will taste too tart at first, but as it sits, the sharp flavors mellow and sweeten. Serve with quesadillas (page 248), scrambled eggs, and omelets.

1 pound tomatillos, husked
2 or 3 green jalapeño or serrano chilies, seeded
¼ cup finely diced red onion
Champagne or rice wine vinegar
½ red or yellow bell pepper, finely diced, about ½ cup
¾ teaspoon fresh lime juice
Salt
Cayenne pepper (optional)
Sugar (optional)
1 tablespoon chopped cilantro

Coarsely chop three-quarters of the tomatillos and puree them with the jalapeños in a blender or food processor to make the base of the salsa. (Do not add water, because the tomatillos will release their juices as they puree.) Transfer to a bowl. Toss the onion with a few splashes of vinegar to draw out their color. Chop the remaining tomatillos and add to the puree along with the onion, pepper, lime juice, and ¾ teaspoon salt. Let the salsa sit for 1 hour to allow the flavors to blend. Season to taste with cayenne if desired and add a little sugar to balance the acidity if necessary. Add the cilantro just before serving.

MAKES 2 CUPS

Salsa Fresca—Fresh Tomato Salsa

This quick and easy salsa is best made at the height of summer, when tomatoes are sweet and juicy and fresh chilies are full of spicy heat. If golden tomatoes are available, combine them with red tomatoes to make a beautifully bright salsa. Roma (plum) tomatoes make a good salsa in the off season.

¼ cup diced red onion
Champagne or rice wine vinegar
1 pound ripe tomatoes, cored, seeded, and chopped
2 or more jalapeño or serrano chilies, seeded and finely diced
2 tablespoons coarsely chopped cilantro
Salt
Cayenne pepper (optional)

Sprinkle the onion with a few splashes of vinegar to draw out its color, then toss with the tomatoes, chilies, cilantro, and ¼ teaspoon salt. Season to taste with salt and vinegar. For a hotter salsa, add more chilies or a few pinches of cayenne pepper.

MAKES ABOUT 2 CUPS

JALAPEÑOS

Jalapeños have plenty of fresh chili flavor, with heat that varies from mild to quite hot—wonderful in salads, soups, stews, and curries. Beware, an otherwise mild-tasting jalapeño can be fiery at the base of the seed pod. Jalapeños are about 3 inches in length with a smooth skin that's either red or green. We use the colors interchangeably, unless the color is specified in the recipe or we're making a green salsa or curry. Cut them in half lengthwise and carefully remove the seeds and stem, then slice, dice, or puree them. Always select jalapeños that are firm—a sign of their freshness.

Salsa Verde

This is a smooth, piquant green sauce—delicious served in the winter with grilled vegetables or Spinach Cakes with Shiitake Mushrooms and Goat Cheese (page 226). In summer, include some basil along with the watercress and parsley.

½ cup extra virgin olive oil
1 scallion, white and green parts, coarsely chopped
1 small garlic clove, chopped
1 packed cup parsley sprigs
1 packed cup watercress sprigs
½ teaspoon salt
2 to 3 pinches of pepper
½ tablespoon fresh lemon juice
1 teaspoon Champagne vinegar
½ teaspoon drained capers, rinsed

Place the olive oil in a blender; add the remaining ingredients and blend until smooth. Serve this sauce freshly made.

MAKES ABOUT I CUP

Pesto

Pesto adds an exhilarating touch to so many of our summer dishes—drizzled over a simple pizza with vine-ripened tomatoes and mozzarella cheese, brushed on a baguette for an eggplant sandwich, or swirled into a potato or sweet pepper soup.

Pesto freezes well, so if your basil is going to seed, make it into pesto. Freeze it, minus the cheese, in small containers to brighten your winter soups and sauces.

¾ cup extra virgin olive oil
1 garlic clove
1 tablespoon pine nuts or walnut pieces
¼ teaspoon salt
⅓ cup freshly grated Parmesan cheese, about 1 ounce
1 bunch of fresh basil, about 4 cups leaves

Place all of the ingredients except the basil in a blender or food processor. Blend until smooth, then add the basil a handful at a time, blending until all of the basil is incorporated and the pesto is somewhat smooth.

MAKES ABOUT 1 CUP

Cilantro Pesto

A little of this bright green sauce goes a long way. Spicy and piquant, it's delicious served with grilled vegetables or on Mexican Pizza (page 180). For fresh chili flavor, add a green jalapeño or serrano chili and omit the cayenne. Walnuts are a fine substitute for the pine nuts.

¼ cup light olive oil or vegetable oil
1 scallion, white and green parts, coarsely chopped
1 garlic clove, coarsely chopped
1 tablespoon pine nuts, toasted (page 263)
1 ½ teaspoons fresh lemon or lime juice
1 lightly packed cup cilantro sprigs with short stems
1 lightly packed cup parsley sprigs, large stems removed
Salt and cayenne pepper

Combine everything but the salt and cayenne in a blender. Add ⅛ teaspoon salt and a few pinches of cayenne pepper; puree until smooth. Season to taste with salt and cayenne.

MAKES ABOUT ½ CUP

Mint-Cilantro Sauce

We serve this fresh green sauce with Spinach and Mung Dal Fritters (page 224), but it also works particularly well with the smoky flavors of grilled eggplant, shiitake mushrooms, and scallions. If you grow your own spearmint, this is the place to use it. This recipe is our version of one of Julie Sahni's in *Classic Indian Cooking*.

½ cup plain yogurt
½ small green bell pepper, coarsely chopped, about ½ cup
1 or 2 green jalapeño peppers or serrano chilies, seeded
1 scallion, white and green parts, coarsely chopped
1 teaspoon grated fresh ginger
Salt
1 packed cup cilantro sprigs with short stems
1 packed cup fresh mint leaves

Puree the yogurt, green pepper, chilies, scallion, and ginger in a blender. Add ½ teaspoon salt, the cilantro, and the mint and puree until smooth. Add salt to taste.

MAKES ABOUT 1 CUP

Tip: Add a pinch or two of sugar if the flavors need to be balanced.

CILANTRO

This tender annual is either loved or loathed with a passion—we happen to love its pungent taste, well honored in so many cuisines. Cilantro is the leaf of the coriander plant and tastes nothing like the seeds. Its fresh piquant character holds its own with hot spicy tastes—sprinkled over a smoky Salsa Roja pizza or tossed with citrus-flavored Chinese noodles. Coriander seeds, toasted and ground, are essential in Indian curries, southwestern polenta dishes, and lentil soups with Mexican spices. The lovely white flowers are delicious in salads.

This very special herb is mentioned in the Bible, and the seeds have been found in Egyptian tombs. It's easily grown directly from seed in light, well-drained soil. Start in the early spring, as soon as all danger from frost has passed—sow every two weeks for a continuous supply. It loves full sun and plenty of water, though it doesn't require heat. Cilantro goes quickly to seed, and once established in your garden, it will naturalize readily.

Basil Aïoli

Sweet basil is a wonderful addition to aïoli. We spread it on sandwiches or serve it with grilled spring or summer vegetables.

¾ cup light olive oil
1 cup fresh basil leaves
1 egg yolk
1½ teaspoons Champagne vinegar
¼ teaspoon salt
1 garlic clove, finely chopped

Place the olive oil and the basil in a blender jar or a food processor and puree. Whisk the egg yolk with a few drops of vinegar until the color begins to lighten; whisk in the basil oil, drop by drop at first, then a little faster as the mixture begins to emulsify. Season with salt, garlic, and the remaining vinegar.

MAKES ABOUT 1 CUP

Chipotle Aïoli

This smoky, spicy aïoli is delicious with grilled potatoes, peppers, and red onions. Chipotle peppers, which are smoked jalapeños, vary from hot to very hot, so take a little taste of the puree before adding it to the aïoli.

1 large egg yolk
½ teaspoon fresh lemon juice
1 cup light olive oil
1 garlic clove, finely chopped
1 teaspoon Champagne vinegar
1 teaspoon Chipotle Puree (page 332)
¼ teaspoon salt

Whisk the yolk and ¼ teaspoon lemon juice together until smooth. Whisk in the oil, very slowly at first, until the aïoli begins to emulsify. After all of the oil has been added, season with the garlic, vinegar, remaining lemon juice, Chipotle Puree, and salt. If the aïoli is too thick, you can thin it with a little warm water.

MAKES ABOUT 1½ CUPS

Honey-Miso Sauce

The flavor of this wonderfully simple sauce will vary depending on the type of miso you use. Choose your favorite—a hearty red or a smooth, light yellow miso—you can even try a combination. Rich sesame oil and honey add depth and sweetness, while freshly grated ginger and jalapeño chilies give the sauce a refreshing bite. Serve with slices of grilled tofu and a sprinkling of toasted sesame seeds.

½ cup mild red or yellow miso or a combination
1 tablespoon dark sesame oil
⅓ cup water
1½ tablespoons honey
1 teaspoon freshly grated ginger
½ teaspoon rice wine vinegar
1 or 2 jalapeño or serrano chilies, seeded and pureed with a little water
Cayenne pepper (optional)
Soy sauce (optional)

Whisk the miso, sesame oil, and water together until smooth. Mix in the honey, ginger, and vinegar; add the pureed chilies. For more heat, add up to ¼ teaspoon cayenne. If you're using mild yellow miso, you may want to add a splash of soy sauce.

MAKES ABOUT 1 CUP

Spicy Peanut Sauce

This smooth, intensely flavored sauce is especially delicious with grilled shiitake mushrooms and eggplant or delicate slices of tofu. The heat of the chilies and fresh taste of lime cut through the richness and pick up the flavors. Garnish these dishes with Spicy Peanuts (page 401) and sprigs of fresh cilantro.

1 tablespoon coarsely chopped yellow onion
1 large garlic clove, coarsely chopped
1 or 2 red jalapeño chilies, seeded
1 tablespoon peanut oil or light vegetable oil
2½ tablespoons soy sauce
1 tablespoon plus 1 teaspoon lime juice
2 tablespoons light brown sugar
1 teaspoon molasses
½ cup creamy peanut butter
¼ cup water
¼ teaspoon cayenne pepper

Place the onion, garlic, chilies, oil, soy sauce, and lime juice in a blender or food processor. Blend until smooth, then transfer to a bowl. Whisk in the remaining ingredients.

MAKES ABOUT 1 CUP

Dipping Sauce

This simple sauce is both sweet and salty. It's handy to have around, and it holds well, so make enough to fill a jar and store it in your pantry or refrigerator. Serve with O Konomi Yaki—Savory Vegetable Cakes (page 228), or drizzle over grilled mushrooms and Japanese eggplant.

¾ cup soy sauce
¾ cup water
¼ cup sugar
6 thin coins of fresh ginger
1 tablespoon dark sesame oil
2 teaspoons cornstarch
¼ cup cold water

Combine everything but the cornstarch and cold water in a small saucepan; simmer over medium heat for 10 minutes. Dissolve the cornstarch in the cold water and whisk the mixture into the sauce. Bring the sauce to a quick boil for 1 minute and continue to whisk. The cornstarch will bind the sauce ever so slightly and give it a silky texture. Remove from the heat and cool, allowing the ginger to steep in the sauce until you're ready to store it. Strain out the ginger and store the sauce in a sealed jar in the refrigerator. It will keep for several weeks.

MAKES ABOUT 1 ½ CUPS

Reduced Balsamic Vinegar

This has to be the simplest, most versatile sauce we make. Balsamic vinegar—the ordinary kind, not the expensive aged vinegar, which is already reduced—is reduced to a thin syrup and brushed over warm frittatas, roasted onions and shallots, and grilled vegetables. The warm, soft flesh of eggplant, mushrooms, and summer squash really soaks up the sweet, tart flavor. The reduced vinegar will hold indefinitely, so make as little or as much as you like.

Balsamic vinegar

In a small saucepan over high heat, reduce the vinegar to half its original volume. (For a more intensely flavored reduction, bring the volume down to one-third.) Be careful that all of the vinegar doesn't boil away as you reduce it. Cool and store in a sealed jar along with your other vinegars or refrigerate.

Morning Breads

and Pancakes

Morning Breads and Pancakes

Morning is a particularly inviting time to enjoy crumbly scones and moist, tender muffins and quick breads just warm from the oven, but of course these comforting pastries are welcome any time of day. Corn Bread with Smoked Cheese and Chilies is a savory treat—it's perfect for lunch with Mexican Lentil Soup with Roasted Garlic and Chilies, or you can serve it for dinner with Southern Rio Stew. Set a piece aside and toast it the next morning for breakfast.

Most quick breads are best served on the day that you make them, but Banana Coconut Bread is different—it's so moist that it keeps well for a few days, while the banana flavor actually develops. You can always make quick bread in advance and freeze it. Scones are surprisingly easy to make; just remember to use a light hand when mixing the dough. To save a little time, make the dough in the evening, refrigerate it overnight, and cut it into wedges in the morning. Take the scones from the oven just as your guests arrive—their buttery rich fragrance will fill the kitchen and awaken every appetite in the room.

Pancakes and French toast are the ultimate crowd pleaser, particularly with a generous serving of fresh summer berries or a heaped spoonful of tart applesauce in the fall. There's never a question about real maple syrup—we always serve it warm. Soak the last slices of stale Sourdough Bâtard in a rich orange-scented batter for wonderfully delicious French toast—you can use fresh bread of any kind, but the porous sourdough soaks up the flavorful batter in the blink of an eye.

orn Bread with Smoked Cheese and Chilies

This spicy corn bread is a favorite, especially for our Sunday brunch. The striking combination of sweet corn, smoked cheese, and fresh chilies gives it exceptional flavor. In summer, whole kernels of fresh corn add bites of chewy texture. Serve with Spicy Black Bean Soup (page 108), Pinto Beans with New Mexican Chilies (page 272), or alongside Southern Rio Stew (page 196).

9 tablespoons unsalted butter
1 ear of corn, shaved, about ¾ cup kernels (optional)
Salt and cayenne pepper
1¼ cups milk
1½ cups unbleached white flour
1 cup fine cornmeal
1 tablespoon baking powder
2 tablespoons sugar
2 eggs
1 ounce grated smoked cheese, about ½ cup
1 green jalapeño or serrano chili, seeded and finely diced

Preheat the oven to 375°F. Grease a 9-inch round cake pan. Melt 1 tablespoon of the butter in a small sauté pan and add the corn, a pinch of salt, and a pinch of cayenne pepper. Sauté until tender, about 5 minutes. Set aside.

In a saucepan, heat the milk and remaining butter together over medium heat until the butter has melted. Remove from the heat. Combine the dry ingredients in a mixing bowl and stir until well mixed. Whisk the eggs together, then whisk them into the warm milk mixture. Pour them into the dry ingredients. Add the corn, cheese, and chilies; stir until just blended. Do not overmix.

Spread the batter into the pan and bake for 20 to 25 minutes, until the top springs back or a skewer inserted in the middle comes out clean.

MAKES ONE 9-INCH ROUND

*O*range-Pecan Scones

Plump currants and fragrant orange zest provide little bursts of flavor in these crumbly, buttery scones. Their surprisingly light texture seems to temper their richness. They're perfect with morning or afternoon coffee.

Zest of 1 orange
3 to 4 tablespoons fresh orange juice
½ cup dried currants
3 cups unbleached white flour
5 tablespoons sugar
1 tablespoon baking powder
½ teaspoon salt
¼ pound cold unsalted butter
⅔ cup buttermilk
1 egg yolk
1 tablespoon milk
¼ cup small pecan pieces, coarsely chopped

Preheat the oven to 400°F. Plump the currants in the orange juice. Sift the dry ingredients together. Cut the butter into small pieces and cut it into the dry ingredients using a pastry blender or 2 knives until it resembles coarse meal. Add the currants and juice. Stir the zest into the buttermilk, add it to the dry ingredients, and stir until the mixture is moistened. You may need to add a little more buttermilk. Do not overmix.

Turn the dough out onto a floured board and gently form into a round about 1 inch high. Cut the round into 8 wedges and place 1 inch apart on a baking sheet stacked on top of another sheet. (The double pan is necessary to keep the bottoms from browning too quickly.) Whisk the egg yolk and milk together and lightly brush the scones with the mixture. Sprinkle with the pecans. Bake until the scones are lightly browned, about 20 minutes.

MAKES 8 SCONES

Variation—Apricot-Walnut Scones: Chop ½ cup dried apricots into small pieces and use them in place of the currants. Plump the apricots in the orange juice and prepare the scones as directed, substituting walnuts for the pecans.

Oatmeal-Raisin Scones

Chewy golden raisins and a hint of orange zest keep the flavor of these hearty scones light.
Enjoy them warm from the oven on a chilly winter morning served with apple butter or
fresh fruit preserves.

½ cup golden raisins
Zest of 1 orange
3 to 4 tablespoons fresh orange juice
1½ cups unbleached white flour
¼ cup sugar
1 teaspoon baking powder
½ teaspoon baking soda
½ teaspoon salt
¼ pound cold unsalted butter
1¼ cups rolled oats
½ cup buttermilk
1 egg yolk
2 tablespoons milk

Preheat the oven to 375°F. Plump the raisins in the orange juice. Sift the dry ingredients together. Cut the butter into small pieces and cut it into the dry ingredients with a pastry
blender or 2 knives until it resembles coarse meal. Add the oats, raisins, and juice, stirring
with a fork to distribute evenly. Add the zest to the buttermilk and add to the dry ingredients, stirring until it just gathers into a ball. Do not overmix.

Turn the dough out onto a floured board; gently shape into a round 1 inch high, about 8
inches across. Cut the round into 8 wedges and place them 1 inch apart on a baking sheet.
Whisk the egg yolk and milk together and brush the egg wash lightly over the scones.
Bake for 20 to 25 minutes, until the scones are shiny and lightly browned.

MAKES 8 SCONES

Banana-Coconut Bread

We often serve this quick bread with cream cheese sweetened with honey, yet it's so moist and flavorful that it can easily be enjoyed by itself. It's best served warm just out of the oven.

1½ cups unbleached white flour
½ teaspoon salt
1 teaspoon baking soda
10 tablespoons unsalted butter, softened
½ cup sugar
½ cup light brown sugar
2 eggs
3 or 4 ripe bananas, mashed, 1½ cups
1 cup shredded unsweetened coconut

Preheat the oven to 350°F. Grease a 9- by 5-inch loaf pan. Sift the flour, salt, and baking soda together. Cream the butter and sugars together until light and fluffy. Add the eggs 1 at a time, beating until the mixture is smooth after each addition. Stir in the bananas. Add the dry ingredients and all but 2 tablespoons of the coconut and mix until blended.
Spread the batter in the pan and bake for 60 to 70 minutes. Sprinkle the bread with the reserved coconut halfway through the baking. The bread is done when a skewer inserted in the center of the loaf comes out clean and the bread is golden brown.

MAKES 1 LOAF

Variation: Substitute 1 cup chopped toasted walnuts or pecans (page 263) for the coconut.

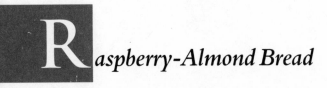

Raspberry-Almond Bread

The sweet tartness of raspberries and crunchy bites of toasted almonds highlight this tender bread, which should be sliced warm from the oven. This bread is gorgeous streaked with the beautiful deep red of the raspberries.

¾ cup whole almonds, unskinned, toasted (page 263)
2 cups fresh raspberries, about a 1-pint basket
¼ pound unsalted butter, softened
¾ cup sugar
2 eggs
½ teaspoon almond extract
1¾ cups unbleached white flour
½ teaspoon cinnamon, preferably freshly ground
1 teaspoon baking powder
1 teaspoon baking soda
½ teaspoon salt
½ cup milk
½ cup crème fraîche (page 359) or sour cream

Preheat the oven to 350°F. Grease a 9- by 5-inch loaf pan. Chop the almonds into small pieces. Sort through the raspberries, but do not rinse them under water.

Cream the butter and sugar together until light and fluffy. Add the eggs 1 at a time, beating well after each addition, then add the almond extract. Sift the dry ingredients together. Whisk the milk and crème fraîche together. Alternately incorporate the dry ingredients and crème fraîche mixture into the batter, beginning and ending with the dry ingredients. Gently stir in the fruit and nuts.

Spread the batter into the loaf pan and bake for about 1 hour. The bread will be lightly browned and a skewer inserted in the center will come out clean when done.

MAKES I LOAF

Variation: For a delicious winter variation, substitute 1 cup dried apricots for the raspberries. Cut the apricots into small pieces and plump them in ½ cup hot water. Drain any remaining liquid before adding them to the dough.

Nectarine-Almond Streusel Coffee Cake

We serve this beautiful coffee cake at brunch throughout the year, varying the fruit with the seasons. Summer is a wonderful time to try berries, peaches, apricots, or cherries. In fall and winter pears and apples add their delicious, subtle flavor. You can also use the batter to make a scrumptious upside-down cake, using the fruit of your choice.

12 tablespoons unsalted butter
1½ cups sugar
Zest of 2 lemons, minced
4 eggs
3 cups unbleached white flour
½ tablespoon baking powder
½ tablespoon baking soda
½ teaspoon salt
1½ cups crème fraîche (page 359) or sour cream
3 nectarines, pitted and cut into ½-inch pieces, about 2 cups
Streusel Topping (recipe follows)

Butter and lightly flour a 10-inch tube pan or 2 9-inch round cake pans. Preheat the oven to 350°F.

In a mixing bowl, cream the butter, sugar, and zest together until light and fluffy. Add the eggs 1 at a time, mixing them completely into the batter after each addition. Sift the dry ingredients together and add them alternately with the crème fraîche. Fold in the fruit and pour the batter into the pan. Cover evenly with the topping and bake until a skewer inserted in the center comes out clean, about 50 minutes for the tube pan, 40 to 45 minutes for the cake pans.

Streusel Topping

This spicy nut topping holds well in the refrigerator. Make a double recipe to keep on hand and store in a sealed container in the refrigerator.

¾ tablespoon unbleached white flour
½ cup light brown sugar
1 teaspoon cinnamon, preferably freshly ground
1½ tablespoons cold unsalted butter, cut into small cubes
¾ cup chopped walnut pieces or almonds

Place the flour, sugar, and cinnamon in the bowl of a mixer or a food processor. Add the butter and process until the mixture resembles coarse meal. If you're using a food processor, transfer the mixture to a separate bowl, then quickly mix in the nuts.

MAKES 1 LARGE OR 2 SMALL CAKES; SERVES EIGHT TO TEN

Variation—Upside-Down Cake: This stunning cake is exceptionally rich and moist. It's a wonderful way to show off fruit, particularly in the summer with juicy peaches, nectarines, and plums. It's also delicious in the fall and winter with tart apples or tender pears. You'll need 3 to 5 pieces of the fruit of your choice, depending on size. Apples and peaches will need to be peeled before slicing. If you're using a small fruit, such as plums, you'll need 5 or 6 of them.

Melt ¼ pound unsalted butter and 1½ cups light brown sugar together over medium heat. Spread the warm mixture evenly over the bottom of 2 9-inch cake pans. Thinly slice the fruit and arrange in the bottom of the pan in a close overlapping spiral pattern. There will be 3 to 4 spirals, depending on the size of the fruit. For an especially beautiful cake, place a wreath of raspberries around the center spiral, tucking the berries in between the fruit slices. (A cup of berries should be plenty.)

Pour the batter over the fruit and bake as directed for about 40 to 45 minutes. Test the cake to see that it's firm in the center before removing from the oven. If the center springs back, the cake is done. (The center needs to be firm to support the weight of the fruit when turned upside down.)

When the cakes have cooled, loosen the sides of the pan with a rubber spatula. Gently turn the cake out onto a plate or serving platter. The fruit will have caramelized with the sugar, and the spiral pattern will have a deep, rich color.

MAKES TWO 9-INCH CAKES

Ginger-Lemon Muffins

These tender, moist muffins are a Sunday brunch favorite, and they couldn't be better. They're filled with bright lemon flavor and the warm spice of fresh ginger. We've adapted this recipe from Marion Cunningham's *The Breakfast Book*.

1 cup unbleached white flour
¼ teaspoon salt
½ teaspoon baking soda
4 tablespoons unsalted butter, softened
7 tablespoons sugar
1 egg
½ cup buttermilk
3 tablespoons grated fresh ginger
Zest of 2 lemons, minced

Preheat the oven to 375°F and butter muffin tins. Mix the flour, salt, and baking soda together. Cream the butter and sugar together in a mixing bowl, add the egg, and beat until smooth. Add the buttermilk and mix until blended, being sure to scrape down the sides. Add the dry ingredients and mix until smooth. Stir in the grated ginger and lemon zest. Spoon the batter into the muffin tins so that each cup is three-quarters full. Bake for 15 to 20 minutes, until the muffins are set inside and turn golden.

MAKES 8 MUFFINS

Corn Cakes

This is our version of Marion Cunningham's recipe in *The Breakfast Book*. These tender griddle cakes are wonderfully light yet full of corn flavor. In the summer months we add kernels of fresh corn sautéed in butter—just right with warm maple syrup. Serve with Poached Apricots (page 364) or sprinkled with fresh raspberries. Be sure to use fine cornmeal to keep the cakes light.

½ cup unbleached white flour
½ teaspoon salt
1 tablespoon sugar
1 tablespoon baking powder
1 egg
4 tablespoons unsalted butter, melted
¼ cup milk
½ cup fine cornmeal
½ cup boiling water
Unsalted butter or light vegetable oil for the pan

Mix the flour, salt, sugar, and baking powder together. In a mixing bowl, whisk the egg, melted butter, and milk together until well blended. In another mixing bowl, combine the cornmeal and boiling water. Stir until well blended. Add the dry ingredients and the milk mixture; mix until thoroughly blended.

Heat a griddle or skillet over medium-high heat and coat the pan with butter or light vegetable oil when it is hot. This is all the butter that should be needed once the pan is seasoned. Turn the heat down to medium. Use about 3 tablespoons batter for each pancake and spoon the batter into the pan. Spread the batter with the back of a spoon if necessary to thin it out a little. Cook until bubbles break on top of the cakes, about 1 to 2 minutes, then turn them over. Cook for another few minutes. The cakes will be lightly browned when they are done.

MAKES ABOUT TEN 3-INCH CAKES

To Add Fresh Corn: Shave an ear of corn and sauté the kernels in a tablespoon of butter until tender. Add several pinches of salt to taste. Sprinkle about a tablespoon of corn on each cake after you've added the batter to the pan, then follow the directions for cooking.

Buttermilk Pancakes

Though these tender, light griddle cakes are perfect served with warm maple syrup and crème fraîche, this basic recipe lends itself to many wonderful variations. Add sliced bananas and toasted pecans to the pancakes just before you turn them or try fresh berries or sautéed apples. They're also delicious served with sliced nectarines and raspberries or blueberries.

1 tablespoon unsalted butter
1 egg
1 cup buttermilk, at room temperature
¾ cup unbleached white flour
½ teaspoon salt
1 teaspoon baking soda
1 teaspoon light vegetable oil (optional)
Unsalted butter or light vegetable oil for the pan

Melt the butter in a small saucepan over medium heat. In a mixing bowl, briskly whisk the egg, buttermilk, and melted butter together. In a separate bowl, combine the dry ingredients; mix until blended, then stir into the buttermilk mixture until the dry ingredients are moistened. The batter will be lumpy.

Heat a griddle or skillet over medium-high heat and coat the pan with butter or vegetable oil when it is hot. Once the pan is seasoned, no more oil should be needed. Turn the heat down to medium. Use about 3 tablespoons batter for each cake and spoon the batter into the pan. Cook until bubbles break on top, 2 to 3 minutes, then turn them and cook until set and lightly browned, about 1 minute.

MAKES ABOUT TWELVE 3-INCH CAKES

Variations

Buckwheat Pancakes: Serve in the winter with warm applesauce and poached cranberries or Cranberry Applesauce (page 363). Make the batter as directed, substituting ¼ cup buckwheat flour for ¼ cup of the white flour.

Buckwheat Banana-Pecan Pancakes: These nutty, sweet pancakes are a Sunday brunch favorite, and we make them throughout the year. The banana sugars caramelize in the skillet, giving the pancakes a wonderful rich flavor. You can also make them with the buttermilk batter.

Make the buckwheat pancake batter. You'll need 1 large ripe banana cut into slices and ⅓ cup chopped toasted pecans. Spoon the batter into the skillet and place the sliced bananas and nuts on each cake before turning.

Apple-Spice Pancakes: These pancakes are filled with tender apples sautéed in butter and the warm spice of cinnamon. A splash or two of Calvados would be wonderful here. You'll need 2 flavorful apples, 1 tablespoon butter, and ¾ teaspoon ground cinnamon.

Use either the buttermilk or buckwheat batter. Peel and core the apples and cut into ½-inch pieces. Heat the butter in a medium-size sauté pan and add the apples and the cinnamon. Sauté over medium heat until the apples are tender, about 7 to 8 minutes. Set aside to cool, then gently fold into the batter. Make the cakes as directed.

CRÈME FRAÎCHE

Crème fraîche is a favorite ingredient—we add it to dishes just before serving to soften and balance the flavors. Unlike sour cream, which breaks or curdles when added to acidic ingredients, crème fraîche remains silky. Try it as a soup garnish or add a spoonful to pastas, risottos, and stews.

It couldn't be easier to make—just allow about 36 hours for the cream to thicken and develop flavor. To make 2 cups of crème fraîche, pour 2 cups heavy cream into a jar or plastic container, add 1 scant tablespoon cultured buttermilk, and whisk or stir the mixture together. Place the container on an upper shelf in a warm part of the kitchen or on top of the refrigerator. Leave the container ajar to help the culture grow. The cream will thicken after 24 hours, and it is usable at this point, but we like to allow another 12 hours for the flavor to develop fully. Cover the container and refrigerate as you would sour cream. The crème fraîche will keep for several weeks. Reserve 1 tablespoon crème fraîche to make your next batch—to keep it going, alternate the crème fraîche starter with buttermilk to freshen the culture.

If you're wondering what to do with leftover cream, crème fraîche is a good solution. A teaspoon of buttermilk or crème fraîche starter is all you need to turn a cup of cream into crème fraîche, extending its life for a week or two.

French Toast

We usually make this French Toast with light, sweet challah, but sourdough bread also works well. It's the spicy cinnamon and orange zest that make the flavor so delectable. Serve with a pitcher of warm maple syrup and warm Applesauce or Cranberry Applesauce (page 363).

4 eggs
1 cup half-and-half or milk
2 tablespoons sugar
Zest of 1 orange, minced
½ teaspoon cinnamon, preferably freshly ground
8 slices of challah or sourdough bread
Unsalted butter for the pan

Beat the eggs, half-and-half, sugar, zest, and cinnamon together in a shallow bowl. Transfer to a shallow dish. Soak each slice of bread in the mixture until moist and soaked through.

Melt enough butter in a large skillet to coat the bottom of the pan. When the butter sizzles, add as many slices of bread as your pan will hold. Cook over medium heat until the bread is lightly browned on each side, making sure that the slices are cooked through. Repeat with the remaining slices.

SERVES FOUR

Variation: A large pinch or two of grated nutmeg or a small sprinkle of ground cloves will add delicious flavor and a bit of spice.

Desserts

Desserts

Of all the seasons, summer is my favorite time for desserts. There's an excitement in the Greens kitchen as the first apricots and cherries appear in crates and flats on our loading dock. These superior fruits bring in the summer season—a time for Apricot-Cherry Crisp, Peach-Blueberry Pie, and fragrant berries of all kinds to serve with Honey Mousse, Crème Anglaise, or simply on their own.

Figs make a brief appearance in June, but their big harvest is really late summer—they linger on through October and disappear quickly when the evenings turn cool. Place them on a warm windowsill until they're perfectly ripe—this is the time to enjoy their succulent flavor. The first Gravenstein apples, French Butter pears, and Bartletts signal that fall is really on its way. We welcome the cooler season with warm Apple-Cranberry Crisp, Baked Apples with Crème Anglaise, and Gingerbread with Poached Apricots and Cranberries. Make an elegant fall or winter compote with poached Bosc pears, quince, apricots, and cranberries.

Meyer lemons and tangerines of all varieties brighten our winter offerings—their freshly squeezed juice makes the most delicately flavored ice creams, sorbets, and pots de crème. Meyer lemons are becoming well known now, and they're available most months of the year. Not to be forgotten are ruby grapefruit, blood oranges, and sweet navels. Rhubarb and the first strawberries, so delicious together, signal spring is on the way with warmer days and the fruits of summer just a few months away.

Applesauce

You can use any kind of apples for applesauce, though freshness and flavor are of course essential. We use red apples whenever possible—their sauce is a beautiful pale rosy color. Sierra Beauty, Jonathan, and McIntosh all have wonderful flavor. Serve applesauce over Buckwheat Pancakes (page 358) with warm maple syrup and a generous spoonful of crème fraîche (page 359).

6 large apples, peeled, cored, and sliced, about 3 pounds
½ cup apple juice or water
Sugar
Juice of 1 lemon

Place the apples and juice in a saucepan. Cook, covered, over medium-low heat, for about 15 minutes, until quite soft, stirring as needed. Remove from the heat and mash with a fork or potato masher. Add sugar and lemon juice to taste, depending on the flavor of the apples. Serve warm, or cool the sauce and refrigerate.

MAKES ABOUT 1 QUART

Variations: You can also use cinnamon or vanilla as a seasoning. Add about ½ teaspoon of either or cook the sauce with a short length of cinnamon stick.

Cranberry Applesauce: The tartness of the sauce makes this a fall and winter favorite. Add ½ cup cranberries to the apples and sweeten to taste, but not too much or you'll disguise the wonderful tartness of the cranberries.

Poached Apricots

These simple apricots are quick and easy to make. We often include them in our winter fruit compotes—their beautiful warm color and chewy texture are just right with poached cranberries (page 365), pears, and quince. For an exceptional breakfast treat, serve the apricots warm over Buckwheat Pancakes (page 358) with toasted pecans.

1 vanilla bean
1 lemon
1½ cups sugar
1 quart water
2 cups dried apricots, about 10 ounces

Cut the vanilla bean in half lengthwise and scrape out the seeds. Using a vegetable peeler, remove 2 to 3 wide strips of zest from the lemon, being careful not to include the bitter white pith just under the skin.

Combine the sugar and water in a medium-size saucepan; bring to a boil, making sure all of the sugar is dissolved. Add the zest, the vanilla bean and seeds, and the apricots to the syrup; gently simmer until the apricots are plump and tender, 15 to 20 minutes. They should be a little firm, because they'll continue to cook in the poaching syrup. Remove from the heat; cool and refrigerate, leaving the vanilla and lemon zest in the syrup. The apricots will hold well in the refrigerator for up to a week.

Variation: The flavor of the vanilla is important here—if you don't have a vanilla bean, its rich, perfumy flavor will be missed, but you can use vanilla extract instead. Add 1 teaspoon extract to the apricots after you remove them from the heat.

MAKES ABOUT 4 CUPS; SERVES FOUR TO SIX

Poached Cranberries

These sweet-tart berries are delightful with warm Gingerbread (page 379) and add sparkle to winter fruit compotes. Like Applesauce (page 363), they can be served with savory dishes to bring out contrasting flavors. The poached berries hold well in the refrigerator, but be sure to reheat them gently so they don't lose their shape.

1½ cups sugar
1½ cups water
1 small orange
¾ pound cranberries

Combine the sugar and water in a medium-size saucepan; bring to a boil, making sure all the sugar is dissolved. Using a vegetable peeler, remove 2 to 3 wide strips of zest from the orange, being careful not to include the bitter white pith. Add the zest and cranberries to the syrup and reduce the heat to medium-low. Gently simmer the berries for 6 to 8 minutes or until they begin to pop, but do not overcook. The berries should be soft but still retain their shape. Remove from the heat and leave in the syrup to cool.

MAKES ABOUT 4 CUPS

Ginger Pound Cake

This lovely moist cake is full of fresh ginger flavor. We serve it in the summer with fresh peaches or nectarines and berries, in the winter with a warm compote of Poached Apricots and Cranberries (pages 364 and 365). It's also wonderful served warm just by itself or with a spoonful of whipped cream.

3¾ cups sifted cake flour, or 3¼ cups sifted unbleached white flour
1 teaspoon baking powder
½ teaspoon salt
1 pound unsalted butter, at room temperature
1 teaspoon orange zest, minced
2½ cups sugar
6 eggs, at room temperature
¼ cup grated fresh ginger
1 cup milk, at room temperature

Preheat the oven to 300°F. Butter and lightly flour a 10-inch tube pan or 2 loaf pans or line them with parchment paper. Sift the flour, baking powder, and salt together. Cream the butter and zest until light and fluffy, about 5 minutes. Gradually add the sugar and beat until the mixture is fluffy again. Add the eggs 1 at a time, being sure that they are well incorporated after each addition. Mix in the fresh ginger. Add the flour mixture alternately with the milk, beginning and ending with the flour.

Pour the batter into the prepared pan and bake for 1¾ to 2 hours, until a skewer inserted in the center comes out clean.

SERVES EIGHT TO TEN

Persimmon Pudding

This rich wintery pudding is our version of Marion Cunningham's recipe from *The Break-fast Book*. Traditionally this pudding is steamed in a bath of hot water on the stove, but ours is steamed in the oven. Serve it warm with Crème Anglaise (page 381) or softly whipped cream.

About 2 ripe persimmons, enough to make 1 cup puree
2 teaspoons baking soda
¼ pound unsalted butter
1½ cups sugar
2 eggs
1 tablespoon fresh lemon juice
1 tablespoon rum
1 cup unbleached white flour
1 teaspoon cinnamon, preferably freshly ground
½ teaspoon salt
1 cup chopped walnut pieces or pecans
½ cup raisins

Preheat the oven to 325°F. Cut the persimmons in half and scrape the flesh out of the skin; puree in a blender or a food processor. Add the baking soda to the puree. (The puree will thicken.) Cream the butter and the sugar together; add the eggs, lemon juice, and rum; mix until well blended. Combine the dry ingredients and stir them in. Add the persimmon mixture; beat until well mixed, then stir in the nuts and raisins.

Pour the batter into a greased bundt or loaf pan. Place in a large baking pan to make a hot water bath, then add enough hot water to come 2 inches up the side of the bundt or loaf pan. Cover the baking pan with foil and bake for about 2 hours, until the pudding is set.

SERVES EIGHT TO TEN

Gâteau Moule—Steamed Chocolate Cake

There is nothing quite like this rich chocolate cake. It's baked in a water bath just like a custard—it's so delicate and moist that it needs to be handled quite carefully when served. It isn't at all difficult to make; just be sure to fold in the egg whites thoroughly but gently. Slightly tart Raspberry Sauce (page 382) is the perfect accent here.

5 ounces semisweet chocolate, chopped
6 tablespoons unsalted butter
2 tablespoons brewed coffee
2 tablespoons water
½ cup sugar
3 egg yolks
2 tablespoons unbleached white flour
½ teaspoon vanilla extract
5 egg whites
¼ teaspoon cream of tartar
Salt

Preheat oven to 325°F. Butter a 9- by 5-inch loaf pan and line it with foil or parchment paper.

Combine the chocolate, butter, coffee, and water in a large bowl and melt over a pan of barely simmering water. Remove from the heat. Whisk ¼ cup of the sugar into the egg yolks and whisk this into the chocolate mixture. Whisk in the flour and vanilla.

Beat the egg whites with the cream of tartar and a pinch of salt until soft peaks form, sprinkle in the remaining sugar, and beat to shiny stiff peaks, being careful not to overbeat. Fold a dollop of whites into the chocolate mixture, then fold in the remaining whites. The mixture should be fairly well blended when done. Do not overblend, or the egg whites will deflate.

Pour the batter into the loaf pan, then place it in a shallow baking dish large enough to hold it. Add enough hot water to make a water bath that comes halfway up the sides of the loaf pan. Bake for 1½ to 1¾ hours. When the cake is done, a skewer inserted in the center will come out with dry crumbs. Cool the cake in the pan, then gently turn it out when ready to serve.

SERVES FOUR TO SIX

Tip: This cake is so delicate that it's difficult to slice—don't expect perfect slices. Heat your knife under hot water, then wipe it dry before slicing.

Raspberries and Figs with Honey Mousse

The flavor of the honey makes all the difference in this mousse, so be sure to use a good one. Light, creamy, and sweetened only by the honey, it's a wonderful complement to fresh figs and late summer berries. Show off the beauty of the figs by serving this family style—loosely arrange the figs on a platter, sprinkle with the berries, and pass the bowl of mousse.

THE FRUIT
1 pint raspberries
1 pint fresh figs: Black Mission, Kadota, or Calmyrna

Sort through the raspberries, but do not rinse them, because water will dilute their flavor. Rinse the figs and cut them in half, leaving the stem ends on.

HONEY MOUSSE
½ cup honey
4 egg yolks
2 pinches of salt
2 cups heavy cream

Whisk the honey, yolks, and salt together in a bowl over a pan of barely simmering water. (Be sure that the bowl is sitting *over* the water, not in it.) Whisk the mixture continuously for 8 minutes, noting how the texture changes as it cooks. For the first 2 to 3 minutes it will be thin and foamy; after 5 minutes it will begin to thicken and the texture will become creamy. Whisk vigorously for a few more minutes, until the mousse leaves thick ribbons on its surface when poured over itself. Set aside to cool. The texture of the cooled mousse will be stiff and sticky and a little difficult to work with.

Whisk 2 tablespoons cream into the mousse, working it until it loosens. Whip the remaining cream until it's firm, fold it into the mousse until it is just incorporated, then whisk the two together. (The cream will lose some of its loft as you whisk it into the mousse.) The texture will be light and creamy, though a little thinner than you might expect.

MAKES 3 CUPS; SERVES FOUR

Lemon Pots de Crème

The expected richness of the custard is lightened by the tart, clear taste of lemon. For an exceptional treat, use fragrant Meyer lemons when they're in season. This dish is most luscious served warm from the oven, but it's also wonderful served at room temperature.

2 whole eggs
8 egg yolks
1¼ to 1½ cups sugar
1 teaspoon lemon zest, minced, about 1 lemon
1 cup fresh lemon juice, about 6 to 8 lemons
2½ cups heavy cream

Preheat the oven to 325°F. In a mixing bowl, vigorously whisk the eggs, yolks, and sugar together. When the mixture is thoroughly blended, whisk in the lemon juice, then the cream. Pour the mixture through a fine-mesh strainer, then add the lemon zest.

Pour the mixture into custard cups or ramekins. Place them in a baking pan and add enough hot water to come halfway up the sides of the cups. Cover the pan loosely with foil and bake until the custard is just set, 40 to 45 minutes. The custard should still be soft in the center when lightly shaken. (It will continue to set as it cools.) Remove from the baking pan and cool.

MAKES EIGHT 6-OUNCE RAMEKINS

Note: The Pots de Crème can be refrigerated, if necessary, but give them plenty of time to return to room temperature before serving.

Ginger Pots de Crème

This distinctive custard is delicate and light, filled with the spice of fresh ginger. For a finishing touch we sprinkle each serving with chopped candied ginger.

½ pound fresh ginger
1 quart heavy cream
½ cup sugar
5 egg yolks
About 2 coins of candied ginger, diced

Fill a medium-size saucepan with water and bring it to a boil over high heat. Peel the ginger and slice it into ¼-inch rounds. Drop it into the boiling water for 30 seconds, then drain it in a colander.

In the same saucepan, combine the cream and the sugar. Over medium-high heat, bring it to the point where it is just barely boiling. When you're sure that all of the sugar is dissolved, add the ginger, then remove the pan from the heat. Cover and let steep for 1 hour. The cream mixture should be infused with ginger flavor. If not, let it steep a little longer. Strain out the ginger and whisk in the egg yolks. Pour through a fine-mesh strainer.

Preheat the oven to 325°F. Pour the mixture into custard cups or ramekins. Place them in a baking pan and add enough hot water to come halfway up the sides of the cups. Cover the pan loosely with foil and bake until the custard is just set, 40 to 50 minutes. The custard should still be soft in the center when lightly shaken. Remove from the baking pan and cool. Garnish with the candied ginger.

MAKES SIX 6-OUNCE CUSTARDS

Apple-Rhubarb Crisp

The tartness of rhubarb is a delightful contrast to the sweet apples and the crunchy texture of the topping. Serve this fragrant, rustic crisp hot from the oven with Crème Anglaise (page 381) or a homemade vanilla ice cream. For a fall variation, try using cranberries in place of the rhubarb.

CRISP TOPPING

This topping holds well in the refrigerator, so make a double recipe and store it in a well-sealed container. It's handy to have around for your next crisp or to sprinkle over sliced fruit for an easy, quick warm fruit dessert.

1 cup unbleached white flour
¼ cup sugar
¼ cup light brown sugar, packed
¼ teaspoon salt
½ teaspoon cinnamon, preferably freshly ground
¼ teaspoon nutmeg, preferably freshly grated
¼ pound cold unsalted butter, cut into ¼-inch cubes
¼ cup chopped walnut pieces

Mix the flour, sugars, salt, and spices together in a bowl. Work in the butter with your fingers or an electric mixer, mixing until the topping is crumbly and begins to hold together. Add the nuts and quickly mix them in.

THE FRUIT

2 medium-size rhubarb stalks, washed and sliced ½ inch thick, about 1 cup, or 1 cup
*   cranberries, about ¼ pound*
2½ pounds apples, peeled and sliced ½ inch thick, about 7 cups
2 or 3 tablespoons sugar

Preheat the oven to 375°F. Wash the rhubarb well, cutting off any brown spots or leaves still on the stalks. If the stalks are especially thick, cut them in half lengthwise before slicing so that all of the pieces are approximately the same size. Place the apple and rhubarb slices in a 9-inch square baking dish, a 9-inch round cake pan, or 6 individual ovenproof dishes. Sprinkle the fruit with sugar to taste (the amount of sugar will vary according to the sweetness of the apples). Level the fruit and cover evenly with topping.

Bake until the topping is golden brown, the fruit is tender, and the juices bubble around the sides, about 40 to 50 minutes. Individual crisps will take about 25 to 30 minutes.

SERVES SIX

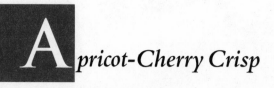

Apricot-Cherry Crisp

We make this luscious crisp in the early summer, when apricots and cherries are at the height of their season. The warm spice of fresh ginger enhances the rich, tangy apricots and the sweetness of the cherries. Serve golden brown and bubbling and spoon lightly whipped cream over each serving.

Crisp Topping (page 372)
1½ pounds apricots, quartered, about 6 cups
½ pound Bing cherries, pitted, about 2 cups
Zest of 1 lemon, minced
1 generous teaspoon grated fresh ginger
½ cup sugar
2 tablespoons unbleached white flour

Preheat the oven to 375°F. Make the topping. Toss the rest of the ingredients together in a mixing bowl and place in a 9-inch square baking dish, a 9-inch round cake pan, or 6 individual ovenproof dishes. Level the fruit and cover with the topping. Bake for 45 to 50 minutes (25 to 30 minutes for individual crisps), until the crisp is golden brown and the juices bubble around the sides of the dish.

SERVES SIX

Peach-Blueberry Pie

Serve this luscious pie warm from the oven, while the juices are still bubbling and the kitchen is filled with its fragrance. It can't get much better than fresh peaches and blueberries, though nectarines, raspberries, or blackberries will make an equally delicious variation. Serve with a generous spoonful of lightly whipped cream or vanilla ice cream.

Piecrust (page 375)
2 pounds peaches, pitted, peeled, and cut into ½-inch slices, about 4 cups
1 cup blueberries
6 tablespoons sugar plus ½ teaspoon
2 tablespoons unbleached white flour
1 egg yolk
1 teaspoon milk

Line a 9-inch pie pan with the dough as directed. Preheat the oven to 400°F.

Toss the peaches with the blueberries, 6 tablespoons sugar, and flour. Add the fruit mixture to the prepared pie pan. Trim the pie dough so that it's even with the edge of the pan and lightly brush the edges with water. Roll out the top crust, lay it over the filling, and trim, leaving ½ inch extending over the bottom crust. Fold the top edge under the bottom edge and crimp together.

Whisk the yolk and milk together to make an egg wash and glaze the crust with it. Sprinkle with ½ teaspoon sugar. Cut a few vents in the top crust for the steam to escape. Bake for 40 to 45 minutes, until the pie is golden, or until the juice bubbles thickly from the vents.

MAKES ONE 9-INCH PIE; SERVES SIX

P*iecrust*

This is our basic recipe, and we use it for all of our fruit pies. As with all pie doughs, keep the butter cold and don't overwork it, or you'll lose the light, flaky texture.

> *2 cups unbleached white flour*
> *¼ teaspoon salt*
> *1 teaspoon sugar*
> *½ pound cold unsalted butter*
> *¼ cup vegetable shortening*
> *¼ cup ice water*

Mix the flour, salt, and sugar in a bowl. Chop the butter into small cubes and cut half of it into the flour mixture, using a pastry blender, a food processor, or 2 knives, until the mixture resembles coarse meal. Add the shortening and the remaining butter and cut them in, leaving ¼-inch pieces. This will help make the dough flaky. Sprinkle with the water, tossing lightly with a fork to moisten it evenly, until the dough holds together. (You may not need all of the water.)

Divide the dough in half and press into 2 balls. Wrap in plastic wrap and let it rest for at least 4 hours, refrigerated. Lightly flour a work surface and roll the dough into circles ⅛ inch thick and 11 to 12 inches in diameter. Place a circle gently into a 9-inch pie pan, being careful not to stretch the dough, or it will shrink when you bake it. You can place the second dough in a pie pan as well or save it for a top crust. Keep the crusts refrigerated until you are ready to fill and bake them.

MAKES TWO 9-INCH CRUSTS

Cranberry Lattice Tart

This favorite fall tart is warm and inviting, with deep red cranberries peeking out of the woven lattice crust. The inspiration comes from the cranberry tart recipe in *The Silver Palate*. Try serving it with homemade vanilla ice cream or lightly sweetened whipped cream.

1 recipe Sweet Pastry Dough (recipe follows)
3 cups cranberries, about ¾ pound
12 dried apricots, quartered, about 2 ounces
1 cup sugar
½ cup water, or ¾ cup plus 1 teaspoon almond extract if you're not using Amaretto or Grand Marnier
¼ cup Amaretto or Grand Marnier
1 egg yolk
2 teaspoons milk or heavy cream

Line a 9-inch pie pan with the dough and cut the lattice strips. Place the cranberries, apricots, sugar, and water in a medium-size saucepan. Cook over medium heat until the cranberry skins pop, about 10 minutes. Add the liqueur and cook for 10 minutes more, then remove from the heat and cool.

Preheat the oven to 375°F. Fill the tart shell with the cranberry mixture. Whisk the yolk and milk or cream together and brush the lattice strips with the egg wash. Lay 6 strips down, evenly spaced, over the filling (using the shorter strips for the ends and the longer ones for the center). Weave the remaining 6 strips into the first strips on a diagonal. Or you can just lay the remaining strips diagonally right over the first strips. Press around the edges of the tart, removing any excess pieces of dough and making sure the ends of the strips are well attached to the edges of the tart. Bake for 40 to 50 minutes, until the filling is bubbling and the crust is golden.

MAKES ONE 9-INCH TART; SERVES EIGHT TO TEN

Sweet Pastry Dough

2⅔ cups unbleached white flour, sifted
½ cup sugar
½ pound cold unsalted butter
2 egg yolks
¼ cup or more heavy cream

Combine the flour and sugar in a mixing bowl. Cut the butter into ¼-inch cubes. Using a food processor, a mixer, a pastry blender, or 2 knives, incorporate the butter into the flour-sugar mixture until it resembles coarse meal. Whisk the yolks and cream together and pour into the flour mixture. With your hands, gather the dough together in a ball. You may need to add up to 2 tablespoons more cream for the dough to come together. Divide the dough in half and press into 2 balls. Wrap in plastic wrap and let it rest for at least 30 minutes in the refrigerator. When it is cold enough to work with, lightly flour a work surface and roll the dough into circles about ⅛ inch thick and 10 to 11 inches in diameter. Place one circle gently into the tart pan. Trim the edges so that they are even with the rim of the pan. Cut the remaining circle into 12 ⅓-inch-wide strips. Keep the crust and the strips refrigerated until you're ready to fill the tart.

MAKES ONE 9-INCH TART SHELL AND ONE LATTICE TOP
OR TWO 9-INCH TART SHELLS

Rhubarb-Strawberry Cobbler

Make this cobbler in the early spring with the first strawberries of the season. The strawberries and tart rhubarb bubble together under the crumbly, light cobbler topping, releasing their wonderful fragrance. Serve warm from the oven with lightly whipped cream.

1 ¼ pounds rhubarb
A 1-pint basket of strawberries, about 1 ½ cups
⅔ cup sugar
2 ½ tablespoons unbleached white flour
Zest of 1 small orange
Cobbler Topping (recipe follows)

Preheat the oven to 375°F. Wash the rhubarb well, cutting off any brown spots or leaves still on the stalks. If the stalks are especially thick, cut them in half lengthwise before slicing ½ inch thick so that all of the pieces are approximately the same size. Wash the strawberries, pat dry, and hull them. Cut them into halves or leave whole if small. Toss the fruit with the sugar, flour, and zest; place in an 8-inch square baking dish, a 9-inch round cake pan, or 6 to 8 individual ovenproof dishes.

Make the cobbler topping and cover the fruit with tablespoon-size dollops of it, using all of the topping. Bake for 35 to 40 minutes, until the topping is browned and cooked through and the fruit is bubbling. Individual cobblers will take about 25 to 30 minutes.

SERVES SIX

Cobbler Topping

1 ½ cups unbleached white flour
¼ teaspoon salt
1 tablespoon baking powder
2 tablespoons sugar
4 tablespoons unsalted butter
1 cup heavy cream

Combine the dry ingredients and cut in the butter with a food processor, an electric mixer, a pastry blender, or 2 knives until it resembles coarse meal. Add the cream and mix lightly, just until the dry ingredients are moistened.

Variation: This cobbler is also delicious made simply with strawberries. You'll need 3 baskets of berries, about 5 cups washed, hulled, and cut into halves or left whole if small. The berries are so sweet that you'll need only ⅓ cup sugar. Toss them with the sugar, 2 tablespoons flour, and the chopped zest of an orange. Assemble the cobbler and bake as directed.

Gingerbread

This delectable cake is surprisingly moist and rich with fresh ginger flavor. Serve it warm as a sweet morning bread or an afternoon treat and it's sure to disappear quickly.

1½ cups unbleached white flour
1 teaspoon baking soda
½ teaspoon salt
1 egg
¼ cup unsulphured molasses
¼ cup dark corn syrup
¼ pound unsalted butter, softened
½ cup light brown sugar
½ cup buttermilk, at room temperature
3 ounces fresh ginger, grated, about ½ cup

Preheat the oven to 350°F. Grease an 8-inch round cake pan. Sift the flour, baking soda, and salt together. Beat the egg in a mixing bowl; add the molasses and corn syrup and beat together. In another bowl, cream the butter and sugar until light and fluffy. Slowly beat in the molasses mixture until smooth, stopping to scrape down the sides of the bowl several times. Alternately add dry ingredients and buttermilk, beginning and ending with dry ingredients. Stir in the grated ginger.

Pour the batter into the prepared pan and bake until the top springs back or a skewer inserted in the center comes out clean, 35 to 40 minutes.

SERVES SIX

Baked Apples Filled with Walnuts and Currants

Serve this homey fall dessert in its own juice or with Maple or Vanilla Crème Anglaise (page 381). The apples are best when served warm from the oven, but they're also delicious re-heated for breakfast the next day.

Be sure to select good baking apples—otherwise, your beautiful baked apples will turn to an exceptionally flavorful "baked applesauce" before they reach the point of tenderness.

¼ cup walnut pieces or pecans, toasted (page 263)
4 medium-size apples: Pippin, Jonathan, Rome Beauty, or other flavorful baking apples
¼ cup raisins or dried currants
Zest of 1 orange, minced
¼ teaspoon cinnamon, preferably freshly ground
2 tablespoons honey or light brown sugar
Apple juice

Chop the toasted nuts when they have cooled. Peel around the top third of the apples, then partially core them, leaving about a ½-inch piece of core at the bottom of each. In a small bowl, combine all of the ingredients except for the apple juice and stuff the apple cavities.

Place the apples in a baking dish and pour in enough apple juice to fill the dish to a depth of 1 inch. Cover and bake for 40 to 60 minutes, depending on the size and variety of apples. Check them as they bake. The apples are done when they can be easily pierced with the tip of a knife. Remove from the oven and drizzle some of the juice over the apples before serving.

SERVES FOUR

Crème Anglaise

The fresh vanilla bean makes all the difference in this simple custard sauce—the bean and the seeds steep together in the warm cream, releasing their perfumy essence. Pour it over fresh summer fruit or try it with warm Apple-Rhubarb Crisp (page 372) or Apricot-Cherry Crisp (page 373).

1 vanilla bean
2 cups half-and-half
¼ cup sugar
4 egg yolks

Slice the vanilla bean in half lengthwise and scrape out the seeds with the knife blade. In a medium-size nonreactive saucepan, heat the half-and-half, sugar, and vanilla bean and seeds until just barely boiling, making sure all of the sugar is dissolved. Remove from the heat, cover, and let sit until the liquid is infused with vanilla flavor, about 30 minutes. Be careful not to oversteep, because the strong vanilla flavor can be overpowering.

In a medium-size bowl, beat the yolks, then slowly whisk in one-quarter of the warm liquid. Add this to the rest of the liquid and cook the mixture over medium heat, stirring constantly with a wooden spoon, until it thickens enough to coat the back of the spoon, about 6 to 8 minutes. Be careful not to overcook, because the eggs will scramble. Pour through a fine-mesh strainer and cool.

MAKES 2½ CUPS

Variations

Maple Crème Anglaise: Excellent with warm Baked Apples (page 380). Substitute 1 cup maple syrup for the sugar and omit the vanilla bean. The maple syrup will not need to be steeped in the half-and-half; just warm it with the cream over medium heat and then follow the instructions for cooking.

Mint Crème Anglaise: For mint lovers. This is particularly delicious with Gâteau Moule (page 368). Substitute 1 cup chopped fresh mint leaves for the vanilla bean and follow the instructions for steeping. Strain out the leaves before cooking the mixture with the yolks.

Espresso Crème Anglaise: This will make the most humble chocolate cake taste extravagant. Substitute ½ cup chopped or lightly crushed espresso beans for the vanilla bean and follow the instructions for steeping. Strain the beans out before cooking the mixture with the yolks.

Rose Geranium Crème Anglaise: Pour this sauce over fresh berries. Substitute 3 to 4 rose geranium leaves for the vanilla bean, crushing the leaves with your fingertips to release their essence before steeping. Follow the recipe for steeping, but taste the steeped cream after 15 minutes. If the rose geranium flavor is strong enough, remove the leaves. If not, continue to steep for 15 more minutes. Strain out the leaves before cooking the mixture with the yolks.

Raspberry Sauce

The tart flavor of fresh raspberries is always appealing, particularly with the rich taste of chocolate. Serve this simple sauce with Gâteau Moule (page 368) or drizzled over berry sorbets or fresh peach ice cream. You can include blackberries or boysenberries or any combination of berries you like.

½ cup water
½ cup sugar
2 1-pint baskets of raspberries, about 4 cups
Juice of 1 lemon (optional)
Framboise or kirsch (optional)

In a small saucepan, bring the water and sugar to a boil, making sure all of the sugar has dissolved. Set aside to cool. Puree the raspberries in a blender or food processor, then pour through a fine-mesh strainer to remove the seeds. Pour the cooled syrup into the berry puree, adding it gradually to taste, depending on the flavor and sweetness of the berries. Adjust the seasoning with lemon juice and framboise or kirsch if needed.

MAKES ABOUT 1½ CUPS

ROSE GERANIUM

The leaves of this scented geranium have a rosy perfume and flavor, but the beautiful pink flowers are unscented. Steep the leaves in hot cream for a delicate ice cream or Crème Anglaise, delightful with the season's first strawberries. Or bury a few leaves in a jar of sugar and sprinkle it over blackberries and sliced peaches—the sweet rose essence will be there, but ever so subtly. The tiny flowers are a lovely accent garnish, snipped fresh from the garden.

All the scented geraniums grow well and easily. In a mild climate they make a lovely hedge—run your hand along the foliage as you walk by for an extraordinary scent. The plants are frost tender, so if your winters are cold, bring them indoors until spring. Start with a plant from the nursery and set it out when the weather begins to warm. Rose geraniums love rich open soil and a sunny position. They enjoy light shearing—just be sure you don't cut them back too far.

Praline Cookies

Adapted from Paula Peck's *The Art of Fine Baking,* these are a favorite at Greens. The buttery caramel flavor of the praline infuses the cookie—it has a wonderful crunchy texture in the crumbly shortbread base. Serve with a creamy dessert like Lemon Pots de Crème (page 370) or Raspberries and Figs with Honey Mousse (page 369).

½ pound unsalted butter, softened
7 tablespoons light brown sugar, packed
½ teaspoon vanilla extract
½ teaspoon salt
2 cups unbleached white flour
¾ cup ground Praline (page 384)

Preheat the oven to 325°F. Cream the butter and sugar together until light and fluffy; add the vanilla and salt and mix again until incorporated. Add the flour and praline and mix until just combined.

Chill the dough until it is easy to work with, about 30 minutes. Roll the dough out to ¼-inch thickness and cut it into shapes, or shape the dough into cylinders about 2 inches in diameter and slice.

Place the slices about 1 inch apart on an ungreased baking sheet and bake for 8 to 10 minutes, until lightly browned. The cookies keep well stored in a sealed container.

MAKES 4 TO 6 DOZEN COOKIES

Praline

This praline has a rich, nutty caramel flavor. We use it in our Praline Cookies, but it can also be sprinkled over poached pears, fresh summer fruit, or ice cream.

2 cups sugar
¾ cup water
½ teaspoon fresh lemon juice
2 cups walnut pieces, pecans, or almonds

Butter a baking sheet.

Stir the sugar, water, and lemon juice together in a medium-size saucepan, off the heat, until well blended. Cook the mixture over medium-low heat until the sugar has dissolved. When the liquid is clear, turn the heat up to medium-high. As the liquid bubbles, wash down the sides of the pan with a brush dipped in water. (This, along with the lemon juice, will help prevent the sugar from crystallizing.) Do not stir the mixture. After about 15 to 20 minutes it will begin to turn golden. At this point the liquid will darken quickly (in 3 to 5 minutes), so watch it carefully.

When it is golden brown, remove from the heat and stir in the nuts with a wooden spoon. Return to the heat and cook just until the caramel liquefies again, then pour onto the baking sheet and spread to a thin layer. When cool, chop by hand or pulverize in a food processor. The praline can be frozen in a well-sealed container.

MAKES 4 CUPS

Tip: The trickiest thing about making praline is to keep crystals from forming in the liquid sugar. Be sure your saucepan is very clean to begin with and brush the sides down with water often as you are cooking the liquid. Do not stir it; stirring will cause the crystals to form. Also, be very careful working with the liquid—it's intensely hot.

Chocolate-Almond Biscotti

Adapted from Lindsey Shere's *Chez Panisse Desserts,* these biscotti are wonderfully crisp and lend themselves to many variations. The nutty flavor of the toasted almonds is a perfect complement to the bits of chopped chocolate.

¼ pound unsalted butter
¾ cup sugar
2 eggs
4 teaspoons kirsch
1 teaspoon vanilla extract
2 cups plus 2 teaspoons unbleached white flour
1½ teaspoons baking powder
¼ teaspoon salt
½ cup almonds, toasted and chopped
¾ cup finely chopped semisweet chocolate

Preheat the oven to 325°F. Cream the butter until fluffy and add the sugar. Cream again until fluffy and add the eggs 1 at a time, beating well after each addition until the mixture is smooth. Mix in the kirsch and vanilla. Combine the flour, baking powder, and salt in a bowl. Beat into the butter mixture until just incorporated. Stir in the almonds and chocolate.

Divide the dough into 3 equal pieces. On a lightly floured board, roll the pieces into long cylinders, about 1 to 1½ inches in diameter. (At this point, the cylinders can be wrapped well and frozen for later baking. Defrost them before continuing the recipe.) Place them on a baking sheet and bake until set and light brown, about 25 minutes.

Cool the rolls and slice diagonally to make ½-inch-thick biscotti. Lower the oven to 300°F. Lay the slices on the baking sheet and bake for 10 minutes. Turn the slices over and bake until dry, about 10 minutes. Cool and store in an airtight container.

MAKES 3 TO 3½ DOZEN BISCOTTI

Tip: Be sure the cookies are completely dried after their last baking, because it's their crunchy texture that makes them so good.

Variation: We often substitute hazelnuts or pine nuts for the almonds or chopped dried cherries for the chocolate, paired with pistachios.

Meyer Lemon Ice Cream

Meyer lemons are exceptionally sweet and fragrant, just perfect for ice cream. They're not easy to come by, unless you have a friend or neighbor with a backyard tree. Serve this delightful ice cream with Candied Citrus Peel (page 388) or with thinly sliced strawberries. You can also make delicious tangerine or blood orange ice cream using this recipe.

3 or 4 Meyer lemons, about ¾ pound
1 cup sugar
1 cup half-and-half or milk
6 egg yolks
3 cups heavy cream
Vanilla extract

Use a vegetable peeler to peel 1 lemon, being very careful not to include the bitter white pith. Place the peel in a nonreactive saucepan with the sugar and half-and-half. Heat the mixture to just below boiling, remove from the heat, and set aside to steep for 10 to 15 minutes. Finely grate the zest of 2 lemons (again, avoiding the pith) and squeeze ½ cup plus 2 tablespoons juice, straining out the pulp and seeds.

Whisk the egg yolks in a bowl until just mixed and pour in a little of the hot half-and-half mixture, stirring constantly. Pour the warmed yolks back into the pan and cook over medium-low heat, stirring constantly, until the mixture coats the spoon, about 10 minutes.

Pour through a strainer into the bowl, then add the grated lemon zest. Let the warm mixture sit for 10 minutes, then stir in the cream and lemon juice. Adjust the seasoning with a few drops of vanilla and more lemon juice if you'd like a tarter ice cream. Chill thoroughly, then freeze according to the manufacturer's directions for your ice cream maker.

MAKES ABOUT 1 ¾ QUARTS

Tangerine Sorbet

Make this refreshing sorbet at the peak of citrus season, when there are many tangerine varieties to choose from. Honey tangerines are certainly our favorite—their juice is a deep orange color, and their flavor is exceptionally rich and sweet—but Mineola, Satsuma, and Fairchild will be good too. Combine different varieties if you like; just be sure to keep as much pulp as you can when you strain out the seeds.

About 5 pounds flavorful tangerines, preferably Honey, to make 1 quart juice
1 cup less 1 tablespoon sugar
Fresh lemon juice (optional)

Finely grate the zest of 1 tangerine, being careful to avoid the bitter white pith. Juice the tangerines and strain out the seeds, keeping as much of the pulp as you can. Place the sugar and 1 cup juice in a nonreactive saucepan. Cook over medium heat until the sugar is completely dissolved, stirring constantly. Combine with the remaining juice and add the zest. If the flavor needs to be brightened, season to taste with a few drops of lemon juice, then chill thoroughly.
Freeze the sorbet according to the manufacturer's directions for your ice cream maker.

MAKES 1 QUART

Variation: This basic recipe also makes ruby grapefruit or blood orange sorbet. If the grapefruit are quite tart, you may need to increase the sugar to a full cup.

Candied Citrus Peel

For a lovely touch, sprinkle a few pieces of Candied Citrus Peel over Meyer Lemon Ice Cream (page 386), Tangerine Sorbet (page 387), or Lemon Pots de Crème (page 370). It's also a tasty sweet bite served on its own.

3 or 4 lemons, tangerines, or oranges or 2 ruby grapefruit
2¾ cups sugar
3 cups water

Use a vegetable peeler to cut the colored rind from the citrus, peeling deeply enough to include some but not all of the white pith. Cut in any shape desired—strips, triangles, or squares. (We cut ours into strips about ⅜ inch thick.) Bring a small nonreactive pan of water to a boil and drop the peel into it. As soon as the water returns to the boil, pour the water and peel through a fine-mesh strainer. Fill the pan with fresh water and repeat the steps once again to leach out all the bitterness in the peel.

In the saucepan, combine 2¼ cups sugar with 3 cups water and bring to a very slow simmer. Add the peel and cook at a slow simmer for approximately 1 hour. Taste a piece to see that it's tender all the way through. Have ready a baking sheet sprinkled with ¼ cup of the remaining sugar. Drain the peel; quickly spread it on the baking sheet and toss, sprinkling with more sugar to coat and separate the pieces. Place the cooled peel in a container with a tight-fitting lid, cover with the remaining sugar, and store in the refrigerator.

MAKES ABOUT ½ CUP

JOHNNY-JUMP-UPS

A tiny viola with a monkey face, this charming blue-violet flower is marvelous tossed into a leafy green salad, as a garnish for desserts and fresh fruit, or candied to decorate a cake.

It's so easy to grow—start from seeds or bedding plants in moist, rich soil with partial shade. Johnny-jump-ups will naturalize in your garden and seed like crazy. Remember where they've been planted; they'll be back on their own the next spring.

Chutneys, Relishes, and Condiments

Chutneys, Relishes, and Condiments

Chutneys and relishes are bursts of bright flavor—whether they spice up or cool down an accompanying dish, they always add sharp contrast and bite. We season our chutneys with a light hand, balancing the taste of fresh or dried fruit with heat and pungent or sweet spices. If you like a fiery chutney, you can always add more pepper, chilies, or fresh ginger. Young ginger is beautifully displayed in San Francisco's outdoor Asian markets—if you can find it in your market, use it; the rosy skin of the delicate hands is so tender and fresh that the ginger doesn't need peeling.

Relishes or pickles are at their best when they're sharp or piquant and lively. Lemongrass Cucumbers lighten the rich flavor of Baba Ghanouj, while Cucumbers with Yogurt and Mint have a refreshing way of cooling down spicier flavors. Have a good white wine vinegar on hand for making pickles and seasoning relishes—rice wine vinegar is always reliable and tasty.

Toasted nuts are a delightful little accent when they're tossed with sugar and salt or a bit of heat. They can be made in advance and stored in an airtight container, but they're so irresistible that they may never make it to your cupboard.

Nectarine Chutney

This simple combination of sweet spices lends itself to the delicate flavor of fresh nectarines, apricots, and peaches. Make this chutney throughout the summer, starting early in the season with apricots and ending with late summer peaches. Select fruit that is ripe and sweet and be sure to cook it lightly. The fresh fruit will make the chutney juicier than one made with dried fruit.

> *1 pound fresh nectarines, apricots, or peaches, pitted and cut into 1-inch pieces (cut the*
> *apricots into wedges), about 3 cups*
> *⅓ to ½ cup sugar*
> *¼ small red onion, finely diced, about ⅓ cup*
> *1 teaspoon grated fresh ginger*
> *¼ teaspoon freshly ground cinnamon*
> *2 pinches of ground cloves*
> *2 pinches of ground mace*
> *2 pinches of cayenne pepper*
> *¼ teaspoon salt*

Combine the fruit and ⅓ cup sugar in a medium-size saucepan; cook over medium heat until the nectarines begin to release their juices, about 2 or 3 minutes. Add the remaining ingredients and cook over medium heat for 10 to 12 minutes, until the fruit is tender. Transfer to a bowl and add sugar if needed. Cool and allow to sit for 1 or 2 hours before serving.

The fresh flavors of the chutney are delicate, so it's best to serve it on the day you make it.

MAKES ABOUT 2½ CUPS

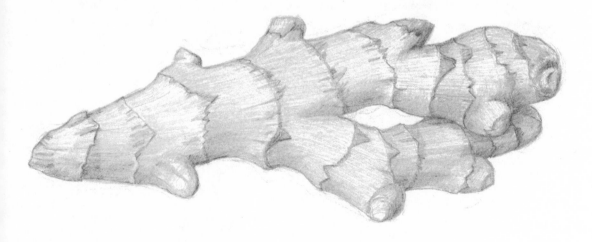

Fiery Pineapple Chutney

Fresh chilies and mint add a lively twist to this spicy chutney inspired by Julie Sahni. We puree part of the pineapple and make it into a sweet-tart syrup, then cook it with chunks of pineapple—cayenne and black pepper add a generous taste of heat. To keep the flavors fresh, the mint is added just before serving. We serve it throughout the winter months with Winter Vegetable Curry (page 190).

1 large pineapple
¾ cup sugar
1½ teaspoons ground cumin
¼ teaspoon cinnamon, preferably freshly ground
¼ teaspoon cayenne pepper
¼ teaspoon black pepper
1 teaspoon grated fresh ginger
1 teaspoon salt
Juice of 1 lemon
1 or 2 jalapeño or serrano chilies, seeded and finely diced
¼ medium-size red onion, finely diced, about ½ cup
1 teaspoon chopped fresh mint

Peel and core the pineapple and cut it into small pieces. Puree 2 cups of it and set the rest aside. Combine the puree, the sugar, spices, ginger, salt, and lemon juice in a medium-size saucepan. Bring the mixture to a boil, then cook over medium heat for 5 minutes, stirring as needed, to make a pineapple syrup. Add the pineapple chunks, chilies, and onion; reduce the heat a little and cook over medium-low heat for 25 minutes. The puree and the pineapple chunks will blend together, with the chunks retaining some of their texture. Transfer the chutney to a bowl and let it sit for 1 or 2 hours before serving. It will keep for at least a week in the refrigerator, but don't add the mint until you're ready to serve it.

MAKES ABOUT 2 CUPS

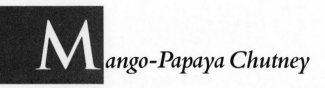ango-Papaya Chutney

We make this fresh chutney in late spring and summer, when mangoes and papayas are in season. It's surprisingly light—with just enough sweet spice and lime to accent the fragrant fruit without overpowering its delicate flavor.

¼ small red onion, finely diced, about ⅓ cup
1 tablespoon Champagne vinegar
¼ cup fresh lime juice, about 4 limes
¼ cup sugar
⅜ teaspoon cinnamon, preferably freshly ground
3 pinches of ground cloves
3 pinches of cayenne pepper
1 mango, peeled, sliced off the pit, and cut into ½-inch pieces
1 papaya, peeled, seeded, and cut into ½-inch pieces

Bring a small pot of water to a boil and drop in the onion for 30 seconds. Drain the onions and place in a medium-size bowl; toss them immediately with the vinegar to draw out their pink color.

Combine the lime juice, sugar, and spices in a medium-size saucepan. Cook over medium heat for 2 or 3 minutes to make a light syrup. Add the fruit to the onions, then pour the syrup over and stir everything together. Let the chutney sit for 1 hour to allow the flavors to blend and soften. Serve within a few hours to retain the fresh, bright flavor.

MAKES ABOUT 2 CUPS

Apricot Chutney

A fragrant blend of spices fills this dried fruit chutney with warmth and rich flavor. This chutney goes well with any of our curries.

½ teaspoon ground coriander
½ teaspoon ground cumin
Scant ⅛ teaspoon ground cardamom
2 pinches of ground cloves
⅛ teaspoon black pepper
¼ cup sugar
1 cup fresh orange juice
½ pound dried apricots, cut into halves, about 1½ cups
1 teaspoon grated fresh ginger
⅛ teaspoon salt
¼ cup golden raisins
¼ cup dried currants
1 fresh jalapeño or serrano chili, seeded and finely diced
1 teaspoon fresh lemon juice or rice wine vinegar

Combine the spices in a small bowl and set aside.

In a small saucepan, dissolve the sugar in the orange juice and cook over medium heat for 3 or 4 minutes. Add the apricots, ginger, salt, and mixed spices; cook over low heat until the apricots are tender, about 10 minutes. Remove the pan from the heat and add the remaining ingredients. There will be some liquid in the pan, but the fruit will absorb it. Transfer to a bowl or container. Allow the chutney to sit for 1 or 2 hours before serving.

The chutney will hold in the refrigerator for a week or two if stored in a tightly sealed container.

MAKES ABOUT 2 CUPS

Cucumbers with Yogurt and Mint

This simple raita is crisp and cool, a good contrast to the rich flavors of eggplant dishes. Serve with Baba Ghanouj (page 52) and wedges of Grilled Pita Bread (page 73) to scoop up the yogurt. If there's mint growing in your garden, this is the place to use it.

1 medium-size cucumber
1 cup plain yogurt
¼ cup chopped fresh mint
⅜ teaspoon salt
⅛ teaspoon cayenne pepper

Peel the cucumber, cut in half lengthwise, and scoop out the seeds. (Removing the seeds will keep the dish from becoming watery.) Dice into cubes about ¼ inch in size. Toss the ingredients together and serve, or make an hour or two in advance and refrigerate until ready to serve.

MAKES ABOUT 3 CUPS

ENGLISH BLACK PEPPERMINT

This exceptional mint has beautiful, deep green leaves with a crisp fresh flavor that's unsurpassed. Sprinkle it freshly chopped in a vegetable stew with southwestern flavors—its sweetness blends smoothly with fresh chilies and pungent cilantro. Whole leaves add zest to a warm spinach salad. It's delicious in a cool cucumber raita. The fine sprigs are an elegant touch for pound cake or a bowl of summer berries. At the end of the day, steep a small handful of mint leaves in hot water for a wonderfully restorative fresh mint tea.

We grow this superior mint at Green Gulch for its strong peppery flavor. It likes a shady warm place, rich soil, and plenty of water and will flourish with no further attention. Grow it under a water tap in a shady part of your garden. Start with a plant or two; they'll send out a profusion of underground runners, colonizing an area quite nicely. In our foggy coastal region, it produces from early spring to Thanksgiving—the leaves grow smaller as the weather cools.

Lemongrass Cucumbers

These tangy cucumbers are a refreshing way to cool down spicy dishes. A touch of sesame enriches their flavor.

1 medium-size cucumber
¼ teaspoon salt
¼ cup Lemongrass Vinegar (recipe follows) or 3 tablespoons rice wine vinegar and
  1 tablespoon fresh lemon juice
1 tablespoon dark sesame oil
1 teaspoon sugar
½ teaspoon hot pepper flakes (optional)

Peel the cucumber, cut in half lengthwise, and scoop out the seeds; slice diagonally ¼ inch thick. Toss with the salt, set aside for 10 minutes, then drain. Toss the cucumbers with the vinegar, oil, sugar, and hot pepper. Serve immediately or refrigerate and serve within an hour or two.

MAKES ABOUT 2 CUPS

Lemongrass Vinegar

Fresh lemongrass is featured in many Southeast Asian dishes and can be found in Asian markets and in the produce section of some grocery stores.

Steeping the lemongrass stalks in rice wine vinegar produces an intensely flavored vinegar that is particularly delicious paired with cucumbers. It will also give a lift to Asian noodle dishes such as Chinese Noodle Salad with Citrus and Spicy Peanuts (page 140) or Chinese Noodles with Green Curry (page 142). The vinegar requires very little time to make and holds for months in the refrigerator. Leave the lemongrass stalks in the jar, discarding them as you use up the vinegar.

¼ pound fresh lemongrass stalks
3 cups rice wine vinegar

Trim the dried outer leaves and upper stem from the lemongrass. Cut the stalks into 3-inch lengths and cut each section in half lengthwise to expose the flavorful core of the lemongrass.

Bring the vinegar to a boil in a nonreactive saucepan. Place the lemongrass in a 1-quart jar with a lid that seals well and pour the boiling vinegar over it. Allow the vinegar to cool, cover the jar, and steep for 2 or 3 days before using.

MAKES 3 CUPS

Sweet and Sour Pearl Onions

These little onions are full of intense flavor, well worth the time it takes to peel them. Served as a pickle, a garnish, or part of an antipasto, they hold well in their syrup. You can make them a few days in advance and refrigerate, but be sure to return them to room temperature before serving. For beautiful contrasting color, combine red pearl onions with the yellow or white variety.

2 10-ounce baskets of pearl onions
½ cup red wine vinegar
½ cup fresh orange juice
2 tablespoons sugar
½ teaspoon salt

Bring a large pot of water to a boil, add the onions, and cook for about 2 minutes. (This will make them easier to peel.) Drain in a colander and rinse under cold water. Trim away the onion tops and hairs at the stem end, leaving the base of the stem end intact, then peel.

Place the onions in a saucepan and add the other ingredients. Bring to a boil, then reduce the heat and simmer, covered, over medium heat until the onions are tender, about 15 to 20 minutes. Use a slotted spoon to remove them from the liquid, then set aside in a small bowl. Continue cooking the liquid until it reduces to a syrup, about ⅓ cup. Pour the syrup over the onions and cool.

MAKES ABOUT 2 CUPS

Pickled Red Onions

These bright pink pickles are a variation of a recipe in *The Greens Cookbook;* we serve them so often that we've included the recipe here. Sharp and piquant, they're delicious with Spicy Black Beans with Chilies and Lime (page 31) or tossed with salads featuring avocado and citrus. They keep well for up to a week covered and refrigerated.

2 medium-size red onions, about 1 pound
1 quart boiling water
¾ cup rice wine vinegar
½ cup cold water
½ teaspoon black peppercorns or whole coriander seed
½ teaspoon hot pepper flakes or a few small whole dried chilies

Slice the onions into ¼-inch-thick rings, then peel away the skin. Separate the onion rings and place them in a bowl. Pour the boiling water over and allow to sit for 2 or 3 minutes. Drain the onions and return to the bowl. Immediately cover with the vinegar and cold water; add the peppercorns and hot pepper. Cover and refrigerate for 1 hour before serving.

MAKES 2 CUPS

Cranberry-Pear Relish

The flavors of this beautiful relish are wonderfully appealing—the sweetness of pears, whole tart cranberries, and the fresh taste of orange. Be sure the pears are fully ripe, so they soften as they quickly cook. Serve with a holiday meal or alongside Pastry Turnovers with Butternut Squash, Leeks, and Thyme (page 232), and a sauté of hearty winter greens.

¾ pound fresh or frozen cranberries, about 3½ cups
½ cup fresh orange juice
½ cup sugar
2 medium-size pears, peeled, cored, and cut into 1-inch pieces
½ to 1 teaspoon finely chopped orange zest

Place the cranberries in a medium-size saucepan with the orange juice and sugar. Bring to a boil, then reduce the heat to medium and cook for about 10 minutes. At this point the cranberries will be cooked through and should still hold their shape. Add the pears and half the orange zest. Cook for 1 minute more, just long enough to heat the pears through, since they will continue to cook with the hot cranberries. Allow to cool, add remaining orange zest to taste, then serve.

The relish will hold for up to a week in a sealed container in the refrigerator. After a few days the taste and texture of the pears will begin to diminish.

MAKES ABOUT 4 CUPS

Variation: A splash of Grand Marnier or Poire William liqueur will give the relish a little added bite.

Spicy Peanuts

These highly seasoned peanuts are a lively addition to our Chinese noodle dishes. We also sprinkle them over grilled vegetables served with Dipping Sauce (page 344) or Mint-Cilantro Sauce (page 339). They require very little time to make and keep for weeks in a sealed container. If the nuts lose their fresh flavor, crisp them in a 350°F oven for 5 minutes. Spicy cashews are a rich variation on this recipe.

1 cup raw peanuts or cashews
½ teaspoon peanut oil
¼ teaspoon paprika
¼ teaspoon cayenne pepper
¼ teaspoon salt

Preheat the oven to 325°F. In a small bowl, toss the nuts with the oil, spices, and salt. Roast them on a baking sheet for about 12 minutes, until they smell nutty. Cool and store in a sealed container.

MAKES 1 CUP

Fire-Dried Walnuts or Pecans

Our good friend Barbara Tropp taught us how to make these irresistibly delicious nuts. This version is a slight revision of her recipe in *The Modern Art of Chinese Cooking*.

The flavor of the caramelized nuts is sweet and slightly salty. Serve them on their own as a tasty little bite or include them in a fall salad of bitter greens tossed with apples or pears.

½ pound plump walnut or pecan halves
2 teaspoons peanut oil or vegetable oil
½ teaspoon coarse kosher salt or ⅜ teaspoon sea salt
2 tablespoons sugar

Place the nuts in a heatproof bowl. Bring a few cups of water to a boil and pour over the nuts; soak for 30 minutes.

Preheat the oven to 300°F. Drain the nuts, pat dry, and spread evenly on a baking sheet lined with parchment paper or paper towels. Dry in the oven for 30 minutes, then reduce the heat to 250°F, turn the baking sheet, and check the nuts every 10 minutes. This will take 40 to 60 minutes depending on the plumpness of the nuts. When they are almost entirely dry, remove from the oven. At this point the nuts can be cooled and stored in an airtight container for a day or two before being caramelized.

To caramelize the nuts, heat the oil in a heavy skillet over medium heat until hot. Add the nuts, stirring gently until evenly coated with oil and warm to the touch. Lower the heat immediately if the nuts begin to scorch. Sprinkle the salt over the nuts and stir, then sprinkle the sugar in slowly, to your own taste, stirring constantly. They should be lively and sweet, with a hint of salt. As you stir, break off any bits of caramelized sugar that cling to the spoon and add them back in. The caramelizing process will take 3 or 4 minutes—the sugar and salt will melt and adhere to the nuts. Serve warm or cool. The cooled nuts will keep for up to 2 weeks in an airtight container.

MAKES ABOUT 2 CUPS

Tip: Pecans are not nearly as bitter as walnuts, so you can skip the soaking and drying steps. Toast them in the oven at 350°F for about 7 minutes, until fragrant, then caramelize as directed.

Appendix

Seasonal Celebration Menus

Planning a special menu can be creative and exciting, but if you're new to vegetarian cooking, it can also be quite daunting. These celebratory menus are based on recipes featured in this book. They're intended to spark your imagination and can easily be simplified or varied as the seasons change. Here are a few of our tried-and-true tips for menu planning.

Always base your menu on what's in season—when you go to the market, take note of what's abundant and fresh. We've suggested two menus for each season. The main course is usually the focus of the meal, so plan it first and then go on to the other dishes—you'll save time by doing it this way. Let your own good taste and common sense be your guide—think about how colors, tastes, and textures work together. Keep in mind how much time you have to make the meal—what can be prepared ahead of time, what needs to be done at the last minute, and what kind of help you can enlist. Plan the meal around dishes that can be made in advance so you can relax and enjoy the occasion.

Spring
Spinach and Mung Dal Fritters with Mint-Cilantro Sauce
Spring Vegetable Curry with Sri Lankan Spices
Cashew Basmati Rice
Fiery Pineapple Chutney
Sliced Mango and Papaya with Fresh Lime

Grilled New Potatoes, Fennel, and Green Garlic with Meyer Lemon Beurre Blanc
Spring Tart with Asparagus and Red Onion
Butter Lettuces and Radicchio with Toasted Pecans and Sherry-Shallot Vinaigrette
Strawberry Rhubarb Cobbler with Whipped Cream

Summer
Grilled Summer Squash and Red Onions with Cinnamon-Chipotle Butter
Stuffed Zucchini with Corn, Chilies, and Smoked Cheese with Tomatillo Sauce and Grilled Polenta Triangles
Romaine Hearts with Avocado, Jícama, Orange, and Citrus-Cumin Vinaigrette
Fresh Berries with Praline Cookies

Sage Focaccia
Sicilian Salad with Roasted Eggplant, Peppers, and Garlic
Spinach Fettuccine with Tomatoes, Crème Fraîche, and Basil
Garden Lettuces and Rocket with Summer Beans, Goat Cheese, and Hazelnuts
Raspberries and Figs with Honey Mousse

Fall

Mushroom Soup with Caramelized Onions
Pastry Turnovers Filled with Butternut Squash, Leeks, and Thyme
Fall Salad of Apples, Beets, Fennel, and Frisée
Gingerbread with Poached Apricots and Cranberries

Artichokes with Lemon and Mint, Beets with Watercress and Orange, Assorted Olives,
    and Warm Gorgonzola Croutons
Fall Risotto with Chanterelles and Late Harvest Tomatoes
Wilted Spinach Salad with Roasted Peppers
Fresh Figs and Chocolate-Almond Biscotti

Winter

Winter Greens with Pears, Walnuts, and Walnut Vinaigrette
Mushroom Lasagne with Mushroom Port Sauce
Roasted Shallots
Wilted Spinach with Lemon and Pine Nuts
Tangerine Sorbet with Candied Citrus Peel

Dolmas, Cucumbers with Yogurt and Mint, Warm Pita Bread, and Oil-Cured Olives
North African Vegetable Stew
Almond-Currant Couscous
Citrus Salad with Bitter Greens
Ginger Pots de Crème

Pairing Wine with Vegetarian Food

by Rick Jones

When Greens opened in 1979, there was serious debate over whether wines would be served at all. But in the end wine won out, and today the restaurant offers one of the most creative and unusual relationships between food and wine in America, with over 300 wine selections.

Pairing wine with vegetarian food requires a new perspective, which is why our food servers are taught to abandon their traditional understanding of food and wine compatibility. Vegetarian food combines many subtle flavors that must be allowed to speak first. Wine then becomes the final seasoning that brings them together. In traditional food and wine pairing, the saturated fats and strong flavors of meat are often overpowering, requiring wines that can return the boldness in a volley for control of the palate. At Greens we look instead for a balance of flavors; the pairing can be a complement or a contrasting taste, but never one that overpowers the food. The complexities of wine with vegetarian food are best enjoyed by emphasizing the simple enhancement of flavors.

Wine is life in a bottle, made up of many components that grow and change over time. When we serve a wine at Greens, our main concern is for its drinkability, that state when all of its components have come together in terms of balance. Fruit, acid, tannin, and alcohol begin as individual voices in a young wine and eventually merge together in harmony. If any one of these components is not fully developed, we often hold the wine in reserve for as long as 18 months for additional aging.

Beyond drinkability, there are no rights and wrongs in the selection of any wine. Wine, like food, is a matter of personal taste, which is why the wine list at Greens has always been chosen by committee. At weekly seminars with the staff, wines are tasted and selected based on popular opinion to ensure a diversity and balance of selection. The wine list is always a reflection of our menu. Over the years Greens has evolved away from a concentration on dairy products to focus on a lighter, more refined balance of flavors, and our wines reflect this change.

Traditional assumptions about wine, such as distinctions between reds and whites, aren't really appropriate for vegetarian dining, except for your personal taste. Begin the process of choosing wine by evaluating the ingredients of the dish. Consider how their flavors affect the dish, for instance the acid content of tomato-based recipes or the hot, spicy flavors of chilies or peppers. Cheese, eggs, and cream give a dish richness; grilled foods add their smoky characteristics. Wine must respond to food, and as these flavors and textures change, so should the wine. Each wine has its own specific style and taste to consider as well. You can't go wrong with a good drinkable wine, and experimenting is a pleasure in itself. Here are the wines we most often recommend.

White Wines
CHARDONNAY
Many cheese recipes, such as Cannelloni or Filo with Spinach, Mushrooms, Goat Cheese, and Pine Nuts, work well with Chardonnay, particularly when the acid is balanced with

a strong fruit backbone. Grilled foods also pair up, like mushrooms and potatoes served with a Basil Aïoli. Be sure to serve this wine chilled. Chardonnays don't pair well with acidic foods like tomato-based dishes, particularly spicy ones. In fact, most strongly spiced foods will overpower this wine. Vinegar- and citrus-based vinaigrettes will present similar difficulties.

SAUVIGNON BLANC

The Sauvignon Blanc vine is a voracious grower, yielding more fruit than most other varietals. While more grapes means more wine for the winemaker, the vine is stressed into ripening all the fruit on its branches. The result can be a wine with pungent grassy and vegetal flavors that is rather unappealing, a difficult companion with vegetarian food.

Quality is crucial in this wine. The best has a smoky, herbaceous, and mineral quality with fruit flavors of ripe melon and figs. This wine can be quite sturdy, standing up to spicy dishes as well as those one might serve with a Chardonnay. Try the Spicy Corn Cakes with Smoked Cheese and Chilies or Enchiladas Rojas.

CHENIN BLANC

The alcohol level is usually low in this wine, making it a great choice at lunch or as an afternoon wine with light snacks. The lighter body does not work as well with big dinner entrées, but this is one wine you can experiment with, since good quality is available at low prices. Spring Risotto with Asparagus and Peas and the Filo Turnovers with Mushrooms and Pine Nuts are good bets.

PINOT BLANC

Pinot Blanc is lighter in style, with fresh appley fruit and good acidity. This dry, fruity wine pairs well with foods of simple, delicate flavors, particularly with foods served at room temperature on hot summer days. We recommend it with the delicate Eggplant and Roasted Garlic Tart or with some grilled vegetables as a first course.

GEWÜRZTRAMINER

This grape is fermented both dry and sweet, with mouth-filling spicy flavors of honey, orange blossoms, and clove. Dry Gewürztraminer is the first wine we suggest to our customers who order the hot, spicy dishes. Its strong flavors stand up to the heat of chilies better than any other white wine. Try it with the Southern Rio Stew or the Polenta Gratin with Salsa Roja. Sweet Gewürztraminers are excellent with dessert.

RIESLING

When fermented dry, the floral richness of the Riesling's fruit can be particularly compatible with vegetarian foods. The relatively low price tag makes Rieslings especially appealing and a source of great satisfaction to those willing to expand their tastes. Like Pinot Blanc, this delicate wine goes well with simple vegetable dishes, particularly in the summer months. Dishes high in acid and seasoning, as well as those with spicy hotness, will overpower it. Some likely companions: Spring Tart with Asparagus and Onion as well as the O Konomi Yaki—Savory Vegetable Cakes.

Red Wines

CABERNET SAUVIGNON

The bold character of this grape provides an abundance of alcohol, acid, and tannin, along with full-bodied fruit flavors of black currant, cedar, and a smoky, herbaceous tone. Cabernet Sauvignon can be a rather hard wine to pair with vegetarian food. Look for a balance of components and stay with heartier foods that match up with the big body of this wine. Polenta and pasta go well, especially those based with tomatoes and olives. Cabernet works with the smoky character of grilled dishes. Recommended recipes: Polenta Baked with Artichokes, Tomatoes, and Olives, the North African Vegetable Stew, or Ratatouille.

ZINFANDEL

This grape has many of the same rich, robust flavors of Cabernet Sauvignon, as well as a certain spiciness all its own. Although it doesn't command the same respect as Cabernet, it's a serious wine that produces spicy berry flavors and can be equally difficult to match with vegetarian cuisine. One advantage: Zinfandel can often be found for a third of the price, making it more accessible for experiments. Again, look for balance in the wine and match it with full-flavored food. Try it with some of the spicier recipes, like Polenta Gratin with Salsa Roja or Creole Mushroom and Pepper Stew.

PINOT NOIR

This wine is noted for its delicate flavors of cherries, raspberries, and strawberries. Look very carefully at the ingredients of your menu, because Pinot Noir can easily be overpowered by sauces, spices, or the tart acid in some tomato dishes. While quality Pinot Noir is very expensive, it goes best with the simplest foods. A perfect blend is pure enjoyment and worthy of a special effort. Try it with Eggplant Filled with Mushrooms, Sun-Dried Tomatoes, and Pine Nuts or, if the tomatoes are particularly ripe and sweet, with the Fall Risotto with Chanterelles and Late Harvest Tomatoes.

MERLOT

This is another rich and hearty wine compatible with the more savory dishes. The fruit can be earthy and smoky, with flavors of cherries and mint. It also provides a certain plumminess that makes it softer and more accessible in its youth, yet the robust body of alcohol and tannin can make it difficult to match with food. Merlot works well with highly seasoned dishes with mild chili and pepper flavors. Experiment with recipes like Spinach Fettuccine with Artichokes, Sun-Dried Tomatoes, and Capers. Merlot also goes well with the rich pastry turnovers, like Pastry Turnovers with Butternut Squash, Leeks, and Thyme.

SYRAH AND RHÔNE VARIETALS

Varietals from the Rhône region of France like Syrah, Mourvèdre, and Grenache are now grown successfully in California. Though they, too, are full-bodied wines, their flavors of rich, smoky raspberry and black currant fruit are blended with a soft, enticing texture, making them compatible with a broad range of vegetarian foods. Syrah, especially, is very versatile; it stands up to the acid in tomato dishes and works remarkably well with rich stews and hearty pastas, polenta, and egg dishes. It's also the best red wine to pair with spicy, hot foods. Gratin of Eggplant, Roasted Peppers, and Garlic, Enchiladas Verdes, and Linguine with Onion Confit, Goat Cheese, and Walnuts are just a few of our recommendations, but don't let this restrict you. The choices are virtually endless.

ITALIAN WINES

Like the Rhône wines, many Italian wines are also ideal because of their great balance of fruit and texture. Tuscan wines like Chiantis made with the Sangiovese grape are especially nice. Wines from the Piedmont region, like Barolo, Barbaresco, and Barbera, can be equally enjoyable, yet be mindful that they can often be rather bulky and tough when young. A Barolo is great with Eggplant Lasagne with Basil or Lasagne with Mushroom-Port Sauce. Try a hearty Chianti with the Pizza with Roasted Pepper Sauce, Leeks, and Olives.

Champagne

Dry champagne works remarkably well with a number of vegetarian dishes. The tartness and effervescence make it a wonderful contrast to rich sauces, like the Meyer Lemon Beurre Blanc. It's perfect for brunch or as an aperitif served with grilled eggplant or shiitake mushrooms. Serve well chilled in fluted glasses.

Beers

Beer is often an excellent companion to vegetarian food, especially if there's a strong ethnic character to the meal. Cold pilsner is a fine choice to go down fast with hot, spicy food. I prefer the body of an ale to pair up with Middle Eastern, Asian, and Indian spices. And I am particularly fond of a slightly chilled porter or stout to go with pizza.

Dessert Wines

After-dinner courses of fruit, cheese, nuts, and chocolate are the perfect companions for vintage and tawny ports. The Gâteau Moule or the Chocolate-Almond Biscotti are splendid with port. The Peach-Blueberry Pie and the Raspberries and Figs with Honey Mousse are the perfect match for sauternes and late harvest white wines.

Serving Wine

The temperature of wine is an important part of its enjoyment with food. White wines should be served chilled to bring out their crispness and enhance the flavors. Yet a wine served too cold will mask all of the fruit until it warms up in the glass. The best serving temperature is around 45°F to 50°F. Red wines are generally best enjoyed when served at 60°F to 65°F, although some lighter-bodied wines like Beaujolais are very pleasant when served with a slight chill on a hot day.

Glasses are an equally important part of the wine experience. Though there are many traditional shapes and sizes for both red and white wine, the common factor in all of them is to provide enough room to allow the wine to be swirled around. This is not an affectation; it gives a wine the opportunity to open up or "breathe," releasing the depth of its flavor. To facilitate this swirling technique, be sure not to overfill the glass.

Low-Fat Cooking

The recipes in this book are not overly rich—we don't, for instance, use creamy salad dressings—but of course we do include dairy products and eggs, oils, nuts, and olives for their essential flavors, using them as sparingly as possible. There are a few things you can do to further lighten the recipes or eliminate the fat altogether.

You can count on citrus juice and zest, vinegars, chilies, ginger, fresh herbs, and capers to brighten flavors. A base of onions and garlic sautéed with a little wine and perhaps dried herbs will deepen flavors and give body to many of the dishes. Dried mushrooms or a puree of roasted garlic or peppers enriches flavors without adding fat. These ingredients can be added to enliven or intensify flavors, whether it's a salad of leafy greens or marinated beans, a simple sauté, a soup, or a stew.

Dishes like Beets with Watercress and Orange use no oil at all, while most of the marinated beans and grains have a very low ratio of oil to vinegar or citrus juice. You can always dress a salad without oil—here's where citrus juice, flavorful vinegars, good Dijon mustard, and freshly cracked black pepper shine.

Most of the recipes use 1 to 2 tablespoons of oil for sautéing (to serve four to six) and occasionally a combination of oil and butter—just enough to keep the vegetables from sticking to the pan. Salt is used in the first stage of sautéing to draw the liquid out of the vegetables. We usually add a little liquid (wine, stock, mushroom soaking liquid, or even water) to the pan to loosen the juices—this way you can use less oil and include every drop of the delicious juices. To sauté without using any fat, begin by steaming the vegetables lightly in a covered pan or skillet, using just enough water or stock to keep the surface of the pan moist until the vegetables release their juices.

Quite a few of the sauces use very little oil and some use none at all—Roasted Pepper Sauce and Tomatillo Sauce can be used in any number of ways and are made completely without oil. The flavor and the freshness of the ingredients are of particular importance here—a splash of balsamic or Champagne vinegar or fresh herbs or chilies can make all the difference to a sauce. Make Mint-Cilantro Sauce with low-fat or nonfat yogurt. Try making lasagne without the herb béchamel or ricotta custard; just be sure to make another half recipe of lasagne sauce. It's a good idea to prepare extra vegetables to replace the ricotta filling. If you're concerned with oil in pasta dishes, see the introduction to the pasta chapter (page 118) for suggestions on using stock.

Cheese can be a real problem in low-fat vegetarian cooking, but you can always use Parmesan, part-skim ricotta, and low-fat mozzarella. Stay away from the creamier cheeses like cheddar, Gorgonzola, Fontina, and young Asiago. A little tangy feta goes a long way in a salad or crumbled over a pizza. (Use the pizza dough variation made without milk.) There are many flavorful tofu products that can be used in place of cheese; savory smoked tofu is an excellent substitute for smoked cheese.

Olives and toasted nuts are wonderful accent flavors, but most of the dishes will hold their own without them. Instead of olives, try using capers for a similar salty, piquant taste. There's plenty of room for variation in most of these recipes, so find combinations of ingredients you particularly enjoy and experiment with them to make dishes that satisfy both your dietary needs and your palate.

Notes on Ingredients

Capers

These tiny bursts of salty, piquant flavor are the buds of the caper bush, which grows on the rugged hillsides above the Mediterranean. They're packed in brine, so rinse well before using. They keep virtually forever in the refrigerator.

Cheeses

Some of the cheeses used in this book will not be available at your local supermarket, so you'll need to go to a specialty cheese shop. It's worth the extra effort; a good-quality cheese will make a memorable dish.

AGED CHEESES—PARMESANS, ROMANO, AND ASIAGO

In recipes that call for Parmesan cheese, we use Parmigiano-Reggiano or the less expensive grana padano, high-quality Parmesan cheeses imported from Italy. Reggiano is made entirely by hand using centuries-old techniques. These cheeses have a wonderful, clean flavor and will make a real difference in salads, pastas, and pizzas, but they are rather expensive and may be difficult to find in some areas of the country. A good-quality domestic Parmesan can be used instead. Grated Parmesan in the can is tasteless and useless. Romano is another hard grating cheese usually made from sheep's milk; it has a sharper, tangier taste than the Parmesans. We use a young Asiago cheese imported from Italy, good for grating and slicing. It's smooth and creamy, although not as soft as Fontina. The imported cheese has a superior flavor, but you can use the sharper domestic Asiago more commonly found in grocery stores in its place. Buy hard grating cheese in blocks and grate it yourself as needed. Store these cheeses wrapped in plastic film in a warm corner of the refrigerator.

BLUE-VEINED CHEESES—ROQUEFORT, STILTON, GORGONZOLA

Each of these imported cheeses—Roquefort from France, Stilton from England, and Gorgonzola from Italy—has its own characteristic stamp. Creamy Gorgonzola makes a mouth-watering pizza or pasta; zesty Stilton or Roquefort makes a wonderful light dessert, crumbled and served with a sliced apple or pear.

CHEDDAR

We most often use an aged white Vermont cheddar that's rich but not too sharp; most orange cheddars are dyed. If you have a favorite cheddar, by all means use it instead. A mild cheddar will work well in most of our dishes, but an extra sharp cheddar is likely to be overpowering.

FRESH CHEESES—MOZZARELLA, RICOTTA, AND CREAM CHEESE

Fresh cheeses are made directly from curds and whey, not pressed, aged, or seasoned. We are lucky to have access to excellent fresh mozzarella and ricotta (sometimes called *ricotta fresca*). With fresh cheeses, the rule is the fresher, the better.

Mozzarella is more commonly seen in a pressed form suitable for grating. For grating, we use a whole-milk mozzarella; you can experiment with the lower-butterfat varieties.

Most of the cream cheese on the market has been stabilized with gelatin. It's worth looking around for a "natural" cream cheese; its light, flaky texture and smooth, fresh flavor are a delight.

FETA CHEESE

Feta cheese is usually made from sheep's milk. It can be French, Bulgarian, or Greek, and each has a different quality—the French fetas tend to be milder. Experiment to find the one most suited to your taste. Feta keeps a long time stored in its brine in the refrigerator.

FONTINA

We use this mild, buttery soft melting cheese in sandwiches, on pizzas, and in omelets. Italian Fontina is the best, but Danish Fontina is also delicious, and it's less expensive and more readily available.

GOAT CHEESE

The zing of a good goat cheese is distinctive, whether it's a young, mild variety, sometimes called *chèvre,* or a stronger-tasting aged one. If you (or your guests) are new to goat cheese, begin with a good chèvre. It's a remarkable addition to a salad or pizza.

GRUYÈRE

The French and Swiss varieties are equally delicious in this Swiss-type cheese known for its mellow, nutty flavor.

PROVOLONE

This aged cheese imported from southern Italy will bring an assertive zest to pizza, lasagne, and baguette sandwiches.

SMOKED CHEESE

Smoked cheese adds a heartiness and variety often welcomed by the vegetarian palate. Many kinds of smoked cheese are now available, and they vary considerably in quality; take a taste before you buy. We use smoked mozzarella, Swiss, and cheddar, and there are good smoked Goudas on the market as well.

Fresh Ginger

The zesty flavor of fresh ginger brightens so many of our dishes—from vinaigrettes to curries, muffins, and desserts. Look for firm ginger in the market, a sure sign of freshness. Unless you're using young ginger (with very tender skin) peel it before grating. You can use the small hole on a hand-held grater or a small food processor for preparing ginger. If using a food processor, slice the peeled ginger into thin coins (cut across the grain to cut through the strings) and finely chop. Ginger will last much longer if stored in a paper bag (rather than plastic) in the refrigerator.

Oils

OLIVE OILS

Extra virgin refers to the first pressing of oil extracted from olives by mechanical means, without the use of heat or chemicals. Dark and flavorful, extra virgin olive oil is a seasoning element in its own right. Brands change from year to year, so seek out a high-quality brand whose taste suits you. Some of our recipes call for light olive oil; this grade is called *pure* on the bottle or can and comes from successive pressings. Pure olive oil is a lighter *color;* the fat content is the same as extra virgin oil's.

Store olive oil tightly sealed away from the light.

PEANUT OIL

We recommend peanut oil for frying, since it doesn't smoke and burn until it reaches a high temperature.

LIGHT VEGETABLE OIL

In recipes that call for a light vegetable oil, we recommend canola, safflower, or peanut.

DARK SESAME OIL

This strong, full-flavored oil lends a characteristic, mouth-watering aroma and taste to many Asian-inspired dishes. Dark sesame oil (made from toasted sesame seed) is more of a seasoning element than a cooking oil, since it's so intensely flavored and it burns at a very low temperature. It's prone to rancidity, so buy a small bottle and keep it refrigerated.

HAZELNUT AND WALNUT OILS

The addition of a nut oil can raise a salad from the merely delicious to the sublime. Find a good-quality brand and keep these oils refrigerated; fragile nut oils turn rancid faster than other oils. Nut oils are expensive, but since we mix them with other oils a little goes a long way.

Olives

Black Niçoise are small, strong-flavored olives imported from France. Gaeta are medium-size olives imported from Italy—we use them interchangeably with Niçoise and sometimes with Kalamatas. Oil-cured (which aren't packed in brine but dried) and Kalamata olives appear in Greek and other Mediterranean dishes and are handy to have on hand. These olives aren't usually pitted, but the pit can be removed easily by pressing on the olive with the bottom of a saucer or cup.

When you can't find good-quality olives, ordinary canned olives can be greatly improved by draining and marinating them for several hours with a flavorful extra virgin olive oil, coarsely chopped garlic, and chopped fresh herbs.

Pepper

We generally use black pepper (Telicherry is excellent), but white pepper and cayenne also appear regularly in this book. A few recipes call for "five-pepper mixture." Available already mixed, it's a combination of black peppercorns, green peppercorns, pink peppercorns (actually Baie rose berries), white peppercorns, and whole Jamaican pepper (allspice).

Saffron

Saffron is the stamen of a certain type of crocus flower; it lends an indescribable delicate aroma and flavor, as well as a rich yellow color, to rice dishes and soups. It's available in threads or ground into a powder; we recommend the threads and soak them in a little warm water.

Salt

We've been using fine sea salt in our cooking since the day the restaurant opened, and we find it works particularly well with vegetarian cuisine. The salt commonly available in grocery stores has been highly processed to remove trace minerals and to keep it from clumping.

Kosher salt has become popular in gourmet cooking; it's a bit milder than fine sea salt, so if you're using it, you'll need to increase the amount slightly.

Sun-Dried Tomatoes

The sun-dried tomatoes we use come packed in olive oil. They have an intense tomato flavor that brings a unique piquancy to a dish. At farmer's markets and specialty stores in some regions of the country you'll find "dry" sun-dried tomatoes; they have rich, sweet flavor and many uses, but are not interchangeable with their oil-packed relative.

Vanilla Beans

Whole dried vanilla beans are a marvelous addition to a dessert chef's pantry. To prepare, use a sharp knife to cut the bean in half lengthwise and scrape out the flavorful seeds. Add the seeds and the bean pod (be sure to remove the pod before serving) to milk or cream for a custard or Crème Anglaise. After flavoring a sauce or custard, store the whole bean buried in a container of sugar. The bean can be reused several times; the sugar will take on a strong vanilla aroma and can be sprinkled over berries, added to whipped cream, or used in baking.

Vinegar

BALSAMIC VINEGAR

Balsamic vinegar is produced in Modena, Italy, and is the stuff of legend. Made from the juice of Trebbiano grapes and traditionally aged (sometimes for decades) in a succession of barrels of different woods, it has been a prized substance for over a thousand years. Although traditionally made *aceto balsamico* is not easy to find and is extremely costly, a perfectly good factory-produced version (irreverently called *industriale* in Modena) is readily available here. Tart, sweet, rich, and deep, it's a unique and versatile ingredient.

CHAMPAGNE VINEGAR

We use this delicate vinegar made from Champagne grapes in combination with citrus juice and zest in many of our vinaigrettes. If not available, substitute a good white wine or rice wine vinegar.

SHERRY VINEGAR

The fine flavor of a good Spanish sherry vinegar makes a remarkable vinaigrette mixed simply with a fruity olive oil, garlic, salt, and some chopped herbs.

RED WINE VINEGAR

The difference between a high-quality aged red wine vinegar and the poor-quality version so readily available in grocery stores is like night and day. It's worth a trip to a specialty store for this essential ingredient.

RICE WINE VINEGAR

This light, clean-tasting vinegar works perfectly in a variety of Asian-inspired dishes.

Wines for Cooking

We often use sherry or wine to deglaze a pan, melting the juices that brown during sautéing so that their dark, rich flavors can be included.

RED AND WHITE WINE

Any good dry red or white wine suitable for drinking is suitable for cooking. It doesn't have to be fancy, and it shouldn't be undrinkable.

SHERRY

When we want the richness and complexity a good sherry brings to a dish, we use a good, dry Spanish sherry, amontillado.

PORT

Port adds a kind of sweet depth and is especially good with mushrooms and in butter sauces. Use a good domestic port for cooking, not an aged tawny port. We use Ficklin.

MIRIN

Sweet cooking sake, available in the Asian section in most grocery stores.

Sources

Seeds and seedlings by mail, farmer's markets, inspiring reading for cooks and gardeners, and more.

Seed Catalogs

Bountiful Gardens
Ecology Action
5798 Ridgewood Road
Willits, CA 95490

> *Ecology Action, a nonprofit organization, offers a catalog with vegetable, grain, and herb seeds to support its work with bio-intensive farming. It offers classes, publishes books, and does research—a worthy endeavor, a fascinating catalog, and good seeds.*

Johnny's Selected Seeds
Foss Hill Road
Albion, ME 04910

> *Johnny's is a great resource for seeds that flourish in northern climates.*

Ornamental Edibles
3622 Weedin Court
San Jose, CA 95132

> *A good source of specialty items that carries all varieties of lettuce and beets.*

Plants of the Southwest
1812 Second Street
Santa Fe, NM 87501

Redwood City Seed Company
PO Box 361
Redwood City, CA 94064

Ronniger's Seed Potatoes
Star Route
Moyie Sorings, ID 83845

> *The best source we know for top-quality potatoes.*

Seeds of Change
621 Old Santa Fe Trail #10
Santa Fe, NM 87501

Seed Saver's Exchange
Box 239
Decorah, IA 52101
   This important organization preserves heritage varieties of seeds.

Shepherd's Garden Seeds
7389 West Zayante Road
Felton, CA 95018
   Offers superior varieties of European vegetables and herbs.

Stokes Seeds Inc.
737 Main Street
Buffalo, NY 14240
   An especially good offering of flower seeds and European vegetables.

Taylor's Herb Garden
1535 Lone Oak Road
Vista, CA 92083
   An excellent collection of live herb plants, many rare and hard to find.

Territorial Seed Company
PO Box 27
Lorane, OR 97451

Other Resources for Seeds and Plants

Green Gulch Farm
Star Route
Sausalito, CA 94965
   Green Gulch operates a year-round coastal plant nursery specializing in flowers and herbs—many varieties not found elsewhere. Green Gulch also offers classes covering all aspects of gardening. Write for a class schedule.

Phipps Ranch
PO Box 349
Pescadero, CA 94060
   Offers a huge variety of high-quality, tasty dried beans. It's a fascinating place to visit; also offers specialty vinegars, dried herbs, and spice blends.

Farmer's Markets

IN CALIFORNIA
The UC Davis Small Farms Center publishes a directory of farmer's markets in California.
For a copy write to:
Farmer to Consumer Directory
Small Farms Center
University of California
Davis, CA 95616

OUTSIDE CALIFORNIA
Contact your Agricultural Commissioner or the city, county, or state director of agriculture to find out about farmer's markets in your area.

Community Gardens

If you live in an urban area, there may be a community garden where you could have a plot. Try calling your local parks and recreation office to find the location. If you see a vacant lot that has been transformed into a garden, stop and talk to the gardeners. The community garden effort is well worth supporting; in San Francisco we have over 60 community gardens.

Recommended Reading

Brennan, Georgeanne. *Potager—Fresh Garden Cooking in the French Style*. San Francisco: Chronicle Books, 1992.

Coleman, Eliot. *The New Organic Grower*. Chelsea, VT: Chelsea Green Publishing Company, 1989.

Creasy, Rosalind. *The Complete Book of Edible Landscaping*. San Francisco: Sierra Club Books, 1982.

Creasy, Rosalind. *Cooking from the Garden*. San Francisco: Sierra Club Books, 1982.

Howard, Sir Albert. *An Agricultural Testament*. Oxford, England: Oxford University Press, 1943.

Hutson, Lucinda. *The Herb Garden Cookbook*. Houston, TX: Gulf Publishing Company, 1992.

Jevins, John. *How to Grow More Vegetables*. Berkeley, CA: Ten Speed Press, 1982.

Kourik, Robert. *Designing and Maintaining Your Edible Landscape Naturally*. Santa Rosa, CA: Metamorphic Press, 1986.

Larkcom, Joy. *Oriental Vegetables—A Complete Guide for Garden and Kitchen*. Tokyo and New York: Kodansha International Press, 1991.

Larkcom, Joy. *The Salad Garden*. New York: Viking Press, 1984.

National Gardening Association. *Gardening—The Complete Guide to Growing America's Favorite Fruits and Vegetables*. Reading, MA: Addison-Wesley Publishers, 1986.

Pellegrini, Angelo. *The Unprejudiced Palate*. New York: Macmillan, 1948.

Pierce, Pam. *Golden Gate Gardening*. Davis, CA: Ag Access, 1992.

Storl, Wolf. *Culture and Horticulture*. Wyoming, RI: Biodynamic Literature, 1979.

Index

Ice cream, Meyer lemon, 386

Jícama
  -orange salad, 63
  and romaine hearts with avocado and
    orange, 20

Kale
  information about/cooking, xxii, 2, 131
  winter greens soup, 103
  winter greens with currants, pine nuts, and
    brown butter, 254
Kumquats, in citrus salad with bitter greens,
  14

Lasagne
  artichoke-leek, 152–53
  eggplant with basil, 150–51
  information about, 118–19
  with mushroom-port sauce, 154–56
Leeks
  fall risotto with chanterelles and late harvest
    tomatoes, 162–63
  filo, mushroom and, with Gruyère cheese
    and thyme, 238–39
  gratin, with potato, fennel, and, 210–11
  grilled, 66, 70
  information about, 85
  lasagne, artichokes and, 152–53
  in lasagne with mushroom-port sauce, 154–
    56
  linguine with chanterelles and, 133
  pastry turnovers with butternut squash,
    thyme, and, 232–33
  pizza with mushrooms and, 172
  pizza with roasted pepper sauce, olives, and,
    171
  risotto with mushrooms, fennel, and, 164–
    65
  soup, basmati rice and, 84–85
  soup, carrot with thyme and, 115
  soup, potato, celery root, and, 104–5
  stock, 84
  tart, olive and, 222
Lemons/Meyer lemons
  beurre blanc, 329
  facts about/growing, xxi, xxii, 47
  in desserts, 362

ice cream, 386
pots de crème, 370
in vinaigrette, 47
Lentils
  French, for salads, 3, 32
  Mexican, soup with roasted garlic and
    chilies, 101
  Moroccan soup, 109
  and Roman tomato soup with mint, 116
  in salad with curry spices and yogurt, 32
Lettuces
  butter, and radicchio with avocado, ruby
    grapefruit, and pecans, 10
  fall greens with marinated mushrooms,
    fennel, and Gruyère cheese, 12
  garden, and rocket salad, with summer
    beans, goat cheese, and hazelnuts, 6
  garden, and watercress, escarole with goat
    cheese and sun-dried tomatoes, 17
  information about/varieties, xxi–xxii, 6, 9,
    12, 17
  See also Romaine; Salads.
Lovage, in stock, 76
Low-fat cooking, how to lighten recipes, 411

Mâche, facts about/growing, 2, 7
Mango
  -papaya chutney, 393
  -papaya salad with citrus-ginger vinaigrette,
    22
  and red and green romaine hearts with
    avocado and ginger, 8
Marjoram, sweet, facts about, 253
Melons
  in late summer salad—figs and, with orange
    vinaigrette, 24
  varieties recommended, 24
Mizuna
  facts about/growing, 2, 41
  in mango-papaya salad with citrus-ginger
    vinaigrette, 22
Mousse, honey, with raspberries and figs, 369
Mozzarella cheese
  about, 413–14
  baguette sandwich with marinated
    mushrooms, roasted peppers, and
    smoked, 300
  potato cakes with scallions and smoked, 223

Metric Conversion Chart

Conversions of Ounces to Grams

OUNCES (oz)	GRAMS (g)	OUNCES (oz)	GRAMS (g)
1 oz	30 g*	11 oz	300 g
2 oz	60 g	12 oz	340 g
3 oz	85 g	13 oz	370 g
4 oz	115 g	14 oz	400 g
5 oz	140 g	15 oz	425 g
6 oz	180 g	16 oz	450 g
7 oz	200 g	20 oz	570 g
8 oz	225 g	24 oz	680 g
9 oz	250 g	28 oz	790 g
10 oz	285 g	32 oz	900 g

*Approximate. To convert ounces to grams, multiply number of ounces by 28.35.

Conversions of Pounds to Grams and Kilograms

POUNDS (LB)	GRAMS (G) KILOGRAMS (KG)	POUNDS (LB)	GRAMS (G) KILOGRAMS (KG)
1 lb	450 g*	5 lb	2¼ kg
1¼ lb	565 g	5½ lb	2½ kg
1½ lb	675 g	6 lb	2¾ kg
1¾ lb	800 g	6½ lb	3 kg
2 lb	900 g	7 lb	3¼ kg
2½ lb	1,125 g; 1¼ kg	7½ lb	3½ kg
3 lb	1,350 g	8 lb	3¾ kg
3½ lb	1,500 g; 1½ kg	9 lb	4 kg
4 lb	1,800 g	10 lb	4½ kg
4½ lb	2 kg		

*Approximate. To convert pounds into kilograms, multiply number of pounds by 453.6.

Conversions of Fahrenheit to Celsius

FAHRENHEIT	CELSIUS
170°F	77°C*
180°F	82°C
190°F	88°C
200°F	95°C
225°F	110°C
250°F	120°C
300°F	150°C
325°F	165°C
350°F	180°C
375°F	190°C
400°F	205°C
425°F	220°C
450°F	230°C
475°F	245°C
500°F	260°C
525°F	275°C
550°F	290°C

*Approximate. To convert Fahrenheit to Celsius, subtract 32, multiply by 5, then divide by 9.

Conversions of Quarts to Liters

QUARTS (QT)	LITERS (L)
1 qt	1 L*
1½ qt	1½ L
2 qt	2 L
2½ qt	2½ L
3 qt	2¾ L
4 qt	3¾ L
5 qt	4¾ L
6 qt	5½ L
7 qt	6½ L
8 qt	7½ L
9 qt	8½ L
10 qt	9½ L

*Approximate. To convert quarts to liters, multiply number of quarts by 0.95.